INDIAN VIDESHINIS

OTHER LOTUS TITLES

Ajit Bhattacharjea	*Sheikh Mohammad Abdullah: Tragic Hero of Kashmir*
Aitzaz Ahsan	*The Indus Saga: The Making of Pakistan*
Ajay Mansingh	*Firaq Gorakhpuri: The Poet of Pain & Ecstasy*
Alam Srinivas	*Women of Vision: Nine Business Leaders in Conversation*
Amarinder Singh	*The Last Sunset: The Rise & Fall of the Lahore Durbar*
Bertil Falk	*Feroze: The Forgotten Gandhi*
Hamish Mcdonald	*Ambani & Sons*
Kunal Purandare	*Ramakant Achrekar: A Biography*
Lucy Peck	*Agra: The Architectural Heritage*
Lucy Peck	*Delhi a Thousand Years of Building: An INTACH-Roli Guide*
Madan Gopal	*My Life and Times: Munshi Premchand*
M.J. Akbar	*Byline*
M.J. Akbar	*Blood Brothers: A Family Saga*
M.J. Akbar	*Have Pen, Will Travel: Observations of a Globetrotter*
M.J. Akbar	*India The Siege Within: Challenges to a Nation's Unity*
M.J. Akbar	*Kashmir: Behind the Vale*
M.J. Akbar	*Nehru: The Making of India*
M.J. Akbar	*The Shade of Swords: Jihad and the Conflict between Islam and Christianity*
Maj. Gen. Ian Cardozo	*Param Vir: Our Heroes in Battle*
Maj. Gen. Ian Cardozo	*The Sinking of INS Khukri: What Happened in 1971*
Madhu Trehan	*Tehelka as Metaphor*
Moin Mir	*Surat: Fall of a Port, Rise of a Prince Defeat of the East India Company in the House of Commons*
Monisha Rajesh	*Around India in 80 Trains*
Noorul Hasan	*Meena Kumari: The Poet*
Peter Church	*Added Value: The Life Stories of Indian Business Leaders*
Peter Church	*Profiles in Enterprise: Inspiring Stories of Indian Business Leaders*
Prateep K. Lahri	*Decoding Intolerance: Riots and the Emergence of Terrorism in India*
Rajika Bhandari	*The Raj on the Move: Story of the Dak Bungalow*
Ralph Russell	*The Famous Ghalib: The Sound of my Moving Pen*
R.V. Smith	*Delhi: Unknown Tales of a City*
Salman Akthar	*The Book of Emotions*
Shahrayar Khan	*Bhopal Connections: Vignettes of Royal Rule*
Shantanu Guha Ray	*Mahi: The Story of India's Most Successful Captain*
Sharmishta Gooptu	*Bengali Cinema: An Other Nation*
Shrabani Basu	*Spy Princess: The Life of Noor Inayat Khan*
S. Hussain Zaidi	*Dongri to Dubai*
Sunil Raman & Rohit Aggarwal	*Delhi Durbar: 1911 The Complete Story*
Sunetra Choudhury	*Behind Bars: Prison Tales of India's Most Famous*
Thomas Weber	*Going Native: Gandhi's Relationship with Western Women*
Thomas Weber	*Gandhi at First Sight*
Vappala Balachandran	*A Life In Shadow: The Secret Story of ACN Nambiar A forgotten Anti-Colonial Warrior*
Vir Sanghvi	*Men of Steel: India's Business Leaders in Candid Conversation*
Zubin Mehta	*Zubin Mehta: The Score of My Life*

FORTHCOMING TITLES

Prateep K. Lahiri	*A Tide in the Affairs of Men: A Public Servant Remembers*
Aruna Roy	*The RTI Story: A People's Movement for Transparency*

INDIAN VIDESHINIS

EUROPEAN WOMEN IN INDIA

Sonia Gandhi . Princess Niloufer
Princess Durru Shehvar . Simone Tata . Sooni Tata
Saint Teresa . The Mother . Margaret Cousins
Sister Nivedita . Annie Besant . Jeanne Dupleix

IAN MAGEDERA

LOTUS COLLECTION
ROLI BOOKS

Lotus Collection

First published 2018

The Lotus Collection
An imprint of
Roli Books Pvt. Ltd
M-75, Greater Kailash II Market, New Delhi 110 048
Phone: ++91 (011) 40682000
E-mail: info@rolibooks.com
Website: www.rolibooks.com

Also at Chennai, & Mumbai

Cover Design: Sneha Pamneja
Layout Design: Bhagirath Kumar
Production: Yuvraj Singh

Photo Credits: Cover, Margaret Bourke-White, Getty Images; Margaret Cousins image Courtesy of the National Library of Ireland; Simon Tata image Sanjay Gupta for Lakmé Fashion Week Winter/Festive 2017; Mirra Alfassa image by Henri Cartier-Bresson.

ISBN: 9789351941361

Typeset in Arno Pro by Roli Books Pvt Ltd and
Printed in India at Repro India Ltd.

In hope and with confidence, this book is dedicated to one of its future readers: Esther M. Magedera

CONTENTS

PREFACE

This is a book about a number of European women who, over the last 120 years or so, have successfully moved to India and made important contributions to life there. The book thus links Europe and India, but will, it is hoped, appeal to readers who, like its subjects, are of many sorts and come from many places.

For readers interested in just one of these women, a good route into the book is to read the Introduction before moving directly to the individual chapter. The chapters, rather than being biographical cameos, are analyses of identity formation. They examine the ways in which these women absorbed themselves in India, sometimes taking on aspects of the identities of the Indians around them and manifesting these in their speech, dress, thought and sensibility. The book shows how they were accepted and also rejected by Indians, and how their various Indian elites mediated their absorption by acting both as their hosts and as their promoters in the new country.

As the world is experiencing hypernationalism and Indian society is living through a period of self-examination and transition at present, Indians and those interested in India need to be particularly aware about how that society is organized. By definition, the nation's elites have been very good at promoting their own interests over many years. This book will demonstrate that one of their most successful strategies has been their porousness: their willingness to integrate non-Indians, and non-Indian women in particular. We may condemn what these elites have done; or the peer groups we belong to might prefer to emulate them; or we may simply be curious about how all this is possible. But it is vital to understand how Indian elites ensure their own continuity by supporting the influential careers of European-born women who work with them, while of course paying lip service to the mantra that they are acting for the good of the nation. If we bracket out their self-interest, we can also see that they are continuing the Indian tradition of accepting foreigners and carrying on, that has been such a prominent feature of the place for centuries.

All of these women either came with or developed special skills that benefitted their elites; many Indian-born women had these skills too, of course, but the unique attribute of these particular foreign-born women was that they were exotically European without being implicated in British colonialism. They were a living illustration of what the future should hold for the Indian nation; they represented an ideal non-colonial relationship between India and Europe and this is why their individual skills were so influential. The approach adopted here allows readers to make their own judgments about the value of these women's contributions. Readers may begin to understand the negative side of a figure that they previously unquestioningly revered, or to comprehend that an oft-reviled foreign woman did after all have some positive effects on Indian society and social cohesion.

For the reader who is interested in the wider issues, the best way to approach the book is to read the Introduction followed by the Prelude, before moving on to the analyses grouped according to the women's domains of activity in India – education, spirituality, business and politics. The Prelude uses the critical self-awareness that is a feature of postcolonial studies to refine the analysis of the ways that these women represent themselves and the ways that they are depicted by Indians (for example in relation to their dress and to how well or badly they speak Indian languages). The approach here goes further than the model of postcolonialism that is usually applied to India, bringing in references to colonialism in Latin America, and also avoiding postcolonialism's frequent tendency to lose itself in its own terminological complexity.

This book aims to be different by combining both an analysis of the language used to describe these women and a focus on real-world processes and phenomena that touch the lives of the majority of Indians – such as voting and property rights. Despite its broad relevance, the book is wary of the tendency of much Western scholarship to apply a grand theory to complex processes in India. The case studies are substantial and representative; but they are also many-layered, covering in depth a wide range, both chronologically and geographically (from New Delhi to Puducherry, via Mumbai and Hyderabad). Each chapter can be read on its own; but it is hoped that readers will be spurred on to further discoveries of women who have similar stories to the one that prompted their interest in the first place. In each case, the photographs and epigraphs set the scene and summarize the diversity of views on the identity of the women concerned. The book thus brings the insights of formal research and scholarship into the dialogue among non-specialists in India, Europe and beyond.

The research that informed this book was done in Pune, Hyderabad and Puducherry, as well as in London and Paris. It sprang from a five-year UK Arts and Humanities Research Council project on French-language representations of India. That project defined the counterintuitive way that this book analyses power, concentrating on the role of the French as minor colonizers in India during the period from 1754 to 1954 – that is, from the year of the departure from India of Joseph-François Dupleix to the cession by the French of Pondicherry – the territory he once governed (with the other French possessions of Chandernagore, Mahe, Yanam and Karikal) – to the Union of Indian States. The project demonstrated the value of an unconventional focus on power during the colonial period. The French were colonizers with sovereignty over these demilitarized pockets of India totalling just over 500 square kilometres, but they were themselves held in check by the British. The resilience of their form of non-absolute power is demonstrated by the French presence outlasting the British Indian Empire; in fact the treaty of cession was not ratified by the French parliament until 1962. The European women in this book assert a similar form of asymmetric power within the Indian elites that support them and whose prosperity they promote.

As a consequence, the Europe presented here is a dynamic and contentious space including its Celtic, Balkan and Ottoman fringes. It is not a stable contrast to India's diversity and supposed unruliness, as it is sometimes portrayed in books on India written by Westerners. While acknowledging the importance of the British colonial powers and of the English language in the period before 1947, the book uses the diverse European origins of these women to move beyond both the binary of colonizer British and colonized Indians and the assumption that Indian Independence marked the end of European activity in India. French-speaking women form the largest subgroup here; but, in addition to the well-known Italian-born Indian politician, there are also women with allegiances to peripheral regions of Europe, such as the Balkans in the case of Saint Teresa, and the former Ottoman Empire in the cases of Princess Durru Shehvar and Princess Niloufer. With Annie Besant, Margaret Cousins and Sister Nivedita, the unique relationship of simultaneous connection and separation between Britain and Ireland helps these three women make their mark in India.

The ten women who feature in this book were chosen to represent the most important domains in which European-born women had influence in India. The long time period studied, going back from 2017 to 1893, allows the reader to arrive at a deeper understanding of how these women, and their supporting elites, co-existed with colonial power structures, were co-opted by nationalism, and then defined themselves anew in independent India.

Personally speaking, one of the most rewarding aspects of writing this book has been the people whom I have met along the way; I would like also to express my deepest gratitude to the existing acquaintances, colleagues and friends who have helped me so much. Completing this book has given me the opportunity of getting to know some of you better and I salute your generosity: Anthony Winder, Priya Kapoor, Deepthi Sasidharan, Robert Young, Margaret Majumdar, Maria Abreu, Fatima Shahnaz, Gobalakichenane, Nandini Das, Manish Unhale, Jogamaya Bayer, Florence D'Souza, the late Guy Deleury, Syed Sayeed, Cécile Jest, Supriya Chaudhuri, Aditi Chopra, Bill Leigh, Neelam Narula, Swati Chopra, Chandreyee Niyogi and

Sanjay Palshikar. Furthermore, I would like to express my thanks to the following institutions and individuals for their support in gathering source materials for this book: Arts and Humanities Research Council, Tata Central Archives, Mother Teresa Center, British Library, University of Liverpool Library, Bibliothèque Nationale de France, Gallica, Rajendra Prasad Narla and Simone Tata.

INTRODUCTION

All the while that Indians were thinking themselves free in the late nineteenth century and long after they achieved freedom in the twentieth, there was another group of Europeans who, for over 120 years, from 1893 onwards, beyond 1947 and up to the present day, bucked the general downward trend of European influence in India. That group comprises European-born women like Annie Besant who arrived in India in 1893, and this book is a study of their lives and careers in the context of the Indian elites that sustained them. The main focus is on how they construct their own identities and how they are represented by the Indians. The tensions within and between competing constructions of 'Indianness', 'Europeanness' and 'foreignness' are signalled by the title, an oxymoron that takes 'videshini', a Hindi word of Sanskrit origin meaning 'foreign woman or women', and pairs it with 'Indian' in a contradiction which is intended to be suggestive.[1] While discourse is important, this will be more than a study of the women at the level of language. Hence the common denominator among the subjects chosen is their influence on Indian society.

Let me introduce the Indian *videshinis*: *Annie Besant,* the co-founder of the Central Hindu College and sometime first female president of the Indian National Congress; *Sister Nivedita (Margaret Noble),* the Northern Ireland-born founder of the Girls' School at Baghbazar, Kolkata; *Margaret Cousins,* the feminist activist and co-initiator of three women's movements, including the All India Women's Conference;

The Mother (Mirra Alfassa), responsible for the early organization of the Sri Aurobindo Ashram and for founding the experimental city of Auroville; *Mother Teresa,* born in what is now Macedonia in eastern Europe and winner of the 1979 Nobel Prize for Peace; *Sooni Tata,* the French-born mother of J.R.D. Tata, whose internationalization of the Tata family and businesses was deepened by *Simone Tata,* the French-speaking Swiss woman who built Lakmé cosmetics into a multi-million dollar enterprise; *Princess Durru Shehvar,* the founder of the Hyderabad Children's Medical Aid Society, born in the Ottoman Empire and an activist for women's rights; *Princess Niloufer* (also a member of the former Ottoman royal family), who donated her divorce settlement to founding the Niloufer Hospital for Women and Children in Hyderabad; and *Sonia Gandhi,* the outgoing Congress Party president who, as any Indian who has an ear open during election campaigns knows, was born in Italy.[2]

Their influence will be discussed fully and critically in the chapters that follow; but, at this stage, suffice it to say that the prime criterion for the inclusion of a woman here is the effect that she has had (or continues to have) on Indian society or social attitudes. Although there may not be total agreement regarding the circumstances that allowed these European-born women to make an impact (far from it in some cases), it is difficult to dispute the fact that an impact has occurred – a fact confirmed by the appearance of four of them on Indian postage stamps; it means that images of these women were (and still are in the case of another stamp depicting Mother Teresa) part of the imprimatur of the Indian state. Thus in the years of their issue – 1963 for Besant, 1968 for Nivedita, 1978 for Alfassa, and 1980, 1997 and 2009 for Mother Teresa – there was consensus in official circles at least about the positive contribution to the nation of these Western women.[3]

Even if we withhold a final judgement, we note that their work has had a transformative effect on four key domains of Indian civil society: education and activism, religion and spirituality, international business and commerce, and state and national politics. If we consider this book as an imaginary train moving across India (quite apt in view of the importance of mobility here), these domains correspond to the four compartments of this book and in each of them sit two or three Indian *videshinis*. We shall find Annie Besant, Sister Nivedita (Margaret Noble) and Margaret Cousins together in 'education and activism', Mirra Alfassa and Mother Teresa, though they are very different from each other of course, share the 'religion and spirituality' compartment, two generations of Tata women are to be found in 'international business and commerce' and, at opposite ends of the 'state and national politics' compartment, sit princesses Durru Shehvar and Niloufer on the one hand and Sonia Gandhi on the other.

This book also analyses the Indian elite who enabled them to have the influence they did. In a fundamental way their influence was made possible because they belonged to elite groups established before their arrival in India. The Indian *videshinis* are studied, therefore, in the context of those elites. None of their compartments, therefore, is 'ladies only'. On the contrary, they are filled with husbands, companions and adult sons. It is also important to note that I am in no way suggesting that the women were elite by virtue of their Europeanness alone; that would be to fall into simplistic positive essentialism. We will see that the women came from a diverse range of socio-economic backgrounds before joining elites in India. Some examples of these elites are: the Roman Catholic Church in India; the Theosophical Society; the Tata family; the Nizamate of Hyderabad; and the Nehru–Gandhi dynasty. The term 'power elite' in this book's title originates in political theory (Wright Mills 1956, 1). Wright Mills's field of study was the United States in the 1950s and his thesis was that members of the elites in politics, the corporate world and academia collaborate and share knowledge between one domain and another, and that this sharing concentrates power even further. While it is not possible to apply these fields to India (and it seems incongruous now that anyone might consider academia as a power broker), Wright Mills's term reminds us that the elites in this book are sub-groups in society – all quite legitimate ones with a stake in the country – whose members will act primarily to further their own interests. The senior deciders within these groups regulate access to the group and have a clear right of veto, making strategic decisions to manoeuvre their power elite into a position from which it can take maximum benefit from wider social trends, such as the increased opportunities given to women to realize their potential and the need for diversification through the internationalization of trade. For example, let us consider the attitude of elites to nationalism in a little detail. At the same time as subscribing to the rhetoric of nationalism, in which India and Indians are considered 'best', elite families maintain their positions of dominance by a practice of ethnic openness which has no problem in admitting suitable foreigners. In sum, restrictive nationalism is for the petit bourgeois; an altogether more relaxed form of cosmopolitan nationalism suits the elite very nicely, thank you.

All of these women had close ties with the leaders of their individual elites, with many of them, such as Annie Besant, Mirra Alfassa, Sister Teresa, Simone Tata and Sonia Gandhi, going on to take up leadership positions in these organizations. They all had a seat at the top table, and for some of them, such as Sooni Tata, Simone Tata and Sonia Gandhi, that forum for decision-making was the 'family dining table'. Family is one of the key themes of this book. Elite Indian families such as the Tatas, the Nehrus–Gandhis, or the Asaf Jahi dynasty of Hyderabad integrate foreign women with comparatively little controversy given the fact that the whole country was and is in a process of national self-affirmation in the period from 1893 to 2017. They join because of a love attraction to one of the members, which is then sanctioned by the wider family at large. Or, as in the case of the Nizam of Hyderabad's family, the marriage was a more conservative alliance between families.

There are cases in which matrimony does not play a role in the integration of the Western woman, such as those of Mother Teresa, Mirra Alfassa and Sister Nivedita. In these cases, however, a 'spiritual senior' with status in India nurtures the woman and acts as her guarantor in the face of any scepticism from those around her. Father Van Exem fulfilled this role for Sister Teresa, Sri Aurobindo was Mirra Alfassa's spiritual teacher and Swami Vivekananda was Sister Nivedita's guide. Once these Indian *videshinis* are established, they evoke a symbolic kinship relationship: thus we have two symbolic mothers to Indians in the Pondicherry Mother (Mirra Alfassa) and in Mother Teresa, and a sister in Sister Nivedita. Indeed both Hindu and

Christian nuns embrace celibacy in order to have a deeper relationship with their deities. The Conclusion examines whether either of these groups – natural mothers and symbolic mothers – has left a legacy through women (in the sense of whether there are women in India today related to them symbolically or by kinship ties who are working in the same domains in which they achieved their prominence).

In order to make the rationale for the choice of these European women clearer, we can see that there is a whole series of women who might have fallen within the scope of this book, but did not. There is Edwina Mountbatten; or the European women who married into princely houses, such as Anita Delgrada, a Spanish flamenco dancer, who married Jagatjit Singh, the maharaja of Kapurthala, in 1910 and Stella Mudge, an English cabaret dancer, who wed his son Paramjit (Teo 2004). The same applies to the cat-obsessed Aryan fascist Savitri Devi 1905–1982, who had Greco-Italian and English parentage and went between India and Europe, campaigning for Hindu nationalism in 1930s Calcutta, for the return of fascism in post war Europe, before spending her twilight years caring for the cats in a Delhi street.* The starting year of the main period covered in this book, 1893, marks the arrival in India of Annie Besant rather than the marriage of Florry Bryan to the maharaja of Patiala.[4] Gandhi's disciple Mirabehn, Madeleine Slade (a rear admiral's daughter), is mentioned in the Conclusion, but only to contrast the limits of her engagement with India (including her departure in 1959) with the depth of that of the Indian *videshinis.*

With only three exceptions, all the women in this book are either living in India at present (Simone Tata and Sonia Gandhi) or ended their days there. Anita Delgrada, Stella Mudge and Florry Bryan will not be included in the chapters of this book because, although theirs are interesting lives, unlike our Indian *videshinis*, their presence in India has not had a lasting effect on Indian society.

---

*Although the prefaces to her 1939 *Warning to the Hindus* and her 1965 allegory for children *Long-Whiskers and the Two Legged Goddess*, profess non-communalism and only an 'aesthetic' interest in Nazism, they are intended to allay the suspicions of the critical reader who will actually find both of these works sympathetic to the nefarious world-views that the prefaces ostensibly sideline.

The mere fact of being a European-born woman living in India is not enough; the figures discussed here lead (or have led) projects which have transformed and renewed India over several years. This focus on context is what distinguishes this book from the previous treatments of European women in India. Anjali Sengupta's *Cameos of Twelve European Women in India 1757–1857* is centred on a different period; Harbans Singh Bhatia's *European Women in India: Their Life and Adventures* presents the women in isolation rather than in their socio-economic context; and the three volumes of Amruta Rao's *Occidental Daughters of Mother India* have a rather narrow and repetitive perspective, with the first volume covering Sister Nivedita and Mother Teresa, the second, Sister Nivedita and Dr Annie Besant and the third, Sister Nivedita and Pondicherry Mother.[5]

Here are some examples of the deeds of four of the Indian *videshinis*. We can see that all of them have a deep-rooted significance. Mother Teresa came to India from Macedonia via Ireland as a simple Loreto nun in 1929, and taught quietly in a Calcutta (now Kolkata) school for eighteen years. All this changed in 1947 when she went public with a radical plan to found a new order whose nuns she insisted would need to 'live like Indians'. The Missionaries of Charity has been an influential and, for some, controversial, part of life in Kolkata ever since.[6]

Edvige Antonia Albina Maino's first contact with the Indian man who would become her future husband, Rajiv Gandhi, was an entirely European affair: she had come to Cambridge from Italy to learn English. Although she appears to have hit it off with her mother-in-law Indira Gandhi when she arrived in India in 1968 (it seems that they spoke to each other in French at first), it was a series of deaths (Sanjay Gandhi's in 1980, Indira Gandhi's in 1984 and Rajiv Gandhi's in 1991) that propelled Sonia Gandhi from the periphery to the centre of the Nehru–Gandhi dynasty. After declining to be appointed as prime minister in 2004, she took up a life post as Congress Party president until December 2017.

Simone Tata came to India in 1955 to be integrated into the life of her new Indian husband, Naval H. Tata. Although her father was an entrepreneur, she only became interested in business in India by listening and learning about what was going on at the heart of the Tata Group. Gradually she took on responsibilities directing cosmetics manufacture and marketing, a field for which her elite life in Geneva and Paris had prepared her. From the 1960s to the end of the 1990s, she was able to develop a cosmetics business, Lakmé, which was the pioneer and market leader in India and which exported to both eastern Europe and the Far East. The business was sold in 1998 for £25 million. Simone Tata then started the Westside retail chain.

Mirra Alfassa visited Pondicherry in 1914; in 1920 she came back to stay and did not leave until her death in 1978. She was sanctioned by Sri Aurobindo to take charge of the day-to-day running of his Ashram in 1923, but she did more than this: she developed it as an organization both in terms of its resident devotees and in terms of the real estate it occupied in the 'White Town' in Pondicherry. By the mid-1930s things got to the point that French colonial authorities stipulated that they could no longer rent more properties; if they wanted more space, they would have to build. Today the Ashram is a thriving centre with 4,500 residents. As with Simone Tata, Mirra Alfassa would not be content with the propagation of one organization. After the death of Sri Aurobindo in 1950 she began to make material and spiritual preparations for a universal town on the outskirts of Pondicherry. Today Auroville has 2,170 residents representing 48 nationalities; its financial status is protected and supported by the Indian state (legally backed up by acts of parliament from 1980 and 1988).

The focus here on these women's influence though organizations active in Indian society and the support of their elites in doing this raises two fundamental questions. The first is a question about evaluating the effects on society of these women's actions and the second relates to feminism and whether other women are the principal beneficiaries of the activity of Indian *videshinis*. Although its subjects are exclusively female, this book has an emphasis which is different from Kumari Jayawardena's *The White Woman's Other Burden: Western Women and South Asia during British Rule* (1995). The organizations of seven of its ten subjects (Sonia Gandhi, Mirra Alfassa, Mother Teresa, Princess Niloufer, Sooni Tata, Simone Tata and Annie Besant) influence both men and women in Indian society. Of course, while

Jayawardena's own approach is avowedly feminist she understands that not all of her subjects are feminists. This position causes a tension within her book. As Mary A. Procida asks:

> Is feminism (or at least Western feminism) thus inherently incompatible with the anti-imperialist struggle? Although Jayawardena professes to analyse her subjects from the perspective of an Asian feminist, she finds no resolution for this difficult paradox. If anything, her sympathies seem to lie with those women who conform most closely to traditional conceptions of Western feminism. The debate has thus far been dominated by the views of (male) Indian nationalists and (female) Western feminists. As Jayawardena notes, the 'key question' to be researched and discussed further is the reaction of Indian women to the efforts on their behalf by their Western 'sisters'. (Procida 2005, 11)

This study responds to Jayawardena's question regarding the reaction of Indian women by including as many relevant female voices as possible. With relation to Sonia Gandhi, in particular, women journalists play a significant role. Journalism has allowed so many women in modern India to communicate to their fellow citizens in large number. In addition, female critics, historians and biographers such as Rupa Chatterjee, Nilima Das and Kamala Ramji are also quoted in these pages. However, the paucity of comment from the female Indian contemporaries of the women active in the earlier part of our period must be acknowledged. The main reason for this is that this book privileges sources in English and other European languages; Indian women in the early part of the period lacked the educational opportunities to acquire enough competence in English to be quoted. They do appear, however, and their insights are extremely valuable; for example, what a certain Mrs J.C. Bose has to say about the inclusive way in which Sister Nivedita used the first person plural in her work with women and girls in Calcutta. Mrs Bose is an atypical case, writing in her own name in English in the *Modern Review* in 1911 (Bose 1911). Furthermore, the words of a Hindi-speaking woman such as the Ashramite Vasudha (she is given no other name) do appear in this book; but we hear her comments as speech reported by another woman, Nilima Das. Despite these difficulties we should not fall into the trap of thinking that this book caricatures women as discourse subalterns; women like Swati Chopra are cited quoting men in the chapter on Mirra Alfassa, and others, such as Manjulika Dubey, have an active hand in shaping the words of elite Indian *videshinis* such as Sonia Gandhi.

Sister Nivedita, Margaret Cousins and Princess Durru Shehvar, whose organizations were engaged in activism to improve conditions for women, had to negotiate in a precise manner with the wider society around them, sometimes at great risk to their own reputations. This is intensified in that they were European-born women (Sister Nivedita born in the north of Ireland as Margaret Noble, Margaret Cousins born in the south of Ireland, and Durru Shehvar in Ottoman Constantinople) acting on behalf of diverse groups of Indian women. It is important to provide the detail about this negotiation; therefore, although gender issues remain an integral part of this book, it would be restrictive to apply a (Western) feminist interpretative grid to the life and work of even the more pro-female of the women subjects in this book (such as Margaret Cousins, Sister Nivedita and Durru Shehvar). Moreover, one would seek in vain for any significant feminist angle in the life and work of Sonia Gandhi and Mother Teresa for example (although Sonia Gandhi's support for the 2010 Women's Reservation Bill is discussed). In sum, then, it is more accurate to analyze gender than feminism, but in tandem with social and economic factors.

One example of where the analysis of these women from a gender point of view must take into account socio-economic factors concerns the issue of their enhanced mobility. All the women in the main body of this book, those who arrived in India from 1893 to 1968, travelled from Europe to India, but they then also kept moving, either within India or between India and Europe (and in some cases both).[7] The wealth and the international dimension of the organizations that these women founded or promoted necessitated international travel. Their secure position in social hierarchies and their support networks among Indian elites meant that they did not need to immigrate to India bringing all their wealth to that land, but could return to Europe to elicit the help of their home networks for the benefit of their Indian causes.

This mobility was both enabled and encouraged by the significant increase in the reliability and the frequency of travel connections between Europe and India in the early part of the period in question. First, there were the shipping lines which were fully utilized by Annie Besant and by Sooni Tata; then there was extensive use of air travel used by Mother Teresa, Simone Tata and Sonia Gandhi.

It is clear that their social position allowed these women to travel in the first place, and that their continued mobility subsequently consolidated and extended their international networks of power and influence.[8] As well as these international links, the women were always concerned to have at least one base in an Indian region or city. Several of the epigraphs that stand at the heads of the chapters that follow go in search of the material traces left by the Indian *videshinis* in their respective localities. If we stand back and consider the corpus of female subjects, we see a representative geographical spread which extends across India: Jeanne Dupleix's money-making colonial enterprise was centred in her home town of Pondicherry. Annie Besant criss-crossed India on her speaking tours, but always returned to her house at the Theosophical Society compound in Chennai (her tomb is found in the grounds there). Sister Nivedita will always be associated with the Baghbazar district of Kolkata, because she founded her school there. Margaret Cousins travelled all over India with her musical recitals and her networking for women's organizations, but her base was in Tamil Nadu, in Kotagiri. Mirra Alfassa's expansion of the Sri Aurobindo Ashram changed the demography of Pondicherry old town, and her founding of Auroville radically altered the land-use of a plateau outside the town. Mother Teresa's Mother House in Kolkata has become a place of pilgrimage and her centres are still active in the city. As befits a member of the commercial elite, Sooni Tata made her home in Mumbai. The same is true of Simone Tata, who lived in a residence called 'Tata Palace' during her early years in the city. Princess Durru Shehvar resided in Bella Vista Palace, Hyderabad, and even after 1948, when she was no longer permanently residing in India, she committed herself to the restoration and renovation of the city's Nizamate heritage. Political campaigning has led Sonia Gandhi to visit all parts of India – in 2004 her odometer reading stood at approximately 60,000 kilometres

– and she has, at different times, represented Rae Bareli and Amethi constituencies.[9] Her national profile and the dynasty to which she belongs, however, have meant that she has maintained New Delhi as her principal residence.

Once again, although in no way belittling the agency of these individual women, which emerges clearly in the chapters below, we shall see how each of them acts as part of an organization. The focus on women in their organizations creates context and enables us to explore the connections between them and various parts of Indian society. They did not work alone in India, but collaborated with Indian men and women as their organizations flourished. Men do not work alone either; but there is sometimes a tendency to view the life of a man in isolation, in particular if the biographer considers that life to be a great one. The women analyzed here integrated themselves into the cultures and society of India and had an effect on Indian life primarily via their organizations.

This study is therefore about personalized history, but also about history at a number of other levels which integrate the individual into structures that are progressively more distant from her. At the first level beyond the individual, these lives are set in the context of the history of the organizations the women founded and promoted. But a fundamental question about their legacy concerns the life-cycles of their organizations. Did those organizations survive the Indian *videshinis*? As mentioned above, these women were integrated into pre-existing Indian elites. The second level concerns the wider social history of India seen through the elites and their relationships with both the British colonial power and with those in favour of liberation from it.

Let us now look at the third macro-historical level. As has already been outlined, the period under consideration in this book straddles the colonial and postcolonial periods: 1893 to 2017 offers a long-view perspective. Writing in 1992 in their *Introduction to Western Women and Imperialism*, Nupur Chaudhuri and Margaret Strobel outline the importance of India: 'Both the length of its history and its prominence as a colonial establishment within the largest colonial empire in the modern world, as well as the range of imperialist policies practised, have make India an attractive area of research' (Chaudhuri and Strobel 1992, 5). The first part of what they are saying restates the family 'jewel in the crown' argument, but it does hold water. As a consequence, 1947 is tied into a historical continuum either side of it. The present study takes in the fifty-four years before Independence, as well as the seventy years since. In doing so, the book aims for an integrative perspective, rather than one which breaks twentieth-century Indian history on the back of midnight on 14 August 1947. The most appropriate name for such an elongated chronological frame is 'pericolonial'.

Why adopt such a perspective? The aim is not to deny the importance of 1947, but rather to acknowledge 'structures of difference'. What does that phrase mean in practical terms? For example, foregrounding 1947 as a simple end to the binary of colonizer (British) versus colonized (Indians) is the grand narrative, but it is not the whole story. Structures of difference, such as the women with Irish allegiances (Annie Besant, Margaret Cousins and Sister Nivedita), allow this book to include additional levels beyond simple comparisons between the Indians and the British. It is important to understand that the intention here is not to posit these structures of difference as a free-standing characteristic which defines all the women in this book; structures of difference are only useful within a specific analysis of the individual woman and how she negotiates her identity between her European origins and her commitment to India (and we shall see in the Conclusion that naturally those European origins also include contact with Britain, Britons and the British Indian Empire). It does indeed appear that the most influential European-born women in India between 1893 and 2017 were of 'non-British' origin. That said, however, the close focus in this book will be on their influence and their identity (in that order), rather than on the problematic notion of 'non-Britishness' that would be required to coalesce around an absence.

Looking more closely at the subjects chosen, therefore, the first thing to note is that no one European nation dominates. The largest sub-group is formed by the three French-speaking (also known as Francophone) women: Mirra Alfassa (born Blanche Rachel Mirra Alfassa in Paris), Sooni Tata (born Suzanne Brière in Paris) and

Simone Tata (born Simone Dunoyer in Geneva).[10] As we can see, this is a linguistic and not a national category as it includes women of both French and Swiss nationalities. While we note that Francophones are the largest group by language, the total of four women with continental western-European origins (the three French speakers plus the Italian-born Sonia Gandhi, whose first conversations with her mother-in-law were also in French) are nevertheless in the minority; they are outnumbered by the six other women who feature in this book. This second group comprises the three Anglo-Irish women who have defined themselves or been defined by others as 'Irish' (Annie Besant, Sister Nivedita and Margaret Cousins), two Ottoman princesses, and Mother Teresa, who was born in eastern Europe.

What is the justification for the unconventional division between western European women on the one side and the heterogeneous group on the other? The second group includes Ottoman and Irish women as well as an ethnic Albanian. It is quite simply to suggest that women from the fringes of Europe also engaged with India and with Indians. Such a plural understanding of Europeanness may be useful in understanding successful cases of female influence in India – particularly in the wake of Dipesh Chakrabarty's thesis, according to which Europe is 'an imaginary figure that remains deeply embedded in *clichéd and shorthand forms* in... everyday habits of thought' (Chakrabarty 2007, 4).

The motive for mentioning this variety of origins of the female subjects in this book is emphatically not to suggest that origin alone dictates influence. Rather, the notions of 'other Europes' and a 'plural Europe' help this book to highlight variations in the conventional periodization of twentieth-century Indian history.

For instance, Mirra Alfassa was only confronted with the issue of choosing between French and Indian nationality in 1954, when the French ceded the sovereignty of Pondicherry to the Union of Indian States (this cession was only ratified in 1962). The same applies to the attention given here to the state of Hyderabad – another region which did not join the Union of Indian States in 1947. Many of the key texts of the 'subaltern studies' school of Indian historiography aimed to include the voices of the Indian masses in the story of the nation; this book attempts in a far more modest way to point to some of the lacunae and discontinuities in the myth of a nation created at the stroke of a single midnight hour.[11]

The aim of this approach is to combine an analysis of discourse with an analysis of more materially based facts, such as the patterns of property ownership by the Sri Aurobindo Ashram in Puducherry old town (found in the chapter on Mirra Alfassa). As a consequence the book proceeds by small, empirically grounded steps, rather than imposing in advance yet another grand theory which purports to offer a bird's-eye view India.

As mentioned above, this study is organized into thematic domains or compartments: education and activism, religion and spirituality, international business and commerce, and state and national politics. The order in which these are presented is chronological, based on the arithmetical mean of the arrival dates for the women grouped into the domains. Thus, the education and activism compartment includes Annie Besant, Sister Nivedita (Margaret Noble) and Margaret Cousins, who arrived in India in 1893, 1898 and 1915, respectively, giving a mean of 1902. Next come Mirra Alfassa and Mother Teresa, *videshinis* involved in religion and spirituality, who arrived in 1920 and 1928, yielding a mean of 1924. After them come the business *videshinis* Sooni Tata and Simone Tata, who reached Indian shores in 1902 and 1955, the mean of which, rounding up, is 1929. The final compartment, representing the domain of state and national politics, houses Princess Durru Shehvar and Princess Niloufer (who both arrived in 1932) and Sonia Gandhi (arrived 1968), producing a mean year of 1944. The point of what may appear to be rather tiresome schoolroom arithmetic is to show that there is an underlying linearity in the organization of the book. If the *videshinis* in a compartment have separate chapters allocated to them, as with Mirra Alfassa and Mother Teresa, this is because the inherent differences between the individual subjects are more important and more substantial than the similarities between them. If, on the other hand, the subjects are grouped together within a chapter, then, while recognizing that they are separate, we place more stress on the similarities between them. This applies in the case of the education and activism compartment housing Annie Besant, Sister Nivedita and Margaret Cousins.

In addition to this background linearity, intended to give the reader the impression of forward momentum and to avoid anachronism, the analysis of the life or lives of the female subjects in each compartment is also presented chronologically. However, for reasons of focus the analysis is selective in terms of which periods of the individual's life are included. For example, in the case of Mother Teresa the detail relevant to the transformation of the nun's identity and her own transformation of the Roman Catholic Church in India is concentrated into the period from 1947 to 1948. This selective focus is far more efficient than a full cradle-to-grave biographical treatment. Indeed, that particular chapter goes beyond the grave, as it were, using posthumous assessments of Mother Teresa to discuss how representations of nationality impact the nun's legacy.

The first chapter after this Introduction is a prelude which takes the example of a woman who will be less well-known to the majority of Indian readers (outside the Union Territory of Pondicherry, that is), in order to test out the method of the book. We shall see that Jeanne Dupleix, born in Pondicherry in 1706, was a highly controversial individual on account of her connivance with the money-making capitalism practised by her husband Joseph-François (governor-general of the French possessions in India from 1742 to 1754) and because of the extreme intolerance she showed to the majority Hindu population (she was a Roman Catholic). One of the most remarkable things about her is that, although she was culturally and politically French to a fault, she was a quarter Indian in terms of her ethnicity. Although this 'Indian blood' greatly exercised French commentators on her, she never allowed it to affect her national allegiances: she was, as the time-honoured phrase has it, 'more French than the French'. The representations of Jeanne show us how an individual's actions can be decoupled from their perceived origins, 'race'. This is an important lesson for understanding the twentieth-century Indian *videshinis*. It is hoped that the study of their complex, problematic Indianness (which is entirely credible much of the time) will make a small contribution towards the way that thinking women and men in India might work out a post-national way of understanding themselves in the world, and the world in themselves.

Jeanne Dupleix is a useful precursor in other respects too; her lack of visibility and eighteenth-century origins allow us to bracket out the question of her influence (which is not analyzed in any detail here) and test the methodology of the present study, refining it in the process. Jeanne Dupleix helps to theorize the issues which affect women's visibility in the first place, such as the way in which women leave a different documentary trace from their husbands, brothers and fathers. This will help us to interrogate the source materials that feature in this book. This matter is considered in detail in the Dupleix Prelude; but suffice it to say at this point that this book uses both writing by these women (autobiographies, correspondence and speeches) as well as documents about them written by others. These range from eyewitness accounts, to journalism, to full-length biographies. It should be understood that in the case of the ego-documents the net has to be cast very widely and encompasses ephemera such as postcards (in the case of Sooni Tata), transcriptions of interviews (Mirra Alfassa) and fragmentary prefatory notes (Sonia Gandhi).[12] On rare occasions, even untrustworthy sources are cited, not for what they actually tell us about the female subjects, but rather for the generic issues about the type of thematic domains in which comment occurs. The chapters on Jeanne Dupleix, Mirra Alfassa and Sonia Gandhi take this one stage further by including fictional sources (novels and films).

The eighteenth-century precursor allows us to introduce the theme of linguistic competence, which was so important for these women. Not only are European-born women often teachers of language in a domestic and professional context; their fluency in the tongue of the other is a marker of their hybridity and of their Indianness (proved by the highly controversial issue of the competence or lack of competence of Sonia Gandhi in Hindi). As we shall see in the Conclusion, on account of the British colonial presence (and its legacy) during the period in question, these European women have a dual linguistic journey. Not only will there be cultural contact with an Indian language (Gujarati in the case of Sooni Tata, Bengali for

Sister Nivedita and possibly also for Mother Teresa); coming to India is also a journey into (Indian) English.

Looking at third-level history concerning the interaction between the precursor's elite and India, we see that the activity of Jeanne Dupleix in the colonial regime of French-controlled Pondicherry encroached on three of the four domains which are considered separately in the main body of this book: religion and spirituality, international business and commerce, and state and national politics (the only one that it does not touch is education and activism). This indicates not only how profoundly asymmetrical colonial relations can be (in Pondicherry, religiously sanctioned, political and economic power was centred in the white hands of a small group of Frenchmen); it also suggests that the elites which supported the Indian *videshinis* all had to negotiate strategies of resistance to colonial rule, while coexisting with the colonial power. They had to engage because that was the only way they could fulfil their primary purpose, which was to preserve their own status in Indian society. In terms of methodology, the convergence of the three domains in Jeanne Dupleix's brand of eighteenth-century colonialism reminds us that, although religion and spirituality and the other three domains form cogent centres of interests, the analysis on Education, Spirituality, Business and Politics is open to crossovers of the lives and careers of these women. These are moments when the women get up and leave the compartments that were allocated them. Thus spirituality and religion will have some impact on politics (we shall see that this might also have been a consideration in the aborted negotiations between Mirra Alfassa, Sri Aurobindo and Sir Akbar Hydari to found her universal city in Hyderabad state in the early 1950s, in an attempt to return some international prestige to post-Operation Polo Hyderabad). The study of the lives of Annie Besant and Sister Nivedita, in particular, suggests that education too is a highly charged political domain in a nation struggling for self-determination and sovereignty.

As we see below, the argument ranges widely in geographical terms too, taking in Madras and Tamil Nadu including Pondicherry (with Annie Besant, Margaret Cousins and Mirra Alfassa), Hyderabad state and city (with Princess Durru Shehvar and Princess Niloufer), Bombay and Maharashtra (with Sooni Tata and Simone Tata), Calcutta (with Sister Nivedita and Mother Teresa) and finally New Delhi with Sonia Gandhi. It is important to avoid the North Indian bias of many English-language books about India. Women like Sonia Gandhi, Annie Besant and Margaret Cousins criss-crossed the country performing at political rallies, public lectures and music recitals. Before we embark on our journey around India, with city street signs guiding us along the way, it is necessary to take a trip back in time to eighteenth-century French-controlled Pondicherry for a *prélude pondichérien*. Our starting point, however, will be modern-day Paris.

Notes

1. I beg the indulgence of readers and scholars of Sanskrit; 'videshinis' is grammatically incorrect, as it is a combination of a Sanskrit stem and English suffix. However, this form has been adopted as the least obtrusive solution to a common problem when Sanskrit words have to be used in writing in English. I am grateful to Rohana Seneviratne for his advice in this matter.
2. At this stage I have reproduced the women's names in the form that is used most commonly in India. Frequently, however, we see that the woman has another name; this is a surface indication of the plural identities of women who are both Indian and *videshinis*. Appendix 1 presents biographical information about the Indian *videshinis* in tabular form.
3. The most recent Mother Teresa stamp is part of the 'Builders of Modern India' series, which includes Rukmini Devi Arundale, B.R. Ambedkar, Indira Gandhi, M.K. Gandhi, Rajiv Gandhi, Jawaharlal Nehru and J.R.D. Tata, all of whom are mentioned in the pages that follow.
4. Outside the European domain there are the marriages of the Australian Joan Falkiner to the Nizam of Palanpur in 1939 and the 1963 union of the United States citizen Hope Cook to the Chogyal of Sikkim. The influence of these women also fails the significance test.
5. See Sengupta (1984), Singh Bhatia (1979) and Rao (1996).

6. A note on the spellings of Indian cities: the modern forms (Puducherry, Kolkata, Chennai, Mumbai, etc.) will be used when the reference encompasses the period after the cities were renamed.
7. See Appendix 1.
8. The only exception is Mirra Alfassa, who appears to have remained in Pondicherry from 1920 to 1973. It should be noted, however, that before she met Sri Aurobindo she had lived in North Africa and Japan.
9. Sanjoy Majumder, 'Why did Sonia change her mind', http://news.bbc.co.uk/1/hi/world/south_asia/3726081.stm (last accessed 11 November 2011).
10. To this group also belongs the eighteenth-century precursor Jeanne Dupleix.
11. The whole notion of 'twilight', commonly used when referring to the period immediately before independence, displays an occidental (or Northern Indian) normative bias; the sun goes down far faster in South India.
12. It is highly probable that Princess Durru Shehvar and Princess Niloufer had Turkish passports, but this cannot be confirmed.

A PONDICHERRIAN PRELUDE: JEANNE DUPLEIX

[S]he is a Nîli [She-devil]. Poets say that there is such a one for each of the four ages … but Madame is all these at once.[1]

– Ananda Rangappillai on Jeanne Dupleix, 1748

A person whom I should refrain from mentioning at all, if she should have had as much influence as is claimed on the injustices and annoyances caused by Joseph-François Dupleix, this minor tyrant.

– Boisserolle, the brother-in-law of Law de Lauriston, 1759

Jeanne, a mixed-race woman of modest origins who became a marchioness and a Begum for a time before dying miserably in Paris from damp and from society's ingratitude.

– Rose Vincent, 1982

By dint of being repeated, these powerful images have ended by taking on the appearance of reality… Nowadays a brand of feminism cultivates this myth. A recent biography depicted Jeanne like a Hollywood star… The governor's wife has done nothing to merit this attention. Most of the protagonists in this story do not even mention her, or if they do so, it is in an indirect manner.

– Marc Vigié, 1993

If you are in Paris or in Google Street View and stand on the Champ de Mars with monsieur Eiffel's landmark towering in front of you, it is not immediately obvious at ground level that to the left and to the right there are six streets named after people who shaped France's presence in India in the eighteenth century. Right here, in a part of the French capital most frequently visited by tourists, it would be pleasant to be able to complete a seamless walk commemorating 'French India'. That is not to be, however, because Paris is a crowded city and its thoroughfares are overlaid with multiple layers of namings; it has many advocates of the dead and famous vying to achieve street-level immortality for those they admire. This has meant that name congestion and about two hundred metres of the avenue Gustave Eiffel – one wonders if he really needed to have a street named after him as well – crossing the Champ de Mars immediately in front of the tower stand in the way of a single French India memory trail.

What you have instead are two adjacent networks of streets in the seventh and fifteenth arrondissements (districts).[2] The first network starts beside the Seine at the Port de Suffren (named after Admiral Pierre André de Suffren in 1905), before becoming the Port de la Bourdonnais (named, also in 1905, after the naval commander Bertrand-François Mahé de la Bourdonnais) and passing the Musée du Quai Branly, which has 138 artefacts from India in its collections. From there, you can continue onto the avenue de la Bourdonnais (named in 1881) and finish on the avenue Silvestre de Sacy (named after the nineteenth-century Oriental scholar in 1908).[3]

The second network begins with avenue de Suffren (an earlier commemoration from 1867). Then there are no less than three memorials to the same person – Joseph-François, the Marquis de Dupleix (1697–1763). His is the prime name in the French Indian pantheon. It is pronounced 'Duplex'. The first memorial is a street (an early designation from 1815); the second a charming square (given its name in the same year).[4] Now you have two options. If you walk south-south-east from Place Dupleix you come to the rue de Pondichéry, a street named in 1892, but which bore the Dupleix surname before that. Walking south-west brings you to the third and most impressive of these memorials to this hero of the French in India – the Dupleix Metro station, which was opened in 1906.

We have not yet encountered the governor general's wife, the true subject of this *prélude pondichérien*; her lack of visibility shows the challenge of focusing on female subjects. She will be introduced in due course; but, in order to grasp her role, one would have to understand her husband Dupleix's significance in the relationship between India and France. Though he was governor of Pondicherry, and thereby the chief authority of all the French trading posts in India, for only twelve years (1742–54), Dupleix is the most prominent figure in the history of the French presence in India, because it was during his governorship and by his direct intervention that the greatest influence, tax revenues and territory were accrued for France. His method was to fight the British, the other European power competing for influence in the Deccan at the time, at the same time establishing alliances with Indian rulers in various regions and getting the Mughal emperor in Delhi to ratify these alliances. French historians generally agree that there are similarities between Dupleix's practice of alliance building and strategies the British employed after Dupleix's recall to France in 1754 (see Vigié 1993, 10 and 532). This means that Dupleix has an extremely important role in the development of a particular method of colonization in India. But we must now consider the role of Jeanne Dupleix, and that of the spouse of colonial administrators in general.

An interesting illustration of the married woman's role is offered by Lu Gwei-Djen, the collaborator and second wife of Joseph Needham, the eminent historian of China. At a dinner for the great man hosted by Neil McKendrick at Gonville and Caius College in Cambridge in 1971, Gwei-Djen is reported to have whispered to her host: 'Joseph may be the bridge between East and West, but I am the supporting arch' (McKendrick 2009, 7). So it is with Jeanne Dupleix. Unlike her husband, no Paris streets are named after her. She does, however, play a supporting role to her husband, as he himself acknowledges in the second epigraph at the head of this Prelude.

In rural northern France, a town called Landrecies, with a population of approximately four thousand, is the birthplace of Governor General Dupleix. A 3.6-metre-high sculpture of her husband by Léon Fagel was erected there in front of the town hall in 1888.

Jeanne Dupleix features in one of the bronze reliefs on the plinth of the monument. This is the only public portrayal of her. The panel shows her tending to the wounded during the siege of Pondicherry by the British in 1748.[5] So whereas her husband now has a metro station in the capital bearing his name, Jeanne Dupleix must be content with a plinth in the provinces.

The life of the Marchioness Dupleix (1706–56) falls outside the post-1893 period of the main subjects of this book, so we shall neither present a detailed account of her life nor give a definitive answer to the question of her influence. Yet she sets some of the terms of the debate around *videshinis*. At a fundamental level, these concern the lack of trustworthy sources relating to their lives. In Jeanne Dupleix's case this has led to controversy: opinions on her are divided. For example, while the plinth shows her caring for the wounded during the 1748 siege, other accounts mention her ordering her militia to confiscate valuables from fleeing civilians. We shall also encounter the ways in which women's supposed multiple allegiances are judged in terms of the languages they speak.

In short, how does one perform 'differentiation'; that is, extracting the meaning of an individual's life from the wider social, cultural, historical and economic context and rehearsing the meaning of that life?

Jeanne Dupleix was born Jeanne Albert in Pondicherry in 1706. She was part of the small French colonial elite that ruled over that territory. She was the eldest daughter of Jacques Albert (1675–1721), a doctor in the French East India Company (La Compagnie française des Indes orientales). Her mother, Rose de Castro (1684–1749), was a Portugese creole. Jeanne Albert was educated in French, but spoke her mother's native tongue as well. Her first marriage was to Jacques Vincens, a Company official, in 1719; she was thirteen years old (this age, though young, was not exceptional for the time). Dupleix probably first met her in 1721, the year of his arrival in India as well as the year of her father's death. Jeanne Vincens, now fifteen, was already the mother of a son, Jacques junior, born in 1720. Jacques Vincens senior and Dupleix were business partners and the extended family welcomed the dynamic new arrival. Their association deepened, as we shall see, to the extent that the whole Vincens family joined Dupleix when he was posted to Chandernagore as the head of France's Bengal trading post in 1731. It was there that Jeanne Vincens married Dupleix in 1741; her husband had died four years earlier.

A year later, in 1742, Dupleix returned to Pondicherry from Chandernagore, accompanied by the ready-made family of his new wife Jeanne, to take up his new appointment as governor general of Pondicherry and head of all the French possessions in India. During the governorships of Lenoir and Dumas the town was a bustling place having obtained a grant to mint rupees and with coral and textile merchants carrying on a brisk interregional trade from Mocha or Muscat to the Philippines. Dupleix, however, was to take this activity to another level.

Dupleix depended on various networks to underpin and extend his power. Now, as governor general, some of these networks were ex officio, such as his staff of administrators employed by the Compagnie des Indes; there was also the key figure of Ananda Rangappillai, his *dubash* or official translator ('du' means 'two' and 'bash' is a particle related to 'language') – the one who calls Jeanne a 'she-devil' in the first epigraph above – as well as the French and native soldiers at his command. There were, however, also private networks, such as that of his birth family: his father, François, was a successful financier and tax farmer, as was his elder brother. The most important support system in his everyday life in India, however, was his domestic network, and the first and foremost person within that network was his wife, Jeanne Dupleix.

As with Jeanne, a marriage ceremony was the starting point of the influence in India of the other five married women in this book: Sonia Gandhi, Simone Tata, Sooni Tata and princesses Durru Shehvar and Niloufer. Compared with those women, however, Jeanne Dupleix has more of everything: more marriages, more languages (between two and four, depending on the source), more children (twelve live births) and more alliances with European countries through the marriages of her daughters (two to French aristocrat husbands, one to an Austrian and even one to a 'Britisher').[6]

This embarrassment of riches suggests that Governor General

Dupleix and Jeanne Dupleix established a form of society in eighteenth-century Pondicherry in which they enjoyed overall control. Though the precise extent of Jeanne Dupleix's role in establishing that society is still a matter of heated debate, it appears that, as a family, the Dupleixes had influence in several domains that are considered separately in relation to the Indian *videshinis* in the main body of this book, domains such as business and politics. The metaphor of the train and its compartments is used in the Introduction to suggest that, even for the later Indian *videshinis*, these domains are connected and that there is a way to pass from one to the other. The Dupleix clan, however, was ultra-elite. From 1742 to 1754, as we shall see, the Dupleixes wielded a form of power, cutting across politics, business and religion, that was close to the absolute power of a monarch (probably why the king and the Company put an end to their reign). The form of capitalism they pursued enriched primarily themselves, by taxing local farmers on the value of their harvests. Under Dupleix these taxes reached the catastrophic level of 50 per cent (David 1999, 48). Furthermore, as discussed below, one of the keenest reproaches to be levelled against Jeanne Dupleix is that during the siege of 1748 she protected only her own faith community, the Roman Catholic Church; indeed, she is accused of using her access to the governor general to lobby actively for the destruction of sacred Hindu sites. The precise nature of her involvement may never be known; while the elite groups provided the prerequisite conditions for the individual woman's action and the power wielded by the Dupleix ultra-elite increased the scope for corruption, corroborated facts would be needed before we could pass judgement.

The challenges about discerning the woman's role also relate to sources. Though Jeanne Dupleix is an elite woman, there are few detailed historical sources about her life. This is acknowledged by Rose Vincent, the author of *Le Temps d'un royaume: Jeanne Dupleix, 1706–1756*, a *biographie romancée* (fictional biography): 'A creole woman, born in India, she did not have any friends in France to whom she could write' (Vincent 1982, 347). Nor did she have professional correspondence with the Compagnie des Indes like her husband.

This paucity of information, however, has deterred neither

biographers such as Isidore Guët and Yvonne Gaebelé nor writers of fiction such as Rose Vincent from writing monographs on her life.[7] Other novelists have written characters inspired by her, such as Joséphine in Dominique Marny's *Du Côté de Pondichéry*, published in 1999. All of them have been captivated by the story of her rise and fall. On the other side of this debate is Marc Vigié, quoted in the final epigraph. From his professional point of view as a historian, the lack of references to Mme Dupleix should be ascribed quite simply to her lack of importance. Vigié laments the myth-making that has spread up around Jeanne Dupleix; in his opinion, even the venerable Alfred Martineau in his four-volume history of Dupleix is not immune to this. For Vigié, Jeanne Dupleix is a woman on the edge of history; the historian who ventures into territory where there are few sources is indulging in myth-making and base fiction.

What should be our attitude to this point of view? It is certainly well-founded. Yet Vigié's dismissive position does not probe what it is about this mixed-race woman's life story which has attracted biographers and novelists. In reviewing what appealed to these writers, first and foremost there is Jeanne's rarity; no other governor general's wife achieved such prominence.[8] Another element is the total reversal in the couple's fortunes after their enforced departure from Pondicherry in 1754. In France they were never able to regain their reputation (it was widely believed that they had been enriching themselves personally).[9]

The methodological point being made is that the analysis of women's lives, in terms of both how they are represented by others and how they present themselves, needs to include a variety of source materials (personal correspondence where it exists, biographies, journalistic pieces, even fiction). Some of these materials, such as the fictionalized biographies of Jeanne Dupleix, are hybrid forms.[10] Indeed, this book also includes the wider mythological context. For Jeanne Dupleix, this means acknowledging that her husband tried to create a myth around her while she was still alive, particularly about her role in the 1748 siege of Pondicherry (see the second epigraph). The Landrecies plinth demonstrates how pervasive this version of events is. Furthermore, at a more general level, although there was no generalized discourse of gender equality in human rights, women nevertheless served to personify symbolic power and the power in France. This is a phenomenon not unique to France; but in France such symbols range from the perennial Jeanne d'Arc (Joan of Arc) to reincarnations of Marianne, the figurehead of republicanism.[11] Jeanne Dupleix's life was so amenable to fiction because it had the three elements of exoticism, tragedy and romance.

In addition to the question of sources, the example of Jeanne Dupleix suggests that the successful differentiation of the roles of women should also revalue the importance of domestic and family space. This follows the thesis of Antoinette Burton's *Dwelling in the Archive,* a study of women's writing about house, home and history in late colonial India. Burton's book emphasizes 'the importance of home as… a material archive for history… in an extended moment of historical crisis' (Burton 2003, 5). Through this Burton 'hope[s] to indicate a pathway out of one of the most vexing impasses of postcolonial history: this apparent dichotomy of "discourse" versus "reality"' (Burton 2003, 5). In basic terms, the dichotomy that needs to be overcome is that between regarding sources as expressions of language with intrinsic contradictions and incoherencies, and viewing them as historical documents which reflect material 'reality' in a more or less direct way. The primary source material of *Dwelling in the Archive* is unpublished memoirs; but the absence of even this sort of document concerning Jeanne's family life means that important information can only be gained from the basic details of the état civil (the register of births, marriages and deaths). Examples of such details are: when she and her offspring were married; what names were given to children; who the godparents of these children were and when these offspring were married, and to whom. But such details are particularly significant in a life as populated by births as Jeanne Dupleix's. They foreground the nascent clan as an efficient form of power elite, particularly because extended family units played an extremely important role in determining and fixing for life the individual's educational opportunities, religion, political allegiances and type of participation in the wider economy. Thus, in eighteenth-century Pondicherry, the family encompassed all the domains, such as education and activism, and religion and spirituality, which we consider separately when examining the lives of the Indian *videshinis.*

We shall now look selectively at Jeanne Dupleix's life in the period from 1721, when she first met Joseph-François Dupleix, to her forced 'repatriation' to France in 1754[12] – a series of snapshots, rather than an exhaustive account. Each links an episode from Jeanne Dupleix's life with a general methodological point relevant to the book.

The first point concerns the differentiation of women, the depth of women's connectivity within their societies. Men have networks through which they exercise power; Jeanne Dupleix, very differently, acquired and exercised power exclusively by virtue of her marital arrangements and family connections. It is important to understand that this way of interpreting women's power and powerful women is a function of the lack of individual opportunities afforded to women in the eighteenth century for acquiring (and increasing their) wealth. Such gender discrimination was still operative in 1893 and continues to the present day, but has declined to a certain extent. We can see the effects of this decline in the fact that opposite the five married *videshinis* (Sonia Gandhi, Simone Tata, Sooni Tata, Princess Niloufer and Princess Durru Shehvar) stand five equally influential women who were unmarried or whose marriages did not have any significant effect on their Indian careers (Margaret Noble, Margaret Cousins, Annie Besant, Mirra Alfassa and Mother Teresa).

At the same time, overemphasizing the family's role creates a pitfall: downplaying the determination, intelligence and success of the individual married women. This caveat is crucial in the case of Princess Durru Shehvar, whose activism in support of Hyderabadi culture in post-Operation Polo Hyderabad occurred after she was estranged from her husband in 1948. Similarly, Simone Tata founded the retail chain Westside in 1998, nine years after the death of her husband Naval H. Tata.

Given the restricted sources already mentioned, Jeanne Dupleix's life reads like a case study illustrating the social function of marriage from the second volume of Michel Foucault's path-breaking *Histoire de la sexualité* (*The History of Sexuality*) (Foucault 1984). The historian is speaking primarily about marriage in ancient Greece, where the woman is passed down through the generations as she moves from the role of daughter to that of wife. A similar instrumentalization needs to be acknowledged in the case of Jeanne.

However, Jeanne's life in eighteenth-century Pondicherry also includes a transfer from husband one to husband two. This occurred following the death of Jacques Vincens in 1737; but the mere fact that Jeanne remarries shows us something about the basic attractiveness of the widow Vincens. This attractiveness derived from a series of elements, social, financial and physical; marriage was not a single one-way contract for Jeanne. The social mores of the time together with her own qualities led to the second marriage.

Let us now illustrate these qualities. According to Vigié, his father's influence meant that Dupleix arrived in India in 1721 better placed than all of his contemporaries; but as the power structures in the administrative centre of France's Indian possessions were rigid, the ambitious young man soon learned that he would have to succeed in a difficult posting to prove himself worthy of a leadership position. Therefore, in 1731, he took up the directorship of the trading post at Chandernagore, in Bengal. It was at this point that the friendly relationship Dupleix had maintained with the Vincens family and with Jeanne moved to another level. Commentators make it clear that before his departure for Chandernagore, Dupleix had found a ready-made family in the Vincens.

It is not surprising that Dupleix wanted a trusted associate to accompany him to Bengal, but it is remarkable that he wanted all of Jacques Vincens's extended family to come.[13] This included Jeanne, her six children, her mother and her two sisters. This letter of June 1732 makes clear the importance of Jeanne's opinion: 'You can show my letter to your wife. Do not do anything without consulting her. Perhaps my suggestions will displease her. If that were the case, it would make me despair; because in all truth my only wish is to be of service to you both' (Gaebelé 1934, 60). The result was that the entire Vincens family accompanied Dupleix to Chandernagore in 1733, a significant cross-regional journey, and remained there for nine years. This was outside the usual convention by which men undertook trade journeys on their own. There has been extensive speculation as to why Dupleix wanted the entire Vincens family to accompany him, with the birth in 1736 of the youngest Vincens child Marie suggesting that Jeanne and Joseph-François may have been in an extramarital relationship while Jacques Vincens was away in France. It is also important to note that the combination of Dupleix's financial resources and the numerous Vincens family was beneficial to both parties, economically and socially. Given that the French were isolated in India at this time, such a ready-made patchwork family offered a clear advantage in terms of quality of life. This was certainly the case in Chandernagore, which was more isolated from the centre of French activity than Pondicherry. It is an interesting paradox that the loneliness of the merchant's life led Dupleix to opt for a form of domestic arrangement quite similar to the extended family still common in India today (similar in terms of its nuclear arrangements, of course, and not on account of its possible extramarital element). Jeanne and her family enjoyed a unique position under the protection of the head of the trading post.

The family's move to Chandernagore resulted in a durable practical union between Dupleix and the Vincens and Albert families. Dupleix's advancement within the company structure was that of a single man with great potential – far greater than Jacques Vincens had ever had, on account of his lack of connections (to establish which, he travelled to France in 1736; the attempt was unsuccessful – he returned from this journey a very ill man, and only lived another few months). Given the protection Dupleix offered, his advancement brought the family advantages. After the death of Vincens in 1737, this alliance only deepened and led to the consolidation of the clan's economic power. Dupleix took on the role of protector–patriarch and Jeanne and her mother Rose probably maintained order among the younger members of the family. Their fortunes were now inextricably linked.

In moving to Chandernagore, Jeanne demonstrated mobility, a crucial characteristic of the Indian *videshinis* in this book. Jeanne Dupleix and the rest of the Indian *videshinis* in this book are remarkable in terms of the range and extent of their repeated travel. It would seem that physical movement is a prerequisite for upward social mobility. Jeanne not only relocated with her whole family and household to Chandernagore from Pondicherry; she also moved back again in 1742, as well as resettling in France in 1754.

In 1741, just as he was to about to marry the thirty-five-year-old Jeanne, Dupleix wrote a remarkable letter to his brother in France. In it he attempts to justify the linking of their family's fortune with that of his future wife Jeanne. The point he is trying to establish is that although she is a mixed-race woman, she is legally French as part of an established tradition in France's Indian possessions. But before looking at the quotation, which illustrates how all of the Indian *videshinis* are defined by the elites that support them, let us consider the ethnic patchwork of eighteenth-century Pondicherry.

The French territory at that time was home to a variety of 'races': white Europeans, primarily French, but also Portuguese; a similar diversity of Indian peoples as today (only in smaller numbers); and also so-called 'cafres' – Abyssinian mercenaries in the pay of the French East India Company.[14] Generally, though, because Pondicherry was under French control, there was a clear polarization between Europeans and non-Europeans. This is clear in the separation built into the town's geography, dividing it into a 'ville blanche' (a 'white town') and a 'ville noire' (a 'black town') with a physical barrier – a drainage canal – between them. This separation came from general customs and from the French wish to create a territory in which they were in the majority. That said, however, although the 'ville noire' was overwhelmingly a Tamil town (with Dalit villages beyond it), there were many buildings inhabited and used by Indians in the so-called 'white town.' One example is that of the Gopurams (which is discussed below in the section about Jeanne's reputation). Another example concerns the dwellings of the servants and cooks of the French inhabiting the area close to the 'white town,' who were also Dalits.

This polarized geography also applied to Jeanne as a person. For herself and for the Indian populations of Pondicherry, although Jeanne was of mixed race, she was a white European in political and cultural terms. However, for Dupleix and the other French people, such as his brother, the situation was seen from a diametrically opposite point of view: Jeanne was a creole, but it was the Indian elements in her make-up which were more visible and which needed to be accounted for. Thus each group saw a different 'other' in the same woman. This phenomenon of multiple otherness is crucial for Jeanne and for the other Indian *videshinis* in this book. It points to the fact that a more complete picture of the woman's identity must include both self-representations and how (and for whom) she is portrayed by others.

Let us now look at her future husband's attempt to explain away Jeanne's difference from a French point of view. The French perspective is a closed circuit here: the arch-colonist Dupleix is writing to another Dupleix, his brother, who farmed the taxes of the French peasants in a similarly exploitative way:

> The children born of a European man and a black woman are called mestizos. According to the edict of 1664, they can be French subjects in the eyes of the law. Their children married to European men are quarter-castes and finally as they progressively increase in whiteness are called creoles. The majority of our employees are married to these creoles whose origins are more or less obscure. Some of them, however, are descended directly from the Portuguese. There are no blacks among Company employees, but only creoles and the sons of white men. (Dupleix 1748)

This singular passage reiterates and confirms the polarized way in which race is seen. An absolute position is expressed in the phrase, 'il n'y a pas de noirs parmi les employés' (there are no blacks among Company employees). These 'noirs' (blacks) are Indian and so the colonial separation is maintained. This absolutism also contains double standards, however, because Dupleix seems to have conveniently overlooked both the Company's Abyssinian mercenaries and Ananda Rangappillai, its translator, when he claims that the French East India Company has no 'black' employees. Moreover, Dupleix aims to account for his future wife's difference from the 'blacks' in terms of a process of whitening, which sees the proportion of her Indian 'blackness' reduced first to 50 per cent in the mestizos (such as her mother) and finally to 25 per cent for the 'quartices' (quarter-castes) such as Jeanne herself. Europeans saw Jeanne in terms of her residual blackness.

Dupleix has thus demonstrated to his brother that his future sister-in-law is at two removes from the 'blacks'; but removed she is. Dupleix is indirectly suggesting that Rose de Castro, Jeanne's mother, was already 'régnicole', which Antoine-Gaspard Boucher d'Argis's 1765 article in the *Encyclopédie* defines as 'a person who is born a subject of the king. This quality is opposed to that of resident of foreign origin or alien' (Boucher d'Argis 1756). Dupleix is implying that the legal definition of Frenchness should take precedence over the racial one.

It is always those in a position of power who define the divisions between those who belong to their group and those who do not. In a 1789 letter to his English friend Ozias Humphrey, the Frenchman Claude Martin (who founded the Martinière schools in Lucknow, Kolkata and Lyon) pleads the same exemption for his Indian concubine 'Boulone' that Dupleix claims for Jeanne. Martin writes: 'My amiable Girl, [whom] I do not Rank among the Blacks, she being whiter than me, and having had as Good an Education as an European' (Martin 1789). Once again we have the general racism confirmed at that same time as the specific exception. Claude Martin's exception is based on the vagaries of skin tone and a claim to a Western education. Even within elites, those who are able to define (generally men) rather than be defined (generally women) are in positions of power. However, this definition is not always polarized in terms of gender. Women such as Mother Teresa define others in their elite; sometimes her definitions will be fair, in other cases they will be less so.

In the chapters which follow, there will be numerous references to ego-documents, in which the women write about their own identities; however, this book sets equal store by judgements about the European-born women uttered by Indians. This is because our main subjects are Europeans attempting to intermesh with Indian cultures and not Indians being granted honorary access to European structures by their husbands (as in the cases of Boulone and Jeanne above).[15] The judgements of Indians (both elite and non-elite) are varied, of course, with some happy to declare the foreign-born women Indian, others stressing their foreignness. These multiple snapshots complement the more sustained self-reflexive ego-documents, sometimes confirming them, at other times contradicting them. The aim in including both is to get a representative picture.

Let us now return to Jeanne Dupleix in 1742. At this point, two elements came together, permitting her and her husband to enjoy exponential social and economic advancement. The first element is Jeanne and her family's homecoming to Pondicherry; the second is her husband's appointment as governor general of the city, the administrative centre of French operations in India. Examining their lives at this time allows us to concentrate on multilingualism, one of the key domains of women's differentiation.

The global significance of women's competence in multiple languages can be signalled by analysing a female antecedent of Jeanne Dupleix, a woman who stands at the crossroads between at least three cultures, and hence goes by at least three names. She is Malintzin for the Mayas and Aztecs, and doña Marina, or La Malinche, for Cortés and the Spanish conquerors of Mexico. Tzvetan Todorov first evokes her plurality of names in his *Conquête de l'Amérique* (*Conquest of America*), when he is examining critically the function of language in colonization (Todorov 1982). After deciding to call her La Malinche, he then goes on to outline the crucial importance of her ability to speak more than one language. Cortés had to dominate both the Aztecs and the Maya, and La Malinche's multiple linguistic competence offered him a unique opportunity. This came about because she was born into the Aztec community, but was sold as a slave to the Mayas and therefore spoke both languages. Todorov also supposes that she eventually learned Spanish as well (ibid., 106); but what is most striking is what he calls her 'conversion culturelle' (cultural conversion), in which she 'adopts Spanish values and contributes all her efforts to making their goals reality' (ibid.). Todorov cannot overstate her importance: 'It is true that the conquest of Mexico would have been impossible without her (or without someone playing the same role)' (ibid., 107).

Is Jeanne Dupleix a French Indian Malinche? Should there be individual recognition of her contribution to Dupleix's system of alliance-building, the system by which he secured French influence over Indian territory by alliances with multiple Indian princes? As we have seen, this was a tactic employed by the British to establish their hegemony in India. Has an enormous historical injustice been done, in that a small exhibition in 1905 was the first and last public commemoration of Jeanne's life (Vigié 1993, 550)? The most probable answer to all three questions is a straightforward 'no'. Despite that, there are relevant comparisons between Jeanne Dupleix and La Malinche, and even between Cortés's interpreter and the Indian *videshinis*.

Just like La Malinche, Jeanne's cultural allegiances never appear to be in doubt. Todorov correctly points out that La Malinche acted on behalf of Spanish colonization in Mexico. However, it appears that her personal loyalty lay not with an abstract idea of nation, but with Cortés himself. She was his concubine. In a similar way, Jeanne Dupleix was always in favour of the French, because the French were intimately connected with the interests of her own family. This situation pertained all the time she was in India and ceased only after she arrived in France. It might be more accurate to say that her loyalty was more to her elite than to France.

These two different centres of interest – the domestic realm and the business of the state – are in conflict as far as the influence of the linguistic competence of Jeanne Dupleix is concerned. Put starkly: was Jeanne an interpreter, her husband's plenipotentiary, or a woman outside the circuits of power? The mainstream historian Vigié will not even accord Jeanne the role of interpreter. While he is prepared to recognize that Jeanne had 'a fairly good education' (Vigié 1993, 468), he insists that she knew only Portuguese and Tamil, and not Persian, the language of international diplomacy in the region. He states that 'when official correspondence came from Arcot, Hyderabad or Delhi [these would have been written in Persian], she had to resort to the Company's interpreters just like everyone else' (ibid.). The implications of Vigié's position are, first, that any advice to Dupleix by Jeanne could not have occurred at the actual time and place at which a message from the Mughals arrived; rather, she would have taken on the traditional female role as a sympathetic ear at home at the end of the working day. Thus Vigié gives precedence to Ananda Rangappillai, Dupleix's *dubash*. The second implication is that her limited command of languages (Tamil and Portuguese) would have forced her to play a secondary regional role, limited to Pondicherry and its hinterland (and the Portuguese possessions in India), rather than that of a stateswoman acting at a 'national' level. If one accepts this, her 'influence' outside her region would have been limited to receiving the financial benefit of the rights to land income given to her and her daughter by Muzaffar Jang (Muhyi ad-Din Muzaffar Jang Hidayat), the *subadhar* or controller of the Deccan.

Writers who argue for her importance foreground her language skills. For instance, in a fictional account of the meeting between Jeanne and Dupleix's military commander, de Bussy, published in 1887, the year before the statue went up on the plinth in Landrecies, Judith Gautier has Dupleix uttering a mock warning to de Bussy: 'Beware of her, she knows all the dialects of India' (Gautier 1887, 174). Gautier then has Jeanne reply: Don't listen to my husband, she said to Bussy in Hindustani, his affection for me leads him astray (ibid.). So here we have the husband's hyperbole being checked by Jeanne herself, but in such a way that it confirms her language competence.

As far as the corroborated historical facts of this matter are concerned, Jeanne clearly spoke and wrote French (though only three letters written by her in Portuguese survive).[16] Of course the key issue is whether, in addition to her mother and 'father' tongues, she also knew Indian languages. This is one of the questions about Jeanne which remains open to debate. Once again, as far as this *prélude pondichérien* is concerned, the main issue is to isolate the domains of differentiation rather than to pronounce on the extent of her language competence.

For Yvonne Gaebelé, generally positively predisposed to Jeanne, this issue should be seen through the prism of orality.[17] For Gaebelé, Jeanne's competence in spoken language was the key factor, and this was transmitted through the distaff side of her birth family by her mother and her maternal grandmother: 'I maintain that she learned how to speak and not to write these languages, because both her grandmother and her mother were completely illiterate; the proof of that is that there is a cross in place of both Johanna's signature on her granddaughter's baptismal certificate and Rose de Castro's signature on Jeanne's marriage certificate' (Gaebelé 1934, 6).

This gendering of language competence is one of the threads running through this book. For example, Sonia Gandhi's competence, or lack of competence, in Hindi has been linked by her political opponents to her suitability for high office and as a residual marker of her foreignness. Sooni Tata's insistence on French and English bilingualism for her five children – while also admitting Gujarati and Hindi into her household – paved the way for a cosmopolitanism that helped to make Tata a successful global enterprise under J.R.D. Tata's chairmanship, which ran from 1938 to 1992. Indeed, she met her husband R.D. Tata in the first place because her mother was his French teacher. As well as high-level language competence as interpreters – for example, Princess Durru Shehvar's mastery of court Urdu and Margaret Noble's excellent command of Bengali – the issue of teaching is important. This is because language teaching, particularly as it relates to children, has over the centuries generally been the domain of women (both mothers and paid female teachers). As well as in the way that language learning was valued by Sooni Tata, the prominence of education is demonstrated by Sister Nivedita's having founded a Bengali-medium school. (Mother Teresa also taught geography in a Catholic Bengali-medium school and Margaret Cousins taught in a Theosophical school.) Annie Besant herself 'took classes in the *Mahabharata* and the *Ramayana* [in the Central Hindu College, the school she co-founded]. Though she considered herself well qualified by her studies to do this, not everyone agreed with her… [O]ne Collegian confessed he thought she talked nonsense on these occasions' (Taylor 1992, 279).

As a final illustration of how the differentiation of Jeanne Dupleix is relevant for the other Indian *videshinis,* let us look at how the different ways in which she is represented act as a self-fulfilling prophecy that caused an extreme divergence in opinions about her. These issues are themselves polarized around a traumatic event in the history of the French enclave of Pondicherry: the French defence of the town during the siege by the British in 1748. The behaviour of Jeanne Dupleix during the siege is the single most controversial issue in the life of the governor general's wife. This incident contains a heady cocktail of civilian meddling in military affairs, the pillaging of one's own side, religious discrimination, and the destruction of the sacred sites of another religious community – as well as selfless care for the French victims and a heroic disregard for one's own personal safety.

Even Vigié, who is generally more than willing to downplay Jeanne Dupleix's influence, acknowledges that Jeanne exerted significant influence in the military domain: she takes it on herself to commit a company of sepoys and her foot soldiers in a breakout raid which fails (Vigié 1993, 282). This raid resulted in the death of Captain Paradis, who was killed by Boscawen's men. Thus Vigié is keen to dispute Jeanne's effectiveness. He states that Jeanne's Indian foot soldiers ('pions', ibid., 281) were responsible for pillaging Indians during the siege. Gaebelé, however, springs to her defence, suggesting that 'if Jeanne had the jewellery and valuables of those fleeing Pondicherry confiscated, it was to deposit them in the treasury of the French East India Company, whose coffers were often empty at this time on account of the war' (Gaebelé 1934, 194).

There is an even more serious charge that continues to haunt the reputation of Jeanne Dupleix: her pleading a case to her husband at the 1748 siege for the destruction of the gopurams of the Iswaran temple. First it is important to note that there is no incontrovertible proof that this heinous act was Jeanne Dupleix's idea; but if Jeanne played a role in it, there are two elements which are significant here. The first, according to Gaebelé (who bases herself on the journal of Ananda Rangappillai), is the gross hypocrisy of Jeanne's presumed position. The gopurams 'are declared to be easy targets for the enemy's artillery and their demolition is ordered, while the bell towers of the various catholic churches are carefully camouflaged (Gaebelé 1934, 197–8). The churches were literally wrapped up in (bales of) cotton wool. Furthermore, it seems totally foolhardy for her to have exacerbated any tensions between the different religious groups within the trading post at a time when they were all subject to the threat of an external enemy: the British.

Even writers otherwise favourable to Jeanne, such as Rose Vincent in her bio-fiction, refer to the way she blindly pursued advantages for her religious community at the expense of others. In *Le Temps d'un royaume*, it is said that Jeanne's 'character was well suited to religion as practised by Father Antonio, a radical faith in the style of the Portuguese, who have always justified their conquests by converting pagans' (Vincent 1982, 277–278). Something very interesting is happening here: a French-speaking writer who is partial to Jeanne Dupleix is ascribing the negative elements in her behaviour to a Portuguese form of Catholicism.

There is a case for suggesting that the Southern Latins are a convenient scapegoat here. Furthermore, a mixed-race woman like Jeanne is extremely susceptible to being made 'other', because negative actions can always be ascribed to the 'other side of her'. There is, however, a striking similarity between the extreme concentration of power in the ultra-elite of Dupleix and his family on the one hand and Spanish colonialism in Latin America on the other. The background to this was that Dupleix's system was bringing more and more land under French influence; but its concomitant was that as Dupleix's personal influence increased, so did the personal tributes and gifts he was able to garner for the transactions and arrangements that were agreed. This was a charmed circle for the members of the elite cabal or clique formed by Dupleix and his extended family – or a vicious circle, if you belonged to one of the Indian populations under their yoke. The situation was further exacerbated by the fact that France was six or seven months distant by ship via the Cape of Good Hope; this meant that directives from the higher authority of the board of directors of the French East India Company took a long time to reach Dupleix. The same delay applied to reports sent from the French possessions in India to the Company's headquarters at the Hôtel Tubeuf in Paris. All this meant that there were no effective checks and balances on the governor general's power.

Indeed, it is rather a coincidence, given that language competence is common to Jeanne Dupleix and La Malinche, that a similar extreme state of affairs existed in Chile during the colonial period from the 1540s to the first decade of the nineteenth century. This has led the contemporary critic Brian Loveman to term this particular form of money-making capitalism 'Hispanic capitalism' (Loveman 1979). As David Hojman writes:

> Three central aspects define Hispanic capitalism. First, it is not competitive but hierarchical and monopolistic. For example, there is no competitive labour market. [South American] Indian labour is organised in a semi-feudal system known as *encomienda* (the Indians paid tribute to the Spanish king in the form of forced labour, with the *encomendero* keeping a share of the output and making sure that the Indians remained Catholic). There is no free international trade. Trade is restricted and monopolised, geared towards supporting the mercantilist aims of Spanish imperialism. Second, and partly as a result of the first aspect, Hispanic capitalism is prone to rent seeking, corruption and extreme inequalities. Third, the philosophical or ideological backbone of Hispanic capitalism is one of intolerance and religious fanaticism. Spanish imperialism and the Roman Catholic Counter-Reformation needed and supported each other. A central expression of this symbiosis was the Spanish Inquisition. (Hojman 2011, 33)

Clearly, there is not an identical match between Dupleix's regime and Hispanic capitalism, because there was no 'French Inquisition' in eighteenth-century Pondicherry, nor any systematic religious persecution, nor forced conversions. However, given that Rose Vincent is a writer who is sympathetic to Jeanne, the reference to the Portuguese brand of Catholicism echoes the perceived obligation of the Spanish *encomendero* to keep his serfs Catholic in Hojman's description of Hispanic capitalism. Vincent uses a perceived cultural difference between the Portuguese and the French to explain Jeanne's intolerance. In fact, the similarities that existed between Chile and Pondicherry suggest that there was nothing essentially Spanish about Hispanic capitalism in any absolute sense. Similar forms of extractive capitalism can grow up wherever the conditions allow it. The form was so radical in Pondicherry that the Dupleixes were only able to exercise it for twelve years, between 1742 and 1754.

In conclusion, how can the analysis of representations of Jeanne Dupleix contribute towards the methodology of this study? An old-fashioned French adage assumes that researchers are men and enjoins them to 'cherchez la femme' (look for the woman) when trying to understand how social processes work. In Jeanne Dupleix's case it is more a case of 'cherchez la famille' (look for the family). Or even, look for the 'families' in the plural, because three levels of family are important: her birth family, the elite family she joins, and the clan she creates through her offspring: Jeanne Albert became Jeanne Vincens, then Jeanne Dupleix, and finally 'Begum' and 'Marchioness'. The influence of the Dupleixes can still be seen today in the way that the geographical extent of so-called 'French India' (l'Inde française) is represented. The apogee of the influence of the Dupleix family is still used as a snapshot of the territory of French India in sources ranging from Wikipedia to the *Oxford Companion to Literature in French* (France 1995, xxii–xxiii). There is no account of the fact that the alliances on which most of this so-called territory depended were fragile (only lasting twelve years); nor of the fact that the territory was not all held simultaneously. Herein lies a caveat for representations of women: differentiation is difficult, and while the precise nature of their position should be seen within their elite, the greater the elite's power, the greater its potential both to be challenged and to invent itself anew.

As we know, the Dupleixes left India for good in 1754, and we will not follow them to France. This book now fast-forwards to 1893 and the arrival of Annie Besant on the coast of Tamil Nadu.

This span of 139 years is marginally larger than the 123 years covered in the main body of this book, which take us from Besant's arrival right up to the present day. Clearly it is impossible to summarize such a large period; in broad terms, however, the main development was the ever deeper penetration of the hook of British colonialism. As for the other Europeans, by 1893 the Dutch and the Danes have retreated, Portugal does not have any ambition to relive the age of discovery in India, and following the Treaty of Paris of 1815 British military force and upheaval at home have brought French dreams of renewed territorial expansion to a definitive end (Magedera 2010, 331–43). The violence during the Uprising of 1857–59 had cast a shadow of fear for Indians and caused anxiety for the British. The ability of the British to repress Indians physically anywhere in the country and the fear of Indians about this potential use of armed force were the reasons why British colonial control was complete. This is the context within which the main chapters of our study begin.

Notes

1. In addition to his enlightening comments on this Prelude, I am very grateful to Gobal Gobalakichenane for locating this entry from 30 June 1748 in the fifth volume of Henry Dodwell's English translation of *The Private Diary of Ananda Ranga Pillai* (Rangappillai 1917, 89–90) and to Chantal Delamourd for confirming the translation, which stresses Rangappillai's view of Jeanne's scheming and vindictive character.
2. These can be followed either by walking the pavements or via Google Street View.
3. The city authorities in Paris host a useful online database which provides information on the history of the names of individual streets: http://www.v2asp.paris.fr/commun/v2asp/v2/nomenclature_voies/. It lists a rue Lally-Tollendal in the nineteenth arrondissement, named after the French general who fought against the British during Dupleix's governorship. In his *Vestiges of the Colonial Empire in France* Robert Aldrich (2005, 27) notes that '275 streets (of about 5,400 in the twenty arrondissements) make explicit colonial references'. The name 'Dupleix' is also found as part of the 'honour-roll of colonists' on the wall of the Musée Colonial (built for the 1931 colonial exhibition); see ibid., 41.
4. The earliest hagiography of the governor general, Claude-Noël Le Fèvre's (1818) *Éloge historique de Dupleix,* dates from three years later. Covering the period 1754–2010, *French Books on India* (François-Denève et al. 2011) records forty-six monographs about him.
5. I acknowledge the kindness of Thomas Guibal, who shared his photograph of Jeanne Dupleix. His website is an excellent resource: http://landrecies.free.fr/
6. Only Mirra Alfassa managed an equal number of marriages: she wed Henri Morisset in 1897 and Paul Richard in 1910 or 1911. Her relationship with Aurobindo Ghose, however, belonged to another order entirely. A note on the term 'Britisher': although it is being used in a jocular way here, its appearance also recalls a time when it was used in anger as part of Indians' verbal retaliation against colonialism.

7. See Isidore Guët's (1892) *Origines de l'Inde française, Jân Begum (Mme Dupleix), 1706–1756,* also available at http://archive.org/details/originesdelindef00gu; and Yvonne Robert Gaebelé's (1934) *Créole et grande dame.*
8. Madame François Martin is the only other woman in a similar position to have a book written about her. See Yvonne Robert Gaebelé's (1937) *Une Parisienne aux Indes au XVIII*[e] *siècle.*
9. It should be noted that Dupleix's life, too, has been the subject of novels, by Judith Gautier (1887 and 1913) and Louis Saurel, whose *Dupleix* is billed on its front papers as 'un prodigieux roman d'aventures' (a prodigious adventure novel) (Saurel 1937, n.p.).
10. The first study to isolate the specific importance of mixed-race women in French-language representations of India was 'Victime ou déesse sexualisée: la représentation de la femme indienne à l'époque coloniale de 1744 à 1930, étude des œuvres littéraires de langue française' (Underwood 2004).
11. French women first exercised their right to vote in parliamentary elections in October 1945 and Indian women went to the polls for the first time in 1951.
12. The word 'repatriation' is in inverted commas because she had never actually been to the country to which she was repatriated.
13. Gaebelé (1934, 59) quotes a letter from Dupleix to Vincens in April 1732 where he mentions that he has also written to Jeanne's mother: 'I have written to Madame Albert. She can be reassured about coming over here and her daughters will find opportunities to set up their own households.'
14. There were however also European mercenaries coming from different regions of German, the Savoy and Switzerland as well as those from Reunion Island, Mauritius and Madagascar.
15. The way that we have seen both Claude Martin and Dupleix argue that their partners are not 'natives' echoes the exceptional status that slave owners established for a very small group of 'key slaves' in the antebellum South of the USA (Tadman 2002, 332–5). These individuals were exempted from physical labour and given an education.
16. These letters were in the possession of Yvonne Gaebelé in 1934. They remain untraceable at present.

17. Orality is also used to depict the character resembling Mirra Alfassa in Catherine Clément's novel, *Les Derniers Jours de la déesse*: 'In contrast to him [Sri Aurobindo], she did not write. Amma would not write, Amma would converse. That is why the bookshop is full of books by disciples' (Clément 2007, 50).

EDUCATION AND ACTIVISM: ANNIE BESANT; SISTER NIVEDITA; MARGARET COUSINS

It has always been somewhat of a grievance to me that I was born in London, 'within the sound of Bow Bells,' when three-quarters of my blood and all my heart are Irish.

– Annie Besant, 1893

[T]o-day let me: Western-born but in spirit Eastern, cradled in England but Indian by choice and adoption: let me stand as the symbol of union between Great Britain and India: a union of hearts and free choice, not of compulsion.

– Annie Besant's presidential address to the Indian National Congress, 1917

What was wanted was not a man but a woman: a real lioness, to work for the Indians … Your education, sincerity, purity, immense love, determination and above all, the Celtic blood, make you just the woman wanted.

– Swami Vivekananda on Margaret Noble, 1897

The government must be mad, or at least prove so if Swamiji [Swami Vivekananda] is interfered with, that would be the torch to carry fire through the country. And I, the most loyal Englishwoman that ever breathed in this country (I could not have suspected the depth of my own loyalty till I got here) will be the first to set it alight!

– Margaret Noble, 1898

> Being Irish, in India neither as a Christian missionary, nor as a British Government servant, nor for any political propaganda, and having already studied and gained much from Indian philosophies... it was easy for me to evaluate strong and weak points in present-day contemporary Indian civilization; and within my first year of landing on Indian soil I was dedicated to the service of India via service to that half of India – its womanhood – which seemed to me the most direct instrument for leverage of the whole people.
>
> – Margaret Cousins, 1941

> Write about the foreign women who come and stick their noses into our affairs. Write about those ladies who came here to suck out the brains of our people, write about Madame Besant, she's a political subject... I do not reproach Sister Nivedita, the valiant companion of Vivekananda, for anything... I do not reproach foreign women for anything if they do not seek to take power.
>
> – The angry pandit, a character in Catherine Clément's novel *Les Derniers Jours de la déesse*, 2006

In Maharashtra, in Andhra Pradesh, and above all in Tamil Nadu, the name 'Besant' has long been visible in city street signs. You will find a Besant Road in Worli, in Vijayawada, and in Chennai's Royapettah and Triplicane districts. Then of course, to the south of them, across the Adyar Estuary, there is also Besant Nagar and the greenery of Besant Gardens. With the possible exceptions of Mother Teresa and Sonia Gandhi, Annie Besant has perhaps the most prominent nationwide public profile of any of the European-born women in this book. She was known across India for her oratory which re-energized an interest in Indian traditions that had been undervalued during the colonial period. This chapter asks whether that prominence is justified and whether figures like Margaret Cousins and Margaret Noble can legitimately challenge it, and on what grounds, given the fact that all three women had an interesting additional layer of identity as all three of them could be considered Irish rather than English by the Indians they met (we will see at the end of this chapter that the decisive element in answering the question about the justification of one of the womens' prominence compared to another is the flexibility with which the women perceive themselves. This something that Maina Singh calls 'layered identity' in the case of Sister Nivedita/Margaret Noble) (Foley and O'Connor 2006).[1] An indispensible preliminary to any critique of Besant's presence in India, however, is an examination of how it began.

Annie Besant died in 1933, before the final shape of independent India was clear; moreover, the secular and sovereign nation founded in 1947 by M.K. Gandhi, Jawaharlal Nehru and Congress was completely different from her vision in the 1920s of home rule on the basis of precolonial religio-political structures. While it is important to acknowledge that, in 1963, she was the first European woman to be commemorated in a postage stamp issued by the Indian Posts and Telegraph Department, it is equally significant to understand that many of her visions for that state were not borne out in the reality of independence. Thus, her current civic memorialization has come about not only because her politics publically valorized Hindu traditions for both Indian and British audiences, but also because she was active in the establishment of new educational institutions in India. Thus in 1898, before she became president of the Indian National Congress (1917) and before she founded the Home Rule League with Lokmanya Tilak (1916), she initiated the Central Hindu College at Varanasi.[2] The 'CHC' was the predecessor institution of Varanasi (Banaras) Hindu University.

This chapter examines the influence on India which takes place at the intersection of education and activism (activism being understood as informal, issue-based political activity without geographical borders; this is in contrast to the party political national or state-specific political activity of the *videshinis* in the last two chapters of this book). In our times a woman like Besant might have made her career in politics alone, but in India between 1893 (the year of Besant's arrival in India) and 1947, education provided both a means of independent income and a way of having a significant effect on Indian society. Education is an ideal domain through which to consider a society in transition. This is because those active in that field need to have a conception of the future development of the country, since they are training its future citizens. Furthermore, the creation of a curriculum forces them to select knowledge from India's past for use in the present. From these value judgements conclusions can be made about the authenticity of the educational endeavour as a political act. As this book privileges a personalized version of history that demonstrates differentiation, this chapter also considers how its educationalist–activist subjects are represented by Indians and how they represent themselves. The chapter achieves differentiation through an analysis of Irishness. Full contextualization for this element will be provided below, but at this stage it is sufficient to note that focusing on Irishness is a key way of considering cultural difference in European-born women active in British India. It can be viewed as both close to, and distant from, Englishness or Britishness. It is this latter characteristic which gives a self-proclaimed Irishwoman greater leeway to define herself in India, particularly as far as her relations with Indians are concerned. For Indians, an Irishwoman might be a type of European 'outcaste' who has the chance to be defined apart from the colonial legacy. We shall see that Besant is the only one of our three subjects who is willing to make political capital of an uncritical and absolute espousal of Irishness.

This socio-cultural potential of Irishness was amplified by political developments in the British Isles. In the forty years from Besant's arrival in 1893 to her death in 1933, Ireland underwent a transition. In 1893 it was still an integral part of the United Kingdom, but it was also the part most at odds with an English-dominated Britain. By 1933, its separation–partition had struck home, changing Britain profoundly, both in itself and as a colonial power.

On account of Annie Besant's prominence in India, the main narrative of this chapter – and of this book – can start on 16 November 1893 with her arrival by sea in Tuticorin, Tamil Nadu. As she progressed northwards, her popular public lectures were not directly political, but provided her own interpretation of themes from Indian philosophy, such as the lecture on renunciation (*tyaga*) that she gave in Kumbakana. According to Anne Taylor's biography, Besant was well-received: in Bangalore, for example, 'the fever of anticipation was so great that offices were closed early for people to go to her lecture'; her dual strategy was to profess 'reverence for their faith' and to urge Hindus to valorize their own traditions (Taylor 1992, 268).

Indians were not the only people listening to her; the British also came. The verdict on her January 1894 lecture in Calcutta in the leader in *The Times* in London was damning; its content was 'essentially an appeal back from the India of the present to the India of the past' and in political terms 'she is merely doing harm in her own way as the British constitution-mongers for India... are doing harm in theirs' ([no author] 1894, 8). These reactions indicate that the British authorities appear to have made the connection between the utterances of the visitor from London and Hindu cultural self-affirmation and its potential to increase the pressure for political self-determination. Indian newspapers reacted differently from *The Times*, with *Amrita Bazaar Patrika* even inviting her to be the leader of a new movement.

This political controversy from her lectures, played out in the public domain, temporarily overshadowed the work of the Indian National Congress, which since 1885 had been gently and genteelly campaigning for the participation of educated Indians in the government of the country. The original core members of the Congress were seventeen British and Indian theosophists, but by 1893, the movement, originally conceived as an all-India institution, had a far broader membership base which had outgrown its theosophist origins. Annie Besant had become a powerful new voice on the Indian political scene.

Suddenly though, in early 1894, in something approaching a public manifestation of *tyaga*, Annie Besant stepped back from a direct involvement in politics in her own right. On 30 March in a letter to the editor of *The Times*, she vehemently rejected any political intent, stating that 'in the whole of my lecturing tour in India I have not in any way meddled in political affairs'; Besant continues that 'the Theosophical Society, under whose auspices I have been working, takes no part in politics, and this fact alone would have excluded me from political speech-making' (Besant 1894). *The Times* even reproduces a copy of the letter she sent to Motilal Ghose, the editor of *Amrita Bazaar Patrika*, the newspaper that had invited her to lead a new political movement, in which she states:

> My own work has always been educational and the generating of enthusiasm for great principles. I have been a pioneer, not a politician; and I lack the practical sagacity and alertness to details necessary for anyone who should take useful part in such work as that which is taken in hand by the National Congress. (Ibid.)

The dividing line she is drawing here between spirituality on one hand and politics on the other is a spurious one, and her modesty about her abilities is false.[3]

Let us take Besant at her word, however, because this allows us to examine the theosophical context to her educational and spiritual project in the period from her arrival to her founding of the Home Rule League in 1916. It is important to understand that although she acknowledged the Theosophical Society as her sponsors, she was also a free agent. Annie Besant's public speaking afforded her a direct means of communicating with people in India. As a European woman, who did not have any allegiances to a particular Indian region, she could gather a broad consensus of Indians around her. This enabled her to function in this period as one of the most important mouthpieces for people's political aspirations. To quote the title of her 1913 series of public lectures, she positioned herself as a person who could 'Wake up, India.'

In September 1893, on the other side of the world and two months before Besant's ship arrived in India, another electrifying public speaker, Swami Vivekananda, had captivated the audience of the World Parliament of Religions in Chicago. He proposed a synthesizing view of Hinduism as part of a universal search for religious truth. Vivekananda's journey to the West, and this address in particular, can be seen as the alternative starting point of this chapter, because the Swami would go on to become the spiritual guide of Margaret Noble (1867–1911) after she met him in London in 1895. This Northern Ireland-born educator–activist is the second main subject of this chapter.

Following her meeting with Vivekananda, Noble had a period of 'mature reflection', lasting one year, in which she probed her increasing engagement with his philosophy. She then decided to come to India and to dedicate herself to working for the Ramakrishna Mission in the field of female education (Reymond 1953, 70).

Noble landed in Calcutta in 1898 and was initiated into the Ramakrishna order as a novice that very year. The name given to her by Swami Vivekananda, Sister Nivedita, meant 'the one who has been dedicated'. From 1898 until her premature death in 1911, Sister Nivedita would both travel across India as a private individual and as a lecturer, be a prolific writer and editor who valorized Indian traditions and supported Indian nationalism (this latter stand became more pronounced after the Swami's death in 1902); she would be important in an artistic movement, the Bengal School and its encouragement of young artists to seek inspiration in Mughal and Ancient Indian aesthetics, and she would play a prominent founding role in Bengal in the field of women's education, founding a school for Hindu girls in Kolkata in 1898.

Let us now return to Besant's activism in the 1890s, which took place in a theosophical context. According to the first article of its 1890-constitution, the goal of the Theosophical Society was to 'form a nucleus of the universal brotherhood of humanity without distinction of race, creed, sex, caste, or colour' (Besant et al. 1891, 65). The Society was founded in 1875 in New York by the Polish aristocrat Helena Blavatsky, the American military officer Henry Steel Olcott and the Irish-American lawyer William Quan Judge. The key issue here is the egalitarian basis on which it was established. A form of equality between Indians and Europeans does indeed seem to have been practised. The Society supported its members' practical research into 'investigating the unexplained laws of Nature and the psychic powers latent in man' without the agency of a divine intercessor.[4] As far as the origin of those conducting this research was concerned, membership was open to both Indians and Europeans. A reason the Society formed a rare forum in that time, in which the two groups could interact as intellectual equals, was that it attracted precisely those Europeans who wished to 'promote the study of Aryan and other Eastern literatures, religions, philosophies and sciences, and to demonstrate their importance to Humanity'.[5] Although the movement was international and boasted a gender mix among its European members, the profile of its Indian members suggests on closer inspection that Theosophy can be described as an Indian elite movement: the language of interaction was English, and only the most privileged echelons of Indian society had access to English at that time. Only the elite, therefore, had the leisure and the economic resources to engage with theosophy. One example was Neelakanta Sastri, a retired high-ranking engineer in the Public Works Department, who built a house near the Society's headquarters in Adyar. His daughter was Rukmini Devi, who went on to become a prominent Indian classical dancer and who married a leading theosophist, George Arundale, in 1920. After her marriage, she was one of the first Indian women to come under the influence of the Society; until that time, the only Indian members (for example, Bahman Pestonji Wadia) were male.

In contrast to Theosophy, the Indian grouping to which Sister Nivedita was associated, the Sri Ramakrishna Movement, founded by Swami Vivekananda in 1897, was a grassroots social organization which grew out of the Hindu saintly tradition. The Movement has two parts: the Ramakrishna Math, or monastic order and 'seminary', and the Ramakrishna Mission, a charitable organization performing social and relief work (including the extremely dangerous plague relief work first done by Margaret Noble in 1899). This work was put on an official legal footing following the Mission's registration in 1909 under the 1860 Societies Registration Act. In doctrinal and spiritual terms, the Movement was founded on the teachings of Ramakrishna Paramahamsa. Upon his death in 1886, his disciples organized themselves into the monastic order that became the Math under the leadership of Noble's future teacher Vivekananda. The prime innovation orchestrated by this Indian monk was to institute a tradition of social service in a separate wing of the Mission. This is embodied by the motto that he designed for it: 'For one's own salvation, and for the salvation of the world'. Although it was a small and relatively new organization when Margaret Noble became a novice nun in its tradition in 1898, it distinguished itself from the start by a non-casteist position in its welfare work. This has ensured its survival today as a non-governmental organization. Furthermore, Vivekananda also championed the cause of women's education, the area in which he wished Noble to leave her mark. These may appear as university liberal modern values and they are in broad philosophical terms, but they have Indian context. In contrast to Theosophy, which was syncretic from the outset, there was no Western influence in the religious foundations and spiritual practice of the Sri Ramakrishna Movement. These foundations and practice are drawn from Vedanta, part of those philosophical, spiritual and religious practices of India which came to be known as Hinduism in the West.[6] The Western internationalizing influence was minimal. We can see that Noble had a profound respect for existing structures and she considered that any social change should be extremely gradual. Furthermore, any initial comparison between Sister Nivedita and Annie Besant in the 1890s must take into account the way that the education of girls and women was circumscribed in an extremely tight set of cultural practices. Whereas Annie Besant bypassed these constraints by focusing on elite education in a form which owed something to the English all-male public school, Sister Nivedita worked within them. For example, the curriculum of Sister Nivedita's school only included limited teaching of academic subjects such as arithmetic (Reymond, 1953, 308). This extreme respect is picked up by otherwise sympathetic Western commentators such as S.K. Ratcliffe:

> There was no attempt [on Sister Nivedita's part] to convert [the Indian woman] to any religious or social system alien from her own; but rather, by means of her own customs and traditions, to develop her in harmony with Indian ideals, the teachers themselves following those ideals… It appeared to some that Sister Nivedita… in her school and in the *zenana* [female residential quarters], was in certain respects a reactionary influence – upholding the *purdah* and child marriage and perpetual widowhood as institutions essential to the preservation of the society which she had learned to admire. But she was far indeed from seeking to maintain the old unchanged. (Ratcliffe 1913, xv)

Sister Nivedita's assimilation of Indian cultural practices was profound and attuned to the society in which she operated. They should not be judged in terms of twenty-first century values In her essay 'The Future

Education of the Indian Women', she asks: 'Have the Hindu women of the past been a source of shame to us, that we should hasten to discard their old-time grace and sweetness, their gentleness and piety... in favour of the first crude product of Western information and social aggressiveness?' (Nivedita 1950, 56). Later, she answers her question by stating that an 'education of the brain that uprooted humility and took away tenderness would be no true education at all' (ibid., 57). In the words of Rabindranath Tagore's 1917 preface to her *Web of Indian Life*, 'she lived our life and came to know us by becoming one of ourselves' (Tagore 1955, xi). Although Tagore stresses 'idealism', 'sympathy' and 'love' in the way that she saw India, he also states that

> we [Indians] have our special limitations and imperfections, and for a foreigner it does not require a high degree of keen-sightedness to detect them. We know for certain that these defects did not escape Nivedita's observation, but she did not stop there to generalize, as most other foreigners do. And because she had a comprehensive mind and extraordinary insight of love she could see the creative ideals at work behind our social forms and discover our soul that had living connection with its past and is marching towards its fulfilment. (Ibid.)

Although, she became more involved in nationalistic and aesthetic causes after the death of Swami Vivekananda in 1902, Sister Nivedita was constantly seeking ways in which to provide for and to improve her school, as well as writing about education in India in general (Nivedita 1950, v).

All the time she worked as an educator in India, Sister Nivedita remained an aspirant in the spiritual domain (first under the close tutelage of Swami Vivekananda and then in terms of an independent quest). We shall see throughout this book that humbleness and modesty are useful qualities for European women to display (whether in a strategic or genuine way, or in a way which is a bit of both) because, for Indians, these qualities mark these women out as different from the colonizers, who are perceived as arrogant. In displaying them, they are not only conforming to an essentialist view of women, but they are also helping their causes by showing respect for the Indian culture around them. For Chandreyee Niyogi, Nivedita's ethos of humility, and her persistent advice to nationalist workers to work from behind the scenes, seem to be part of a complex philosophical and socio-cultural understanding of the position of women in India and the symbolic use of the term 'woman' as an ideal of 'femininity' in post-Enlightenment discourses, which had also used tropes of 'the Hindu' and 'Mother India' with a host of metaphysical and devotional associations known to devout Christians like Tolstoy in his 1908 'Letter to a Hindu'.[7] Sister Nivedita, then is adept at negotiating her identity and the essentialization of it by others in a way to achieve her personal goals which included helping both other women and Indians at large.

Sister Nivedita's humility as seen by others can be found in the following humorous anecdote, found in the writings of Sri Chinmoy (1931–2007). Whether it is actually true or not is immaterial (it is not found in the various primary sources consulted for this book), because it shows how humility has useful strategic effects:

> In this connection let us cite here an incident that actually took place in her life. The milkman who would daily supply her with milk asked her one day to give him some advice on religion. On hearing it her eyes widened with surprise. 'You! You are an Indian. You need to have a piece of advice from me? Is there anything that you people do not know? You are the descendant of Sri Krishna. Accept my salutation'. (Chinmoy 1985, 172)

The story resembles a parable, because there is already a link between Krishna and milk. It is almost as if Nivedita's claim that she has nothing to teach the milkman is tacitly acknowledging that he could be a manifestation of the deity. In this she shows her knowledge of and respect for traditions and symbolically use them to elevate the common man.

In Swami Vivekananda, Sister Nivedita had a teacher to whose teachings she remained faithful throughout her life. His premature death in 1902 at the age of thirty-nine did not throw her off course; on the contrary, it seems to have compounded her determination to fulfil the task he had set her. After his death she aimed to feel 'this living presence of our Master' (Nivedita 1910, 514). Her activity for the Movement was limited to one specific field: women's education, a task given to her by Swami Vivekananda. She thought herself qualified neither to influence the future direction of the monastic order, nor to found her own allied organization. (This marks her out from both Annie Besant and the women we consider in our next compartment, Mirra Alfassa and Mother Teresa.) Her role for the Mission was confined to running a single educational institution as well as some actual teaching.

If Margaret Noble was an energetic individual willing to conform to the religious vow she had made and to be known as Sister Nivedita, Annie Besant was no less enthusiastic; but she had the added dimension of a self-promoting nature.[8] As mentioned above with reference to Chandreyee Niyogi's comments, this is not only a temperamental difference between the women, it occurred often enough in Sister Nivedita's fields of activism to be considered a strategy. Whereas Sister Nivedita favoured an approach based on scholarship and dialogue (such as her joint lecture with Romesh Chandra Dutt at the Mahajan Sabha in Madras on 4 February 1902, which was later published as 'India Has No Apology to Make').[9] This is in contrast to Annie Besant, who in the second epigraph above, asks that she 'stand as the symbol of union between Great Britain and India'. This posturing indicates the extent of her egotistical self-regard. Besant was a person who sold herself at the same time as she pushed her causes. Moreover, unlike Sister Nivedita, she campaigned in her own name and led the movements that she acted for: the Central Hindu College from 1898, the Theosophical Society from 1907, the Home Rule League from 1916 and the Indian National Congress in 1917. Indeed, she also co-founded the Central Hindu College and the Home Rule League.

Besant confronted the British authorities directly and was interned in a government house in Ootacamund (Udhagamandalam, or Ooty) from June to September 1917. Although she was careful never to act entirely alone and had Indian collaborators in all her enterprises, she was successful in leaving her personal mark on Theosophy in India. If we look back at the Society's 1890 constitution we see a reference to a 'nucleus of a universal brotherhood' (Besant et al. 1891, 65). The word 'nucleus' indicates that theosophists were aware that they would have to start with a small and committed group of adherents. It was this inner circle to which Besant belonged. Moreover, it was the future direction of this group that she sought to influence directly in 1909 by engineering a spiritual succession for her brand of Theosophy. She and Charles Leadbetter would do this by means of a 'world teacher' for Theosophy, in the person of Jiddu Krishnamurti.

The 'world teacher' would have been a first among equals, reducing the power in the nucleus to a single individual allied to her, certainly as far as Theosophy's external relations were concerned. In one sense, it might be argued that, in putting forward Jiddu Krishnamurti as a new central figure, Besant and Leadbetter were seeking to reproduce for international Theosophy the influence that Swami Vivekananda had had in the West sixteen years earlier. The key difference was that, as opposed to the Swami, who acted in his own right as the spiritual inheritor of Sri Ramakrishna, Krishnamurti had Besant and Leadbetter as his spiritual parents (indeed she had actually become his legal guardian in 1910 when he was about fifteen). From 1898 to 1929 – from the foundation of the Central Hindu College to Krishnamurti's renouncement of the world teacher role and his withdrawal from Theosophy – Annie Besant remained close to networks of power. She was also instrumental in the arrival of many Britons to India for Theosophical work. One of them was Belfast-born James Cousins, who was accompanied by his feminist activist wife Margaret (1878–1954). She is the third woman of Irish heritage with whom this chapter is concerned.

Margaret Cousins marks herself out from Annie Besant and Sister Nivedita because she arrived in India in 1915. Although this might appear to place her in an entirely different generation from the other two, there is a sense in which she is following in their wake. So the question is, would she adopt an approach closer to Besant, her husband's sponsor, or one that resembled Sister Nivedita's? Although Sister Nivedita had been dead for four years by the time Cousins reached Madras, the latter mentions that she had already been introduced to the elder woman's writings while still in Europe:

> Lady Sybil Smith told me that Lady Minto [a former lady-in-waiting to the Queen] had personally known Sister Nivedita, an Irishwoman, Margaret

> Noble by birth-name, who had become a devotee of Swami Vivekananda and who wrote beautifully about the philosophy, life and people of India. (Cousins and Cousins 1950, 170–1)[10]

In the Theosophists, Cousins shared the same initial support group as Annie Besant; indeed it was at the invitation of the latter that she came to India in the first place. This offer of employment, however, was initiated by supernatural intercession: following

> a meeting of a special group of Theosophical students who met in Birkenhead … I received a strong intimation, known only to myself, that Jim [James Cousins, her husband] should write to Mrs Annie Besant in India offering her his services as a journalist … his services and mine were at her disposal if needed. A couple of months later Jim received an equally short note from her, dated March 6, 1915, asking us to come to Adyar for three years. (Cousins and Cousins 1950, 242)

Although Cousins appears to have maintained an interest in the occult her entire life, the diversity of different religious traditions amongst Theosophists meant that she did not have to renounce overtly any individual religious allegiances she had to Protestantism.

She and her husband James soon left Besant's side at Adyar and went to Mandanapalle (near Chennai) to teach at the theosophical school there. She taught English and her husband was principal. Yet Cousins was to become known for her influence not directly through Theosophical education, but through a more generalized form of activism which focused on women's rights: 'Margaret Cousins was one of the most illustrious women leaders who played a mighty role in shaping the women's movement in India' (Ramji 1977, 1). One of the constants in Cousins's activism and influence is the connection that she made between female liberation and women's education. In her own words:

> Without adequate education the women of India cannot expect to rise to their full powers, and with the present standard of literacy in their own language, only two per cent, it can be seen that the matter of education is

> of the utmost importance ... Legislators have not yet fully wakened to the national value of educated womanhood. They are under an illusion that girls should wait for education until all boys are first provided with it. But this differentiation is going to lower the respect in which the mothers of the next generation will be held by their children, and this is a step right against all the fine tradition of India's past veneration of motherhood. (Cousins 1923, 10)

Her commitment to this issue was clear from the start of her life in India, when 'she decided to send a deputation and present a memorandum to [E.P. Montagu] the Secretary of State for India when he visited the country in 1917' (Ramji 1977, 1). From the other side of the fence, Montagu commented in his diary: 'We had an interesting deputation from the women asking for education for girls, more medical colleges' (ibid., 1–2).

Where Besant wanted to be the mother of organizations, Cousins was their midwife, part of a team helping them come into being. As Barbara N. Ramusack states in Cousins's entry in the *Dictionary of National Biography*, she 'worked tirelessly to identify with Indian women as a colleague, to develop organizational and propaganda infrastructures which Indian women could utilize to pursue their own agendas... she sought to be a builder of bridges between women' (Ramusack 2004). This was the case with her work to establish the All India Women's Conference in 1926. If the advancement of Indian women was well served by the change, Cousins was quite content to see the organization she had helped to found being disbanded or merged into a new, more powerful body acting at a national level. Rather than founding a series of organizations in different fields in the manner of Besant, Cousins's organizations developed in an organic manner, being cultivated and blossoming before being grafted onto another broader stem. This serial development covers the merger of the Abala Abhivardini Samaj (Weaker Sex Improvement Society), founded around 1916, with the Tamil Women's Association, to become the Women's Indian Association; this organization used female education as a campaigning platform, before itself becoming a national body, the All India Women's Conference (AIWC).[11] Cousins

> appealed to educated women to form local committees to be subsequently synthesized into a pan-Indian organization. They were called upon to express their views on female education and to help formulate a concrete scheme for the system they wanted to establish. The response was enthusiastic and a series of conferences was held in twenty-two different places between September and December 1926. (Ramji 1977, 3)

In 1943, when the AIWC was secure and her own health declining, Cousins manifested a genuine *tyaga* (so unlike the tactical retreat of Annie Besant from politics in 1894 which was accompanied by a letter to *The Times*): 'direct participation by me was no longer required, or even desired, by the leaders of Indian womanhood who were now coming to the front' (Cousins and Cousins 1950, 740).

Annie Besant campaigned in good faith; but maintaining her own status within a group of overwhelmingly male colleagues was very much part of everything that she did. She had garnered influence for herself and her ideas by adopting proven methods for gaining power, both within India and outside it. These methods included the founding of organizations which could potentially have a mass membership, while also having an elite constituency (in the shape of the Theosophists), and the training of a nominated successor. Critics of Besant have pointed to her linking of Aryanism with a caste bias which made Brahmins her favoured group to carry through the national project. As we have seen, this is against the spirit of the 1890 constitution of the Theosophical Society, which disavows casteism in its aim to 'form the nucleus of a Universal Brotherhood of Humanity, without distinction of race, creed, sex, caste or colour' (Besant et al. 1891, 65). Besant sees things differently:

> I have had a vision of your mighty [Brahmana] caste going forward to the feet of India, the mother taking off the coronet of privilege from your own heads and laying it down in sacrifice at her feet. I have dreamt that the great act of national sacrifice, once accomplished, splendidly performed, India, the Mother, would stretch out her hands in blessing and say to her children who made the sacrifice: 'Go back to your people and take your rightful place again as leaders still.' (Besant 1918, 5, quoted in Geetha and Rajadurai 1995, 1769)

It is telling that the Central Hindu College that she established was a single sex school for boys: 'she wanted to raise standards though leadership by an elite' (Taylor 1992, 315). This is in stark contrast to Sister Nivedita's school which aimed to uplift girls and widows, two disadvantaged groups at that time.

Although not in direct competition with the Kolkata-based Nivedita, Besant owed it to her ambition to make a public announcement in 1904 about her position on female education.[12] She claimed that she had wanted to get involved in the education of girls from her arrival in India in 1893 and justifies the delay thus: 'many thoughtful Indians begged us to wait until we had secured the confidence of the Hindu community, so that no suspicion could arise with regard as to our objects' (Besant 1913b, 318). Despite what is in effect a holding statement, Annie Besant never did found an educational establishment for young women, as did both Margaret Noble and Margaret Cousins. From June 1919 to April 1920, the latter was the founding headmistress of the National Girls' School in Mangalore (Alan Denson 1967, 24). So to answer the question set out above, Cousins's activism is far closer to Sister Nivedita's than to Annie Besant's (though it is more focused on the role of women in Indian society). As can be seen from the quotation above, referring to 'the matter of education [as] of the utmost importance', her chosen sphere of activity was to change the role and status of women. During the twentieth century nationalism was the big debate, but there are signs in the twenty-first century that the status of women may be becoming recognized as the issue around which a national debate can crystallize, whether this be framed in terms of gradual progress or as a national emergency which needs to be addressed. Therefore, it is possible that the contribution of Margaret Cousins might now be given the recognition it deserves.

Let us now consider representations and self-representations of Besant, Nivedita and Cousins from the perspective of the connection with Ireland which they have in common. Stepping back for a moment, though, how was it that Irishness could be important for their organizational effectiveness in India? There may be plenty of academic debate regarding the proper description of the relationship between

Britain and Ireland in this period, but it is certainly true to say that being Irish attracted a certain kudos between 1893 and 1947. This was because the Irish train heading towards independence was further down the line than its Indian counterpart. As a consequence, these women potentially had, on account of their place of birth or their heritage, a way of constructing their identity as different from Englishness, the dominant and most frequent form of European identity in India at that time. As the support for self-determination slowly gathered among groups of Indian and Irish people in the second half of the nineteenth century, these women were able to call on their Irish ethnicity as a positive quality in their activity in India. This central part of the present chapter shows how their different experiences of Irishness, and the debates that were taking place throughout the period about a type of national identity that was separate from imperial Britain, influenced these women's cultural contact with Indians.

The closeness between the two main islands of the British Isles over the centuries means that is impossible to provide a single comprehensive definition of Irishness. Much academic ink has been spilt in unproductive discussion about whether or not the relationship between Britain and Ireland was a colonial one. This is less useful than to focus on its practical elements and to point, as Christine Kinealy does, to the paradoxes within it (Kinealy 2006, 77). In this chapter we see individuals born in Ireland (Margaret Noble in the north, Margaret Cousins in the south – both with Protestant parents) or partly educated there (Cousins, Noble and also Reginald Dyer, the commanding officer during the Jallianwala Bagh massacre). Another way of defining Irishness is through parentage; and there is also, of course, elective affinity, where people chose to foreground a certain aspect of their ancestry. The first epigraph shows how Annie Besant's Cockney birth in London is a source of some 'grievance' to her. All of these factors are relevant for Besant's self-perception. Before this issue is pursued, it is important to examine Irishness in India in general historical terms, by reviewing the involvement of people born on the island of Ireland in the British Indian Empire.

At the outset, this overview states categorically that many thousands of Irish people were active participants in the enterprise of empire. The first significant influx into the British Army of recruits born in Ireland occurred during the Seven Years War (1756–1763). 'Between 1757 and 1763, almost 17 per cent of recruits were from Ireland – 825 out of a total of 4911' and in 1857 'considerably more than half of the Company's white soldiers were Irish' (Mokyr and Ó Gráda 1989, 90 and Cadell 1953, 79, quoted in Holmes 2000, 248). The importance of this war in securing British hegemony over larger and larger areas of the country and neutralizing the threat from France is well known. Indeed Winston Churchill called it the first 'world war' (Bowen 1998, 7). Many of these soldiers and their regiments had a reputation for extreme brutality. Thomas Bartlett notes that 'the emergence of a separate name for them, "Rishti", to separate them from the "Angrese", the English – was more a warning to the natives than a gesture towards Irish sensitivities' (Bartlett 1997, 22). Two cases from the Punjab illustrate this. In 1857 the Irish-born soldier John Nicholson was responsible for ordering 'mass executions in which mutineers were blown away from the mouths of cannons' and, following the Jallianwala Bagh massacre in Amritsar in 1919, the Irish-born lieutenant governor of the Punjab, Sir Michael O'Dwyer, declared his support for the commanding officer Reginald Dyer '(the son of an Irish brewer, who had been educated in County Cork)' (Holmes 2000, 237 and 239).[13] The grisly footnote to O'Dwyer's declaration in favour of Dyer was that in 1940, twenty-one years later, the former governor was assassinated in London by a Sikh, Udam Singh.

Although being born in the north or south of Ireland, areas where the Celtic part of the culture was subjugated over many centuries, was no insulation against people of Irish origin oppressing Indians, it is still worth examining possible reasons for the collaboration between the Irish and the British. Such an examination will reveal the imperial context in which Besant's, Nivedita's and Cousins's Irishness is deployed.

In his research on the Irishmen who worked for the Indian Civil Service, Scott B. Cook mentions the 'balancing act of justifying Irish equality (with the British) and superiority over the Indians' (Cook 1987, 521, quoted in Holmes 2000, 238). This 'balancing act' might partly explain both the complicity of O'Dwyer and even the brutality of a military man like Nicholson. Great Britain at the time was a multinational nation, but one in which there was clearly a dominant partner: England. Empire gave those who originated from what could be broadly termed the Celtic fringe of Britain the opportunity to demonstrate that they were equal to those from the British core. They often did this through discrimination and violence directed against Indians. It should be noted that in acting in this way the people of Irish origin were confusing imperial ideology with the sacred temple of national belonging (itself a myth of course) into which the core Britons (and especially the English) could retreat when it suited them. Expressed playfully, this temple was home to the core Britons' *esprit de corps*.

Colonial abuses by ethnically Irish people should not be ignored and Elleke Boehmer makes a compelling case for the importance of Kali-worship in Sister Nivedita's 'attempt to authenticate herself as a Hindu' (2002, 59); but how European-born women were perceived and the structures of potential allegiance that were different from the British colonizer remain important. In addition, as Michael Holmes notes, these structures had a certain pedigree: the 'spread of nationalist ideas in the latter half of the nineteenth century brought a new element in Indian–Irish relations' (Holmes 2000, 242). This took place in a broader cultural context in which Western Romantic scholarship on comparative mythology claimed to discern connections between ancient Indian and Celtic myths.[14] In India in particular, people of a nationalist disposition, whatever their own political *parti pris*, could attempt to draw internationalist comparisons between the claims for self-determination in Ireland and those at home. In the case of the subjects of this chapter, in spite of the differences between them, both the way that Sister Nivedita was deemed by her guru to be an Irishwoman and Besant's Irish heritage and self-declared elective affinity with the Celtic nation contributed to these two women's ability to participate actively in Indian intellectual debates when living in India. This was the situation which pertained from 1898, the year Noble arrived in India, until her death in 1911. Annie Besant's participation would further intensify after 1913 with a series of public lectures entitled 'Wake up, India' (Besant 1913a, 11). In the same year, Margaret Cousins and her husband moved to Liverpool, the city which was to be their port of departure for India two years later.

As we read in the third epigraph, Swami Vivekananda rates Margaret Noble's Celtic blood as the most prized of her qualities, the one which would enable her to do her work in India without being reproached for being English (given what has been said about potential allegiance above, Vivekananda's concern is focusing not only on his own perception, but on that of the Bengali masses to whom Sister Nivedita will minister). In this way, Sister Nivedita could bring new ideas to the country, particularly those inspired by the New Education Movement. Inspired by the writings of Johann Heinrich Pestalozzi, the Movement envisioned a pedagogy which was child-centred and recognized the rights of minors. In short, her Irishness meant that she could import Western ideas, including some from the salons of London, without English colonial baggage. As Krishnan Dutta notes, Swami Vivekananda had benefitted from

> a western-style education mixed with a traditional Hindu upbringing... imbibed mainly from his mother... As a student at Presidency College and later in the General Assembly's Institution (now Scottish Church College), [he] read western literature ranging from Shakespeare to Jules Verne. In history he studied the French Revolution [and] Maspero's history of Egypt. (Dutta 2008, 108)

It appears that he wanted Margaret Noble to provide an education for girls in Kolkata which, while it did not seek to reproduce this dual elite-school tradition in its content because Nivedita's curricula remained Indian focused and basic in their academic ambition, the education would, on account of Noble's involvement, benefit from a cross-cultural perspective in the way that it was pedagogically framed.[15] Indeed, for Noble, the child-centred pedagogy as she conceived it was not alien to India:

> The Kinder-garten lessons of Europe, then, might be described as a series of *bratas*... they deal in the first place directly with the concrete object.

> These objects are introduced by means of stories. In the course of the lesson or 'play' – or *brata* as it might be called – some definite act is performed repeatedly… [T]he European thinkers and observers – Pestalozzi, Fröbel and Cooke – assuming that it is general knowledge of the world that makes man, turned to the same field of study, little children at play, in order to find out from it how the child might be made to acquire the knowledge and gain a mastery of the world. (Nivedita 1950, 119–20)

Did practical reasons determine Vivekananda's essentialist definition of Margaret Noble as Irish, taking into account the orthodox Hindu circles in which his disciple would have to work? Was this a knowing reduction of the complex identity of his disciple? This unfortunately appears not to have been the case as far as his vision of her Irishness is concerned – he also defined Bengalis in what sound today like stereotypical and essentialist terms in the following comments he made to Nivedita:

> Perhaps you will understand my people better than anyone, the Bengali and the Irish are races after the same pattern. They only talk and talk, and play with high-sounding words. These two peoples excel in grandiloquence, but they are incapable of doing anything when it comes to real practical work. Besides, they will spend all their time barking at each other and tearing each other to pieces. The English are right in criticizing us. To raise the standards of the masses, we must educate them. It is only thus that we can build a nation. (Reymond 1953, 169–70)

This passage suggests that Vivekananda's essentialism was not only limited to Nivedita's Irishness, but was also an integral part of the way that he perceived other ethnic and regional groups. At one level, the Swami's lacerating tirade is making a distinction between the Bengali masses and himself as a man of action. In reading passages such as this, the sense of his frustration at the current situation and the enormity of the task ahead of him appear clearly and it must be said that he burnt himself out trying to make progress. It does seem, however, that the irony that the Swami is himself a Bengali appears to be lost on him. The Swami's mind has been opened to multiple cultural influences by his education and travel to the West, but his role as the leader of a mass movement in the Hindu tradition means that he is seeking to adapt his elite experience for the many. There is no record of what Nivedita, his 'Irish' interlocutor, thinks about his stance. This is because instead of providing authentic quotations, Reymond in her biography dramatizes the protagonists' thoughts by means of free indirect discourse, paraphrasing the subject's thoughts. However, it is possible to reconstruct Noble's views using her correspondence for example. As is clear from the fourth epigraph of this chapter, she avoids essentializing discourses of that sort, preferring multiple allegiances she maintains at the same time in an equally heartfelt manner.

Swami Vivekananda, however, is not the only person to pronounce Sister Nivedita 'Irish'. Lizelle Reymond, her first French biographer, refers to her as an 'Irishwoman' twice (Reymond 1953, 19 and 134) and once as Vivekananda's 'Irish disciple' (ibid., 102). Jean Herbert, who translated the biography in 1953, mentions Irishness in her preface when recounting a scene from her own experience of Indian life, which shows the high regard in which Sister Nivedita is held by Indians:

> Several years ago, in a large city in India, I attended a theatrical performance by a remarkable traveling company, semi-professional, made up of some sixty children. At the end of the play the director of the company invited me to the religious service which was always celebrated by the young actors before they had their supper. On an improvised altar behind the scenes had been placed portraits of various gods, prophets, and great men: Gandhi was neighbor to Buddha, and Sri Ramakrishna's portrait stood close to a Botticelli Madonna. Among all these serene faces, the one which most attracted my attention was that of a Western lady; and my hosts brought the picture to me so that I might look at it closely. It was an Irish woman who had died a few years before, after devoting all her life to India. (Reymond 1953, 11)

In addition to her guru, her biographer and her translator, Swami Gambhirananda (1889–1988) – the publisher of the 1955 edition of the *Web of Indian Life* – uses his preface to call her 'the brilliantly gifted Irish disciple of Swami Vivekananda' (Nivedita 1955, n.p.).

In contrast to this tendency to essentialize Margaret Noble, Annie Besant's tendency to focus on herself and on her own image meant that the latter's relationship to Irishness would always be configured in a more self-reflexive way. It appears that, in the case of Sister Nivedita, Irishness was a quality which was always imposed on her by others and never one the nun directly claimed for herself. In contrast, Besant's autobiographical texts such as *Autobiographical Sketches* (Besant 1885) and *Annie Besant, an Autobiography* (Besant 1893 – written before she travelled to India), actually thematize Irishness. Carol Hanbery MacKay argues that the references to her Irishness are more precise in the second book:

> Initially the author of *Sketches* happily acknowledges her Irish heritage and describes in detail a range of family members who variously influenced her, but by the time she writes *An Autobiography*, her political involvement with Ireland leads her to streamline the anecdotal Irish relationships and reclaim her Irishness in her own right. (Hanbery MacKay 2001, 122)

In the later text she is naming Irishness in a direct manner and being a 'self-claimant to a much maligned ethnic identity' (ibid.). Thus it was in the 1893 *Autobiography* that Besant wrote: 'I feel playfully inclined to grudge the English blood they put into my father's veins, with his Irish mother, his Galway birth, and his Trinity College, Dublin, education', later elaborating:

> as a child I was mystical and imaginative, religious to the very finger-tips, and with a certain faculty for seeing visions and dreaming dreams. This faculty is not uncommon with the Keltic races, and makes them seem 'superstitious' to more solidly built peoples. (Besant, 1893, 14 and 24–5)

In these two passages Besant uses terms such as 'they' and 'more solidly built peoples' to construct her Irishness in terms of its difference from what we presume to be English and Englishness (attributes she does not define). Although these documents were written before Besant came to India, it is important to mention them, because they shed light on the narrative strategies she uses in relation to Irish cultural identity.[16]

The first of these strategies concerns a nation's future cultural renaissance. She writes of Ireland: 'Blessings on the ancient land once inhabited by mighty men of wisdom, that in later times became the Island of the Saints, and shall once again be the Island of Sages, when the Wheel turns around' (Besant 1893, 15). Apart from the obvious reference to the wheel of life in this passage, Besant's theosophical world view compares the ancient civilizations and lost knowledge in Ireland with a vision of Theosophy's role in reactivating Indian classical philosophy for the future nation of India. Furthermore, 'the Sages', who were once in control in her image of ancient Ireland, equate to the Brahmins in the Indian setting. They have been initially displaced by foreign conquest (Mughal in one place, British in the other) before a renaissance in which they re-establish their rule.

The second element of comparison is Blavatsky's notion that 'an avatar, a teacher would appear to show how Ireland would be freed from Anglo-Saxon rule (as India would be freed)' (Tuohy 1976, 32 and Kuch 1986, 106, quoted in Taylor 1992, 253). Blavatsky was Besant's spiritual guide; and this idea of the avatar–teacher is extremely close to Leadbetter and Besant's 1909 vision of the spiritual renewal in India promised by the 'world teacher', Jiddu Krishnamurti.

Third, and in addition to these high-level theosophical parallels, Besant's political writing reproduced both the names and the precise constitutional objectives of organizations that had first surfaced in Ireland. This third element relates to both the Home Rule Movement she co-founded in 1916 and to the less well-known National Convention of India, a form of estates-general, that met 'several times In Delhi between 1923 and 1925' with Besant as its general secretary (Taylor 1992, 320). Its name mirrors the National Convention of Ireland. Given that the concrete connections between the Irish and Indian movements were minor and generally limited to public expressions of support, her aim in mirroring the names appears to have been to harness them together symbolically. She seems to have wanted the Indian manifestation to draw strength from its Irish predecessor and to box in the British from the East as well as from the West.

Margaret Cousins uses her Irishness in a different, but equally interesting, way. The first aspect is that she is very clear on the sectarian divide she was born into, referring to 'my birth in Western Ireland of Protestant Unionist parents, though I myself became convinced of the justice and necessity of Home Rule for Ireland even if it in effect transferred power to Roman Catholic hands' (Cousins 1941, 7).[17] This shows Cousins would not let her condition at birth determine her position on political questions. We shall see that this same uncompromising refusal of determinism, whether in matters of gender, reproduction, or politics, marks her out throughout her life – unlike Besant, who uses her Irishness to claim both an affinity with spirituality and a solidarity with a group she suggests had always been oppressed (though we know that some Irish people were also oppressors in colonial India). Cousins did affirm her Irishness, but used it in a pragmatic, rather than essentialist, way. For instance, in the first years of her mobilization of women, she says that 'Irish hospitality' led her into inviting Indian ladies to tea, a function which under the title of 'light refreshments' was happily outside caste restrictions on 'food' (Cousins and Cousins 1950, 298). Her use of Irishness here claims a form of cultural difference that enables her to cut through prescriptive dietary restrictions and get Indian women talking to her and to each other. Gretta Cousins, as she was known to her friends, recounts an individual case in which she configures her closeness with an Indian woman at the moment of the latter's death. The woman, perhaps rather predictably, is of the Brahmin caste, but Cousins defines her own Europeanness via Irishness: 'The Brahmin lady… passed to Swarga [heaven] from the arms of her Irish sister – an utterly unorthodox thing to do' (Cousins and Cousins 1950, 299). This is a personal, playful and performative self-depiction, rather different from Swami Vivekananda's ideological and instrumentalized contructions of Sister Nivedita's Irishness.

Comparing the constructions of Irishness in the cases of Annie Besant and Sister Nivedita, we can see that they are inversely proportional to each other: where the theosophist's Celtic essence is self-attributed, the nun's is the result of the discourse of others. It is significant that there is an almost total absence of the terms 'Irish', 'Ireland' and 'Celtic' from Sister Nivedita's works which appeared in book form.[18] Given the fact that her spiritual guide, her biographer,

her translator and her publishers all refer to her as Irish, the complete absence of terms denoting Irishness from her three autobiographical texts (*Studies from an Eastern Home* [1913], *The Master as I Saw Him; Pages from the Life of Swami Vivekananda* [1910] and *Notes of Some Wanderings with the Swami Vivekananda* [1913]) amounts in effect to a contradiction of her spiritual guide's essentialist view of her.

If we now compare Annie Besant's legacy, first with that of Sister Nivedita and then with that of Margaret Cousins, we see that in institutional terms Besant's appears to be the more substantial by far when viewed in pan-Indian terms. Besant built lasting capacity in Indian educational institutions. Whatever reservations one may have about its initial caste exclusivity, the Central Hindu College was quite simply the right organization at the right time. After Besant's death in 1933, and after 1947, it had enough resilience to develop according to the country's needs. Indians had taken a stake in it, and it survives today as a school with a national profile.

Returning to Sister Nivedita, her legacy and posthumous presence is found most predominantly in West Bengal in the Bengali language. It ranges widely from cultural manifestations such as the acclaimed 1962 film, directed by Bijoy Bose, *Bhagini Nivedita*, winner of the Golden Lotus at the National Film Awards, India. Many girls are named after her, pupils across the state are taught about her life, and the biographies written about her by Pravrajika Muktiprana in Bengali and Pravrajika Atmaprana in English are widely sold. Many girls' schools in West Bengal display her portrait. It may be that traces of her name, in comparison with Besant, are less prominent in national civic life, but across the generations in West Bengal her memory is very much alive. This presence is also widespread in geographic terms, not being limited to the major conurbations of the state such as the statue in Baghbazar Park, Kolkata, unveiled in 1993. For instance, there are statues of Sister Nivedita and Swami Vivekananda at a junction of the Grand Trunk Road in the north part of Chandannagar (Hooghly). It is, however in Mysore that a district, Niveditha Nagar, has been named in her honour. Kolkata does, however, celebrate the nun in the name of a colony in the city's Patipukur district and in the Nivedita Bridge which opened in 2007. In Bosepara Lane, Bagbazar, the original site of her school is indicated by a plaque. Sister Nivedita's educational legacy does thrive as the Ramakrishna Sarada Mission Sister Nivedita Girls' School, located at 5 Nivedita Lane, Kolkata.[19] Once again, however, the prominence given in the name of the school to 'Ramakrishna', followed by 'Sarada', with Sister Nivedita in third place, gives an indication of her position in the hierarchy of the institutions she founded when under Vivekananda's tutelage. This notwithstanding, the institution is held in high regard across Kolkata, for its ethos and for its academic results.

She is, however, not part of the official constellation of central figures in the Sri Ramakrishna Movement. The Movement has developed into an important organization in India and in 2012 had nineteen branches in countries outside India. The three main figures in the movement are Sri Ramakrishna, Sri Sarada Devi and Swami Vivekananda. Being a disciple of Swami Vivekananda, and not of Sri Ramakrishna himself, however, might explain Sister Nivedita's lack of first-rank prominence within the organization.

Given the breadth and depth of their writing, an appreciation of the legacy of these three European women of Irish origin would not be complete without factoring in Annie Besant's, Sister Nivedita's and Margaret Cousins's texts. Besant continued to publish on theosophical subjects after 1893; *Occult Chemistry: Clairvoyant Observations on the Chemical Elements,* written with C.W. Leadbetter, was published in 1919. The conclusion of this work demonstrates the typical mix in Besant's theosophical writings, almost unreadable today, of claims to provide a new previously occulted dimension of the real, paired with an indication that the final truth is still over the horizon. Here is an example of their style:

> [I]f we wish to have a right view of the realities underlying manifestation in this universe, we must to a considerable extent reverse the ordinary conception as to what this matter essentially is. Instead of thinking of its ultimate constituents as solid specks floating in a void, we must realize that it is the apparent void itself which is solid, and that the specks are but bubbles on it. That fact once grasped, all the rest remains as before. The relative

> position of what we have hitherto called matter and force is still for us the same as ever; it is only that, on closer examination, both of these conceptions prove to be variants of force, the one ensouling combinations of the other, and the real 'matter,' *koilon*, is seen to be something which has hitherto been altogether outside our scheme of thought...
>
> What *koilon* is, what its origin, whether it is itself changed by the Divine Breath which is poured into it – does 'Dark Space' thus become 'Bright Space' at the beginning of a manifestation? – these are questions to which we cannot at present even indicate answers. Perchance an intelligent study of the great Scriptures of the world may yield replies. (Besant and Leadbetter 1919, 66)

The final words of the conclusion enjoin the reader to take up the form of study of 'Eastern and Aryan literatures' which is outlined in the theosophical constitution of 1890. As Anne Taylor suggests, these works by Besant have not stood the test of time and read like nonsense today. Although Blavatsky's 'life and personality remain the subject of serious research and speculation... [t]here is no school of Besant' in Theosophy (Taylor 1992, 332) – though, as we have seen, the Central Hindu College was a 'Besant School' in its early years.

Compared to Besant's writing, Noble's 'educational journalism', written primarily for an Indian English-speaking audience, was more critical, more substantial and more 'theoretical', as one would say nowadays.[20] In essays such as 'Some Problems of Indian Research' (reprinted in *Footfalls of Indian History*) she deals with key epistemological questions. The 'Indian people' she says, must engage in the

> rewriting of their own history... [but] this, in accordance with the tacit rule of modern learning, will have to be carried out, not by one, but by a combination of individuals; in other words by an Indian learned society... To recognize the geographical unity and extent of the great whole we call India is not enough; it is imperative also to understand how it came to be. (Nivedita 1956, 169)

For her, Vincent Smith's *The Early History of India* was 'a compendium summarizing for and opening to the Indian worker the results achieved by the European organization of research' (ibid.).

Sister Nivedita also had the ambition to provide a corrective view to Western opinions about an absence of historical writing in India: 'We are often told that Indian literature includes no histories... Even if this is true... we must remember that India herself is the master-document in this kind [sic]. The country is her own record' (Nivedita 1956, 6). She continues by concluding two things. The first is that '[i]f India itself be the book of Indian history, it follows that travel is the true means of reading that history' (ibid., 14). This is a plea for the inclusion of current empirically based knowledge in an accurate image of India. The second element is a privileging of domestic space, which, exactly as Antoinette Burton was to argue in *Dwelling in the Archive* (2003), is one of the ways of foregrounding women's history: 'It will be from amongst the records of home and family-life that light will be shed upon the complete history of Bengal' (ibid., 7). These are profound words. It is possible, therefore, to argue that Noble's work to create a new perception of India at home and abroad was more scientifically rigorous than Besant's, because it was based both on historical sources and on observation.

The publication history of Sister Nivedita's books is significant in itself, in that it demonstrates the importance of her thought for others both before and after her death in 1911. There are three phases to this history. First, in Sister Nivedita's lifetime, articles which first appeared as journalism were collected and published in book form. Under the auspices of Advaita Ashrama, the publishing arm of the Ramakrishna Math and Ramakrishna Mission, a second wave of publication followed her premature death.[21] This phase occasioned the commemorative prefaces by Rabindranath Tagore and S.K. Ratcliffe quoted in this chapter. Then, soon after independence, her works on education and Indian history were published again, because they were judged to form part of the national dialogue about the future development of the country. This manifestation of the relevance of her work more than fifty years after the bulk of it was written is evinced by the following volumes: *Religion and Dharma* (1952), *The Web of Indian Life* (1955) and *Footfalls of Indian History* (1956). Soon after their publication, these three volumes and another entitled *Hints on National Education in India,* published by the Math's Udbodhan Office in Kolkata, were deemed to be suitable as gifts of the Indian High Commissioner to British university libraries, such as the one at the University of Liverpool. These publications, and the twenty-first century academic interest in the sociological and historical content of Nivedita's life and work, suggest that her afterlife in the reception by others might range more widely than Besant's, which is confined to the history of the middle phase of the struggle for Indian independence.[22] This is because Nivedita is less linked to an elite esoteric movement than Besant.

Although it is less than a third of the length of Annie Besant's forty-year engagement with India, the thirteen-year period during which Margaret Noble became Sister Nivedita is worth valorizing across India and not only in West Bengal. This worth stems from the discursive historico-sociological content of her work and from the integrity of her activity within her school when she was alive, rather than from the survival of the institution. It is this dual activity, though more circumscribed than Besant's, that provides a valuable model of a practice of hybridity in a pericolonial context.

There are five aspects to this practice. First, Sister Nivedita's public dedication of her life in India was not only to an individual, Swami Vivekananda, it was also to a task. When he died, Sister Nivedita understood that her work had to continue. This dynamic of devotion is not found in Annie Besant; in order to understand it better, it is necessary to briefly compare it to the dedication of Mirabehn (Madeleine Slade), the most well-known of M.K. Gandhi's Western female disciples. Although the personal closeness between Nivedita and Swami Vivekananda is important, there is a fundamental difference here between Nivedita's functional dedication and the exclusive personal dedication of Mirabehn. In *Going Native: Gandhi's Relationship with Western Women,* Thomas Weber shows that Mirabehn was an unusual disciple because

> Madeleine *went* to India to be at the feet of Gandhi, the new object of her devotion. Most of the others who 'went native' for any extended length of time also revered the Mahatma, but were engaged in furthering his ideals

> rather than obsessively wanting to tend to him personally. They were in India to do good work and met Gandhi along the way. With the exception of Margarete Spiegel [who remained in India but moved away from Gandhi's influence], those who did go to India to be at the feet of Gandhi, their 'guru', stayed for a much shorter time than Mirabehn. (Weber 2011, 190)

Much of Mirabehn's activity in India, 'promoting sanitation and teaching carding and spinning' (ibid., 200) in villages, was done as placements directly assigned by Gandhi, rather than as independent organizational activities. (The Indian *videshini* in this book, although dependent on their elites, generally had much more scope than Mirabehn had to organize their own activity in India in a way that corresponded to their own talents.) This is very different from Sister Nivedita's proven expertise. She had set up her own school in Wimbledon in 1892 and was invited to come to India by Swami Vivekananda to dedicate herself in exactly the same domain. After Gandhi's murder, Weber tells us that Mirabehn 'did not seem to find her place in the new India, people let her down, she did not have the drive and clout to make her projects work in an objectively measurable way' (Weber 2011, 215). After the Swami's death, Sister Nivedita continued in her task. In 1959, eleven years after the assassination, Mirabehn finally left India. After his death and the absence of direction from her life, her work in India did not have a great deal of lasting influence – certainly much less than that of both Annie Besant and Sister Nivedita. While the reason for the lack of Mirabehn's influence in India cannot be reduced to Britishness, that quality was important for her activity when Gandhi was alive. The personal dynamic is crucial – Weber demonstrates this clearly. Mirabehn is also important for what she represents as the daughter of an establishment figure (Rear-Admiral Sir Edmond Slade), and as someone who dedicated herself to Gandhi.

In contrast, contemporary commentators were struck by the way in which Sister Nivedita identified with the Indian women with whom she came into contact in Kolkata. This is the second aspect of a practice of hybridity in a pericolonial context. In addition to Tagore's comments quoted above, Ratcliffe quotes a Mrs J.C. Bose, who comments on the nun's particular form of linguistic identification:

'[S]he had so completely identified herself with us that I never heard her use phrases like "Indian need" or "Indian women"; it was always "our need", "our women." She was never an outsider who came to help, but one of us who was striving and groping about to find ways of salvation' (Bose 1911, 487). In addition to this use of a unifying first person singular pronoun, Sister Nivedita maintained a complex inner life which she reconciled with her identification with Indians.

A central question regarding this inner life is her Christian faith and whether or not she converted:

> Once, in 1911 (that is to say after her death), the Swami Nirmalananda was asked, 'Tell us something about Nivedita's conversion to Hinduism.' 'What do you mean?' he responded. 'Vivekananda made a greater Christian out of her. She always remained herself, and was great therefrom.' (Reymond 1953, 359)

Her funeral was conducted in Darjeeling according to Hindu rites; but as Reymond elaborates, 'ashes were buried amid the honeysuckle in the family grave in Great Torrington [Devon], under the sign of the cross' (Reymond 1953, 389). Both the non-conversion and the funeral in two traditions suggest that Sister Nivedita did not supplant Margaret Noble. We see evidence of this phenomenon in the fourth epigraph. There Noble states and then intensifies an expression of loyalty to England at the very moment at which she tells her correspondent in London that she will be performing a treasonous act of sedition against the crown.

Third, although Sister Nivedita had a good knowledge of India and had travelled widely throughout the country, giving lectures in both Madras (1902) and Bombay (1904), in terms of the institutions she founded, her activity was limited to West Bengal. It is above all in the Bagbazar district that she seems to have had a direct effect on the population through her educational and welfare work. She was locally centred and not peripatetic within India in the mode of Annie Besant (she did, however, travel away from India to lecture on the country and its people in Europe and America).[23] The Ramakrishna nun would travel overseas and have holidays (she died at Roy Villa in Darjeeling), but the school was her principal organization; it remained in the same street in Kolkata in her lifetime.

It is this local dimension which leads us to educational activism and to the fourth and fifth aspects of Sister Nivedita's practice of hybridity. Clearly, her work took place as part of the activities of the Sri Ramakrishna Mission and thus was firmly anchored in an Indian tradition; but she was also able to make a particular contribution to the education of women. The fourth aspect is that she was able to raise funds, both in India and internationally. The school received international funding from the American disciple of Swami Vivekananda Sarah Thorp Bull as well as '800 Rupees from the Maharajah of Kashmir' (Reymond 1953, 88 and 179).[24] The fifth aspect is closely related to the fourth and comes about because, while she was an Anglo-Irish woman who proclaimed herself as Indian in her language and deeds, she was considered to be exclusively Irish by her mentor Swami Vivekananda.

Having now considered the components of Sister Nivedita's hybrid identity, a look at the wider significance of her activity confirms that hers is probably the only attempt by one of the European women in this book to develop a grassroots movement not totally dependent on a single elite grouping, be it religious, spiritual, economic or political. The precarious nature of that endeavour is confirmed by the difficulties she experienced in getting funding for the school. Sister Nivedita wanted to remain independent and would only accept funding if it came without preconditions. As a consequence, she was not able to keep the school open continuously. Her activity in this domain is a thoroughly modern attempt to combine the local, the national and the international. This is reflected in the Indian internationalist perspective of a description of her activity written in 1900 for potential American donors: '[O]nly World-Service is true Home-Service' (Sister Nivedita 1950, 82).

Ultimately, because their traces in Indian public life can be said to be lighter than those of others (such as Annie Besant), a full account of the hybridity of the two Margarets, Noble and Cousins, should include the domains of their activism and their writings on the one hand and of their inner spiritual lives on the other. In the first domain they combined a respect for the singularity of India with an understanding of the European perspective and contribution to nation building via schooling. Margaret Noble, however, influenced greater numbers of Indians than Margaret Cousins through Noble's activist contacts in freedom movements, in her journalism, her historical writing and her lectures. In terms of their inner spiritual lives, they both embraced devotion to Indian-based goals, while never renouncing or repudiating the non-Indian tradition from which they had come.

Margaret Cousins has another domain of activity in which she was a pioneer, but this is one in which she initially worked with the colonial authorities. It is not well known that in 1922 Cousins became the first female honorary magistrate in India (sitting at Saidapet Courthouse in Madras). What is all the more remarkable is that she was nominated to this position despite having been convicted and imprisoned in both London and Dublin for damage to property in direct feminist action. The action in England took place on 21 November 1910 and the events in Ireland occurred at the start of 1913 (Denson 1967, 23 and Cousins and Cousins 1950, 177–9). Both involved throwing stones to break the windows of government buildings: the prime minister's residence in Downing Street and 'the windows of Dublin Castle, the official seat of English domination'; Cousins comments: 'That sound of breaking glass on January 28, 1913, reverberated round the world and did what we wanted... We were the first women prisoners on behalf of women's demands for their sex in a Home Rule setting' (Cousins and Cousins 1950, 188). (The rationale of this form of action was 'no taxation without representation' [Cousins and Cousins 1950, 175]). From there it was but one step to 'break[ing] the windows of the houses of Cabinet Ministers, the property of tax-payers of whom thousands were women' (ibid., 177).

However, Cousins's work for the courts was far from an uncritical collaboration with colonialism. It was during the civil disturbances of the early 1930s that the uncompromising nature of Cousins's stand for women came through. In 1932 she travelled to the United States of America, 'where she spoke at several meetings held against the imprisonment of Mahatma Gandhi, Mrs Gandhi and Sarojini Naidu' (Ramji 1977, 3). Back in India, the first female honorary magistrate was arrested and imprisoned in Vellore Women's Gaol for addressing an illegal political meeting.

These acts are typical of Cousins's ability to put aside her ego in campaigning for a just cause. Her support for Gandhi in 1932 is all the more significant given her strident opposition to his actions two years earlier, when he appeared to forbid women from taking part in civil disturbance. Her position, expressed in an open letter, is as cutting as it is eloquent:

> Gandhiji has left the care of his Ashram entirely to women. This division of sexes on a non-violent campaign seems to us unnatural and against all the awakened consciousness of modern womanhood. In these stirring critical days of India's destiny there should not be water-tight compartments of service. (Ramji 1977, 3)

Cousins instinctively knew that if women were not actively involved in the freedom struggle, there might well be a problem with the de facto recognition of their rights when independence finally came.

Judged by the standards of human rights aspired to in many twenty-first century nations, Cousins's writings are probably less well known than those of the other 'Irishwomen' in this chapter. In *The Awakening of Asian Womanhood* (Cousins 1922), she clearly demonstrates that she finds the practice of child marriage intolerable: 'Ignorance makes slaves. Slave-mothers produce craven children' (ibid., 23); and 'The Vedic ideal of marriage discloses itself as an adult and freely chosen partnership of a man and a woman' (ibid., 41).

While she campaigned for women's education and for women's rights in general, Margaret Cousins was attuned to the elite culture in colonial India. One of the prime vectors for contact with this culture was Western classical music. In the summer of 1937 in Ooty, where the wealthy went to escape the lowland heat, she recounts how she plays to one of the subjects of a later chapter of this book, 'Turkish Princess Niloufer of Hyderabad: what an embodiment of beauty of mind and soul', Cousins exclaims, while also collecting funds and members for the AIWC (Cousins and Cousins 1950, 703). As she puts it, 'My piano-playing, which I kept up by daily practice, and Jim's light baritone singing and his original verse, brought us invitations to tea and dinner parties' (ibid., 725). However, while she was accepted in both these and Indian circles, she does recount an occasion on which an Englishwoman who is a member of the Missionary Society expresses hostility towards her as a 'wicked Theosophist' (ibid., 725). In the subsequent description, Cousins shows that she can also triumph over the woman on her own terms and describes herself as 'a better Christian' than her adversary (ibid.). This demonstrates that Cousins, like Sister Nivedita, cherishes a freedom of conscience in her own inner spiritual life. She belongs to as many camps as is necessary for the fight. The angry pandit in Clément's 2006 novel quoted at the head of the chapter is a caricature, but expresses understandable Indian hostility towards women who apparently helped themselves (to status) as they helped Indians to gain their sovereignty.

Towards the end of their 'duography', the joint autobiography she wrote with her husband, Cousins, who was frequently in poor health after she began to write the book on 'St Patrick's Day, 1940' (Cousins and Cousins 1950, 729), also wonders about her legacy:

> What had we done that was worthwhile? We had pioneered for the liberation and elevation of womanhood and for culture and beauty in education and life. But to what effect? Much had been accomplished; or it seemed much when you had your eyes on it. But when you raised them and looked at the vast area of necessity, what had been done seemed as nothing. (Ibid., 728)

One wonders what her reaction would have been to the fact that AIWC membership currently stands at 100,000.

There is no street-sign legacy of Margaret Cousins in India. This lack of civic memorialization is only mitigated by her commemoration within the headquarters building of the AIWC in New Delhi. At least here, at the heart of an organization that she helped to found, one of the rooms in the library has been named after her. It is important to add, though, that when she fell ill both the state of Madras and Nehru as prime minister made ex gratia payments for her medical care and for her material needs. Part of the citation mentioned her 'sacrifices in the service of freedom for the women of India' (Denson 1967, 11). In the light of this, and given the fact that Annie Besant and Sister Nivedita were commemorated by Indian postage stamps in 1963 and 1968 respectively, it is rather surprising that to date in India there have been no public advocates campaigning for a stamp commemorating the activism of Margaret Cousins.

And what of Sister Nivedita, who died suddenly in Darjeeling in 1911? She was only forty-four; her spiritual teacher had died at the age of thirty-nine. When the last moments came, she might have cast her mind back to Calcutta, where her school was admitting pupils only sporadically due to the scarcity of funds. In her biography, Barbara Foxe details the relentless series of personal losses that befell her in 1911: Sarah Thorp Bull died, then Bhuvaneshvari Devi, Swami Vivekananda's mother, then Devi's mother, Vivekananda's grandmother, then Olea Bull, Sarah's daughter, passed away; following that two once-faithful teachers at the school, Christine and Sudhira, left to teach at the Brahmo Girls' School (Foxe 1975, 218–9). Nivedita must have had a crushing sense of her life's work as incomplete. How much progress had been made in the task that Swami Vivekananda has set her? The school did not survive her death. Despite the discontinuity in the institutions she founded, the school was re-established by the Sri Ramakrishna Mission. In terms of authenticity, political edge and intellectual depth, Sister Nivedita's is probably the greatest legacy, though that of Annie Besant has had the greatest surface sheen.

Annie Besant left this world in 1933 at the ripe old age of eighty-five (a full twenty years after Sister Nivedita's passing). Though she was by no means as active in the public domain in the last fifteen years of her life as she had been previously, and though Jiddu Krishnamurti's dissolution of the Order of the Star in August 1929 had been a serious blow to her, Besant was ensconced in the citadel of Theosophy. She knew that she would be buried at the centre of Adyar. There was nothing which would have suggested to her that her legacy for India and Theosophy was anything less than secure. Indeed, as we have seen, her recognition is high, even if her reputation does not quite justify it.

The Mother (Mirra Alfassa) and Mother Teresa, the subjects of the next two chapters, are the two European-born figures (male or female) who have had the greatest influence on spirituality in India during the period between 1893 and 2017.[25] Before we examine their lives and the construction of their identities, let us review briefly the historical context.

Spirituality is one of the key ways in which Indians have conceived of themselves through the ages. Indeed, it was such a feature of the identities of a majority of Indians before the twentieth century that it is not useful to speak of identity as distinct from spirituality. The separation between the two is a mode of thinking more prevalent in the West than in India.

In addition to this India-specific perspective, the longevity of the importance of spirituality in the relations between Europe and India is also undisputed. Spirituality manifests itself in several different forms at several different times. At the most fundamental level is the distinction between the Western knowledge of Indian-based spiritual traditions and the influence of Christianity in India. Though generally separate, these two modes, the first mainly spiritual and the second mainly religious, are both changed in their cross-cultural encounter. The chapters which follow analyze the first via Mirra Alfassa's engagement with the integral yoga of Sri Aurobindo and then the second via Mother Teresa's renewal of the Roman Catholic Church in India.

As far as Christianity is concerned, the third-century text *Acts of Thomas* presents India as an outer horizon in the aspiration of Christianity. The document recounts the journey to India of St Thomas, his founding of churches on the Keralan coast, and his martyrdom by Vasudeva (the last great Kushan emperor), who ruled the area covering present-day Afghanistan, Pakistan and northern India from approximately 191 to 225 CE. As this story ended in the Christian's death (another tradition says that he died from natural causes), it was taken up again in another account in the early twelfth century. That narrative alludes to a small Christian community in India led by a charismatic leader, Prester John. These accounts served to posit a Christian domain beyond the core zone of Islam in the Middle East.

In doing this, India, the Eastern horizon on the road to China, took on a partly Christian hue that was more palatable to co-religionists in the West. Furthermore, the existence of this community – described in utopian terms as a place that was both rich and just – provided an impetus for Christians to carve paths through and beyond the core Islamic lands in competition with the global spread of that religion.

Every century since the twelfth has seen the European countries developing different forms of engagement with India and revising or adding to those which have gone before. This engagement may take place via the accounts of individual travellers or groups of travellers, the most influential being those of Marco Polo, who passed though India on his 1271–95 journey. As Kate Marsh has shown, for the period from 1754 to 1815 'the increase of British administrative power in India functioned, paradoxically, as a means of establishing notions of French colonial identity' (Marsh 2009, 2). For specific thinkers like Voltaire, this identity included a precursor of what would now be called an 'anti-colonial' critique. In the article 'Des Brames' (On Brahmins) in his 1773 *Fragments sur quelques révolutions dans l'Inde*, Voltaire constructs this binary using 'the ancient Brachmanes and their [supposedly] degenerate successors [the Brahmins]' (ibid., 119).

The dual process of the contact between Christianity and Indians, as well as the engagement of Europeans in Indian religious traditions, continues alongside the institutions founded by Mother Teresa and Mirra Alfassa. The Beatles' brief stay in Rishikesh in 1968 was a late manifestation which promoted the diversified landscape in which there are a few million European-born followers of Indic-origin traditions (such as Hinduism and Buddhism, to name but two) in the West and '68.189 million' Christians in India (Frykenberg 2008, vii). Our case studies will cover the roles of Mirra Alfassa and Mother Teresa in three concrete manifestations of this cross-fertilization in Indian society. Their influence can be measured in terms of the numbers of people who actively subscribe to their views. For instance, there are the more than 5,000 Indian-based nuns, brothers and priests in the family of orders associated with the Missionaries of Charity,[26] as well as the 2,000 Ashramites in Puducherry town and the 2,000

Aurovillians outside it. Let us now proceed to Puducherry, the unique spiritual site of both the Ashram and Auroville. There is no place quite like it in India.

Notes

1. That is the reason why this chapter will use 'Sister Nivedita' and 'Margaret Noble' interchangeably, but preferring 'Sister Nivedita' as she herself did after she took her vows in 1898.
2. Until December 2017 the position of Party President for life was held by Sonia Gandhi, the final subject in this book. With the exception of Rashbihari Ghosh's twenty-four-month tenure in 1907, the presidency was held by the incumbent for one year only. Will Rahul Gandhi also hold the position for life? This hardly seems likely and thus there are clear limits to the stability of dynastic succession in the Congress Party.
3. In the course of her letter, Besant embraces the 'spiritual' on twelve occasions and rejects the 'political' and 'politics' no less than eighteen times.
4. Objective 3 in paragraph 3 of article 1.
5. Objective 2 in paragraph 3 of article 1.
6. This is confirmed by the lack of prominence given to Sister Nivedita in the Mission's website. Only two sentences are devoted to her, as part of Swami Vivekananda's influence on 'world culture': http://belurmath.org/swamivivekananda.htm#World%20Culture (accessed 11 November 2011).
7. Chandreyee Niyogi, correspondence with the author, April 2013. M. K. Gandhi had Tolstoy's letter translated and published it in his newspaper *Indian Opinion* on 18 November 1909.
8. A note on the name Sister Nivedita/Margaret Noble: it is possible to search library catalogues with either names as the search term. In 2012 the British Library catalogue yields 48 and 75 results respectively. The same search in the catalogue of the National Library of India produces 66 and 18 documents respectively, although 37 of the entries are displayed in the form, 'Noble, Margaret Elizabeth (Sister Nivedita)'. This indicates that, despite national variations, both names are still known and propagated, unlike the case of Anjezë Gonxha Bojaxhiu / Mother Teresa whose later consecration is the main name widely recognized in the public domain.

9. Pravrajika Atmaprana (ed), *The Complete Works of Sister Nivedita*, 5 vols, Calcutta: Ramakrishna Sarada Mission and Sister Nivedita Girls' School, 1955, vol. 2, pp. 460–69.
10. Indeed Cousins recounts that she read all 'Vivekananda's book (sent by Lady Sybil Smith)' during her incarceration in Holloway Jail with other suffragettes for smashing the windows of 10 Downing Street, the residence of the prime minister, David Lloyd George (Cousins and Cousins 1950, 180).
11. These developments have been traced by Manmohan Kaur in his *Role of Women in the Freedom Movement 1857–1947* (1968, 198–201).
12. Sister Nivedita's biographer recounts how her subject met Annie Besant twice in Almora in June 1898 (Reymond 1953, 121). The two women, however, did not see eye to eye. Just as in the accounts of the meetings between Besant and Margaret Cousins in *We Two Together* (Cousins and Cousins 1950, 111), Nivedita and Besant agreed to disagree in their discussion about the need to convince the British in Britain of the need for home rule in India.
13. A full account of Nicholson's activities has been written by Anthony Bishop (1967–68, 277); T.G. Fraser (1996, 88–89) gives a good summary of O'Dwyer's life.
14. Godfrey Higgins, *Anacalypsis, an attempt to draw aside the veil of the Saitic Isis; or, an inquiry into the origin of languages, nations, and religions*, London and Glasgow, n.p. 1878 and Edward V.H. Kenealy, *The Book of God*, London: Trübner, 1867
15. Boehmer uses the term 'cross-national' at the heart of her study (Boehmer 2002, 1).
16. In 'England and Ireland', written in the context of the First World War, she makes parallels between the ways in which both India and Ireland 'forget the evils' of colonialism to rally to England's defence, 'because loyalty and patriotism, and belief in the splendid immortal soul of England… outweigh all transitory wrongs' (Besant 1914, 46). The article is reprinted in *War Articles and Notes* (London: Theosophical Publishing Society, 1915). In her 1917 presidential address to the Indian National Congress she refers to poverty and the dependence on subsistence agriculture in Ireland as the 'direct results of the destruction of its wool industry by Great Britain' (Besant 1917, 15).

17. She elaborates a little on this position in her biography: 'We were Protestants and Unionists and my father a Government official... I belonged in my heart from the beginning to the fighters for freedom' (Cousins and Cousins 1950, 25).
18. The following texts contain no occurrences of these terms: *Religion and Dharma, Studies from an Eastern Home, Love and Death, The Web of Indian Life, The Master as I Saw Him, Notes of Some Wanderings with the Swami Vivekananda* and *Myths of the Hindus and Buddhists.* There are only two passing reference to Irish culture in the *Footfalls of Indian History* (Noble 1915, 35 and 130).
19. There is also a Sister Nivedita School in Ameerpet, Hyderabad.
20. 'Educational journalism' is the phrase of S.K. Ratcliffe, who notes that the articles collected in *Religion and Dharma* were first published in Calcutta's *Modern Review;* Swami Yogeshwarananda adds that Nivedita also contributed editorials to the Ramakrishna Movement's publication *Prabuddha Bharata* (Nivedita 1952 [1915], v).
21. Advaita Ashrama is located in Uttarakhand on India's northern Himalayan border. Twenty-four titles by Sister Nivedita are currently in print at the Advaita Ashrama: https://www.advaitaashrama.org/book/list (accessed 11 November 2011).
22. Recent publications include Alak Bhattacharya, *Nivedita: Synthesis of East and West* (2010) which focuses on her contribution to the Bengal Renaissance, Sudeshna Basak, *Glimpses of the Past: Essays on Sister Nivedita, and Her Contemporaries* (2004) which notably explores her connections with Bihar, and Raj Kumar, Rameshwari Devi and Romila Pruthi (eds), *Sister Nivedita: Social Revolutionary* (2003).
23. Although outside the time frame of this book, the case of Annette Ackroyd (1842–1929) also underlines the importance of Sister Nivedita. Ackroyd built up significant contacts with Indian supporters; indeed Aurobindo Ghose's father chose to give his son the middle name Ackroyd after her. In a similar way to Sister Nivedita, Ackroyd 'started the Hindu Mahila Vidyalaya (Hindu Ladies School) in Calcutta with ten pupils and two teachers' (Jayawardena 1995, 72). The school opened its doors in 1873. However, the colonial context around her and the lack of any alternative pro-Indian form of social organization limited her freedom of action. Jayawardena recounts how Ackroyd married the

liberal-minded civil servant Henry Beveridge. Although Beveridge was sympathetic to her pro-feminist views, the marriage resulted in her closing the school and moving with her husband from one placement to another across India. Sister Nivedita's school was only intermittently active, as we have seen; but she continued the project until the end of her life.

24. The chapter on Princess Durru Shehvar and Princess Niloufer examines the extreme local magnification of agency that can be achieved by the elite of a princely state in India acting on its home turf.
25. The only other name which might possibly be mentioned alongside theirs is that of Amy Carmichael (1867–1951), the Northern Ireland-born Protestant missionary who ministered and offered sanctuary to orphans in Dohnavur, Tamil Nadu, for fifty years from 1901 to 1951. Her orphanage, the Dohnavur Fellowship, still operates today. Carmichael's influence on individual Indians cannot be contested, but she did not have the national reputation of Besant, Sister Nivedita, Alfassa or Mother Teresa. In addition, Carmichael's works are devotional in nature and do not take wider Indian history, geography or spiritual traditions into account.
26. The family consists of both nuns (who number about 4,500) and brothers (each with their respective lay and contemplative orders, though these do not actively serve the poor). Their mission is 'to go in search of the souls of the poorest of the poor through the apostolate of prayer'; see http://www.mcpriests.com/11_family.htm and http://laymc.bizland.com/whoweare.htm (accessed 11 November 2011). Self-submitted population statistics for Auroville are available at http://www.auroville.org/society/av_population.htm (accessed 11 November 2011) and those for the Ashram at http://www.sriaurobindoashram.org/ashram/saa/index.php (accessed 11 November 2011).

RELIGION AND SPIRITUALITY: THE MOTHER

Blanche Rachel Mirra Alfassa was born in Paris on February 21, 1878. Her father Moïse Maurice Alfassa, a banker from Adrianople, had married Mathilde Ismalun in Alexandria in 1874. Both were of Sephardic Jewish origin, though neither religious … In the 1860s, everybody in [Port Said] town seemed to have something to do with the Suez Canal. Maurice Alfassa had been sent to Egypt by an Ottoman bank with a stake in the multinational venture. He prospered for a while, but things became difficult when the country slipped into political and financial chaos. In 1877, Maurice, Mathilde, and their young son Mattéo settled in Paris. Mirra, who was born the next year, was proud of her Middle Eastern heritage, but she never considered herself anything but French.

– Peter Heehs, 2008

Blanche Rachel Miriam (Mirra) Alfassa (1878–1973), later known to some of her followers as 'The Mother' is considered a Hindu spiritual leader by a large group of followers in India … I will explain the history of this distant relative of mine. I will explain that she was a Jew, a lost Jew… She was proselytized and led off by new age Hindu thought which was popular in the early 20th century among some in the French intellectual circles. She had lost her ancestry, her religion, her culture and her roots.

– Shelomo Alfassá, 2006

> I belong to no nation, no civilization, no society, no race, but to the Divine. I give obedience to no master, no ruler, no law, no social convention, but to the Divine.
>
> – Mirra Alfassa, 1920

> From the first time I came to India – in 1914 – I felt that India is my true country, the country of my soul and spirit ... I am French by birth and early education, I am Indian by choice and predilection. In my consciousness there is no antagonism between the two; on the contrary, they combine very well and complete one another.
>
> – Mirra Alfassa in 1954, on the passing of Pondicherry from French sovereignty into the Union of Indian States

> It is France that can connect Europe with India. There are great spiritual possibilities for France. She will play a big part in spite of her present bad condition. It is through France that the spiritual message will reach Europe. That is why I chose France for my birth, although I am not French.
>
> – Mirra Alfassa, undated quotation, between 1955 and 1961

> The moment one enters the life of the Ashram and takes up the Yoga he ceases to belong to any creed or caste or race; he is one of Sri Aurobindo's disciples and nothing else. Race prejudices, caste feeling, pride of sect or contempt of other religions have no place here.
>
> – Sri Aurobindo, 1929, the eighth of fourteen 'Rules and Regulations of the Ashram'

These epigraphs illustrate some of the contradictory yardsticks used to measure the national, religious and spiritual identity of the subject of this chapter: the Mother (or Mirra Alfassa, to use her non-spiritual name).[1] When she first came to India in 1914, national identity was experienced in a very different way from today because the Indian nation did not yet exist and because passports and visas were not necessary for travel. Yet this was no anonymous free-for-all; travel was the preserve of a small group of individuals who could afford it and Mirra had travelled from Paris to Pondicherry, from an imperial capital to the administrative centre of the French trading posts in India. It is natural to find contradictions in the way that others see Mirra's identity and this is demonstrated by the first two epigraphs, but the third, fourth and fifth epigraphs illustrate that she herself found national identity at odds with the profound spiritual quest she had undertaken with Sri Aurobindo in Pondicherry. This chapter focuses, not on that personal spiritual journey, but on 'Mirra in the world' and how she constructed no less than two different spiritual organizations (the Sri Aurobindo Ashram and Auroville) which still survive today. Her steel, her almost monomaniacal self-regard and the curious pragmatic use of her Frenchness emerge in the fifth epigraph: 'That is why I chose France for my birth, although I am not French.' It is this paradoxical post-national use of national identity that this chapter will pursue.

The chapter proceeds chronologically from 1910 to 1988 and beyond. The key years in this progression are 1910, 1914, 1920, 1926, 1947, 1950, 1954, 1956, 1968, 1973, 1980 and 1988. These years include three orders of event: the macro-historical (such as the independence of India in 1947 and the cession of French sovereignty over Pondicherry to India in 1954), the personal (the first meeting between Aurobindo Ghose and Mirra Alfassa in 1914, Mirra Alfassa's taking up of permanent residence in Pondicherry in 1920, the death of Sri Aurobindo in 1950, and the death of Mirra Alfassa in 1973), and the institutional, that is, the history of the Ashram and Auroville (with Sri Aurobindo passing the day-to-day running of the Ashram to the Mother in 1926, the Mother's first overtures to ashramites about the project that was to become Auroville in 1956, the opening of Auroville in 1968 and the universal city coming under the control of the Government of India in 1980 and 1988). The apparent clarity of chronology needs to be balanced by one caveat though. The documents that relate to events occurring in these specific years were often written after the fact and bear the marks of interpretation with the benefit of hindsight.[2] Wherever possible, therefore, these accounts will be interwoven with contemporary eyewitness accounts, not with the assumption that the latter are neutral in some way, but to retain, where relevant, both unexplained elements and others which are critical of Mirra Alfassa, while acknowledging her great importance as a spiritual leader. Despite these reservations, however, the logic of year order is a helpful place to start.

In common with other chapters, the crucial questions that will be answered here can be boiled down to agency; that is, how did Mirra Alfassa come to do what she did in India as a person born outside it? In pragmatic terms, this will cover two chronologically separate, but intertwined issues. The first being the analysis of the stages of her journey to great influence at the centre of the Ashram, arguably the only spiritual project in twentieth-century India, important enough to the state to be subject to an Act of Parliament. The second is her extraordinary use of her position of Mother in the Ashram as a springboard for Auroville, her own related internationalist project. We are dealing with institutions in brick and mortar, so at times this chapter will display both a materialist edge and a negotiation with French and British imperialisms and the emerging Indian national state in the period from 1910 to 1988. It will, however, concentrate on how Mirra Alfassa saw herself, how others saw her, her growing influence until her death and, in a final posthumous section, how her reputation has been maintained since.

1910 Mr Ghose and Monsieur Richard

How is it possible to have 1910 as a start date, when Aurobindo Ghose and Mirra Alfassa did not meet until 1914? The answer is simply about presenting the right context. In tracing the acts of this Indian *videshini*, it is essential to include her emergence and how her influence was mediated through others. This understanding of an individual through the networks that support her is a constant in this study and defines its contribution to life-writing studies. This essential element of prehistory, occurred in 1910 in the form of a meeting in Pondicherry between Mirra's then husband, Paul Richard (1874–1967), and her future spiritual guide Aurobindo Ghose. In papers written mostly in the early 1950s and published as memoirs by his academic son in 1987, Paul Richard states that a friend from Parisian legal circles casually offered him 'my place as candidate for the [legislative assembly] elections for Pondicherry' (Richard 1987, 55) which represented in Paris all five of the French territories in India as a single constituency. There is, however, some uncertainty as to Richard's own role here, because he arrived in Pondicherry only three weeks before the elections, which took place on 24 April, and does not figure in the results list published in the *Journal Officiel* (the official gazette) on 6 May 1910. Be that as it may, the official reason for Richard's trip was political and sanctioned by the French nation state. The personal aim, however, was very different; Paul Richard describes it in the following spiritual terms:

> Before reaching Bombay, I had a dream about receiving a telegram from Pondicherry telling me that all plans for the election had changed. When I arrived in that city a telegram was waiting for me, and the message was exactly what I had seen in the dream. Thus the practical justification for my coming to India had vanished, but the real reason was about to become manifest. I continued my journey south to Pondicherry as if nothing had happened to change my plans. As soon as I arrived, I asked several people if they could direct me to a wise man, as that was what I had come to find. (Richard 1987, 55)

Ghose had arrived that very April from Chandernagore. He had yet to take up a spiritual role openly. He was living discreetly, in the house of Sundara Chettiar, a wealthy Tamil resident who sheltered and protected him for the next six months. While there is a heavy sense of destiny here, the meeting between the two men can be said to have spiritual significance for Richard (and, as we shall see, for his wife Mirra), because in Aurobindo, he found a man who had the command of English and French and a profound knowledge of Western classical thought. This enabled Richard to begin a dialogue about Indian spirituality with someone who was familiar with his cultural tradition. It can further be speculated that Aurobindo's Western education would be able to deliver knowledge which could be relayed to other people such as Richard's wife, who had been engaged on a Kabbalah-inspired spiritual quest for six years before her marriage to Paul in 1911. There is no surviving correspondence between husband and wife, but the knowledge from Sri Aurobindo that Paul Richard would have passed back would have been transferrable and not relevant to him alone because only he had experienced it.

For Sri Aurobindo's part, in a letter to Motilal Roy in April 1914 Ghose noted that he had been in 'material and spiritual' correspondence with the Richards 'for the last four years'.[3] Thus, although she was not present at the 1910 meeting, here we have Ghose backdating his contact with both Mirra and Paul Richard to the time of the first meeting with Paul. Another piece of evidence which substantiates contact with both Mirra and Paul Richard from 1910 emerges in a letter by Sri Aurobindo dated 20 March 1935. Here he mentions that Mirra Alfassa's brother Mattéo, who had first entered the French Ministère des colonies in 1898, intervened on his behalf in 1911. Around that time the government of British India sent an extradition request for the former radical Aurobindo Ghose to the Ministère des Colonies in Paris. Mattéo Alfassa, however, made sure that the matter was not pursued. Sri Aurobindo expresses it thus: 'We used outward means of a very slight and simple character [i.e. getting the Mother's brother (Governor in French Equatorial Africa) to intervene with the Ministry]' (Aurobindo 1997a, 31). Richard describes the event in different terms, stressing the active role of himself and his brother-in-law: '[o]ne day my brother-in-law, who was in charge of a section of the colonial office, told me that he had received a letter from the British government requesting execution of an order of extradition against Aurobindo [...]. My brother-in-law of course knew about my close association with Aurobindo, and when I asked what he had done with the order [...] he winked at me and said, "I left it lying in my drawer"' (Richard 1987, 60). In both Sri Aurobindo and Paul Richard's accounts, there is no direct mention of Mirra Alfassa, but she is present residually in Aurobindo's 'we' and in the term 'brother-in-law', a relation by marriage. These accounts by men demonstrate two points. First, how the default setting for history elevates the agency of those who cast themselves in roles within its narratives, and those actors are frequently men, as in the cases of Paul Richard and Mattéo Alfassa. Second, however, Indian *videshinis* such as Mirra Alfassa can be written back into history in retrospect when they have taken on significant roles, as happens in Sri Aurobindo's account. The wider point is that Mirra Alfassa appears to have been able to demonstrate her practical usefulness to Sri Aurobindo even before she met him as a spiritual seeker.

1914 Madame Richard and Mr Ghose

In an entry in her *Prayers and Meditations* of 3 April 1914, Alfassa expresses the significance of her 1914 meeting with Aurobindo in transformational existential terms: 'It seems to me that I am being born into a new life'. She says that she is 'stripped of my entire past' and that she is like 'a new-born child whose whole existence is yet to be lived' (Alfassa 1987a, 116). What was that past? Mrs Paul Richard had been pursuing a spiritual quest with her husband as part of the *Mouvement Cosmique*. That small Parisian group was originally based around Max Théon, and practised a new version of the Kabbalah. As in the case of the 1910 visit, the spiritual was combined with the secular and practical. The Richards had come to Pondicherry in 1914 for political reasons. Paul Richard had resubmitted his candidature for the Pondicherry seat in the French National Assembly. After the confusion of 1910, in 1914 there is a clear record in the gazetteer (*Journal officiel*) of his putting himself forward to join the France-based governing elite. At a time when travel was so much more complicated and time-consuming compared with today, these members were usually the political equivalent of absentee landlords, who would leave for Paris, once elected. It can be speculated that the Richards would have done things differently if elected. According to Nolini Kanta Gupta, one of the inner circle of adepts who joined Sri Aurobindo from Bengal, Mirra Alfassa actively campaigned for her husband in 1914. One of her earliest experiences of India was going to the nearby enclave of Karaikal in search of votes.[4] This officially sanctioned role in this French-controlled territory was not to be, however. Sri Aurobindo, although he had given up an active role in the struggle for Indian independence, was certainly engaged in Paul Richard's electoral campaign and refers to it in letters to Motilal Roy:

> I send you today the electoral declaration of M. Paul Richard, one of the candidates at the approaching election for the French Chamber. [...] If Richard were to become deputy for French India, that would practically mean the same thing as myself being deputy for French India. [...] Of

> course, there is no chance, humanly speaking, of [his] being elected this time. Richard has come too late; [...] Still, it is necessary, if it can at all be done, to stir things a little at the present moment and form a nucleus of tendency and, if possible, of active result which would be a foundation for the future and enable us at the next election to present one or other of these candidates with a fair chance of success. (Aurobindo 1970c, 442)

Paul Richard's political ambitions came to nought, however. The extent of his failure in 1914 was magnificent: he polled 231 votes compared with the successful candidate's 33,154 – though, as in previous (and future) years, this result could partly be attributed to intimidation and electoral fraud such as the buying of votes. As before, if the official position was not granted to them, the Richards had the resources to pursue their private intellectual and spiritual projects with Sri Aurobindo.

In addition to her political work mentioned above, Mirra had a role in the *Arya*, a magazine on spirituality that was conceived as a bilingual enterprise, with a French version appearing as *Revue de Grande Synthèse*. Paul Richard's memoirs write Mirra out of the trio and relegate her to the role of his secretary: 'Aurobindo and I had the double task of writing and also translating on another's work. Meanwhile I also continued dictating to Mirra my manuscript entitled *Le Pourquoi des Mondes*' (Richard 1987, 67). A role as facilitator is belied, however, by the fact that her name appears alongside those of Aurobindo Ghose and Paul Richard on the title page. The months between May and August were intensive ones for all three of them: in that short time, according to Heehs, the trio went from the idea of a magazine to the actual publication of the first number of the *Arya* on 15 August 1914, Sri Aurobindo's birthday (ibid., 256–7).

Macro-historical forces brought an end to this period of intellectual collaboration between the three of them. War broke out in Europe and with all fit men being expected to contribute to the war effort, the Richards made plans to return to France. The French version of *Arya* foundered, but the English edition with the three contributors' names on it ran until 1920, the year of Mirra Alfassa's return to Pondicherry from Japan, where she had been living with

Paul Richard who had secured work as a promoter of French exports. However, her activity for the magazine must have primarily been in terms of editing, translating and some writing, though to a lesser extent than the other two male contributors. It is interesting to note that the first issue of the magazine also envisages an expansion of the group around Sri Aurobindo. This mention of expansion is important because it heralds that there will be organizational change. That would be the task to which Mirra would devote her life and in which she would be so successful. At this early stage, the organization is called a 'Society' rather than an Ashram: 'The Society has its headquarters at Pondicherry with a reading room and library. A section has been founded at Karaikal and others are likely to be opened at Yanam and Mahé' (Aurobindo, Alfassa and Richard 1914, 58). Also important is that the geographical locations proposed here are those of the French possessions in India and so the expansion envisioned in a French and English bilingual publication is particularly coloured by French colonial geography. This means that the public dissemination of Sri Aurobindo's thought went hand in hand with the zones of French influence in India. Conversely, this shows that French people such as Mirra and Paul Richard could play and would play active roles within this development. Furthermore, British India was not seen as a zone in which to extend their influence (this development in a zone of influence outside the Raj is an issue to which we shall return). These intentions to expand also demonstrate that spiritual development was tied from the start to organizations and places in which those paths of the mind and spirit could be followed. The trio put their names to this. Thus there was a need for the 'Society' to expand before the time Mirra Alfassa took up residence in Pondicherry in 1920, before she built up the Ashram from 1926 and before she founded Auroville in 1968. This need was left in abeyance due to the geopolitical effects of the First World War, but, clearly in 1914 there was a practical leadership role there to be filled.

1920 Mirra Alfassa and Dorothy Hodgson

Recalling the quotation from 1914 where Aurobindo praises the couple as 'European Yogins who have not been led away by Theosophical and other aberrations' (Aurobindo 1970c, 442), we note that Sri Aurobindo does not pass individual judgement on Mirra Richard separately from her husband, referring to Richard and 'Madame Richard' together. Things were to prove very different when the Richards returned to Pondicherry on 24 April 1920. Before that year was out, the strong bond between Sri Aurobindo and Paul Richard would be over and the magazine *Arya*, on whose title page the trio's names had appeared, would be finished. The marriage of Paul and Mirra Richard would be over and their relationship irretrievably finished. Paul soon left Pondicherry, never to return; Mirra stayed there, never to leave.[5] In bald terms, Mirra Richard became a disciple of Sri Aurobindo. However, her gender and her cultural connections with France gave her a special role in the group of people around Sri Aurobindo. For Mirra, in 1920, the spiritual is seen very much in personal terms as a link between herself and Sri Aurobindo, in the context of a disciple's devotion to him. The manuscript of A.B. Purani's *Evening Talks with Sri Aurobindo* (Purani 1982) is the only account we have of the final crisis between Mirra and her husband. The notion of a unity between Mirra and Aurobindo emerges here, but there was disruption to be endured before it could be fully realized:

> One day P.R. [Paul Richard] came & asked him in what way he (A.G [Aurobindo Ghose]) related to Mirra. He said she was his disciple. But what was her attitude towards him? He said in whatever way the disciple will aspire for me he will get me as such – Suppose she claims relations of marriage? "Well she will have that". (Purani 1982, 76)[6]

These words show that Sri Aurobindo had accorded an exclusive space to Mirra Alfassa. Here for the first time we see a person, Sri Aurobindo, putting Mirra Alfassa centre stage. Sri Aurobindo does not mention his own intentions in the matter, saying that he was only replying to her wish to be a disciple. Paul Richard could do nothing about this situation; the husband could not deny Mirra's free will, nor, it seems, could he live with the implied exclusivity of her choice to be a disciple of another man. Paul soon left for the Himalayas and then returned to France, before settling in the United States of America. Mirra Alfassa was now free to stay in the place to which she had returned. There is no contemporary record of her thoughts on this matter, but in the entry for 5 November 1961 in Satprem's 6,000-page Mother's Diary (*Agenda de la Mère*, Satprem 1997), she refers to this period as a 'tragicomedy' and to Paul Richard as a 'vibhouti' (emanation) of an 'Asura' (a negative force).[7] It was clear by this stage that Mirra Alfassa had emerged from the shadow of her husband, with whom she had travelled the spiritual path and whose ultimately fruitless political ambitions she had supported. Sri Aurobindo, the teacher in whose ambit she now found herself, already had a radical political past behind him and was ready to offer her a spiritual example to follow.

In 1920 Mirra Alfassa did not live within the accommodation shared by the community. She lived in the company of Dorothy Hodgson, an Englishwoman she met in Japan and who is said to have considered Mirra as her 'guru' (Srinivasa Iyengar 1978, 182). In being a woman and having a follower herself, Mirra Alfassa was different from the early male seekers in Sri Aurobindo's community. In 1922, following a storm which damaged their house, it was agreed by Sri Aurobindo that both women would move into the shared accommodation. Hodgson would come to be known in the Ashram as Datta and Mirra Alfassa would become the Mother.

1926 Sri Aurobindo and the Mother

In both spiritual and institutional terms, 1926 was a watershed year. Sri Aurobindo devoted himself to his spiritual quest and withdrew from regular contact with *sadhaks*, announcing, in a joint address with the Mother, that she was going to be his emissary on earth – not only would she be responsible for the day-to-day running and development of the community, she would also serve as his principal conduit to the outside world. Clearly, this was a transformational step for Mirra Alfassa. She now had sole responsibility for the organization of the institution and for its expansion. What is more, she drew that authority from an unimpeachable source, one who provided the fundamental spiritual justification of the whole project. Finally, she now controlled the flow of information between Sri Aurobindo and the community.

Although the transition to her new status must have been

discussed and planned in detail, there is no record of those discussions between Sri Aurobindo and Mirra Alfassa; what we do have are general contextualizing remarks by Sri Aurobindo relating to the period and contemporary accounts of how it was justified and presented to the other adepts in the community. An example of the first is found in Anilbaran Roy's unpublished journal. It recalls Sri Aurobindo's description of the whole of the 1926 period and how important Mirra Alfassa was: 'I progressed for myself, but could not do much by way of helping others. Then came the Mother and with her help I found the necessary method' (Srinivasa Iyengar 1978, 201). It is also important to consider the accounts of the transformation of Aurobindo's experience into wider institutional change. This is because the spiritual dimension in which they function and the language in which they are couched were not only used to anchor the new order in the Ashram in which Mirra became a dominant force, they were also recycled by Mirra Alfassa thirty years later in 1956, when she began to prepare the Ashram for the development of Auroville, her universal city project, which took material form in 1968.

The confluence of the personal and institutional in the transformation on 24 November 1926 is confirmed by Nilima Das, who refers to the 'following comment dictated [by Sri Aurobindo] a few days before 5 December 1950 when he died':

> It is only then that Sri Aurobindo started his Ashram. What happened on the twenty-fourth of November prepared the possibility of this descent [of the Overmind to Earth] and on that day he retired into seclusion and entered into a deep dynamic meditation. (Sethna 1999, 11)

On that November evening in 1926 (later known by ashramites as Siddhi Day, *siddhi* meaning 'perfection' or 'attainment'), Mirra Alfassa assembled the *sadhaks* and an intense spiritual experience occurred and was performed and interpreted by both her and Sri Aurobindo. In his *Life of Sri Aurobindo*, A.B. Purani describes how, on the evening in question, collective meditation with around twenty people was followed by a ritual in which each *sadhak* was blessed by Mirra, who was sitting on a stool in front of Sri Aurobindo's chair (Purani 1958, 217). Collective meditation was not uncommon, but the second more performative element, in which Mirra Alfassa took an active role, was. According to Sri Aurobindo's interpretation of the performative ritual, something positive for the community and the world (that Aurobindo called 'the Supermind') could descend to Earth. He, however, would have to withdraw from the world to facilitate its passage. While he was in this state, there would be a division of labour in which Mirra Alfassa would organize and manage the community which sustained all of them.

Three days after the event, Haradhan Bakshi, who had also been present, gives the following account of what Sri Aurobindo is supposed to have later said about the practical implications of this spiritual experience: 'Mirra is my Shakti [female principle]. She has taken charge of the new creation. You will get everything you need from her. Give consent to whatever she wants to do' (Bakshi [no date], 240). The comments are perhaps not the precise words of Sri Aurobindo; but 'new creation' suggests we are dealing with a new beginning in terms of the organization.

This introduced a new form of organization in which Mirra Alfassa was anointed as the head of the collective in all practical matters. Her executive power is clear in these accounts, and Bakshi's words indicate clearly that there are at least two aspects to her agency. The first is that she will provide for the individuals, nurturing them; the second is that they will obey her unquestioningly. These two qualities were cemented in her new appellation: the Mother. However, the transition was gradual, with Sri Aurobindo's brother Barin, among others, using an intermediate form, 'Mother Mirra'.[8]

As signalled above, the material dimension of bricks and mortar is important in understanding Mirra Alfassa's journey from outsider to the central organizing authority at the heart of the Ashram. A brief review of the physical development between 1911, when Sri Aurobindo rented a first property in the rue Saint Louis, and 1939, when the Ashram under Alfassa began the construction of the Golconde dormitory block, will make it clear how effective she was in the task that she took on. As readers who have visited Puducherry might know, the Ashram property is recognizable by the light grey colour of its facades; the definitive city map produced by the Indian

National Trust for Art and Cultural Heritage (INTACH), situates the Ashram at the block bordered by the following streets: rue de la Marine, rue François Martin, rue Saint Gilles and Mannakula Vinayagar Koil Street (the former rue d'Orléans). The buildings in this substantial compound which are now the headquarters of the organization were acquired for the Ashram's use in piecemeal fashion from 1922. This was the year in which Mirra took up residence with Sri Aurobindo, accompanied by Datta. Before that time the Ashram rented buildings across the city. For example in rue Saint Louis (first rented in 1911), rue des Missions Étrangères (1913) and rue François Martin (1913). After 1922, when Mirra Alfassa and Dorothy Hodgson physically entered the community, the location of the Ashram became more concentrated in the location described above. While a 'compound' was beginning to be created, there was still provision made for expansion because the property at 41 rue Saint Martin (now called the Guest House) was not released but retained for housing new devotees.[9] A 1927 letter from Barin Ghose also provides details on Mirra's power of action in real estate matters. Once again this relates to the purchase of the Meditation House: 'She at once began negotiating for the purchase of the house. The owner wanted as much as Rupees 14000, an exorbitant sum for it. Mother said money wasn't of any consequence as this house meant so much for the future of the colony. So it was purchased and repaired for Sri Aurobindo to live in.'[10] This account gives few details about where the money came from, but it certainly appears to be the case that Mirra Alfassa had the executive authority to spend it on behalf of the community. In a letter to her son, André Morrisset, dated 16 January 1927, Mirra draws up a form of balance sheet: 'Our community is growing more and more; we are nearly thirty (not counting those who are scattered all over India); and I have become responsible for all this; I am at the centre of the organisation, on the material as well as the spiritual side, and you can easily imagine what it means. We already occupy five houses, one of which is our property; others will follow. New recruits are coming from all parts of the world.'[11] Mirra's position here is unassailable. Seven years later a significant increase in the number of seekers is confirmed by Sri

Aurobindo in a letter dated 9 May 1934, mentioning that they are now '150 Sadhaks' (Aurobindo 1997a, 518) and no room for more. Clearly Mirra's involvement in the organization had brought about a transformation in its size.

She had acquired, expanded and managed a real estate portfolio, but began to move into design and construction. In 1934 the British began to apply pressure on the French to investigate the financial structure and accounts of the expanding Ashram, which was by then skewing the market for rented property in Pondicherry by its need for houses for its new *sadhaks*.[12] As had happened in 1911, Mattéo Alfassa intervened on Sri Aurobindo's behalf, writing a letter to the *Ministère des colonies* that confirmed that the Sri Aurobindo Ashram was a spiritual venture and not a political one that needed its accounts investigated. As had happened before, on this occasion too, Mirra Alfassa's brother was able to deflect the British pressure. In 1939, one of the seekers, Nirod, recalled Sri Aurobindo's tribute to Mattéo Alfassa's role in the survival of the Ashram: 'It is men like him who built up France and also made it possible for the Ashram to continue here. Otherwise I [Sri Aurobindo] might have had to go to France, or else to America and supramentalize the Americans' (Nirod 1966–86, vol. 1, 360). The material pressure on real estate in Pondicherry had not changed, however, and following a report by the French governor of the enclave, it was decreed that 'if they [the Ashram] wanted more space, they would have to build' (Heehs 2008, 372). This led the Mother to plan and begin, in 1935, the construction of Golconde, a communal residence which was completed ten years later. It is possible to speculate that this name is a discreet acknowledgment of the fact that the lion's share of the building costs was covered by a donation from the government of Hyderabad.[13]

It is significant, given the future development of Auroville, that Golconde was not a residence for herself and Sri Aurobindo, but a dormitory for prospective ashramites. The aim of the Mother was expansion through numbers. In architectural terms, Golconde is a statement of architectural modernism, and in his praise for it Sri Aurobindo singles out the Mother's involvement, while alluding to a French architectural tradition as a guarantee of quality:

> In Golconde Mother has worked out her own idea through Raymond, Sammer and others… architects and people with architectural knowledge have admired it… one spoke of it as the finest building of its kind in all Europe or America, and a French architect, pupil of a great master, said it executed superbly the idea his master had been seeking for but failed to realize. (Das 1980, 117–18 and Aurobindo 1970b, 230)

Further details of the Mother's active role in the design of the dormitory emerge in a 2005 report for the American Institute of Architects by Pankaj Vir Gupta and Christine Mueller. After examining the correspondence on Golconde, they stress that the architects 'consulted with the Mother on all aspects of the design' (Vir Gupta and Mueller 2005, 150).

In the 1920s and 1930s, she strove constantly to expand the Ashram, by renting, purchasing and adapting properties. In the Golconde expansion plans, the Mother moved to another level and gained valuable experience for Auroville, working her ideas out with the French architect Roger Anger. Dominic, a Canadian architect living in Auroville since 1997, confirms that Golconde was a prototype and the Mother's close involvement in the project a dry run for Auroville.[14]

Now we have a better understanding of her journey from outsider to the central organizing authority at the heart of the Ashram between 1910, 1926 and into the 1930s, it is important to get a deeper sense of why this came to pass. This will help us grasp how she was able to mobilize so many people around her and abroad in the realization of Auroville, a second project, behind which she was the driving force.

Accounts by scholars and contemporary witnesses explaining why she was able to have such a prodigious level of influence invoke the depth of the relationship she had with Sri Aurobindo (the analyses of Ashis Nandy and of Leela Gandhi are particularly pertinent here, though these two scholars lay significantly different emphases). Eye witnesses confirm that the Mother was able to reproduce the intensity of this relationship with others who became personally committed to her as disciples. Although she would always say that she was acting only as a conduit for Sri Aurobindo's spiritual work, we will see that this commitment was sought by her and anchored in a ritual with the individual. None of these explanations, however, gives enough significance to the French language and French culture and politics in Mirra Alfassa's trajectory of influence in a place that was under French sovereignty until 1954. This chapter ties places (namely Paris and Pondicherry in 'French India') into her deeds.

Returning to the explanations by scholars and eyewitnesses for Mirra Alfassa's influence, we start with Ashish Nandy, who constructs Mirra as filling a symbolic lack in Sri Aurobindo's psyche. No mention is made of 1910 and the return in 1920 and the background motivation of the French elections. Instead, Nandy writes that '[T]he West had one more decisive intervention to make in Aurobindo's life. In 1914 Mirra Paul Richard, at that time an attractive Frenchwoman of thirty-seven, joined Aurobindo, leaving behind her home, husband and children' (Nandy 1983, 94).[15] Nandy is a peerless scholar, but this initial inaccurate portrait of Alfassa compresses the period of their acquaintance and simplifies it into an almost passive act of devotion on her part (when it was more like a spiritual partnership). Of course, in 1914 she was a Westerner and disciple who did not have the cultural and linguistic background to have a pre-existing understanding of the tradition from which Aurobindo's integral yoga stemmed.[16] As we have seen, however, Mirra's gradual separation from Paul Richard was preceded by two failed attempts for the Richards and Ghose to work together as a trio in the political and in the academic domains (with Paul's attempts to get elected and the publication of *Arya/Grande Revue de Synthèse*). The period from 1910 when Mirra first heard of Sri Aurobindo, to her moving into the Ashram in 1922, was actually a lengthy apprenticeship in which she proved her worth as an advisor, administrator and chief executive. What is more, as we have seen, through her brother, she had the contacts in Paris to defend the interests of the Society and the physical entity of the Ashram on what was French soil. Admittedly, Nandy does describe Mirra Alfassa as 'the powerful, committed woman from Europe' (ibid., 95), but then deploys a psychoanalytically influenced symbolic interpretation of why Mirra Alfassa was effective:

> For him, the freed East [himself] had at last met the non-oppressive West symbolized by [Mirra Alfassa] the Mother… The West once separated him from nearness, love and nurture [Nandy is alluding here to the extreme Anglophilia of Aurobindo Ghose's father, Dr Krishnan Ghose, and the fact that he sent him away from the family to be educated in England]. Now a part of the West had returned to put him in touch with them… [D]iscovering the East in oneself by losing oneself in the East-in-the-West [in the Mother] became a transcendent goal and a practical possibility. (Ibid., 95–6)

This interpretation provides one account of the personal psychical dimension of Sri Aurobindo's quest in meditation and for his impulse to unite with the Mother. Nandy summarizes the impulse as 'when you are completely identified with the Divine Mother and feel yourself to be no longer another and separate being' (ibid., 96). His analysis is Sri Aurobindo-centred and, like that of Paul Richard's memoirs quoted above, partially writes Mirra's agency out of the story. The 'non-oppressive West' must be understood not only in personal terms but also political ones as the protection that French sovereignty over Pondicherry could offer the growing Ashram (which would carefully position itself as an exclusively spiritual project).

Furthermore, Ashis Nandy calling Mirra Alfassa 'the East-in-the-West' is accurate, in the limited sense that it engages with her understanding of the Indian spiritual tradition as carried forward by Sri Aurobindo; but it does not acknowledge the specifically French dimension which she encouraged, by holding French classes for Ashram children for example. Therefore a corrective interpretation needs to be given: Mirra Alfassa's 'West' was not Sri Aurobindo's. His was largely British, steeped in the classics, and hers was French-dominated, though not in a chauvinistic sense and, if anything, it was more global than his, with cross-cultural influences drawn from Jewish and near Eastern traditions as well as a strong Japanese Buddhist influences.

Much of this richness, left out by Nandy, is included in Leela Gandhi's *Affective Communities: Anticolonial Thought, Fin-de-Siècle Radicalism, and the Politics of Friendship*(2006). Gandhi's account has the welcome intention of showing a mutuality between Sri

Aurobindo and Mirra Alfassa, providing both Alfassa's thoughts on their first meeting, which, as we saw above, were transformative in an existential sense, and what are said to be Aurobindo's thoughts, which are quoted as 'I was going to say what you have said – She is a great soul always with you.' Leela Gandhi quotes these words from Sri Aurobindo's *Record of Yoga, I* (Pondicherry: Sri Aurobindo Ashram, 2001), 10:1402, but there is a slight problem with this account, as it is a piece of 'automatic writing' in which the personal pronouns are not easily attributable to individuals. For instance, the 'you' could be Mirra Alfassa, or it could be Paul Richard or it could even be Sri Aurobindo himself. The 'she' could be the Divine mother, rather than Mirra Alfassa. This problem about knowing exactly to whom this text refers, or whether it is referring to individuals at all, is illustrated when the quotation is put in its wider context which shows a masculine third person singular, 'he':

> What? I suppose you have had relations. Then? One of those who prepare, but are not prepared. Oh, let him do his own work, he does it well. Do not try to give men more part than the Divine Being has given them. That would do him harm, to try to make him more than himself. Friendship is blind. Love, but do not govern your actions by a partial affection. I was going to say what you have said. She is a great soul always with you. He was necessary to her force. Yes, in certain limits. In another sense than the Theosophist, she would have to be dissolved to be useful otherwise than she is. I don't mean physically. Everything is possible, but all is not intended. No, help her by your thought & let the result be what it will. You come back to the action. Yes, but the Review is only a means; its success depends on what I told you at the beginning. In your case, the mechanical forces of matter are nothing; it is the inner powers that must work & fulfil.

The 'he' here could be a case of Sri Aurobindo referring to himself in the third person or he could be referring to Paul Richard. The wider point is that, while Gandhi's account does rightly elevate Mirra Alfassa's role, an accurate interpretation of the situation in 1914 cannot yet be reduced to Sri Aurobindo and Mirra Richard as a spiritual couple because, as the wider quotation shows, another person or at least another point of view is present: there is you, me, her, and he. The passage above is not a stable dialogue, but something which resembles a record of highly contradictory feelings. How, for example are we to understand Aurobindo's phrase 'she would have to be dissolved to be useful otherwise than she is', if the 'she' is simply Mirra Alfassa in an uncomplicated sense? This leads Gandhi (in common with Nandy) also to compress the process by which the future Mother of Pondicherry gained her influence: 'Mirra Alfassa returned finally to Pondicherry in April 1920, where she became in due course the Mother of the devotional Ashram community and Sri Aurobindo's spiritual collaborator' (Gandhi 2006, 119). The 'in due course' suggests that there was a natural progression here, that once Sri Aurobindo, provided the spiritual authority, there would be no impediment to the development of the Ashram, but that implication too underplays Mirra Alfassa's dynamism. Clearly, nothing would have been possible without Sri Aurobindo's spiritual authority as a galvanizing force, but, as we have seen, the work and the physical interaction with outside agencies such as property owners and architects was Mirra Alfassa's domain. Sri Aurobindo wrote up these interactions praising the mother, but did not directly take place in them himself.

The scope of Leela Gandhi's study is highly ambitious, arguing for hybridity and for the importance of the politics of friendship. She criticizes the latent Kantian binaries behind Nandy's critique of Mirra's running of the Ashram as making it 'politically conservative and a means of oppressing the people around' (Nandy 1983, 95 and Gandhi 2006). As Gandhi puts it: 'Our conception of the "political" or "ethical" is in many ways hopelessly circumscribed by the secular, rational calculations which underscore the movement of modern European thought – from Europe "out" into the (post)colonial world' (Gandhi 2006, 116). Leela Gandhi is arguing that the meeting of minds such as Aurobindo's and Mirra's can generate new hybrid forms of association informed by Indian spirituality. She is correct about the unique institutional expression of the association between Mirra and Sri Aurobindo, but it is important to add that it did grow up in a place and in a politics that was dominated by a colonial relation.

The crucial point is that France was a minor colonizer controlling a disparate territory across India of just over 500 square kilometres. In the period when the Ashram grew, a well-connected French-born person such as Mirra Alfassa was perfectly placed to draw on the support network that the French offered. Therefore, although he incorrectly reduces Mirra's role, Nandy is right to criticize the running of the Ashram. However, instead of the Ashram being a 'means of oppression', as Nandy implies, the unequal economic relations had two causes. The first, as is so often the case in this book which analyzes elites, was the fact that its adepts saw themselves as an elite seeking a higher spiritual truth. Others could service them in this enterprise. This is clear from a letter by the Mother of 23 August 1930 to her son André in which she states that for between eighty-five and a hundred ashramites, 'the number of paid workers of the Ashram (labourers and servants) has reached sixty or sixty-five' (quoted in Van Vrekhem 2004, 111). Furthermore, the Mother exploited existing colonial trade routes between France and Pondicherry. In the same letter, she states that the Ashram has a 'general stores containing a variety of goods, nearly all imported from France' (Das 1980, vol. 2, 59–60). Oppression of others is a serious charge and it should not have happened, but the benign nature of the relation between the Mother and the other *sadhaks* was not extended outside the wider Ashram community. That community felt that it had to take care of its own interests. Mirra Alfassa had no option but to use her French contacts in this French territory. This was because the young Ashram was still held in suspicion by the British colonial authorities. As they did in connection with the real estate question, the French authorities would also intervene to warn the Ashram when it was seen to be exploiting its important economic force in the trading colony. There was, therefore, a fundamental separation between the Ashram and other communities in Pondicherry, but, equally, it was the Ashram's responsibility to mitigate this.

1950 The Mother alone

If the Ashram and its organization had been enough for Mirra Alfassa, she could have secured her legacy in the modern history of spirituality in India by continuing to maintain the Ashram for what were to be the twenty-three years from the death of Sri Aurobindo in 1950 to her own death in 1973. Had she done this, she would have been only a preserver and protector of Sri Aurobindo's legacy, in the manner of many spouses who create foundations, research centres and museums that aim to perpetuate the legacy of their eminent partners. Evidently, building a monument was not in her style; she was a powerhouse. Be that as it may, it should not be forgotten that Mirra Alfassa was seventy-two years old when Sri Aurobindo died in 1950. Despite her age, it was with characteristic energy (and like Sister Nivedita after the death of Swami Vivekananda) that Mirra Alfassa did not allow herself to by deflected by Sri Aurobindo's death; she did not withdraw from the world in favour of her *sadhana* (spiritual practice), but pushed forward her next project. Its name, Auroville, is both cosmic and French, as it was the 'town' ('ville' in French') of the 'dawn' ('l'aurore' in French), but the pseudo-prefix 'auro' in the name also links it back to Sri Aurobindo, although its form and goals were all the Mother's own.

The central question that this chapter is aiming to answer is how Mirra Alfassa achieved the establishment of both the Ashram and Auroville. The answer, as we are seeing, is linked to Sri Aurobindo, as Nandy and Gandhi have proposed, but her cultural difference, as someone with no birth connection to India and as a Frenchwoman in Pondicherry, are crucial elements which have not been understood sufficiently in other accounts. Since the British authorities assumed that Aurobindo Ghose had been involved in the Alipore bomb plot, he had to stay away from any activity that could be seen as political and in support of the struggle for Indian self-determination. If he did not, they would certainly push again for his extradition. Aurobindo Ghose maintained an interest in both international and national politics. So much is clear from his letters and in particular from his correspondence and comments about how he saw Paul Richard as his political surrogate. Ghose, however, could not and did not want to pursue this interest actively by interaction with those in power. Hence his two-stage spiritual quest, which involved seeking out sanctuary in Pondicherry in 1910 and withdrawing from active involvement in the Ashram in 1926.

Mirra Alfassa had a completely different starting point as someone who was apolitical and not involved in the freedom struggle at all. The crucial point is that the space for the Ashram was outside British colonial hegemony. A Calcutta satellite at Bhowanipore had been given up in 1925 (after foundering for three years), but it emerged in a talk given by the Mother in 1965 that plans had been discussed to resite and expand the Ashram in Hyderabad, a princely state which was not directly under British colonial rule. This might have been possible if the Nizam had taken the project under his wing.[17] The plan involved setting up an ideal town with Sri Aurobindo himself living at its centre. In 1965 she does not give the precise date when this plan was abandoned. One part of the talk, however, suggests that the key factor in the abandonment was the death of Akbar Hydari, the prime minister of Hyderabad state: 'Sir Akbar died and that was the end of it, the matter was dropped' (Alfassa 1977, 44). The mention of this death, which occurred in 1941, would mean that plans were afoot in pre-Operation Polo days. This might well have been the case because, from Hyderabad State's point of view, attracting a renowned international institution such as the Ashram would add to the state's prestige and also perhaps its claim to independence (we see in the chapter on Princesses Durru Shehvar and Niloufer that since 1857 Hyderabad had had a tradition of positioning itself with an eye to the wider geopolitical situation). Of course, the political status of Hyderabad was very different from that of Pondicherry because it had no European 'hinterland', although it did try to establish one through the matrimonial links to the former Ottoman Empire via the marriage of its crown princes to Princesses Durru Shehvar and Niloufer, who were closely related to the Caliph. For Mirra, the rationale for transplanting the Ashram to Hyderabad might have been be similar.

From its unorganized start in 1910, the Ashram was a pan-Indian institution drawing men mainly from Bengal to Pondicherry. Mirra Alfassa's cosmopolitan background took this openness to difference to another level by bringing in an internationalist dimension. Before she began the Auroville project, she had to create the rationale for it among the ashramites, her main home constituency. The task for her was to make the case for an organization which was different from the Ashram and, most challengingly, to take the other ashramites with her. A schism would have endangered the future of both the current and the planned institutions. The more closely one looks at the care with which she created the narrative of Auroville and the different threads of that story – the historical, the organizational and the spiritual – the stronger is the impression that the Mother's comments about Auroville in these years were orchestrated and not spontaneous. It is this threefold narrative of Auroville which is an unacknowledged part of Mirra Alfassa's importance as a spiritual leader in India.

Let us first consider the historical dimension. It cannot be forgotten that the years between the 1940s and the 1960s were crucial in terms of the public history of India, encompassing the war years, partition, independence and the aftermath of both, including the assassination of Mahatma Gandhi. India was an independent and sovereign nation, but Pondicherry was in limbo until 1954, still nominally under French rule, although there were several regions in which the situation was immeasurably more tense, one of these being Jammu and Kashmir. In September 1948, just over a year after independence, the new Indian state intervened militarily to bring the princely state of Hyderabad into its control. In 1951, after a referendum, Chandernagore, the French enclave and former sanctuary of Sri Aurobindo, was absorbed into the Indian state of West Bengal. It was clear that the French (and also the Portuguese) would have to manage the decolonization of their enclaves. In short, the territory was living on borrowed time as the state of India unfurled around it. Despite the significant diplomatic tensions and the sense in some right-wing political circles in France that the decolonization was rushed and might have been negotiated on better terms, the fact that there was a resolution of the sovereignty question in 1954 was of great benefit to the Ashram because it preserved the importance of cultural institutions in a one-state-with-two-nationalities solution. As is clear from the Mother's statements on her desire for dual nationality in this chapter's epigraphs, she did not stand above such issues. As a leader, she took care to protect the Ashram's position by making contact with Nehru and inviting him to the Ashram in 1955.[18]

It is important to understand that in seeking to preserve the status quo for the Ashram, she was also anxious to preserve the role of non-Indians (people such as the Frenchmen Pavitra and Satprem) already active within it. That is, she wanted to avoid for Pondicherry what had happened to Hyderabad in 1948. She was correct about the resolve of the new state to assure its territorial integrity. This resolve would be demonstrated in the forcible decolonization of Goa by the Indian army in 1961 (Operation Vijay), which involved the evacuation of Portuguese citizens. In macro-historical terms, it is possible to speculate that what she envisaged was the need for the Ashram to spawn an institution which would not be merged into India in such a way that there would be no trace of the pluralistic cultural heritage which had been a part of the Ashram under her leadership and under French sovereignty.

Moving on now to the organizational thread, the first comments which belong to it were made by the Mother in 1952 in front of a live audience in the Ashram. The fact that this talk was published only in 1977 might well mean that this was a speculation that the Mother intended for ashramites and not for the general public. It may be the case, therefore, that here the Mother was experimenting with ideas. She proposes an event more than a permanent institution, but adopts the principle of using the built environment to represent different nationalities side by side in one place. Mirra Alfassa outlined that

> A kind of world-exhibition has to be organised in which all the countries will be represented in a concrete and living manner; the ideal would be that every nation with a very definite culture would have a pavilion representing that culture. (1977, 9)

These kinds of showcase projects in which world cultures were packaged and co-opted into serving a narrative of national glory were a dominant feature of British, French, Hapsburg, Australian, Spanish, Belgian and US American metropolitan cultures from the nineteenth century onwards.[19] This resulted in a series of thirteen such exhibitions around the world (starting with the Great Exhibition of 1851 in London). What the Mother envisioned was an internationalization of the Ashram by bringing other cultures to it in the form of architectural and cultural samples on what might be called the 'pavilion principle'. The first question that would have occurred to her audience would have been 'where will this world-exhibition take place?' It would have marked a clear departure from the organic growth that had been a feature of the Ashram thus far. It would also mark a departure from anything that had happened in Pondicherry, or even in India for that matter. The only comparable events would have been the Indian-focused celebrations of the British Empire at the Delhi Durbars. The model that Mirra was following was an European one which stressed an internationalist dimension. It is possible to say this because the best manifestation of the pavilion principle evident in the 1952 world exhibition speech had taken shape in Paris over more than two decades. In 1925 an international student city, the Cité internationale universitaire, was established on the edge of central Paris.[20] By 1953, a year after her world exhibition speech to the ashramites, there were halls of residence representing thirty-two different countries, including Sweden, Mexico, Morocco, Japan, Lebanon and Canada. The architecture of several of these residences was conceived in such a way as to pay homage to respective national architectural traditions, in a similar way to what she was envisaging in Pondicherry. While it is quite clear that the roots of the pavilion principle go back to British exhibitions and their overly imperial intent which was copied and adapted in the French colonial exhibitions (the *expositions coloniales*), there is an important difference between Alfassa's and colonial plans.

This was because after the First and Second World Wars the idea was adapted to provide accommodation in Paris for students as part of a project to foster international understanding in the wake of global conflict. The Mother was using this very continental model of international residences – there are no international student cities in Britain – to foster the global dimension of her ideal town. Student lodgings were also part of the 1952 world exhibition plans. The Mother mentioned that in addition to the national pavilions '[a] lodging house also could be attached, large or small according to the need, where students of the same nationality would be accommodated' (Alfassa 1977). In 1952, there had not been a universal exhibition since Brussels in 1935 and so there was an impetus to re-establish the tradition in the post-Second World War era in a way that was as free as possible of imperial connotations. These plans for a World Exhibition in Pondicherry never came to fruition and their structures would have been temporary, but her ambition to house people of different nationalities in one place is an important indication that she was thinking ahead about building in an international manner.

1954 The end of 'French India' and the start of the idea of Auroville

In 1954, the Mother told the ashramites about a dream that she had had. The dream does not suggest that the evolution of the Ashram is finished, it does not call the *sadhaks* to begin the search for an alternative place, but it does relativize the position of the Ashram: it would no longer be unique. This is because the Mother's dream sets out the spiritual possibility of another place that is a more complete form of the spiritual development begun in the Ashram. Thus in her celebrated account of her dream she says that

> [t]here should be somewhere upon earth a place that no nation could claim as its sole property, a place where all human beings ... could live freely as citizens of the world ... In brief, it would be a place where the relations among human beings, usually based almost exclusively upon competition and strife, would be replaced by relations of emulation for doing better, for collaboration, relations of real brotherhood ... The earth is certainly not ready to realise such an ideal ... yet, this dream is on the way to becoming a reality. That is exactly what we are seeking to do at the Sri Aurobindo Ashram on a small scale. (Alfassa 1977, 7)

The Mother's dream announces the goals of a potential new project, while stating that the Ashram is a small-scale version of it. We can see that the scale of the project has increased exponentially here and that the responsibility is global; but the ashramites were probably not concerned, because the words 'should be a place somewhere' stress the notion of possibility. No mention is given yet of who will be responsible for such a project. The only concrete reference to reality is one which takes the audience back to the Ashram as a small-scale expression of the pressing global need. Mirra Alfassa knew that she had to work with the Indian government and actively courted its many leaders. By 1966, two years before the inauguration of the 'universal city', Mirra Alfassa's lobbying had been successful to the point that the Government of India recommended Auroville at the international forum of the United Nations Educational, Scientific and Cultural Organization: 'The Government of India moved a resolution on Auroville at the UNESCO General Conference held in Paris from 25 October to 30 November 1966.' The resolution was approved by the Conference and the Ashram is commended for 'set[ting] up a cultural township... where people of different countries will live together in harmony in one community and engage in cultural, educational, scientific and other pursuits'. It is noted that 'pavilions... represent the cultures of the world... by presenting different schools of architecture'. Furthermore, UNESCO 'expresses the belief that the project will contribute to international understanding and the promotion of peace' ([no author] 1968b, 12). This quotation illustrates that the government was fully on board this prestigious project and had espoused the pavilion principle to create on Indian soil what amounted to a multinational embassy for world spirituality.

After the macro-historical and organizational threads, let us now go back in time to 1956 and consider the final thread, which is the spiritual one. Evidently for a community such as the Ashram, this was going to be crucial. In her New Year's message that year, Mirra announced rather mysteriously that 'the greatest victories are the least noisy' (Das 1980, 275). Then, on leap year day of 29 February 1956 she made it known that '[d]uring the Evening Meditation, I went up into the Supermind' (ibid., 279). She was careful to use a term that was semantically similar to Aurobindo's 'Overmind', but nevertheless not the exact term because that would have equated her experience with his. Both Aurobindo in 1926 and Alfassa in 1956 further explain their respective terms 'Overmind' and 'Supermind' as manifestations of the 'supramental force'.[21] She also evokes the presence of Sri Aurobindo at this time by means of her linguistic difference from him, she as a native speaker of French and he as a speaker of English, the language that they used as a common medium. She said, 'It is interesting to note that the words "the Time has come"... were heard by me in English and not in French. It was as if Sri Aurobindo has spoken them' (ibid.). Here she is narrating spiritual content as if Sri Aurobindo, who had been dead for over five years, was speaking. In the weeks and months that followed the leap year experience, she generalized this experience. It is possible to see a series of carefully constructed similarities between the spiritual event that the Mother was narrating and events thirty years earlier in 1926, where she was anointed and appointed as the executive head of the Ashram.

In response to a question regarding the implications for other ashramites of her ascent 'into the Supermind' (Das 1980), the Mother uses the words of Jeanne d'Arc, arguably the best known female figure in the history of France: 'I could almost say as for the banner of Joan of Arc: "You have shared in the labour, you will share in the Glory"' (Alfassa 1987b, 139).[22] In these words she is including the others in her struggle; they may be instrumentalized at the same time, but there will be a positive result, glory even for them.

If we compare 1956 with 1926, it is clear that this time, in 1956, there was not the spontaneous recognition among the ashramites that a major spiritual event had occurred. This meant that the Mother had to take the community with her by explaining in greater detail the process by which it would be relevant: 'When this individual event has happened in a way that proves sufficient to create a possibility of a general kind, it is no longer a "descent", it is a "manifestation"' (Das 1980, 283). She did this, not through collective meditation with a small group of people, as Sri Aurobindo and she had done in 1926, but during a large-scale communal meditation on the Ashram sports ground and through a series of elaborate descriptions of what had occurred to her.

1956 Auroville is a 'new world'

The Mother's statement of April 1956 makes the importance of this year clear: 'un monde nouveau est né' (a new world is born) (Brosse 1984, 180; Das 1980, 273 and 277). This was taken further by evoking changes in the physical nature of people which can be part of Sri Aurobindo's integral yoga. The result would be momentous – something that might be described in more conventional terms as human evolutionary change:

> What Sri Aurobindo has promised … is that the time has come when some beings among the elite of humanity who fulfil the conditions necessary for spiritualization will be able to transform their bodies with the help of the supramental Force … so as no longer to be animal-men but become supermen. (Alfassa 2000, 25; Das 1980, 299)

Just as Alfassa had referred to the global importance of her project in institutional terms, now in the spiritual thread she invoked an elite. There is a paradox here. This is because, at the same time as launching a discourse of universalism and internationalization, welcoming all countries into the focus of the Ashram's activities after 1956, the Mother also suggests that those who actually enact that new beginning should see themselves as an elite. In logical terms, the elite and the universal might appear to be irreconcilable opposites; but openness to all countries, with only a self-selecting group of those countries' citizens actually coming to Pondicherry to join the new enterprise, is an accurate description of what happened from 1956 to the inauguration of Auroville in 1968. At the official opening ceremony, as confirmation of its international mission, a handful of earth from 124 countries was poured into a commemorative urn at the centre of the circular parade ground. The ceremony itself was attended by delegates and officials from around the world. The Mother gave a rousing speech that offered those who answered her request to come to Auroville an enhanced sense of self-worth. One way that the mother reconciled the apparently diametrical opposites of the elite and the universal was to imagine forerunners of the new institution as superior extra-terrestrial beings who have come to Earth. This may initially strike one as very strange, but it fits in entirely with Mirra Alfassa's logic. Alfassa outlines the Auroville project using a range of metaphors: an 'immense hotel', a 'zone', a 'ship' (Das 1980, 301, 306 and 307) and a 'mooring point' (point d'attache). Her 1958 invocation of an extra-terrestrial elite is anchored with futuristic references to a vision in which 'at the wharf several very tall beings were posted. They were not human beings, they had never been men before' (Alfassa 1987c, 273). She refers to 'certain individuals, who are the pioneers, the vanguard… [and who] enter into communication with the new Force' (Alfassa 1987b, 133). In these interpretations of the 'new world', intended to galvanize ashramites to support the new institution, we have seen that Mirra Alfassa resorts to several different types of narrative. Even her spiritual narrative, however, has an element of concretization within it, albeit in terms of a fantasy story of non-human beings. In her 2012 article, Jessica Namakkal provides a cogent critique of the marginalising force of the Alfassa's future focused discourse on the indigenous Tamil population. The discourse 'reinforced and reinserted colonial hierarchies' (Namakkal 2012, 62). Namakkal goes on to state that 'this emphasis on the future was to the detriment of understanding of the past' (Namakkal 2012, 62) in which the Tamils owned land that the Auroville project sought to purchase.

The key to Mirra Alfassa's influence in these two ventures (the Ashram and Auroville) lies not just in the minutiae of planning and organization at which she excelled, but also in her ability to tell a convincing narrative which uses the particular historical fact of a territory under the influence of a non-British European power (until 1954) to anchor a particular form of institutional organization with the spiritual practice of integral yoga. She would also extend the institutional elements to include project planning on an international scale. She would pitch for projects that would usually be organized at national level. For example, in 1965 the Mother mentions her plans to host the 1980 Olympic Games in Pondicherry: '[T]welve years later [than 1968] we would hold the Olympic Games in India, there. So we need space' (Alfassa 1977, 42). Mirra Alfassa was, therefore, one of great mythologists and impresarios of her time. Both the narrative of her new role in the Ashram in 1926 and her outlining of the concept of Auroville in 1956 reserve an unalienable place within them for Mirra Alfassa as a woman in control because she alone had told the initial story. However, the crucial way in which she exercises this agency is through the spiritual authority of Sri Aurobindo. In 1926, he publicly gave Alfassa *carte blanche* to operate the Ashram as she saw fit this did not alter during his lifetime and his death in 1950 set this position in stone. Mirra was a nurturer and a seeker and an absolute leader. One presumes that if she were ever criticised for her institutional strategy and day-to-day decisions (though there is no published public record of such criticism by the *sadhaks*) she could always refer to the agreement of 1926 and the absence of any negative comment by Sri Aurobindo after that. Namakkal rightly adopts a critical position in terms of the unintended negative effects of Alfassa's utopian ideals on the Tamil villagers living in the area that Auroville now occupies (even if many of those effects were caused not by the Mother herself, but by her followers): 'Both Tamil land and labour were essential to the building of Auroville, although, once sold, they [the Tamils] had no longer any claim to the products of their labour' (Namakkal 2012, 77). There is, therefore, a cast-iron logic about the Ashram and the start of Auroville. They are manifestations of his integral yoga by Mirra Alfassa, his agent on earth. The unique nature of Mirra Alfassa's status is confirmed by the relative chaos that followed her death in 1973. An examination of Auroville's development after Mirra Alfassa's death is important in assessing the value of her work for India in the twentieth century and up to the present day.

1973 The foundress is no more

A former associate of the Mother, Michel Montecrossa, advances the following account of Auroville in this period: 'The spirit prevailed for some years but began to change after 1976. The Auroville community split into various groups and bitter, increasingly violent conflicts eroded the original inspiration' (Montecrossa 2010, 85). The direct connection that Mirra Alfassa had had with Aurobindo's spiritual authority and her record of success in the execution of the plans for the Ashram and for Auroville could not be reproduced by other members of the Ashram, despite the seniority of some of them, such as N.K. Gupta who had been there even before Mirra's first visit in 1914. These old men were neither appointed nor anointed by Aurobindo. Other younger figures such as Bernard Enginger, also known as Satprem, with whom the mother had a particularly close relationship, could not take on her mantle and became embroiled in disagreements. The most serious of these related to Mirra Alfassa's supposed relationship with senior Ashramites.

One of the key points of discord was the dispute between Satprem and the trustees of the Ashram surrounding Satprem's wish to publish *l'Agenda de la Mère* (*Mother's Agenda*), thirteen volumes of taped conversations he had had with the Mother, in entirely unedited form. The most shocking allegation concerns comments supposedly made by the Mother in 1971 in which she doubts the commitment of certain unnamed members of the Ashram who were allegedly waiting for her to die so that they could live in peace, supposedly by integral yoga. Whatever the sound files show, this content and Satprem's position as the person who wished to disseminate it were both controversial. It is certain that this dispute was part of a period of extremely strained relations between the Ashram and Auroville, because it polarized some of the ashramites and Aurovillians. Satprem was no longer welcome in the Ashram and left for Auroville after the Mother's death. He characterized the Ashram as part of the old thinking, a spiritual museum of forms of resistance ('musée spirituel des résistances') (Brosse 1984, 174). Democratic organization of the two institutions was attempted, but given their separate politico-legal locations (the Ashram being in the Union Territory of Pondicherry and Auroville in the state of Tamil Nadu) and the lack of a formal institutional arrangement and a person such as the Mother to link them, the result was infighting. Claims and counterclaims involving corruption began to surface in the late 1970s. They are summarized in the preamble to the emergency legislation of 1980:

> [A] Committee was set up under the chairmanship of the Lieutenant-Governor of Pondicherry with representatives of the Government of Tamil Nadu and of the Ministry of Home Affairs in the Central Government, and the said Committee had, after a detailed scrutiny of the accounts of Sri Aurobindo Society, found instances of serious irregularities in the management of the said Society, misutilisation of its funds and their diversion to other purposes.[23]

1980s and beyond In Mirra's memory

Michel Montecrossa states that '[b]y the 1980s the level of violence became so strong that the Indian government intervened' (Brosse 1984, 174). He then goes on to suggest, controversially, that the takeover of Auroville was a form of nationalization in which the primarily spiritual purpose of the township was corrupted (this point of view is also explored in Monique Patenaude's 2004 novel *Made in Auroville*). For Montecrossa, the emergency measures of 1980, under which Auroville was temporarily taken into state control, 'expropriated the project and changed it into a touristic government-controlled business, combined with educational and rural development endeavours' (ibid.). This point of view would be contested by the Government of India and many Aurovillians, who would stress that the spiritual mission remains primary. They are right, but the juridical–legal context of Auroville is clear; it may be an autonomous body, but it is under the jurisdiction of the Ministry of Human Resource Development of the Government of India.

The intervention of the Indian state, however problematic for spirituality, was and is a measure of the value placed by Indians far beyond Pondicherry on Mirra Alfassa's vision of a universal spiritual embassy on Indian soil. The idea of Auroville is so important that an Act of Parliament was considered necessary to preserve it. One of the early expressions of the respect that many in India had for Mirra Alfassa was the postage stamp issued in 1978 to celebrate the centenary of her birth. It was the first time for ten years that an Indian stamp had been made to commemorate a European-born woman, namely since the Sister Nivedita stamp was issued in 1968. It was clearly a tribute, but it was also the start of the official appropriation of her legacy.

Of all the Indian *videshini* in this book, Mirra Alfassa is perhaps the most cosmopolitan. All through her life, she avoided being pinned down by one single national identity, whether French or Indian. As we have seen, her dual allegiances, doubled cultural understanding and twin support systems helped her embed two major spiritual institutions in India. This account has argued for the importance of the French cultural component of Mirra Alfassa's composite identity, but not at the expense of the others. Her 'Frenchness' was decentred and non-metropolitan; in a word, it was globalized, with an Indian tint. It had, however, advantageous links back to that non-British part of Europe which acted as a support to the Ashram and Auroville in the period of their establishment. The first was founded outside British India and the second was able to secure a small degree of autonomy via its international development agenda.

The Indian and French components in the Mother's composite identity are like tiles in a mosaic; each is wholly dependent on the other for its effect, but without both tiles the picture is incomplete. This creed of hers, quoted by Champakal, appears in the fourth epigraph at the start of this chapter (Champakal 1976, 61). Viewed positively, this can be called cosmopolitanism. It means that Mirra Alfassa is one of the people who have most completely realized Michel Hulin's expression of how India can function as a way of thinking about otherness. Hulin's hypothesis is: 'India could be the spiritual motherland of those people who feel themselves to be foreigners' (Hulin and Maillard 1996, 19). It is very important to understand that, for the Mother, this 'foreignness' is not alienation, it is multiple belonging. It is also a way of growing spiritual projects which had (the case of the Ashram in Pondicherry before 1947), or which have (in the case of Auroville), a similar type of plurality to the one that so distinguished Mirra Alfassa, the prime mover in their creation (with Aurobindo as their perpetual and essential spiritual guarantor).[24]

This plurality was present in the Ashram between 1926 and 1947, an institution under French sovereignty in British India. Without Sri Aurobindo, its unique location and Mirra Alfassa the Ashram would not exist today. For the Ashram this plurality became diluted after 1947 and further after 1954 and also in certain monopolistic economic practices followed by the Ashram from the 1930s onwards, particular as far as real estate and land use is concerned. In 2017 at the time of writing, it exists only in a residual way in the form of the Ashram's property and its positive reputation in India and around the world. This plurality was also present from the founding of Auroville in 1968 to the administrative annexation of the universal city in 1980. The plurality remains in terms of its multinational demographic profile. Clearly a new nation, India, has asserted itself in terms of the governance of the institutions founded by Mirra Alfassa. The Ashram and Auroville, however, may still have one more lesson to teach India and the world. This is because, despite (the tacit support of the French occupying power in the case of the Ashram), the Mother was able to create one of the few communities in India which has developed a post-national expression of the global. In the multi-ethnic potential super-nation that India has become, Auroville's practice of a pluralistic nationalism (however imperfect it has been) may be of value to the country and to the world in the future.

We have considered Mirra Alfassa's life as a quest to organize spiritual practice in the real world and have seen the support that she received in doing this both from Sri Aurobindo and from the French-speaking elites in Pondicherry and Paris. So despite her claims that she was beyond national identity, she did use her connections in France to protect Sri Aurobindo and expand the Ashram and to make Auroville a more complete international project. Let us now move on to a case where a European-born woman was able to harness nationalist sentiment in 1947 and establish a religious movement which renewed Roman Catholicism in India. Mother Teresa's order, the Missionaries of Charity is, of course, a very different organization from Auroville; however, in common with the universal city, it thrives on account of an international dimension. Let us now consider how it regulates that internationalism in a strict way in order to preserve orthodoxy.

Notes

1. Depending on context, and as a reflection of her plural identities, this chapter will refer to its subject as Mirra Alfassa, Mirra Richard, Madame Richard, the Mother and Mother Mirra.
2. Two additional complications are that the publication dates of these documents were frequently later still and that they were edited by committees representing institutions created by these individuals. These committees were presumably protecting the good reputation of the individuals and institutions concerned. In saying this I am in no way imputing censorship, but merely suggesting that the editorial process is not immediately transparent. No academic study has been dedicated to the textual history of key texts such as the *Sri Aurobindo Centenary Library* and the *Complete Works of the Mother*.
3. http://www.sriaurobindoashram.org/research/show.php?set=doclife&id=29 (accessed 11 November 2014). These are found

in the 'Sri Aurobindo, the Mother and Paul Richard 1911–1915' section of the Ashram Archives' 'Documents from the Life of Sri Aurobindo'. This letter has no exact date, but it continues: 'He and Madame Richard are rare examples of European Yogins who have not been led away by Theosophical and other aberrations' (Aurobindo 1970c, 442). Aurobindo's calling Theosophy an 'aberration' confirms the scepticism regarding the direction it took under Besant and Leadbetter, discussed in the previous chapter. Sri Aurobindo's subsequent comment about Richard alone is the most telling; he describes Richard 'as a European who is practically an Indian in belief, in personal culture, in sympathies and aspirations, one of the Nivedita type' (Aurobindo 1997b, 196). Sri Aurobindo had known Margaret Noble and her devotion to the work of Swami Vivekananda in his final years in Kolkata.

4. *Reminiscences* (Gupta 1969, 76); accessible among the 'Documents in the life of Sri Aurobindo' at http://www.sriaurobindoashram.org/research/archives.php (accessed 20 July 2010).
5. As we will see in a later chapter, this decision to return for good after a period away from India was repeated in the life of another Indian *videshini*, Sonia Gandhi, in 1980.
6. We frequently see others using the nation of unity with reference to Mirra. For instance, Madam Okhawa, a friend from Japan, writes about Alfassa's ability to foster a feeling of deep communion between herself and others: 'She came from the far off land of France. But it was my feeling that she was all along, like me, a daughter of Japan. I could swear that she was my very sister when she wore a kimono' (Das 1980, 192). In an interview conducted by Swati Chopra, Georges Van Vrekhem, the Mother's biographer, describes an Ashram ceremony in which 'you took a ring to her and she would put it on your finger. I, very naturally, extended the ring finger of my left hand. She was surprised and said: 'On that finger?' Afterwards, she told her son [André Morrisset], whom I knew rather well, that it symbolized "a mystical marriage."' See http://www.lifepositive.com/spirit/masters/sri-aurobindo/georges-van-vrekhem.asp (accessed 20 July 2010).
7. See http://mother-agenda.narod.ru/ (accessed 11 November 2011). Many Ashramites and Aurovillians do not consider Satprem's account to be trustworthy.

8. In a letter dated 1927 on the acquisition and intended purchase of the Mediation House, quoted in *Sri Aurobindo Ashram*, 1998, 11.
9. An inhabitant of 1960s Pondicherry, who wishes to remain anonymous, claims that these rented buildings were painted a light saffron colour. The tensions caused by this occupation and acquisition of land are outlined at the end of this section.
10. In a letter dated 1927 on the acquisition and intended purchase of the Mediation House, quoted in *Sri Aurobindo Ashram*, 1998, 11.
11. The Collected Works of the Mother, Volume 16, p. 3. *Sri Aurobindo Ashram*, describes how the community first rented and then purchased the following buildings: the Library House (rented 1922, bought 1929), the Rosary House (1925 and 1937), the Secretariat (1926 and 1929) and the Meditation House (1926 and 1927; the Meditation house was the first building purchased).
12. This is confirmed by Philippe Barbier Saint Hilaire (2001, 139).
13. The discussion of Auroville below mentions the plan to relocate the Ashram to post-Operation Polo Hyderabad.
14. http://www.auroville.org/thecity/architecture/collect_housing/linesofforce.htm (accessed 20 July 2010).
15. Nandy is wrong about 'children'; Mirra Alfassa had only one child, André Morrisset.
16. Integral yoga refers to a series of practices developed by Sri Aurobindo and Mirra Alfassa which aim for a holistic form of transcendence that encompasses what is conventionally known as both the body and the mind. These practices are summarized in Sri Aurobindo's *Letters on Yoga*, collected in volumes 22, 23 and 24 of the Sri Aurobindo Birth Centenary Library (SABCL) (Pondicherry: Sri Aurobindo Ashram, 1970–72).
17. This may well be same relocation of the Ashram to post-Operation Polo Hyderabad referred to by Michel Montecrossa (2002, 37): 'Shortly before 1950 the Mother envisaged the foundation of an Ideal City in Hyderabad where she could live together with Sri Aurobindo.'
18. Kamaraj (the chief minister of Tamil Nadu), Lal Bahadur Shastri and Indira Gandhi were also in the party: http://www.sriaurobindosociety.org.in/mother/mother7.htm (accessed 20 July 2010).

19. The principle was partly realized in Auroville over the years in the Indian and French pavilions, but also in the building styles of the inhabitants' houses (Brown 2000, 12). It was perpetuated by Puducherry's presence at the 2010 Shanghai Expo (one of only four non-Chinese cities selected to present its record of the 'Protection and Utilisation of Historical Heritages').
20. This development was formalized in institutional terms three years later following the signing of an international convention, when a Bureau des expositions universelles (World Exhibitions Bureau) was set up in Paris in 1928.
21. The Mother's words are quoted by Das (1980, 273) and Sri Aurobindo's comments are reproduced in K.D. Sethna's, *The Development of Sri Aurobindo's Spiritual System and the Mother's Contribution to It* (1999). See the works of the disciples in the E-library at www.motherandsriaurobindo.org (accessed 11 November 2011). See also Sri Aurobindo, *Letters on Yoga*, vol. 1, pt 1 and *The Mother's Agenda*, vol. 1 1951–1960)
22. The Mother is paraphrasing Joan of Arc's words when her inquisitor asked why she had the effrontery to have her banner present at the coronation of Charles VII: 'Il avait été à la peine, c'est bien raison qu'il fût à l'honneur' (It had borne the burden, it had earned the honour) (Twain 1896, 381). The burden referred to is a self-effacing reference to Joan's magnificent campaign against the English.
23. http://indiacode.nic.in/fullact1.asp?tfnm=198059 (accessed 20 July 2010).This legislation was revised in the Auroville Foundation Bill in 1988 and the first bill of 1980 was repealed in 2001. See http://indiacode.nic.in/fullact1.asp?tfnm=198059 (accessed 20 July 2010).
24. The epitaph drafted by the Mother on their common tomb in the Ashram expresses their symbiosis well: 'Without him, I do not exist, without me he would be unmanifest' (translated).

RELIGION AND SPIRITUALITY: SAINT TERESA

I'm leaving my dear house / And my beloved land / To steamy Bengal go I / To a distant shore … Goodbye, O mother dear / May God be with you all / A Higher Power compels me / Towards torrid India … The ship moves slowly ahead / Cleaving the ocean waves, / As my eyes take one last look / At Europe's dear shores.

– Saint Teresa, a poem written en route to India, 1928–29

During the year very often I have been longing […] to identify myself with Indian girls completely

– Saint Teresa, a letter to Archbishop Périer that outlines her plans for the Missionaries of Charity for the first time, January 1947

She is of Slavic origin and consequently I fear that she is sometimes a bit exaggerated, maybe excited. But that is only a personal impression and I would find it difficult to prove the reason of that impression.

– Ferdinand Périer, Archbishop of Calcutta, in a character reference for Saint Teresa, 1948

I am aware that Mother M. Teresa had not always been understood well and that in the opinion of a few she is not considered very highly, perhaps even not favourably, owing chiefly to her previous education, different in many

> ways from the one imparted in other countries of Europe: she is Yugoslav by nationality.
>
> – Ferdinand Périer, in January 1948 letter to Mother Gertrude, Superior General of the Loreto Order, supporting Saint Teresa's request to leave the Order

> By blood and origin I am all Albanian. My citizenship is Indian. I am a Catholic nun. As to my calling, I belong to the whole world. As to my heart, I belong entirely to the heart of Jesus.
>
> – Saint Teresa to a journalist in Oslo, 1979

> Mother Teresa was an Indian citizen and she is resting in her own country, her own land … The question [of her remains being transferred from India to Albania] does not arise at all.
>
> – Vishnu Prakash, a spokesman for the Indian Ministry of External Affairs, 2009

Though Sonia Gandhi may be more widely known in India, it is Saint Teresa who has the largest global profile of any of the Indian *videshinis* in this book. Although she passed away in 1997, her prominent position is reinforced by her 1979 Nobel Peace Prize, her almost fifty years leading the Missionaries of Charity from 1948 to 1997, her canonization in September 2016 and the continuing global recognizability of the blue-bordered, white saris of the nuns of her order. The epigraphs above illustrate that, despite her visibility, there are open questions about her identity as a European and as an Indian.

In the first epigraph she bonds with Europe at the moment of her departure on her missionary journey to South Asia in 1928. The third and fourth show that her superiors in the Church perceived a distinction between Western and 'Slavic' Eastern Europeans, though acknowledging, as in epigraph three, that such an ethnically determined description of her temperament was 'difficult to prove'. Her Indianness too was full of contradictions. As suggested by the final two epigraphs, recorded in a time after both her order of nuns and the Union of Indian states were founded, it seemed to be limited to citizenship. In January 1947, however, as recorded in epigraph two, she describes a desire for an almost mystical union with Indian women. These shifting representations of identity form the backdrop to this analysis of her achievements.

The first and foremost of these achievements is the 1948 establishment of The Missionaries of Charity Order, a global organization with around five thousand women and men who have dedicated their lives to its goal of serving those in the greatest physical need. The Order has a multiple presence across India and remains headquartered in Kolkata. In the minds of many non-Indian readers, though, the Order is inseparable from the care of a large number of the city's poor in the five decades after Independence. Towards the end of this chapter, we will see that the size of this number and the form of care are still a matter of some controversy.

Readers might think that the Missionaries of Charity was Saint Teresa's supporting elite, but that is only true after it became well-established in India in the 1950s. This chapter focuses on the remarkable feat of how she created this order of nuns from *within* the Roman Catholic Church in India, while criticizing the Church for its elitist tendencies.

In chronological terms, the chapter focuses on the years between her birth in 1910 and the official foundation of her order in 1948, with a very close focus on two relatively short periods where her life was radically transformed. In keeping with the aim of this book to provide a broader perspective on 1947, it will end with an analysis of her posthumous reputation and how national identities resurfaced in a diplomatic row in 2010 between India and Albania about her mortal remains. The first of the short periods runs from 1925 to 1929. During those years, she left her home in Skopje, what is now Macedonia, and travelled to Ireland, trained there and left again for India. The second period of close focus covers the time between 13 January 1947 and 8 January 1948. In those eleven months and twenty-five days, she mounted and won a struggle to convince the Church hierarchy to let her leave her then religious order and found a new one based on her perception of Indian needs and how she could help Indians address them.

There are numerous biographies which focus on her leadership and the work of her order, the Missionaries of Charity, from its 1948 foundation to her death in 1997 and beyond – some are glowing with praise and others are more critical.[1] The initial focus here, however, will be on the pre-1948 period before the order became self-sustaining. During this time, it was the wider Church that was her elite and her source of both financial and moral support, but, as we have seen with reference to the 'Slavic' comments above, there was also a great deal of ambiguity about her status in this early period.

Her story is so crucial for the wider story of spirituality and religion in India because of the timely way that she harnessed her idea for a new religious order to the narratives of national rebirth that were so prevalent in India in the momentous years around 1947. We will see that her private correspondence (published for the first time in 2007) displays a considerable depth of what should be called a critical political understanding of India and the Church in India before and on the cusp of Independence.[2] This political content will surprise those who thought her interventions were limited only to religious matters and only capable of a rather superficial level of analysis. Her grasp of contemporary Indian history is noteworthy, but her more substantial achievement was creating and growing new religious order that was unique in the 500-plus-year history of the Catholic Church in India.[3]

The reason why it was more substantial is because she occupied a lowly position within the Church when she arrived in India in 1929 and for nearly twenty years afterwards, until she was in her late thirties. Sister Teresa, as she was known before her final nun's vows in 1937, was a member of an Irish order of nuns, but she was not an Irish sister. The first order to which she belonged, the Institute of the Blessed Virgin Mary, commonly known as the Loreto sisters, had provided her with the common basic training for missionary work, but her origins in the eastern periphery of Europe marked her out from the vast majority of other recruits.

1910 Born in Europe's East

In order to fully appreciate Saint Teresa's achievement in building a powerful organization in India, and then to present a fair critique of some if its inherent structural problems, we will analyze parts of the journey to India of an Albanian-speaking girl born in 1910 in Skopje, which was then in the Ottoman Empire, where Roman Catholics such as Anjezë Gonxhe Bojaxhiu (her birth name) were in a religious minority.[4] Indeed, I will argue that this experience of being in a minority and an outsider due to her Eastern European origins in the Irish religious order, were both crucial in her making the leap of thought necessary to create an Indian-centric organization within the Roman Catholic Church, a multinational organization which had grown over its long history from an institutional base in Western Europe.

The account that follows is organized chronologically and begins in Skopje in 1910. The biographers of Saint Teresa do not agree on the principal profession of her father. Three different ones are mentioned by three different biographers – her official biographer, Navin Chawla, suggests that he was a merchant, Anne Sebba also mentions that he had other 'wide-ranging business interests', owned 'several houses' and had a 'partnership running a pharmacy' (Sebba 1998, 10–11)and Chatterjee believes that he was a local building entrepreneur (2003, 116). All existing accounts, however, do suggest that Nikola Bojaxhiu had a certain status in the local community, where he 'sat on the town council' (Spink 1997, 4).

Although she was only nine at the time of his death in 1919, it is probable that as a child, Bojaxhiu had some awareness of her father's prominent local status. More significant for her later life of action is that in the aftermath of her father's death she experienced the painful ending of that position of privilege and a radical change of circumstances. The most important change was that she saw her mother struggle and then succeed in providing for the remaining four family members on her own, by setting up a home-based embroidery business. It is important simply to note that Bojaxhiu's childhood provided a powerful positive gender role model of a woman exerting herself independently and successfully to secure family finances in the wake of a crisis.

It is certain that Gonxhe Bojaxhiu's decision at the age of sixteen to leave her mother and older sister and brother would also have meant one less mouth to feed, but this economic dimension is not explored in depth in the existing biographies, because the missionary narrative of the young woman's desire to save souls is so well-documented and compelling (Sebba 1998, 19 and Spink 1997, 10). The exact process by which she came to the Loreto Sisters (the Institute of the Blessed Virgin Mary), rather than to another order that sent missionaries to India, is not known in detail. Whether it was a positive choice, or the only option that the contacts in her local church could offer, is unknown.

It is, however, worth looking more closely at the bare facts of her joining this order. She could have decided to join one of the established religious orders in Eastern Europe. This would have enabled her to remain relatively close to the language and culture of her birth, but the religious institution that she entered was one that prepared young women for missionary work in India. More than that, it was located over three thousand kilometres from her home. When she decided to train as a missionary she knew that she was entering a two-stage exile, the first transplanting her from home and the second sending her away from Europe. In common with most missionary journeys, it would effectively be a one-way ticket, because it would be too far to go back on a regular basis.

In addition, and as confirmed in the third epigraph above, where the archbishop mentions her Slavic heritage, although she had been a Loreto Sister for nearly twenty years at the time these words were written in 1947, in the 1920s she would have been joining an institution which had no tradition of integrating novices from her background.[5] Her application documents for the Institute of the Blessed Virgin Mary further illustrate her foreignness in linguistic terms. They give a snapshot of her language mix as a fifteen-year old in 1925. 'I know Albanian', she writes, 'which is my mother tongue, and Serbian, I know a little French, English I do not know at all' (Kolodiejchuk 2007, 14–15). Though this linguistic palette was not unusual for a conventionally educated young woman born in Skopje at the time, the main internal language among the Loreto Sisters was English and, in the field, there was an established tradition of the nuns in the order teaching in the medium of English.[6] Her initial lack of English meant that she was a linguistic outsider in the order and would not be able to take part in the order's principal activity of teaching in that language in prestigious convent schools such as the ones in Entally and Darjeeling.

Thus, before her departure to India, she knew that she would only be allowed to teach in Bengali-medium schools. Saint Teresa had a uniquely innovative idea of founding a religious order where Indians were in the majority in both receiving and giving care. Her correspondence, analyzed below, shows that her nineteen years (from 1929 to 1948) teaching in these schools in Bengali led her to know the majority Indian society better, rather than only its Anglophone elite. This subaltern experience, therefore, fed into her perceptive historical analysis of the comparative estrangement between the Roman Catholic Church and the wider population in India in the 1930s and 1940s.

In 1928, once she had been accepted by the order, at the age of around eighteen, she embarked (presumably alone) on a prodigious railway journey across Europe in a west-bound carriage from Skopje to the Loreto headquarters in Ireland. One could call that train Bojaxhiu's 'Occident Express' – it was a journey that presumably passed through the metropolises of Paris and London. Her terminus was Dublin and her final destination was Rathfarnham Abbey on the western Catholic Celtic fringe of Europe. She had thus moved from one edge of Europe to the other.

Her stay with the Loreto nuns at Rathfarnham was not a long apprenticeship. It lasted from September to December 1928. It started her novitiate and helped her to begin gaining a basic knowledge of English to use in her missionary work. It is important to acknowledge the importance of those months for the future Saint Teresa. In Ireland, for the first time, she experienced her religion in a region where members of that faith were in the majority. This was entirely different from the Skopje of her birth, where the Muslim Ottomans the extended family of princesses Durru Shehvar and Niloufer, subjects of a later chapter of this book – held power, and where Orthodox Christianity was also a large group.[7]

Nationalism was also prevalent in the civil society at the time she arrived in Ireland. She found herself in a country whose struggle for freedom from Britain was under way, but whose independence did not yet exist on a constitutional basis. As we shall see, Saint Teresa first publically mentioned the idea of establishing a new order of nuns in 1947, a time when India was in a similar position to that of the south of Ireland in 1928. In Ireland she might have chosen to inform herself about the political situation from the Irish nuns and novices around her, or she might have laid greater emphasis on her own spiritual preparations for entering the religious order.[8] No causal link between Ireland and India can be proved, therefore, but her later correspondence in India shows that she did take an active interest in the society around her. It is possible that she might have done the same in Ireland.

1928 Departing for India

In December 1928 Sister Teresa set off on a sea voyage from Ireland to Calcutta. It is interesting to note that the early Mediterranean stage of this eastward journey would have taken her past her former Balkan home. The poem she wrote on board the ship (quoted in the first epigraph of this chapter) demonstrates that, though her experience of Europe was very diverse, an idea of belonging to Europe was anchored in her consciousness as she departed to India. In her world view, India was a place on the very edge of the 'Christian world' (Teresa 1929, 3).

Her future work in India as a missionary for the order was not only a job, but a vocation for life.[9] Other stanzas in the poem express her situation clearly: 'I'm leaving my old friends / Forsaking family and home / My heart draws me onward / To serve my Christ… In return [for her sacrifice], I ask of Thee / O most kind Father of us all: / Let me save at least one soul – / One you already know' (Kolodiejchuk 2007, 16–17). The lines in this poem express her desire to save souls in order to save her own soul. This is the personal imperative which was later to drive the creation and expansion of her new religious order. However, this is not only an act of faith tied to an act of will, the poem also mentions numbers of souls and contains, therefore, an inbuilt positive attitude to growth. This is part of the missionary dynamic and seems to say 'saving one soul is good for my soul, but saving two is even better and saving thousands of souls is better still'. This dynamic seems entirely in harmony with capitalist growth.[10] It is this expansionist tendency that so offended (and still offends) adherents of other religions in India.

1929 to 1948 Years of training and work in Bengal and 1947 The unique idea for a new order

The nineteen years from her arrival in January 1929 to the final permission from the Archbishop of Calcutta to leave the Loreto sisterhood and to found the Missionaries of Charity in January 1948 was a time of further training and hard work. There were two years of novitiate before she began teaching at St Mary's Bengali Medium School in Calcutta in 1931.

In 1937, in a letter to Father Franjo Jambrekovi, her former confessor, she mentions her happiness at being about to take her final vows which would anchor her for life in her practice of poverty, chastity and obedience in the Institute of the Blessed Virgin Mary (the Loreto Sisters). It was during this period of stability and after her final vows that she made her first regular Sunday visits to the poor in Calcutta's slums, noting, in an article about her missionary activity published in Skopje, that 'I cannot help them, because I do not have anything, but I go to give them joy' (Teresa 1937, 25).[11] Mother Teresa, as she was known after her final vows, had to use her own initiative to solve frequent problems with food supply to the school during the war years. She was made principal in 1944.

As in the case of Mirra Alfassa, the accounts of key events are often recorded long after they occurred. This applies to the case of her unique idea to found a new order. In 1970, when Mother Teresa was well-known in India and gaining ever more recognition across the world, she was interviewed about her personal history by the BBC journalist Malcolm Muggeridge.[12] It was during this period that Mother Teresa mentions how the idea to help the poor of Calcutta came to her in a train journey from Calcutta to her annual retreat in Darjeeling on 10 September 1946.[13] Since this analysis concentrates on the mechanics of how a respected but relatively isolated member of the Loreto Sisters was able to influence an organization as big as the Roman Catholic Church, this inspirational explanation of it all coming to her in the northbound train will be left aside. Instead we will concentrate on the fiery exchange of letters between Teresa and her Archbishop, Ferdinand Périer.[14] The precedent for this approach is found in a letter by Archbishop Périer to Teresa, dated 7 April 1947. In it he asks her to bracket out her religious visions for a moment and to give him something that in modern parlance would be called a 'business plan' for the new order of nuns that she was proposing: 'It is not desired to have a long description of what you fancy you will be able to do. What we [the archbishop and the advisors that he would consult in Rome and in India] want to know in a few words: the aims, the means, the rules, the recruitment, the possibilities of success [Périer underlines the items in this list] [...] if we start something it must be able to achieve the object for which it is started – that's what I call the success' (Kolodiejchuk 2007, 71). In what follows, there will be numerous references to this nine-point 'business plan' which she completed and sent to him in June 1947.[15]

January 1947 to January 1948 Correspondence between Saint Teresa and Périer

Before beginning the analysis, a summary of the entire twelve-month correspondence is needed in order to show how far apart Teresa and Archbishop Périer were at the start, and her formidable persistence in convincing him and the Church hierarchy that her plan was viable.[16] The correspondence begins with a long letter to the Archbishop dated 13 January 1947, followed by a reminder letter by Saint Teresa, dated 25 January. The response is a holding letter from Archbishop Périer (19 February), stating 'this is far too important a question to be solved or to be assessed on the spot, or in a day or month' (Kolodiejchuk 2007, 59). There follows an entreaty by Teresa (written sometime between 20 February and 7 March) for the Archbishop to bring her request to the direct attention of the pope during a forthcoming trip to Rome. Once again, in response, Périer requests time to reflect: 'The question is far too important for the Church to decide all at once. It may take months, it may take years...' (ibid., 64, dated 7 March); but Teresa's response requests action: 'Your Grace, let me go, and give myself for them, let me offer myself and those who will join me for those unwanted poor' (ibid., 65, dated 30 March). She backs this up with a reference to the papal encyclical, or guidance, of 6 January 1946, in which Pope Pius XII pleaded for the 'Care of the World's Destitute Children' (ibid., 369). She puts a direct question to Périer: 'What would he [the pope] say, if he saw your poor, the poor of the slums of Calcutta? Do something about this before you leave [...]' (ibid., 67). Périer replies on 7 April that he is 'rather astonished' by her descriptions of his inaction. As mentioned above, he asks her to draft a business plan and says that 'I have absolutely no power to let you start this kind of work' and that 'the matter must necessarily go to Rome' (ibid., 70). Teresa replies with her nine-point plan on 5 June 1947. Périer left for an annual stay in Europe and she heard nothing until October when he returned and wrote to her that 'it will still take a little while before I can conclude the whole thing' (ibid., 84).[17] Teresa then sought to meet him in person (ibid., 59). Périer did not grant her request, but asked for further clarification on practical issues via Father Van Exem, Teresa's spiritual advisor.[18] She provided this to him on 19 October 1947 and continued to maintain that the 'grave reason' that Périer needed to garner support for the project in Rome should be the 'salvation of souls' (ibid., 87). On 24 October, Teresa wrote to the archbishop again, literally begging him to 'let me go' (ibid., 91). On 7 November, she wrote yet again 'Like the woman in the Gospel here I come again – to beg you to let me go' (ibid., 93). On 3 December, she edited and sent him a summary of her thoughts and the Voices that she had heard that year. This was sent via and addresses Van Exem and not Périer. She also provides practical details of recruits: 'two Yugoslav girls [...] six Bengali girls – The Belgium girl' (ibid., 100). Both Périer and Van Exem were born in Belgium and so this may have been Teresa's attempt to show dedication to her plan from someone in their former homeland. Finally, on 6 January 1948, Périer met her after mass at the Loreto convent and gave his consent for her to begin the project.

The first letter written to the archbishop by Teresa on 13 January 1947 is an extremely important document and worth examining in depth. This is because it provides a new vision for the Roman Catholic Church in India.[19] It was a vision that was perfectly timed to respond to the humanitarian need in Bengal that followed the famine of 1943 and the communal riots of August 1946. This situation would later be exacerbated by the refugee crisis following Partition.

The letter to the archbishop opens with Teresa's admission that 'strange thoughts and desires have been filling my heart' (Kolodiejchuk 2007, 47). Following established practice, in which nuns raise matters of personal faith with their 'spiritual director' (ibid., 81) before taking them to a higher authority in the Church, she states that she has already discussed her mystical experiences and resulting radical request to start a new order of nuns with Father Van Exem. She then says that he first 'told me he thought it was God's inspiration – but to pray and remain silent over it' (ibid.). This was a judgement that the 'strange thoughts and desires' were fundamentally positive, but that she should wait for further comment from her superiors in relation to the request that accompanied them. Teresa then reveals her spiritual director's authorization to speak to the archbishop. Van Exem is said to have told her that 'You [Teresa] will write to His Grace [the formal way of addressing an archbishop] as a daughter to her father [...] telling him how it all went, adding that you talked to me [Van Exem] and that now I think I cannot in conscience prevent you from exposing everything to him [to the archbishop]' (ibid.). Before she begins, Teresa stresses her absolute obedience to the archbishop and that she will respect any decision that he might come to in the matter: 'at one word that Your Grace would say I am ready never to consider again any of those strange thoughts which have been coming continually' (ibid.).

She then launches into her account: 'During the year very often I have been longing to be all for Jesus and to make other souls – especially Indian, come and love Him fervently – to identify myself with Indian girls completely [...] I thought [it] was one of my many mad desires. I read the life of St M. Cabrini – She did so much for the Americans because she became one of them. Why can't I do for India what she did for Amer [America]? She did not wait for souls to come to her – she went to them with her zealous workers. Why can't I do the same for Him here?' (Kolodiejchuk, 2007, 47–48).The wider project is not explicitly about conversion; to say that would be to impute intentions to Saint Teresa which are not overtly present in this letter. There is, however, a sense in which the aims of the enterprise is to get a large number of 'souls' who are not acquainted with her God to 'love' that God 'fervently' (ibid., 47).

The most remarkable aspect here is the account about how she came to make her request and the authorities she quotes in support of it. Teresa not only invokes scripture in her letter, but also makes a reference to biography. The life story of Saint Frances Xavier Cabrini is referred to here as a model to follow. She was also known as 'Mother Cabrini' and she lived from 1850 to 1917. She was the nun who founded a religious order and took care of the spiritual and material needs of many thousands of Italian immigrants to the United States between the late 1880s and her death in 1917.

Father Brian Kolodiejchuk, the priest who argued the case for her beatification and canonization (her postulator) and the editor of the 2007 book that published these letters for the first time, gives a very brief summary of Saint Frances Xavier Cabrini's life in an endnote. She was a nun of Italian origin who cared for Italian immigrants to the United States from the end of the 1880s. However, neither he, nor any of her biographers, have paid enough attention to the close parallels between Saint Teresa and Saint Frances Xavier Cabrini, the first naturalized citizen of the United States to be made a saint. This is no casual reference by Teresa; on closer inspection, it is clear that she has taken the Italian-American's life as a model for her own project as far as two practical items of strategy are concerned.

Before we consider these items, further research into the Cabrini biographies shows that the account of Cabrini given in Cyril Martindale's 1931 life, *Mother Francesca Saverio Cabrini,* displays a remarkable similarity to Teresa's plans.[20] Among the seven biographies published in and before 1946, only Martindale directly describes Cabrini's life as a model for other young women: 'I hope that some of my readers may be girls: I hope they are girls who get enthusiastic about others girls swimming channels and flying half way around the world. [...] I end, then, by hoping that many who read about M. Cabrini may become members of her Institute, or at any rate women of the same spirit and heart as hers' (Martindale 1946, xv). These are sidelong references to the achievements of women in secular society: swimmer Gertrude Ederle and the aviatrix Amelia Earhart (Ederle was the first woman to swim the English Channel in 1926 and Earhart flew alone across the Atlantic Ocean in 1928). Given that Teresa refers to Cabrini as a model, she is definitely aspiring to be a woman 'of the same spirit and heart as hers [as Cabrini's]' (ibid., xv). Specific parallels between Martindale's account of the two saints' letters will be analyzed as they arise below; let us now consider other parallels between these two female religious leaders.

The first of these is found in the similarity between the names of the two women's orders. The Italian-born nun founded the 'Missionary Sisters of the Sacred Heart of Jesus'. In a letter to Archbishop Périer, Teresa reveals that she has considered two names for her order: the 'Missionaries of Charity' or 'Missionary Sisters of Charity' (Kolodiejchuk 2007, 50 and 51). The second of these is close to that of Saint Frances Xavier Cabrini's order.

The second parallel relates to the quotation above and Teresa's comment about her Italian-born predecessor doing 'so much for the Americans because she became one of them'. This rather abstract notion has an eminently practical expression. Cabrini became a United States citizen in 1909, thus adopting the citizenship of the nation of her prime field of charitable activity. Teresa would receive permission from Périer to begin her project on 6 January 1948 and became an Indian citizen in the same year. She did this although there was absolutely no need for her to do so from a Church or theological perspective. As we know from the cases of other Indian *videshinis* such as Sonia Gandhi, the nationality question is often a controversial one. As we have seen, Mirra Alfassa's nationality appears to have remained French, although she espoused Indian identity. Saint Teresa, however, was the only Indian *videshini* who made a clear choice of Indian nationality as soon as it was possible for her to make it.

There is, however, a crucial difference between Frances Xavier Cabrini's field of operation and what Teresa was proposing to do in India: Cabrini and her helpers were ministering to Roman Catholics in a foreign land, whereas in Teresa's venture in India, Indian Christians would be helping non-Christians in their own soon-to-be-sovereign homeland. This dual role for Indians is clear because, after a passage in which she acknowledges the difficulty of this task for her, Teresa reveals the particular role that is reserved for young Christian women of Indian origin within the organization. Here she uses italics to quote the voice that she has been hearing: '*I want Indian nuns [...] who would be so very united to Me [to Jesus] as to radiate My love [the love of Jesus] on souls*' (Kolodiejchuk 2007, 48). She is stressing the spiritual side, but setting her proposals in a wider context; it also makes sense to found a new order with Indians caring for Indians at a historical moment when national self-sufficiency was the order of the day.

Teresa has a Church-centric institutional point to push home to the archbishop here; namely, that her proposal cannot be realized from within the Loreto Order to which she belonged at the time of writing in January 1947. She recounts a dialogue that she believed she had with Jesus 'Our Lord' to stress that a new order of Indian nuns would be necessary for the task: 'I tried to persuade Our Lord that I would try to become a very fervent holy Loreto nun [...] – but the answer came very clear again. *I want Indian Missionary Sisters of Charity – who would be My fire of love amongst the very poor – the sick – the dying – the little street children. [...] and the Sisters [...] would bring these souls to Me*' (Kolodiejchuk 2007, 48–49). So Indians are on both sides of the binary here: caring and cared for, but within a new organization created by the Catholic Church in India and with Teresa at its head. Her position at the head of an order would transform her from a Loreto Sister to a 'Superior General' in her own order; from a foot soldier of Christ, she would become a general.

Not only is the name of the new order introduced in the letter, but so is its dress. In the following extract Mother Teresa's voice of Jesus not only simplifies the appearance of the sari, it also interprets this anachronistically as an exclusively humble form of dress, similar to that worn by Mary, the mother of Jesus: 'You [the nuns] will dress in simple Indian clothes or rather like My Mother dressed – simple and poor [...] your saric [sic] will become holy because it will be My symbol' (Kolodiejchuk 2007, 48–49). In sartorial terms, therefore, the Church would spawn a Western–Indian hybrid form of nuns' dress.

At this midpoint in the letter, just as in the expression of obedience to the archbishop's final decision which prefaces it, Mother Teresa pulls away from the main line of her argument to tell her superior how fearful she is regarding her own role in the mode of operating that she is proposing for the new order of nuns: 'The thought of eating, sleeping – living like the Indians filled me with fear' (Kolodiejchuk 2007, 49). Mother Teresa uses her voice of Jesus to answer the question: '*Do not fear – I shall be with you always*' (ibid.). She then returns to her argument, embellishing it with a point on how the Catholic Church in India needed to renew its mission for social reasons. Mother Teresa uses her voice of Jesus to stress the need for a ministry to the poor, in contrast with contemporary Church structures in India which she believes mainly cared for elites: '*[G]ive Me the souls of the poor little street children [...] If you only knew how many little ones fall into sin every day. There are convents with numbers of nuns caring for the rich and well-to-do people, but for My very poor there is absolutely none*' (ibid.).[21] The letter continues with two subtitled sections: 'The Call' – the religious goals of the nuns, and 'The Work' – their activity in serving those goals. In 'The Call', Saint Teresa envisages a deepening of the spiritual life of these Christians who would 'complete one full year of true interior life' with 'perfect poverty'.

These elements of vocation and activity are familiar features of religious orders around the world, but the unique recurrent element in Teresa's proposal is living in an 'Indian' way: 'To be an Indian – to live with them – like them – so as to get at the people's heart' (Kolodiejchuk 2007, 50). The words 'Indian' and 'Indian-minded' are mentioned no less than fourteen times in the letter; ten times by Sister Teresa speaking for herself and four times by the voice of God. Crucially though, this Indianness was conceived in a non-exclusive way as far as recruitment was concerned (otherwise it would have defeated the unstated objective to grow the Missionaries of Charity): 'In the order, girls of any nationality should be taken – but they must become Indian-minded – dress in simple clothes' (ibid.). The nuns will follow a path of self-sacrifice, becoming 'Indian victims for India', yet they will of course receive respite from their hard task in a home base: 'So as to renew and keep up the spirit – the Sisters should spend one day in every week in the house – the Mother house of the city' (ibid.).

As far as the work is concerned, there is no mention of conversion, but, in common with the Indian *videshinis* Sister Nivedita and Margaret Cousins (and with Annie Besant, though to a lesser extent because she preferred elite education), elementary education is the first pillar: 'No boarding schools – but plenty of schools – free – up to class II only [...] The school should be only in the very poor places of the parish, to get the children from the streets, to keep them for the poor parents who have to work' (Kolodiejchuk 2007, 51). Saint Teresa rejects boarding schools because they are too close to what was currently being maintained by orders such as the Loreto Sisters in India at that time.

The second pillar, helping 'the sick and the dying' was to become the mainstay of the order; the nun 'who will take care of the sick – she will assist the dying – do all the work for the sick – just as much if not more, what a person gets in a hospital – wash them and prepare the place for His coming' (Kolodiejchuk 2007, 51). It is important to note that there is no mention of curing the sick here; the help, comfort and Christian love are given to people who are dying. The aim is to care for them on the way to death and thereby gain their souls. She also does not say whether the dying person has any volition in this process, but for the new order, the alleviation of the suffering of the dying is at the heart of the charitable act. Seen in isolation, there is both a theological and a humane rationale to such a project. However, as we will see in the next section when we examine critics of the Missionaries of Charity, wider moral objections can be raised about it at an ethical level.

1947 to the mid-1980s A historically robust core mission threatened by institutional growth?

Périer's twelve-month-long consideration of her request forced Teresa to elaborate her justifications of each point in her January 1947 letter to the archbishop. We have seen from Teresa's own early experiences how fundamental language learning is for the work of a nun. In the nine-point business plan, dated 5 June 1947, she elaborates on this, saying that new recruits 'must be able to learn or know the language of the country thoroughly [...] for whatever nation they enter that people's language and ways must be theirs' (Kolodiejchuk 2007, 75).[22] The nuns of the Missionaries of Charity, therefore, would go into the field equipped with linguistic tools. For non-Western recruits to the order, Teresa envisaged an automatic placement decision which was simple: 'if a Tamil enters – she shall be given work amongst the Tamils – a Chinese amongst the Chinese and so on' (ibid.). This pragmatism is different in form, but no less rigorous than the placement in a Bengali-medium school that she had to take up in the Loreto order. For its members, therefore, the new order would have an inflexible code.

In the quotation from the business plan below, Saint Teresa develops arguments relating to nationalism which represent probably the most profound historical analysis in her published writings. Here, in response to Périer's probing question 'whether it is not possible to obtain this end by congregations already in existence?', she outlines what she perceives as the ambiguous position of Indian nuns in Roman Catholic orders in India. Can existing orders fit the bill?

> No. First, because they are European. When our Indian girls enter these orders – they are made to live their life – eat, sleep, dress like them [Europeans]. In a word, as the people say – they become 'Mems' [memsahibs – white, European women associated with colonial power in India]... Second – as much as those Sisters try to adapt themselves to the country, they remain foreigners for the people – and then there are the rules [of the existing religious orders] – which do not allow them so to say, be one of the people. They have their big schools and hospitals – in all these the souls have to come or be brought to them. While the Missionaries of Charity will go in search, live their days in the slums and streets. Close to the people's heat – they would do the works of Christ in their very homes [the homes of the poor]. As our Lord himself says [here Teresa is quoting the voice who she believes spoke to her], '*There are plenty of nuns to look after the rich and well-to-do people – but for my poor, there are absolutely none.*' [...] He [Our Lord] asks for Indian Nuns – dressed in Indian clothes – leading the Indian life. – Whoever desires to be a Missionary of Charity will have to become Indian, dress like them, live like them'. (Kolodiejchuk 2007, 76)

Critics of Saint Teresa, such as Christopher Hitchens, have claimed that she was ignorant (Morgan, Hitchens and Ali 1994; Hitchens 1995); they have also implied that she was stupid. The response above suggests that they are wrong. What we have here is an intelligent analysis of socio-economic groups across Catholics of Indian and European origin in India. According to Saint Teresa, when Indian women entered the religious orders that existed before the Missionaries of Charity, they were turned into foreign women, *videshini* estranged from their social origins. In her opinion, this Europeanization should be stopped at all costs. Her answer to this problem was to found in an order of nuns that embraced more radically the vow of poverty that all nuns have to take. Seen in isolation, this logic is irreproachable. It works like an impregnable logical lock at the heart of the organization. There will always be extreme need somewhere in the world and this is the supreme and eternally valid defence for the existence of the Missionaries of Charity (but we will see that there has been criticism of how they respond to this need).

Her organization would employ Indians, enhancing their Christian spiritual life, but would also keep them 'in the field' with contact with the Indian masses. It is not hard to see the appeal of such an analysis in a time when there was widespread extreme poverty in India and when there was soon going to be a transition from one political system to another. The potential for the proposed new order to reconnect Christianity in India with the people, thereby renewing it, was probably also evident to those in the Church hierarchy. There is, however, no published record of the application of historical criteria by Archbishop Périer or by Teresa's spiritual director Van Exem. Nevertheless, the latter states that the project 'all came from God' in a letter to the Archbishop (Kolodiejchuk 2007, 90).[23] In the correspondence, Périer also describes the proposal as 'important' on two occasions. Kolodiejchuk also mentions that after Périer made his decision he wrote to the Superior General of the Loreto Order on 13 January 1948, saying 'that by withholding my consent, I would hamper the realization, through her, of the will of God' (ibid., 102).

If we look more closely at Saint Teresa's analysis of the existing 'European' orders of nuns, we can see that there is a problematic assumption behind it, which is that all Indians joining these orders will be of such low socio-economic status that joining such an order will be a form of social advancement. 'They get more than they give', as she puts it (Kolodiejchuk 2007, 48). This is clearly an inaccurate generalization. Indian Christians come from all socio-economic groups and joining an organization with communal living, little or no individual property and a vow of poverty is not going to be an enhancement of social position for all of them, even if their material needs such as food, clothing and shelter would now be taken care of by the Church. In passing, we should note that Teresa's vision for the Indians joining her order is very different from the mystical union that she outlined for herself at the start of her first letter to the archbishop recorded in this chapter's second epigraph, where we recall that she says that she has 'been longing [...] to identify myself with Indian girls completely' (ibid., 47). We note this inconsistency in passing because it appears to have been largely resolved in the subsequent development of the order. Demographics and the fact of being headquartered in India meant that the majority of the nuns were and still are of Indian origin. With reference to the fifty-year period from 1947 to 1997, the biographer Meg Greene states that 'all but three' of the 119 nuns in the order were Indian (2004, 92). Teresa's successor as Superior General was an Indian-born nun, Sister Nirmala Joshi (born in 1934).[24] The reason for mentioning this inconsistency at all is because it reveals that the global interconnectedness and huge financial resources of the Church mean that elitist practices are a constant risk, even if the primary aim of the new order is to negate that risk.

In her business plan, Teresa is also aware of the issue: 'If girls with high qualifications desire to enter – they may come but that will not make them whatsoever different. They will have to be one of the Sisters. If rich – them, but not their money. I need missionaries – souls are not bought' (Kolodiejchuk 2007, 75). Here she is claiming that, in intention at least, her order will be outside the economic system. This is a radical claim, but ultimately a futile one. This is because no organization can function without financial resources, and this correspondence was aimed precisely at securing that backing.

Saint Teresa's business plan insists that the whole new order would be embracing poverty. In proposing this, she was setting up a high ideal. It was an aspiration that the nuns would be close in location and at a similar material level to the people they cared for. It was a levelling process and a corrective to what she saw as the existing forms of social separation between Indian Christians and the wider population. There were two inherent dangers in this proposed levelling dynamic which were fundamental to the criticism that was later directed at the Missionaries of Charity by Chatterjee in his 2003 study, *Mother Teresa: The Final Verdict*.[25]

First, however much resources the order initially received from the Church and however much money it could raise itself, it would need to avoid enriching itself because that would raise it too far above the social groups that it was to care for. During Saint Teresa's lifetime, her international fundraising success – Reuters estimated it at thirty million US dollars annually (Sebba 1998, xvii) – meant that this was a real challenge. As far as its income was concerned, the Missionaries of Charity was able to draw on these global funding structures as the order expanded between the 1950s and the 1990s. These international funding structures and recruitment are the hallmark of Indian elites. The Church and the Missionaries themselves share these characteristics with the other very different elites in this book, such as the Tata Group and the Auroville Foundation.

The expansion can be divided into two phases. The first, from 1959 to 1965, was within India, with new branches opening in Delhi, Jhansi, Ranchi and Bombay. The second phase began with Pope Paul VI's granting the order the status of a Society of Pontifical Right in 1965. This crucial event meant that the Missionaries of Charity could now officially expand overseas. In that year the order established a home in Cocorote, Venezuela. By the time of Saint Teresa's death in 1997, the Missionaries of Charity had branches in over 130 countries.

Aroup Chatterjee takes up this funding issue, suggesting that too much of the fund is directed to the reserves and expenses of the order. In his book, Chatterjee levels scores of documented charges against Saint Teresa and the Missionaries of Charity. For example: 'I hope people who send Mother Teresa money realize that much (most) of the money is spent in the upkeep of nuns and Brothers, and in the training of priests' (Chatterjee 2003, 222). He provides photographic evidence (ibid., facing p. 276) of the use of 'ambulances', not for humanitarian purposes, but to 'ferry nuns, often to and from places of prayer' (ibid., 382).

The second danger relates to rigidity of the principles of the order versus the societies in which it works, which are subject to positive change. In order to maintain its moral integrity and to justify its own existence as well as its radical difference from the religious orders that went before it, the Missionaries of Charity would need the provision of social welfare in India to remain at a low level. Around Calcutta, in the short and medium term after 1947, the situation actually got worse because partition meant that privations, shortages and famines of the war period were followed by a refugee crisis. In these circumstances, organizations such as the Missionaries of Charity would not be able to take the poor people out of poverty, but only care for them within it. However, as we might remember, this crisis-level minimal support dictum was built into the order's mission by Saint Teresa from the very start. The activity of this order from its foundation to the present day is palliative and not transformative, failing to tackle the causes of the crisis. Its very rationale meant that it could set its sights low.

In saying this, the aim is not to belittle the incalculable amount of human care that the Missionaries of Charity and their lay staff and volunteers have given to vulnerable people over close to seventy years now; it is merely to say that the logic lock with which it was founded by Saint Teresa gave it very specific limits and a responsibility to serve only the most disadvantaged groups in society.

Since it grew out of the Roman Catholic Church, an independently funded multinational entity which acted as elite, her new order was financially self-sufficient and not dependent on the Government of India for its core funding. The only external authority to which it referred was the Church at large. These parameters did not change during her lifetime and there was no built-in provision for future change. The order is still very much active in Kolkata today, but it carries out its work alongside a plethora of city, state and other non-governmental organizations. The humanitarian situation now is very different from that in the 1950s and 1970s. Although not acknowledged in the rules of the Missionaries of Charity, this seems to be indicated by a practical shift to admit the elderly homeless into the refuge for the dying in Kalighat.[26]

A corollary of the order's inflexibility in terms of its mission is that its critics in Kolkata, most notably Aroup Chatterjee, greatly regret the way the city has been portrayed in the West through the optic of the work of the Missionaries of Charity. Chatterjee is not a lone voice here; Amit Chaudhuri notes in his *Calcutta: Two Years in the City* that 'Calcutta had become, as the Americans might say, a dump. By the early eighties, Mother Teresa's profile as the face of eternity was so widespread that, in the Western world, this great city (*mahanagar*) of modernity, with its many contradictions and exacerbations, was seen as a present-day Galilee, a place of supernatural cures, of lepers awaiting the miraculous touch' (Chaudhuri 2013, 86).It was Chatterjee, however, who did calculations which he claims show that the city's net loss of tourist and inward investment income versus the spending of the Missionaries of Charity in the city up to 2003 was over fourteen billion US dollars (Chatterjee 2003, 153). One can accept these figures or dispute them, but it does seem that a separation had developed between Kolkata and the Missionaries of Charity since it began its overseas expansion in 1965.

At one level, Kolkata is the home of the organization, its institutional centre and the place where it was conceived, took root and grew. In terms of posthumous memorialization after Saint Teresa's death in 1997, it is the place where her remains are buried. Roman Catholics around the world consider the Mother House at 54a A.J.C. Bose Road as a shrine. And yet, the Missionaries of Charity began to be configured internationally after only seventeen years of work in India; this was shorter than the time Saint Teresa had spent working in Bengali-medium schools. As we have seen, the battle to establish the order took place in the Calcutta branch of a multinational organization, the Roman Catholic Church. What happened during that international expansion from the 1950s to the 1990s and beyond was that the

Missionaries of Charity developed a network that reproduced a smaller, but nonetheless significant, portion of the complexity of its mother institution (130 branches around the world). As a consequence, a mismatch arose between the order and Kolkata. It could be said that the order, while caring for many thousands of desperate people in the city, has objectified Kolkata and the real suffering of a small portion of its people for a Western audience.

This objectification has been used to gain funds and volunteers for charitable work in Kolkata, but also to grow the organization across the world. In the same way that the Church provided the seed corn funding for the Missionaries of Charity, each new international implantation was probably funded by Missionaries of Charity capital, backed by donations from the country in question. This suggests that, allied to the moral value of alleviation of suffering and the provision of care, however basic, the greatest success of the Missionaries of Charity was its own growth as an institution. Particularly in the late 1970s and 1980s, perhaps due in no small part to the Nobel Peace Prize awarded to Saint Teresa in 1979, the organization perpetuated itself at a rapid rate. A great deal of this growth was global. It brought committed Christian women and men into the religious life in cognate organizations such as the Missionaries of Charity Sisters – Contemplative (founded in 1976), the Missionaries of Charity Brothers – Active (founded in 1963) and Contemplative (founded in 1977), the Missionaries of Charity Fathers (founded in 1984), the Priest Co-Workers of Mother Teresa, Corpus Christi Movement for Priests (founded in 1983), and the Lay Missionaries of Charity (founded in 1984). The last organization exists for committed non-clerical people. From the early 1950s, Saint Teresa had an effective strategy for bringing on board individual lay members. She used a rhetoric of plurality for practical fundraising purposes. It was a performance of a plural identity in Christ. In it she would share her own first name with an individual who accepted the order's goals. This is illustrated by her taking on Jacqueline de Decker, a Belgian nurse and social worker, as her 'second self' for whom she would pray, while the 'suffering member' would 'share in all our prayers, works and whatever we do for souls' (Kolodiejchuk 2007, 147). On 17 October 1954 she opens a letter to Decker thus: 'My Sister Jacqueline Teresa' (ibid., 155). Brian Kolodiejchuk explains that the theological basis for the practice of the second self comes from Father Alphonsus Rodriguez (ibid., 375, note 65).[27] The practice brought outsiders into the body of the order without the need for a physical presence in India.

All of this overseas recruitment and personal fundraising suggests the development of a dual emphasis. The order was working for itself as well as for the poor. In Kolkata, Aroup Chatterjee maintained that only 5 per cent of the nuns were from the city (2003, 391).[28] In addition, he suggests that many conversions did not take place in the city and that the novices were drawn to join the order from areas with larger Christian populations such as the states of Kerala, Goa and Tamil Nadu.

The general direction of Chatterjee's assessment is confirmed by Jack Praeger, a medical doctor who briefly worked for Saint Teresa in the 1970s before founding his own medically focused charity Calcutta Rescue. Praeger makes an important point about the growth of the order by linking the expansion to proselytism outside Kolkata: 'If she had concentrated on Calcutta, she would have been forced to compromise on her proselytizing activities' (Praeger 1982, 79). This critical view correctly suggests that in organizational terms, her greatest achievement was not conversions in Kolkata, or India, where cultural sensitivities were and remain acute. Rather, the Missionaries of Charity are a resounding success as an internationalized movement funding themselves, but with a deliberately limited programme of work giving a little to those who have absolutely nothing. An extremely tight operating strategy such as this maintains both donations and surpluses.

1979 to 2001 Secular nationalist representations of Saint Teresa in Albania and India

At the same time as the complex institutional processes described above were going on around the world for the Missionaries of Charity, in India and Albania there was a firming up of the projected image of the order's foundress. This is another manifestation of the eternal potential of hardened national identities to resurface whatever the complexity of an individual's identity. In the same way, water always has the potential to develop solid ice, if the temperature falls low enough.

In India there was a national–international projection of Saint Teresa, with no less than three Indian postage stamps carrying her image (whereas the other Indian *videshinis* who are presented in stamps – Annie Besant, Sister Nivedita and Mirra Alfassa – get only one stamp each). These stamps continue to send her likeness around the world in the name of India and its national postal service.

On the other side of the world, in Albania, a nation of three million people, a similar process also began. Albania was tying Saint Teresa to Albanian national identity. In 2001, the international airport at Rinas, serving Tirana, was renamed 'Aeroporti Nënë Tereza' (Mother Teresa Airport). In the main square and in front of the university in Tirana, statues of the nun were erected. Although the place is relatively small in terms of global aviation flows, having an airport named after her means that Saint Teresa has achieved the holy grail of memorialization referred to in the *prélude pondichérien* of this book. She joins the likes of Netaji Subhas Chandra Bose and Charles de Gaulle, trumping Jeanne Dupleix with her plinth and Margaret Noble with her reading room. Although the homage paid to the other Indian *videshinis* named in Besant Gardens in Kolkata and Mirapuri village in Italy are impressive enough, as are the hospitals in Hyderabad named after Princess Durru Shehvar and Princess Niloufer, the renaming of the airport confirms Saint Teresa's global profile mentioned at the very start of this chapter.

1997 to 2003 A partial posthumous transformation within the Church

Saint Teresa died in Kolkata on 5 September 1997, three days after Diana, Princess of Wales. As a consequence, her death was under-reported in the Western media, but it was the subject of great media interest in Kolkata and in India more widely. Usually, there is a five-year waiting period before the Church considers beatification, but Pope John Paul II dispensed with this and the process began in 1999. As befitting a multinational organization, the process involved scrutiny in Europe (in the Vatican) of events in India. The key event in the process was the supposed curing of a cancerous tumour in Monica Besra in 2002, after the application of a locket containing a picture of Teresa. This event was approved as the necessary miracle by the Congregation for the Causes of Saints in the Vatican. Pope John Paul II beatified Mother Teresa in 2003, only six years after her death. Her official title became 'Blessed Teresa of Calcutta'. On 17 December 2015, Pope Francis certified the second miracle required for Teresa's canonization. The subject of this miracle is a mechanical engineer from the Brazilian city of Santos. In 2015, a Vatican medical commission pronounced that the engineer had fully recovered from a life-threatening brain tumour in a way that they said could not be explained in conventional scientific terms. The man's wife had, however, spent months praying to Teresa on behalf of her husband, and thus in the way of miracles it was agreed that Teresa had interceded. In September 2016, Saint Teresa was canonized in Kolkata, less than nineteen years after her death – this is extremely fast and has only been bettered in modern times by former pope and name patron of Krakow airport, John Paul II. As a comparison, the cause of Saint Teresa of Lisieux took twenty-eight years and was considered extremely fast in the 1920s. For many Christians in Kolkata and particularly for the nuns in her Order, however, Teresa has been venerated as a saint since her death in 1997.

2010 Her birth centenary and an international debate about the location of her remains

So, for the Church, Saint Teresa has been inscribed into a holy narrative, the final chapter of which has already been written, though for non-religiously minded people the Church version was just one narrative of many. Other narratives include the story of the Eastern European outsider analyzed above and the Albanian national heroine and Indian citizen examined below.

At the height of her Nobel Prize fame, in 1979, Saint Teresa voiced multiple hybrid and co-existing identities to a journalist in Oslo. These are quoted in the fifth epigraph. However, after death her identity was subject to the reassertion of national allegiances. Her centenary was the trigger for a diplomatic disagreement between

Albania and India over the question of the location of her remains. On 9 October 2009, the prime minister of Albania, Sali Berisha, issued an official press release requesting India to return the remains of Saint Teresa to Albania in time for the hundredth anniversary celebrations. Prime Minister Berisha's justification for the request was a 'humane' one: it was proposed that she be buried next to her mother and sister in Tirana. The city and the country were closed during the Hoxha dictatorship from 1944 to 1985, and after leaving them in 1928 Anjezë Gonxha Bojaxhiu did not see her mother and sister again; they died in 1972 and 1973 respectively.

There was a slight problem with Prime Minister Berisha's request. We recall that our subject was born not in Tirana, Albania, but in Skopje, a city in the Republic of Macedonia that made no claim to her ethnic origin. So the politician in Tirana was making a claim on the basis of language community and her cultural affiliation at birth and for the first eighteen years of her life until she took the train to Ireland in 1928. Saint Teresa was being elevated to a peerless position in the narrative of the post-Hoxha Albanian nation. Although the plans for a museum have not yet borne fruit, there is a Mother Teresa pavilion in the Albanian National History Museum on Skanderberg Square in the heart of Tirana. The permanent exhibition there, with its photographs of Saint Teresa meeting Princess Diana and Ronald and Nancy Reagan among others, pays homage to her as a global celebrity who is part of the Albanian national story.

In India the reaction to the Albanian prime minister's request saw both the Roman Catholic Church in Kolkata and the secular state defend India as her final resting place. On 17 October 2009, Reuters quoted Father Sukhendu Biswas of St Mary's Church in Kolkata, who said:

> It is not acceptable to the people of India. It is the wish and desire of Indian people that her mortals [sic – mortal remains] should remain in the headquarters of Mother Teresa. The people of the world have accepted it. The headquarters is the place where she has operated her ministry and this has become a holy shrine to Kolkata, people of India and people of the world.[29]

It is interesting that this statement applies a multi-polar and pluralist rhetoric similar to that of Saint Teresa's 1979 comments in Oslo.[30] The 'people of the world' are quoted on two occasions, acknowledging that she is a universal Indian, an Indian citizen of the world. The official reaction from the Indian state is simply based on the legal choice she made in 1948 and is recorded in the final epigraph.

Conclusions

In answer to the open questions at the start of this chapter about Saint Teresa's identity figured along national lines, we can say that her Eastern European origins are significant. They are a powerful example of the 'different difference' of the Indian *videshinis* in the present study. This difference is distinct from that of the white women associated with colonial power. We have now seen how Irish-, Eastern European-, and French-influenced identities are part of the way that these Indian *videshinis* gain superior insight into India.[31] Furthermore, in the decades either side of 1947, these different European women are recuperable by Indians in a more positive way, when compared with the more polarized forms of difference between Indians and most white British women.

Despite its reforming impulse, we have seen that there was a fundamental inconsistency in Saint Teresa's Missionaries of Charity Project. She appeared to promise the Church souls, but the process by which they were won was not clear. No one could object to the care she proposed, but clearly, multiple conversions without consent were not possible after 1947. The only souls to which she could lay claim, were not those of living Indians, therefore, but those who departed this life under her roof. The old missionary logic is bankrupt in an independent nation. The agency and positive decisions of those Indians who are to be converted need to be taken into account. This could not be done and Kolkata was not converted, though compassionate care was offered and is still being offered. In the wake of her failure to understand the future of India, though she had provided such a powerful critique of its missionary past, her organization turned in on itself. Paradoxically, this occurred during the same period that it expanded internationally. The Missionaries of Charity 'International', as they developed from 1965, however, had their own inner stasis. They developed the characteristics of a self-serving elite while maintaining their limited core mission. In the final analysis, it is simply untenable to be faithful to an individual's 1947 vision for fifty years and more in a nation that has changed as much as India, even if that individual is Saint Teresa. The Missionaries of Charity were beholden to the larger Church organization around them. They developed regressively towards that previous model, rather than overcoming it by refocussing on the changing situation of the poor. In its own terms, the silent harvesting of souls at the moment of death was not enough to grow the organization, not only in absolute terms, but in harmony with the needs of post-Independence India. The Missionaries of Charity have suffered mission creep. As they expanded their network, the original 1947 reforming rationale slipped away and the soul count on which it was based did not increase significantly in Kolkata. In common with other orders, today there is little or no expansion in member numbers.

All the while, in Nirmal Hriday in Kalighat and in other centres, the moral integrity of Saint Teresa's original idea of ministering to those who have nothing is maintained and practised year after year; not exclusively by nuns, but mainly by lay volunteers.[32] In *The Rumour of Calcutta: Tourism, Charity and the Poverty of Representation*, John Hutnyk admits that he 'largely ignore[s]' the "religious" volunteers [...] in favour of travelers and volunteers from [Praeger's] Calcutta Rescue group' (1996, xi). Hutnyk is, however, scathing about what he calls 'the World Bank/IMF/comprador elite/hegemonic order which perpetuates exploitation and oppression' and also about the ignorance of these 'volunteers who thought their activity was significantly different from mainstream tourism' (ibid., 220 and 215). Hutnyk speaks sense about the wider system; however, as a materialistic critique, his study remains insensitive to the power of the caring touch and comfort of words exchanged between the volunteers and inmates of Kalighat (although the touch is not generally accompanied by analgesics and the words are not always translated into Bengali). Though the context could not be more unequal, because the volunteers are living and have homes and resources, the touch given and the words spoken have meaning for both parties. The sainthood of Teresa, latent in Muggeridge's representations of her in the 1970s and obvious in the way that Kolodiejchuk used the moniker 'Saint of Calcutta' in the subtitle of his edition of her letters, a full nine years before her canonization, is now official. It will become clear in numbers and actions of the Kalighat volunteers in the next decades whether the 2016 canonization represented a plateau, or the beginning of the end of charities of the Missionaries of Charity type in Kolkata. Now that the official status of Teresa has stabilized, there is a chance that an Indian Roman Catholic may be challenged to found a new order adapted to the needs of the city and the nation in the twenty-first century. Given Saint Teresa's example, she may find a Church that is still willing to listen and act.

Notes

1. Eileen Egan (1985), Anne Sebba (1997), Kathryn Spink (1997), and Meg Greene (2004). There will also be references to the contrarian views of Hitchens (1995) and Chatterjee (2003).
2. *Come Be My Light: The Private Writings of the 'Saint of Calcutta'/Mother Teresa.* Father Kolodiejchuk, M.C. deserves praise for putting the nun's correspondence in the public domain in 2007.
3. The only comparable organization is the Franciscan Missionaries of Mary, established by the Frenchwoman Hélène-Marie-Philippine de Chappotin (1839–1904), who arrived in Madurai in March 1865. That order had a troubled early history with schisms, although at its peak in the 1950s it had grown to eleven thousand nuns in seventy countries.
4. Her name is pronounced 'An-yay-zay Gon-ja Bo-ya-ji-u'.
5. Sister Gabriela, who knew Bojaxhiu from her childhood in Skopje, is the only other Eastern European Loreto Sister mentioned in Saint Teresa's private letters.
6. It is a fascinating coincidence of history that the Anglophile family of Aurobindo Ghose sent him to the Loreto School in Darjeeling as a boarder in 1877. Peter Heehs comments that Aurobindo's work contains few memories of this period, except a 'curious inner experience. "I was lying down one day," he said in 1926, "when I saw suddenly a great darkness rushing into me and enveloping me and the whole of the universe." This "darkness" stayed with him for the next fourteen

years, most of which were spent in England' (Heehs 2008, 9). It seems that for him there was a continuity of spiritual darkness between the convent school and his subsequent education in England (though he achieved academic success in the Western system). Exactly sixty years after Aurobindo entered the school, a Loreto novice called Teresa made her vows in the school chapel and entered the order. This coincidence whereby the same place can be imbued with associations which are diametrically opposite in nature, Aurobindo's 'darkness' and Saint Teresa's sense of belonging, is part of the greater ambivalence of the cultural contact between Europe and India. As we know, though, transformation is part of extraordinary lives: Sri Aurobindo overcame the 'darkness' through internal yoga in Pondicherry with Mirra Alfassa, and Saint Teresa left the Loreto order for her Missionaries of Charity.

7. According to a 2010 report in the archives of Associated Press, two-thirds of Albania's 3.2 million people are Muslim. Accurate figures for the Orthodox and Roman Catholic minority are not known, but the estimates for the latter are of the order of 15 per cent (http://www.aparchive.com, accessed 30 April 2015).
8. It is possible that Sister Teresa might have known of the existence of St Enda's School, Rathfarnham, occupying the imposing Hermitage building half a mile down the road from the Loreto convent. The school was founded by the Irish nationalist Patrick Pearse in 1908; it moved to Rathfarnham in 1910, the year of Bojaxhiu's birth, and so was well-established by the time she arrived in the Dublin suburb. There is no documented record that Sister Teresa had contact with St Enda's; however, if she was aware of its existence, she might have relativized her future task as a missionary educating within and for Christianity. She might have grasped that an education based on nationalist principles was also possible. I am grateful to Paul O'Hanrahan for bringing my attention to this possible point of contact between Irish nationalism and Saint Teresa's early history.
9. In a letter to the Cardinal Prefect of the Sacred Congregation of Religious in Rome, written in February 1948, she submits a petition for secularization, and signs herself with her dual identity: 'Sister Teresa, IBVM/In the world (Miss) Gonxha Bojaxhiu' (Kolodiejchuk 2007, 116). The options open to her when leaving the Loreto Sisters were

either exclaustration or secularization. Exclaustration would have allowed her to retain her vows as a Loreto nun and to return to the order if her new venture did not succeed. Sister Teresa insisted, however, on petitioning the Church for secularization, thus irrevocably leaving her order (ibid., 108). She had already made a similar clean break before, when she left her Eastern European home in 1926.

10. Kolodiejchuk's edition of Saint Teresa's letters quotes the following reminiscence of her from the late 1970s by an unnamed sister in her order: 'Mother [as she was known then] one day brought a map of Europe and spread it before me... Then she started to count the countries where [the Order did not yet have a presence]... she was in dead earnest that a "tabernacle" should be opened in each country of the world' (Kolodiejchuk 2007, 304).
11. Saint Teresa, *Katolike Misije*, October 1937, 25 (quoted in Kolodiejchuk 2007, 365).
12. These interviews coincided with a period in which Muggeridge became a Christian and they were published under the title *Something Beautiful for God*.
13. Saint Teresa repeats this claim in her Easter and Christmas addresses to the Missionaries of Charity in 1996 (the year before her death).
14. Ferdinand Périer, a Jesuit, was born in Antwerp, Belgium in 1875 and died in Calcutta in 1968.
15. The term 'business plan' will be used to draw attention to the international funding structure behind the local work of the Missionaries of Charity.
16. A tabular summary is found in Appendix 2.
17. There is a slight problem with the dates of these two letters in Kolodiejchuk's edition. He states in a footnote that Périer wrote to Teresa on 24 October 1947, but her reply in which she refers to his letter is dated 1 October 1947.
18. Céleste Van Exem, a Jesuit, was born in 1908 in Brussels, Belgium, and died in 1993 in Calcutta.
19. The frontispiece of Kolodiejchuk's books reproduces the first page of the letter in which we can see how well-composed and neatly written it is.
20. London: Oates & Washbourne, 1931. Given that she did not speak Italian, it is unlikely that the source of her knowledge was any of the

publications in that language from the 1930s. These books are [no author], *Viaggidella Madre Francesca Saverio Cabrini, narrati in varie sue lettre* (Milan: Bertarelli, 1935), Emilia De Sanctis Rosmini, *La Beata Francesca Saverio Cabrini* (Rome: [n.p.], 1938) and Nello Vian, *Madre Cabrini* (Brescia: Morcelliana, 1938). Furthermore, given her testimony that even food supplies were disrupted by the war and its aftermath, it is highly likely that the following books published in Europe and the United States in 1944 and 1945 would not have reached Calcutta in time for her to read and use them in her project: *Frances Xavier Cabrini: The Saint of the Emigrants*, written by a 'Benedictine of Stanbrook Abbey' (1944), Theodore Maynard's *Too Small a World* (1945) and Lucile Papin Borden's *Francesca Cabrini: Without Staff or Scrip* (1945). The length of time that it took for books to reach India also makes it less likely that Bojaxhiu might have read, before she wrote the letter to Périer, any of the publications which appeared in 1946, the year of Cabrini's canonization, such as Eliy Mac Adam's *Saint Francesca Cabrini* (Dublin: Anthonian Press, 1946).

21. Saint Teresa's words here echo Martindale's account of the fundamental reason for Saint Frances Xavier Cabrini's project: 'One of her dreams showed her the Italians of the United States' and that 'practically nothing 'Italian' was done for them' (Martindale 1931, 25). In addition to the notion, familiar in spiritual discourse, of dreams being an inspiration, these words are close to Saint Teresa's desire for specifically Indian-focused aid.
22. This echoes Martindale's account of the importance of both the native and the national language for effective charitable work (for this work with new immigrants in the United States the relevant languages were Italian and English): 'M. Cabrini was not blind to the obvious – namely, how gravely insufficient for her work was a knowledge of Italian' (Martindale 1931, 52). Martindale soon elaborates this need for dual linguistic competence with reference to those in receipt of Saint Frances Xavier Cabrini's charitable work: 'She was right and wise, I am convinced, in wishing Italian to be taught in all her schools to little ones who had never talked anything else. I cannot believe that it is a prudent plan to try to change all of a sudden any immigrant child into the nationality within which it lives. American, therefore, should be the primary language of her school; but Italian, definitely second' (ibid., 54).

23. Dated 26 October 1947.
24. Sister Nirmala led the order from 1997 to 2009 and was succeeded by the German-born Sister Mary Prema Pierick (born in 1953), who joined the Missionaries of Charity in 1980.
25. Krishna Dutta's *Calcutta: A Cultural History* mentions that Saint Teresa's 'death anniversary is hardly commemorated and no street has yet been named after her', explaining that 'if her order wishes to reconnect her name with the city that made her famous in a positive way, it should devote itself to looking after the poor as well as the dying by offering proper medical care. The Missionaries of Charity owe that to Calcutta' (Dutta 2008 [2003], 174 and 175).
26. 'The hospice for the dying not only takes terminally ill people. A good part of the beds is occupied by elderly people who otherwise would have to go back to a lonely life on the streets.' Wim Klerkx, 'Teresa's Volunteers', a photo-reportage, 1998. See http://www.wimklerkx.nl/EN/PROJECTS/TV.html#14 (accessed 1 April 2015).
27. Father Alphonsus Rodriguez (1538–1616) was the author of *Ejercicio de Perfección y virtudescristianas* (1612 and 1616). It was a standard used in the training of those who entered holy orders. It is highly probable that Saint Teresa was familiarized with this work during her novitiate. I am grateful to Professors Ernst Hofhansl and Josef Weismayer for this information on Rodriguez.
28. Unfortunately, Chatterjee does not say where he gets this figure.
29. http://www.blinkx.com/watch-video/mother-teresa-body-dispute/u1z_l6F2U0-FGO-jAhCu2Q (accessed 24 March 2010).
30. See Egan 1985, 111.
31. Subsequent chapters will show that this was also the case with Simone Tata, a Swiss woman, the Ottoman Turkish princesses and for many Congress supporters of the Italian-born Sonia Gandhi in the 1990s and early 2000s.
32. 'Together with several paid labourers, volunteers do the lion's share of the daily work in the hospice. This leaves the hands free of the 6 sisters who permanently live here, to engage in other projects in the area.' WimKlerkx, 'Teresa's Volunteers' a photo-reportage, 1998. See http://www.wimklerkx.nl/EN/PROJECTS/TV.html#7 (accessed 1 April 2015).

The Theosophist and Indian nationalist Annie Besant was born in London in 1844 to parents of Irish origin. She arrived in India in 1893 and died in Adyar, Chennai in 1933.

The historian and disciple of Swami Vivekananda, Sister Nivedita was born Margaret Noble in Dungannon, Northern Ireland in 1867. She came to India in 1898 and died in Darjeeling in 1911.

The magistrate and women's suffragist Margaret 'Gretta' Cousins (far left) was born in Boyle, Southern Ireland in 1878, settled in India in 1915 and died there in 1954.

The fundraiser and founder of a religious order, Saint Teresa was born Anjezë Gonxha Bojaxhiu in Skopje Macedonia in 1910. She came to India in 1928, ending her days in Kolkata in 1997.

The writer and founder of spiritual and utopian organisations, Mirra Alfassa, was born in Paris in 1878, first visited India in 1914, before settling in Puducherry in 1928. She remained there until her death in 1973.

The homemaker and dynasty builder Sooni Tata was born Suzanne Brière in Paris in 1880. She journeyed to Mumbai in 1902 where she set up a family home. She died in Paris in 1923.

The cosmetics entrepreneur Simone Tata was born Simone Dunoyer in Geneva Switzerland in 1930. She visited India in 1953 and settled in Mumbai two years later, where she still spends most of her time.

The social reformer, Ottoman Princess and Hyderabadi Queen-in-waiting, Durru Shehvar was born in Istanbul in 1914, spending her adolescence in Nice, France. She arrived in India in 1932, left in 1952 and passed away in London in 2006.

The women's hospital founder and Ottoman and Hyderabadi Princess, Niloufer was born in Istanbul in 1916 and spent her adolescence in Nice, France. She arrived in Hyderabad with her cousin Princess Durru Shehvar in 1932, left India around 1952 and died in Paris in 1989.

The elite politician Sonia Gandhi was born Edvige Antonia Albina Maino in Lusiana, Italy in 1946, she flew into India in 1968 and is still active in New Delhi, where she resides.

Sonia Gandhi photographed during Christmas with her mother-in-law Indira Gandhi and husband Rajiv (standing, right), and brother-in-law Sanjay (standing, left).

INTERNATIONAL BUSINESS AND COMMERCE: SOONI TATA AND SIMONE TATA

I, who am neither fish nor fowl here [in Bombay], a Frenchwoman for the Parsis and a Parsi for the Frenchwomen, have to be extremely careful; when one is the object of almost everybody's gaze, the slightest fact … sprouts feet and runs along by itself, getting bigger as it goes.[1]

– Suzanne Brière (Sooni Tata), Mother of J.R.D. Tata, on her first months in Bombay, 1904

I was very Europeanized; I'd lived half in Europe, in Japan, India and France. I wanted to have a wife who would be as comfortable in India as elsewhere. I was waiting to find a girl who was like me, half and half, where there were foreign parents.

– J.R.D. Tata (Sooni Tata's eldest son) in 1986, on his international childhood and youth from 1904 to 1925

Don't worry about the Tata name. It won't suffer if strangers are introduced into the shrine or home … In India, there is no Bird in Birds & I doubt if there be any Killick or Nixon in K & N. The principles of 'Transfusion', by which an external limb planted in a living body may keep the body as a whole alive & functioning, will also avail the Tata Firm; bring new blood and worth, bring more shoulders to bear the new burden.

– B.J. Padshah of Tata Group to R.D. Tata (Sooni Tata's husband and J.R.D. Tata's father), 1918

Geneva [the Swiss city of Simone Tata's birth] was never really associated with 'cheese and cuckoo clocks' in the mind of people. Geneva had its own identity which was quite international, due to the presence of the United Nations, a number of international organizations such as the ILO [International Labour Organization] and WHO [World Health Organization] and, of course, the Red Cross.

– Simone Tata (née Dunoyer), 2011[2]

The impact of World War Two started with the defeat of France and its occupation. For a family with so much French blood, it had a terrible impact.

– Simone Tata, 2011

Naval [H. Tata] found the Lakmé name in 1951, long before we were married. He was hunting for a name for the proposed Tata venture into cosmetics and, whilst in Paris, attending a performance of *Lakmé* at the Opera, he found it to be just the right name for this new company, a happy blend of France and India.

– Simone Tata, 2011

The country [India] really fascinated me and during my trip in 1953 I travelled alone across the country by plane, train and bus. I met many Indians of all types ... they were also very curious to find a young European woman travelling alone, more so since most foreigners had long since left India and the age of the backpackers and hippies was still a long way off.

– Simone Tata, 2011

I started at the top in a non-existent industry.

– Simone Tata, 2005 (on joining the Lakmé board in the early 1960s)

The name Tata would also convey a certain awe which kept people at a distance. It was somewhat counterproductive. Being a woman, a Tata, and a foreigner is quite intimidating.

– Simone Tata, 2008

> Yes it was sometimes difficult to be a 'Tata, a woman and a foreigner in business'. Some people found it hard to take me seriously. Others thought I was just a figurehead, akin to what is known today as a 'Brand Ambassador'. And there were hardly a couple of women in India's business world in a leading position. In the company, however, it was not difficult to establish myself.
>
> – Simone Tata, 2011

> The Tatas are a reconstructed family who adopt and cobble together people to make a family. That way they do promote talent rather than blood relations.
>
> – Gita Piramal, 2008

For Indian readers, the Tata Group with its four hundred thousand employees worldwide and annual turnover of nearly seventy billion US dollars hardly needs an introduction.[3] Neither does the Lakmé cosmetics brand, not least because it has been sponsoring the annual Lakmé India Fashion Week since 1999.[4] The brand is currently owned by Hindustan Unilever Limited, but it was founded within the Tata Group in 1952, was grown by Simone Tata, the main Indian *videshini* subject of this chapter and finally sold by Tata Group to Hindustan Unilever for $45.5 million in 1998. Simone Tata (née Dunoyer) was born in Geneva, Switzerland, in 1930 and married Naval H. Tata in 1955. She joined the Lakmé board on a part-time basis in the early 1960s and became managing director in 1964. As we will see, Simone Tata's significance should not be measured only in terms of Lakmé's value in dollars in 1998, nor should it be calculated by the fact that, after Lakmé's sale, she also founded another successful company: Trent – Tata Retail Enterprises.[5] Her inclusion here is justified because of a contribution to cultural change within India from the 1960s to the 1980s and beyond. In that period her company played a significant role in increasing the acceptance of manufactured cosmetics by middle-class Indians, and today it is still one of India's most trusted cosmetics brands.[6]

This chapter adopts a chronological approach, and as it does so it positions Simone Tata's period at the helm of Lakmé from 1964 to 1998 within two time periods, one shorter and one longer. The aim is to set the particular Swiss-French components of Simone Tata's contribution to Lakmé in a wider context, namely that of the Tata Group and the Tata family, her sustaining elites.

The shorter of the two is the full life cycle of the cosmetics company from its foundation in 1952 to its sale in 1998; this demonstrates the extent to which, after 1964, she shaped the strategy of a business which was a wholly owned subsidiary of TOMCO (Tata Oil Mills Company) and which began after Jawaharlal Nehru suggested to the Tata Group that newly independent India needed to manufacture cosmetics domestically in order to forestall foreign exchange problems. We will find out what she brought to the enterprise from her Swiss French upbringing and youth, and how her time in India in the Tata Group and in the Tata family has changed her. The nature of her contribution in terms of Lakmé's commercial strategy, products and marketing will thus be brought into sharp individual focus. The resulting composite internationalist picture includes Indian, Swiss, French and US elements. In the shorter time period, an openness to people and knowledge outside the India–Britain binary, such as the practical knowledge of cosmetics from France that Simone Tata possessed, was an important element of Lakmé's success and wider cultural influence in India.

The longer time period sets Lakmé within the wider history of the Tata Group as a whole since its foundation in 1868. This long-view notion of 'Tata time' helps us understand the wider internationalist company culture that allowed Lakmé and the Swiss-born Simone Tata to influence Indian perceptions about cosmetics and to achieve commercial success.[7] This takes us beyond the post-colonial axiom that business is global and investigates how the key players in Tata Group developed internationalism for Indian business in the context of colonial power relations. This approach underlines this book's 'peri-colonial' focus on several decades either side of 1947, showing how those at the helm of Tata Group understood Indian nationalism, but acted internationally for business and family. This two-pronged approach, being in India and also in the world beyond colony and colonizing country, is one of the hallmarks of the Indian elites of this book.

In the longer time period, the analysis of Tata Group's openness to people and knowledge outside the India–Britain binary steps back one and then two generations to show how Tata Group's expansion strategy, under its founder J.N. (Jamsetji) Tata, during the colonial period sought out the expertise of non-British business partners from the US and Japan for commercial advantage.[8] There is, however, more to this than commercial strategy alone. The group's diversified recruitment strategy was mirrored in one branch of the Tata family in the way that a Frenchwoman, Suzanne Brière, married R.D. Tata at the start of the twentieth century. This woman became the second wife of Jamsetji's cousin.[9] Therefore Suzanne Brière, who became Sooni Tata in 1902, functions as a precursor to the Swiss woman, Simone Dunoyer, who became Simone Tata in 1955. As the family tree at the start of this chapter shows us, Naval H. Tata, Simone's husband, was the adopted son of Navajbai Tata, the wife of Jamsetji's younger son Ratanji Tata.

The details of the presence of Suzanne Brière at the heart of the Tata family from 1902 to 1923 are not well known, and this chapter will remedy that lack.[10] We will see how her entry into the family increased its international exposure via the multilingualism and dual residency of herself, her husband and her five children in India and France.[11] One of those children was her French-speaking and partly French-educated son J.R.D. Tata, who massively increased the global reach and value of the company during his chairmanship from 1938 to 1991. In this period, the Tata Group grew in sectors with global markets such as soda ash, steel and hospitality and the launch of its new international ventures such as Tata Indian Airways, which brought non-Indians to India and took Indians abroad. J.R.D. Tata, speaking in 1976, understood that narrow nationalism in the 1940s and 1950s, be it French, Indian or Indo-French, did not succeed as a commercial strategy for Tata Group: 'I told Mr Chirac [then French prime minister] I had always felt sorry that my youthful ambitions in the early part of my career, to promote Indo-French industrial co-operation, had not fructified.' The middle and later part of J.R.D. Tata's career at the helm of Tata Group saw him seeking out opportunity wherever it lay in the world. This brings us full circle, because J.R.D. Tata's chairmanship intersected with Simone Tata's years leading Lakmé from 1964 to 1998, and thus Lakmé's success in selling Indian-manufactured cosmetics domestically and in Eastern Europe was an element of this.[12] Let us, however, first go back to the nineteenth century and consider the start of the larger time period.

1868 to 1904 Jamsetji Tata builds businesses in India and alliances beyond the British Empire

Naturally, given the historical datum that the enterprise was established under British colonial hegemony in 1868, the commercial contact between Tata Group and the United Kingdom was significant. Jamsetji knew that the immediate future of the company would be defined by its co-operation with the British Empire. This co-operation had a commercial component because Jamsetji equipped the mill with British machinery, the most technically sophisticated in the 1870s. It also had a cultural component as evinced by his decision to call his new textile venture Empress Mills on 1 January 1877, the date Queen Victoria was proclaimed Empress of India. As he co-operated with the British in India, however, Jamsetji also had extensive contact with the rest of the world, travelling to Hong Kong in 1857, China in 1861, Palestine in 1873, and to Japan in 1893.[13] The notes he took about the linguistic repertoire of the guests in a Palestine hotel during his 1873 visit stress the importance of languages other than English:

> They all spoke French amongst themselves, it serving as a common language to all. None of them spoke English ... I think that it is quite necessary for a man who has extensive travels in view to acquire knowledge of Arabic and French besides English ... French is understood in almost all countries of Europe. (Nath, Vithalani and Vatsal 2004, 18)

These notes suggest that he was attuned to the fact that others understood the world in a medium other than English and this was a 'necessary' strategy to grasp the world more fully. In personal terms, he continued to travel and to maintain relations with other countries, as well as having an active dialogue with the British in India. Tata Central Archives hold copies of his letters to high-ranking government officials such as Lord Reay, Richmond Ritchie, H.H. Risley, and Lord George Hamilton (the Secretary of State for India). J.N. Tata declined the baronetcy the British offered him, but accepted an honour from the Japanese emperor Mutsuhito (ibid., 19).

The next generation of Tatas maintained this strategy of co-operation without dependence. After Jamsetji's death in 1904, his sons Dorab and Ratan Tata accepted knighthoods (Dorab in 1910 and Ratan in 1916).[14] They also displayed remarkable persistence, however, by raising the funding in India for a major steelworks, which had been actively pursued by Jamsetji since the 1880s. From 1906 to 1911, the Tata Iron and Steel Company (TISCO) was founded by the two brothers, despite the fact that 'London investors were not prepared to risk their capital in ventures controlled by Indian entrepreneurs even with the reputation of the Tatas' (Morris 1983, 590). The fact that they took only 'three weeks to find £1.63 million in Bombay' demonstrated both the Tatas' independent business acumen and the effectiveness of Bombay as an alternative capital market (ibid., 591). According to the economic historian Ramprasad Sengupta, the establishment of TISCO 'represents the most important instance of entrepreneurship of Indian private capital in the twentieth century' (Sengupta 2007, 499).

At the same time as Jamsetji grew his steelworks project, a hydroelectricity power station, the idea for an Indian institute of higher learning, and his cotton mill (strategically renaming it Svadeshi Mills in 1887), he also laid the foundations for a luxury hotel in 1898. The Taj Mahal Hotel opened its doors in Bombay in 1903, a year before Jamsetji's death.

1898 to 1923 The Tata family in France and 'France' in the Tata family

The Tata commercial presence in France began in 1898 when Manchersha Godrej was sent to establish a small trading company at 47, rue Lafitte.[15] Jamsetji had R.D. Tata, the third member of the second generation (with his sons Dorabji and Ratanji), based there, where he learned French. In this language learning, R.D. Tata was realizing the French part of Jamsetji's 1873 assessment of the necessity for 'a man who has extensive travels in view to acquire knowledge of Arabic and

French besides English' (Nath, Vithalani and Vatsal 2004, 18). This interest in France is an example of Jamsetji's strategy of developing parallel business interests and contacts outside the British Empire. As well as learning the French language, R.D. Tata would meet his future wife through that activity and build a long-standing family, and small but highly significant commercial relations with France. Contemporaneous with Taj Mahal Hotel in Mumbai, the investment in Hardelot, a purpose-built exclusive holiday resort on the French Channel Coast in 1905, would anchor this branch of the Tata family and the group in France for nearly fifty years. The section which follows analyzes the crucial role of R.D. Tata's French wife in establishing and maintaining that base and connection with France. These were to be a formative influence on their son J.R.D. Tata, because it was in Paris and Hardelot that he became better acquainted with aeroplanes and automobiles. As he puts it: 'My first important memories from the point of view of a growing child [...] were about cars and aeroplanes.'[16] Later, in 1925, R.D. gifted his son a Bugatti, which he drove from Paris to Hardelot on country roads in five hours flat, even changing one spark plug en route. 'Everybody was mad over the car', J.R.D. enthuses, 'but nobody as mad as myself.'[17] Before the First World War, as a younger child, he notes that 'occasionally a Blériot aeroplane would land on the beach [in Hardelot], to everyone's great excitement. It was flown by his chief pilot, Adolphe Pégoud, the first man to loop the loop. From then I was hopelessly hooked on aeroplanes and made up my mind that come what may, one day, I would be a pilot.'[18]

Sooni Tata was born Pauline Suzanne Geneviève Valentine Brière in Paris on 26 May 1880; she was the daughter of Mathilde Brière (née Tribout), who taught R.D. Tata French. The couple had a civil wedding in France in 1902 and a Parsi wedding in India in 1903. Though Sooni Tata did not found or run any organizations like the other Indian *videshinis* in this book, she merits consideration as a precursor to the ultramodern way in which she, her husband and their five children lived life between Europe and India and between a selection of languages and cultures which belonged to each continent. Her correspondence, which will form the basis of the assessments about her, reveals a woman who had a good general education. Her mother's address in the rue Debrousse in the nineteenth district of Paris suggests a prosperous socio-economic standing. In 1902, it might be expected that a woman with this background marrying a man whose family had the great wealth of the Tatas might move to India and set up home there. The Tatas did this, but maintained not only a second and third residence in France (in Paris and in Hardelot), but, as we will see, frequently moved between the two countries.[19] They even stayed in other countries as well, such as the period from 1917 to 1918 when Sylla, J.R.D. and Sooni Tata lived in Japan. We have seen in the Introduction that mobility is one of the hallmarks of the Indian *videshinis*. Indeed, the frantic rhythm of family life of Sooni and R.D. Tata resembles that of many globalized NRI (Non-Resident Indian) or PIO (Person of Indian Origin) families in today's jet age. Given that they did this from 1902 up to Sooni Tata's death in 1923, their mobility represented a significant logistical undertaking. With her characteristic eye for a humorous anecdote, Sooni Tata tells her mother of one of her more precipitate departures from Indian soil: 'This morning I have had what you might call a fright. It was a quarter past eleven and Ratan burst into the room to tell me that our ship was leaving at twelve noon. The little one was not yet dressed and my hair was in a terrible state.'[20]

1902 to 1907 Marriage, mobility, multiple country residency and multilingual space

Let us first consider the period from 1902 to 1907, for which there is a full record of the couple's itinerary. The ports of call of Sooni and R.D. Tata between August 1902 and December 1907 make for a dizzying succession of stop-offs: in 1902, Czech Republic (Carlsbad), Switzerland (Montreux), London, the United States (New York City and the Niagara Falls), Mumbai; in 1903, Mussoorie, Mumbai, France (Vichy and Paris), London, France (Marseilles), Mumbai; in 1904, France (Nice), London; in 1905, France (Paris, Chamonix and Marseilles), Mumbai; in 1906, Matheran, Mumbai, France (Marseilles), Mumbai; in 1907, Panchgani, Mumbai, Poland (Warsaw), Russia (Vladivostok), Japan (Osaka, Buzen, Nikko, Tokyo, Sagami, Tokyo, Osaka, Kobe), China (Shanghai), Hong Kong, Singapore, Sri Lanka

(Colombo).[21] In the first five years of their marriage, therefore, the Tatas led a semi-nomadic life along international trade and tourist routes. In a characteristically witty turn of phrase drawn from her correspondence with her mother, Sooni Tata passes comment on her traveller's life as she gets ready to leave Mumbai once again: 'The trunks are becoming more and more of a second home to me, I dare say, you'll not find me anywhere else; I live in them!'[22]

This almost perpetual movement between August 1902 and December 1907 could be a function of their wealth and privilege, and the fun evident in postcards that were sent from the United States (such as the card from New York reproduced earlier[23]) suggest that the trip there was part of their honeymoon. Their globetrotting was not always for fun.[24] The movements were partly dictated by concerns about Sooni Tata's health and by R.D.'s professional commitments, such as his involvement in mining in Japan (thus perpetuating Jamsetji's strategy of non-dependence on the British Empire). This is evident in the itinerary from Warsaw to Japan to Colombo in 1907. Already in 1905, after the birth of their first two children (Sylla in 1903 and Jehangir – J.R.D. – in 1904), Sooni Tata's letters record the physical strain of travel for her: 'It is this accursed mad rush which forced me to return to France and medical science which I hope will get me back on my feet again and give me back the strength I have lost.'[25] This illustrates that travelling is enjoyed most when the traveller is in good health and that this was not always the case for her.[26]

Coming to India is also a coming to English for all of these *videshinis*, and the same applied to Sooni Tata. On board the *SS Imperatrix* on her way to Mumbai in December 1902, the letter that she writes to her mother musing on what she would do if they saw each other again underlines that she has entered a multilingual space in which English dominated:

> We would chat in my beloved and beautiful French, which I am forced to abandon somewhat to speak English, as, unfortunately, French is not understood by all. With Ratan [R.D. Tata] I cannot speak the same French as with you, mother dearest, I have to use exact and correct words which leave no room for ambiguity.[27]

In the first sentence here, Sooni is literally regretting the absence of her mother tongue, in the second part she notes that she does speak French with her husband, but that the level of his language competence is not that of a native speaker. A 1906 letter written by R.D. Tata to his mother-in-law in French suggests that he had a good command of the language. His French is virtually error-free and he uses a variety of registers (both formal and colloquial) (Sooni Tata 1906a).[28] As for Sooni Tata's competence in English, a note she wrote in English in 1903 to Meherbai Tata (the wife of Dorabji Tata) survives; this allows an objective assessment of her level of competence in the language at the start of her marriage. The letter is quoted here exactly as it was written:

> I receive your kind letter with great pleasure. Ratanji is in Paris since six weeks and you must think how happy I feel. We have now an 'épouvantable' wather [sic] always raining and windy and cold. I hope I was in India! We are all well and expecting something new next week probably – Ratanji and Navajbai will return in India end of September and we hope to see you and Dorabji in Paris very soon. We look for a larger apartment and if we find one, we shall be very happy to receive you to leave with us. How are you getting on and Hirabai and Jamsetji? I hope she feels better now, it is so painful to see her suffer so much. Hoping to hear from you very soon. I send you and Dorabji our best love and kindest regards. Believe me always your very sincere Soona [sic] R. Tata.[29]

We can see Mme Tata's command of English was passable (though far less competent than her husband's ability in French). There is a vocabulary breakdown in the use of 'épouvantable' instead of 'terrible', several spelling mistakes ('leave' for 'live', for instance) and the register used is basic, littered with stock phrases. The content, however, shows how integrated she is within the core of the Tata family. It is not surprising that in later years her English skills improved as an ancillary effect of her married life, which took place partly in that language. In a later letter, dated 8 June 1906, she notes that English words come to her before those of any other language (Sooni Tata 1906b).

Her arrival in Bombay in 1902 was a time of excitement for her, but also one of upheaval. She was delighted by the warmth with which she was welcomed into her husband's family. It is important to stress that she was not coming to India to settle there permanently, rather it would be just one of her residences (as the itinerary above confirms, she returned in 1903, 1905 and 1906). She found that the house of her mother-in-law was a multilingual space and noted a cacophony of languages: 'the Gujarati of my mother-in-law that I do not understand, the pidgin French of a children's nurse who uses the familiar form to address me and to whom I do not listen, and the bickering with the rest of the servants who do not understand me.'[30] Even more than this, as we see in the first epigraph, she has a sense that she is not only in between cultures, but also that everyone is scrutinizing her:

> I, who am neither fish nor fowl here, a Frenchwoman for the Parsis and a Parsi for the Frenchwomen, have to be extremely careful; when one is the object of almost everybody's gaze, the slightest fact … sprouts feet and runs along by itself, getting bigger as it goes.[31]

Despite being in a multilingual environment that she cannot completely penetrate, she is in a society that values learning and actively engages in it: 'The ease and determination with which Parsis learn languages are extraordinary.'[32] This factor governs her future attitude to languages, including non-European languages. Thus the new Mrs Tata soon resolves to follow the example given and be neither cautious nor passive. She begins to learn Gujarati: 'Mother dearest, yesterday I studied Gujarati for an hour and a half (it's difficult).'[33] The fact that she mastered at least the script is illustrated by the postcard dated June 1905 where French words are written in Gujarati characters. These years embedded in this branch of the Tata family a linguistic and cultural multiculturalism informed through travel.

1903 to 1923 The multilingual childhood of Sooni Tata's children

This constant travel and multilingual environment implicated not only Sooni and R.D. Tata but also their growing family: Sooni Tata had five children between 1903 and 1916.[34] In 1906, once the fraught period of her two elder children's birth and earliest infancy was past (health concerns dominate even for this family, which had access to the best health care available at the time), one of the key markers of their progress was language development.[35] It may be objected that language is one of the universally acknowledged yardsticks of childhood development and that the Tatas represent nothing unusual here. It is important to note that Sooni Tata mentions not only what the children say when they start to speak, but the language in which they speak it. The children's development, therefore, is not measured in absolute terms – terms which might be conveyed by the words, 'today my little girl/boy said a three-word sentence', for example; rather, it is a case of multilingualism being the norm. Sooni Tata comments on her son's language repertoire at the age of three, with both curiosity and delight. He speaks 'a mix of Gujarati, Hindi and English'.[36]

In the following extract from 1907, the mother mentally reviews the linguistic progress she expects her daughter Sylla and her son Jehangir (J.R.D.) Tata to have made during their stay with their grandmother in Paris, and also reflects on the sacrifice of having to send them away from her:

> When I think that Sylla is going to be four soon! She is a little lady already and how funny and entertaining she will be when we see her again, and dear Jehangir? He is about to turn three, what change we will see in him, he will be able to speak like a grown up. When I think about all that I am losing by not seeing them, I am seized by an unspeakable melancholy and I would like to leave immediately and rush over to you, with Ratan of course.[37]

Sooni's two eldest children were sent to live with their grandmother in France, where they spent most of their time during their childhood and young adulthood, between 1907 and 1923.[38] Sending the children to France had a linguistic purpose; it anchored French as one of the children's 'mother tongues' – indeed, there is an anecdote that whenever J.R.D. Tata was heard counting, he did so in French (Lala 1992, 54). J.R.D. Tata confirms the family's common language: '[B]ecause my mother was at first not familiar with the English language, the language used by all of us was French' (ibid., 17).

Sooni Tata's nurturing and love of her five children is evoked by J.R.D. Tata as her legacies to him and his siblings. In response to the question from the interviewer M.V. Kamath about his memories of his mother, J.R.D. Tata replied: 'Wonderful memories of great love and admiration... [S]he also had an ability to cart up to five children from one place to another, finding homes and ruling the family with love and a very great efficiency' (Kamath 2004a, 4–5).[39]

In parallel to this interpersonal relation that privileged French, there was also a grounding in France for R.D. and Sooni Tata's branch of the family. In 1905, there began a business association between R.D. Tata and Sir John Whitley, a British entrepreneur who had purchased four hundred hectares of coastal land on the French side of the English Channel (called 'La Manche' in French) and who in 1902 had taken over the development of the prominent neighbouring resort of Le Touquet.[40] R.D. Tata was a member of the board on this project, suggesting a major commitment by Tata Group to the hospitality sector in France as well as in India. One of the major achievements that the group's founder, Jamsetji, saw completed in his lifetime was the Taj Mahal Hotel in Mumbai. The project at Hardelot also benefitted from the increasing official warmth in the relations between France and Britain in the wake of the Entente Cordiale of 1904. The aim was to build on undeveloped land a private coastal resort with exclusive leisure and commercial facilities. The English-language publicity for the project shows that Whitley had secured the patronage of the King and Queen of England, and the corresponding French-language documentation mentions the King and Queen of Belgium as well as the British monarchy.[41] Alluding to its fine, firm sand beach, the exclusive resort billed itself as 'the queen of beaches and the beach of queens'.[42] This patronage and the entirely private basis on which the resort was created contributed to its exclusivity.[43] The development of Hardelot from 1905 onwards represented a first for India: it was most probably the first time an Indian company had invested in Europe; not only did R.D. Tata have villas constructed for his own use, the Tata Group also invested in six other properties and in commercial premises of the resort.[44] The first name of the street on which these were found was 'Avenue des Indes' or 'India Avenue'. In order to maintain architectural quality and a unified appearance across the resort, the villas were mostly designed by Louis-Marie Cordonnier, the architect of the Peace Palace in The Hague (this building is now home to the International Court of Justice). The villa Paulette in the centre of Hardelot became the main summer residence of Sooni and her children and of R.D. Tata when the latter was not travelling on business.[45] The investment in Hardelot property by the Blériot family and the presence of Baron de Zuylen de Nyevelt de Haar, the president of the Automobile Club de France, on the honorary board of the resort, meant that Hardelot was a place where an indirect form of technology transfer involving planes and cars took place.[46] It was here that J.R.D. Tata first became acquainted with and gained an insight into the functioning of automobiles and aviation. In this, however, J.R.D. was very much following the interests of his mother. Sooni Tata functions as a precursor and a path-breaker for him as well as for Simone Tata. In addition to being the first woman in India to hold a driving licence from 1905, Madame Tata took to the skies on a pleasure flight from Hardelot Beach on the French side of the English Channel in July 1913. At the controls of the monoplane carrying the mother of four was Edmond Perreyon, one of Louis Blériot's team of pilots.[47]

The commercial aviation introduced to India by J.R.D. Tata, in the form of Tata India Airways, gave the context for the first meeting between Simone Dunoyer and Naval H. Tata at an Air India reception in Geneva in 1953: the future Mrs Simone Tata worked for the airline briefly as a member of ground staff in the early 1950s. Although flying is associated with modernity, until the start of the twenty-first century it was an activity that marked the elite out from the masses. Alluding to Rajiv Gandhi's career as an airline pilot, one of his political detractors, Madhu Dandavate of the Janata Dal (Secular) said: 'It began with Rajiv, he came into politics straight from the airport. With Sonia it is worse' (Chatterjee 2000, 149).[48] This last comment alludes to the negative perceptions of air travel and its association with elitism.

Suzanne Brière's entry into the Tata family, the multilingualism of the family group, and the multiple residences at Mumbai, Hardelot and Paris gained a transnational identity between nations for Sooni and R.D. Tata and their children. This was crafted and offered by the parents to the children in their early childhood (whereas the two parents had to work hard to acquire these skills). In 1924, J.R.D. Tata begins a letter to his father in French, quoting a limerick he has written in English, after which he effortlessly switches to English and continues the letter in that language (J.R.D. Tata 1924a). In the 1986 interview with M.V. Kamath, J.R.D. Tata refers to three occasions where his transnational identity comes into play: 'I had dual nationality, I was born a French man [sic] in France and was treated as a French man. In India as an Indian. A British subject presumably.' 'I was a French soldier and I'd been brought up as a French boy so I had dual patriotism' (Kamath 2004b, 3 and 5). Moreover, it is clear from J.R.D.'s slips of the pen that the metropolises of Mumbai and Paris were very close to each other in his mind map. In a letter to his father, the son writes: 'Tu dois être maintenant de retour à ~~Paris~~ Bombay' (You must be back in ~~Paris~~, Bombay by now) (J.R.D. Tata 1924b).[49]

Given the physical distance which frequently separated members of the family (J.R.D. Tata's military service in France between 1924 and 1925 is a case in point), an obligation to practise written communication appears to have been inculcated into the children (just as Sooni Tata had herself felt obliged to write two pages a day to her mother for more than four years). Languages were used in active communication – different languages for different members of the family. Such communication requires a great initial investment to establish and an effort to maintain; however, it is an efficient method to bind members of the family together, because the material support of the letter becomes a keepsake and a token of affection in itself. Seen in the round, each member of the family of Sooni and R.D. Tata has a particular linguistic constellation made up of four elements (English, French, Gujarati, and Hindi), in a hierarchy of competence that differed for each person. As a consequence, the family's philosophy of language consisted of communicating in such a way that the palette of languages was maintained and improved.

This period during which France was their country of principal residence in terms of time spent there each year lasted until 1923, when R.D. Tata came to France to bring his children back to India after the death of their mother. After his military service in France from 1924 to 1925 J.R.D., however, was sent to England to improve his English and to continue his education with a view to going to university. For the scion of an industrial family such as the Tatas, an apprenticeship with the company was more important than higher education, and J.R.D. Tata did not take up a place at Gonville and Caius College, Cambridge University (the subject he was to study is not known), but was called back to Bombay in December 1925.

1906 to 1931 Internationalism and Tata Group

Despite living only till the age of forty-three, and with an active involvement with the Tata family for only twenty-one years from her marriage in 1902 to her death in 1923, we have seen the effect of Sooni Tata's active engagement with India while remaining grounded in France. Crucially, her children were all provided with the lived experience and linguistic competence to get knowledge of France and the West from the inside. Jimmy and Sylla died young, but Darab, Rodabeh and Jehangir (J.R.D.) Tata would all use those qualities within the Tata Group according to their own different levels of ambition and competence.[50] Looking towards the future, the Tata Group was able to be such a supportive elite for Simone Tata from the 1960s because within the organization there were individuals with other traditions of internationalism at the heart of the group.[51] As we have seen in the case of J.N. Tata, internationalism within the group is not limited to those who, like the Tata siblings, were brought up in a multicultural environment. Burjorji Jamaspji Padshah was perhaps the most complete early example of this Indian-born internationalism after the group's founder. Padshah was born twenty-five years after J.N. Tata in 1864 and became the founder's ward in 1880, after the early death of his father who was J.N. Tata's best friend from Navsari in Gujarat.[52]

On account of his interdisciplinary education, winning prizes in the arts and sciences at Elphinstone College, and his periods of study in Bombay and Cambridge, J.N. Tata appointed Padshah to be the group's representative on the project to found an Indian institute of higher learning. From 1896 to 1898, Padshah toured universities in the United Kingdom, the United States and in Europe to research the best model for India.[53]

After J.N. Tata's death in 1904, Padshah continued to perpetuate the founder's practice of bringing diverse global talent into the business. So, if we look at 1906, we can see a letter Padshah wrote to R.D. Tata in which he argues from a purely business point of view for an increased multinational dimension to the firm's commercial activities ([no author] 2005a, 1–5):[54]

> We all absolutely agree with you [R.D. Tata] that we need to travel outside India for promising recruits & thank you for your indication of the French Ecole de Mines [sic]. Perhaps it is not so difficult as it looks to secure a capable English-speaking French man [sic] to organise the exploration of minerals. (Padshah 1906)

This correspondence relates to the confirmation of the quantity and quality of the iron ore deposits which were so crucial in making TISCO a functioning enterprise in the period from 1906 to 1911. In addition to recruiting on the basis of competence, we also see the continuation by Padshah of J.N. Tata's strategy of diversification in recruitment beyond the British Empire. In the following letter, dated 23 July 1918 and quoted in this chapter's third epigraph, we see Padshah again making the case for the integration of foreign expertise in terms of a dynamic fusion strategy for the company's human capital. The expressions used here, such as 'shrine or home', show the intersection between family and business interests at this point in the history of Tata Group. The biological metaphor of transfusion, now more commonly called transplant if organs are involved, sees the company as a body that can receive parts from various other individual sources.

> Don't worry about the Tata name. It won't suffer if strangers are introduced into the shrine or home. There is no Armstrong or Whitworth in the firm of Armstrong or Whitworth; a few shares may be held by a Maple in Maples, but the management is in other hands; the Caesars very soon ceased to be

> of the family of Julius & were ultimately Spaniards, Greeks & Barbarians & Germans. The Caesars early took Associates when the empire grew too big for one Autocrat. In India, there is no Bird in Birds & I doubt if there be any Killick or Nixon in K & N. The principles of 'Transfusion', by which an external limb planted in a living body may keep the body as a whole alive & functioning, will also avail the Tata Firm; bring new blood and worthy, bring more shoulders to bear the new burden.(Padshah 1918)

Leaving the accuracy of Padshah's views on companies mentioned to one side, the key issue here is that these letters are addressed to R.D. Tata; thus, when it comes to evaluating Sooni Tata's overall contribution to the international diversification of the Tata Group, we can see that, while her activities were confined within the domestic sphere, they are one step further, because the multilingualism, multiple residency and international experience of her and her young family is already a reality.

Sooni Tata probably did not know about B.J. Padshah's letter and its content, but her husband was the group director to whom the letter was addressed. He was the common link displaying diversity in both the domestic field and continuing to develop it in his commercial ones; his family life with his wife and children provided a successful fully functioning practice of internationalism in the domestic context. Both, the first meeting between Suzanne Brière and R.D. Tata around the turn of the twentieth century, and the early international education of Sylla and J.R.D. Tata, took place in a domestic domain: the Parisian apartments of Suzanne's mother Mathilde Brière. This apartment in the rue Debrousse in the sixteenth district within close reach of the right bank of the Seine was the classroom and the nursery of internationalism in this branch of the Tata family.

This domestic internationalism is highly gendered. Mathilde Brière's role as the teacher of R.D. Tata and J.R.D. and Sylla Tata, and the choice of the French and Gujarati speaking ayahs mentioned above, indicates that, as was usual for wealthy families in the first decades of the twentieth century, language learning both inside and outside the family was frequently the preserve of women.[55] It was their role to teach children mother tongues and to mint the currency of cultural contact. Therefore looking at how languages are transmitted across the generations is a way of valorizing the female and the domestic sphere, and of getting beneath the male-dominated surface of the well-known Tata family tree.[56]

What emerges, overall, is three constituencies of internationalist diversity in the company and family. First, there is the internationalist mindset of Indians (such as B.J. Padshah and J.N. Tata), who arrived at that position through a mixture of education and travel. This could be called 'intellectual internationalism'. Within this category, R.D. Tata took this form of internationalism to another level by marrying a non-Indian, studying languages and by long periods of residence abroad. Second, there are individuals such as the children of R.D. and Sooni Tata who have a deep level of hybridity based on language competence and lived experience during childhood. Though there is some overlap with the first form when these people become adults, this could be called 'cultural internationalism'. Third and finally, there are a host of individuals brought into the group from the global North since the TISCO days, some as consultants for their special expertise for a limited period, and others becoming or recruited as group employees from the start. The Americans Charles Page Perrin, the metallurgist who supervised the initial choice of Sakchi for the Tata Steel Works, belonged to the first category and his countryman T.W. Tutweiler, general manager at the works from 1916 to 1925, belonged to the second, as did his Irish successor J.L. Keenan who first worked for the group as a blast furnace foreman in 1913. In the words of B.J. Padshah, this constituency represents what can be called 'transfusional internationalism'. We will see that Simone Tata is a special case in that third category. Her achievements demonstrate a crossover from the domestic to the commercial domains. Like Sooni in 1902, Simone Tata would enter the Tata circle via the domestic route in 1955; but her talent, family contacts and practical experience of cosmetics were utilized to maximum effect because of the earlier combined effect of both intellectual and cultural internationalisms.[57]

To conclude the discussion of Sooni Tata, let us speculate on how her particular brand of internationalism might have influenced the group's early ethos. Mobility, multiple residences and linguistic competence are important for their wider impact on the development of an internationalist perspective in the Tata Group as a whole. While the history of economic activity in South Asia has always included an important international dimension (one only has to consider the histories of the various European East India companies and external colonialism and conquest though the ages), the Tata Group has a particular place within the history of international business in India: it was one of the first India-based international companies in private hands. The readiness of Jamsetji Tata to approve the integration of new French blood into the family in the first years of the twentieth century is telling. In considering why this was so, the question of the role of the 'Parsiness' within the Tata Group initially comes to the fore. Might it have been that, among leading members of the Tata Parsis, an awareness of their own non-majority status in India made them willing to enter into tangential minority-to-minority alliances outside India (such as the admission of the Frenchwoman Suzanne Brière into such a prominent position within the family)?

There are several caveats to be borne in mind when raising this apparently confessional issue. The first is that there should be a clear separation between separate sectors: the situation of Sooni Tata and her opinions and self-image; the wider Tata family; and finally the wider company ethos. As far as the last of these is concerned, any 'Parsiness' within the group of companies should certainly not be thought of as sectarianism; working for the benefit of special interest groups goes against everything that Tata stood and stands for and, furthermore, it negates the basic commercial imperative of the enterprise to impact the lives of as many people as possible. Secondly, the potential role of 'Parsiness' in the business ethos of the Tata Group probably has little to do with the Zoroastrian religion in any strict theological sense. This is because the majority of employees are of other faiths and, because it is a minority and a non-proselytizing faith; few non-Parsis have a profound insight into it.

Once these limits have been set, 'Tata Parsiness' loses its specific ethnic, cultural and confessional attributes and retains only one element – a sense that this company is different from other companies of comparable size in their home base of India. The diffuse nature of this sense of difference from other companies can be quickly invested with positive qualities, because it can be understood in different ways by different company employees. Of course there are quantifiable elements on which the sense of difference rests, the most important of these being that Tata charitable trusts hold 65.8 per cent of the residual value of the Tata Group.

As far as Sooni Tata and the early twentieth century are concerned, it appears clear from the self-projections of R.D. Tata's wife and the way she brought up her children that she conceived of the elite in far more exclusive terms. For her the Tata elite was also a Parsi elite. In the many references to the Parsis that dot her correspondence, it is apparent that she saw herself as having married not only into a wealthy family, but also into a religious and quasi-ethnic group which she assumed to be set apart from and above society at large, both in India and more widely. Her sense of pride at being French and her confidence in the superiority of her taste compounds her attraction for what she understood as the privileged socio-economic situation of the Parsis.[58] This accounts for the way in which she enthusiastically practises a cultural 'Parsi' identity. She had to have a Parsi marriage ceremony, had herself photographed in Parsi dress, learnt basic Gujarati, and even signed her private letters to her mother 'Soonaï' or 'Sooni', rather than using her birth name, Suzanne.

However, it is also clear in her choices about her children's upbringing that she and her husband strove to distinguish themselves, and particularly their offspring, as a super-elite within the Tata–Parsi elites. It is this project of internationalization through moulding the linguistic and cultural diversity of her children that Suzanne Brière bought into when she became Sooni Tata, and it is here that her indirect contribution to the diversification of the whole Tata Group at a crucial moment in its history needs to be better acknowledged. But how is her contribution to be judged? Other than as a casual translator from French into English and as a procurer of business information for her husband, she did not play any official role in the day-to-day activity of the company (this is very different from Simone Tata, who developed a successful business within the group).[59] Thus, because of the unquantifiable nature of her contribution, her role is best described in terms of 'secondary human capital.'[60] Sooni Tata, therefore, is one of the group's intangible assets.

Her desire to live life with her family in a multilingual and transnational setting was important for the company. As we have seen in her sadness at being separated from her children (J.R.D. Tata was not even three when he went to live with his grandmother in Paris), she was prepared to sacrifice direct contact with her children in pursuit of this internationalist ideal. Clearly, the opportunity to enrich family life and her children's upbringing with this amount of international experience was only available to a small minority of individuals in the first two decades of the twentieth century. Even within the Tata family, Sooni and R.D.'s branch was the only one to avail itself of it to the point of creating 'cultural internationalism', combining travel, language competence and long-term dual or multiple residency during the childhood of their offspring. This is illustrated by a brief contrast of the domestic arrangements of the other two main partners of the Tata Group after J.N. Tata's death. Dorabji Tata resided mainly in Bombay, apart from two years at Cambridge University between 1877 and 1879; he married the Parsi Meherbai Bhabha and they did not have children. J.N. Tata's second son Ratanji Tata travelled frequently between London and Bombay in the fifteen years before his early death in 1918 at the age of forty-seven, but was educated exclusively in India and married the Parsi Navajbai Sett. Although in 1906 he bought York House, a mansion in Twickenham, the couple did not bring up any children there. The child that his wife Navajbai adopted after his death in 1918 was Naval Hormusji Tata (1904 to 1989), the husband of Simone Tata. Though it was to increase exponentially during his years in the Tata Group, the early international experience of the young man confined itself to a short course in accountancy in London in 1930. This was the year of Simon Dunoyer's birth.

1930 to 1954 Simone Dunoyer before Tata

This Indian *videshini* was born in 1930 in Geneva, Switzerland. As the fourth epigraph records, there is a firm basis for her opinion that Geneva is an international city. The International Committee of the Red Cross was headquartered there from 1863, the Labour Organization from

1920 and the World Health Organization from 1948. Let us consider her background and upbringing to see if there are any internationalist parallels linking her to India or to the 'cultural internationalism' of Sooni Tata and Sooni's children. Her father, François Ernest Dunoyer, ran a successful chemicals business and her mother, Alice, ran their 'big house with large grounds, three kilometres from the centre of Geneva' (Simone Tata 2011a).[61] She recalls that her mother 'always attracted a lot of people, cousins, nephews and friends' and that 'our house was always full of people' (ibid.). Though Simone Dunoyer's parents were both born in Geneva, the two families were of French origin. Her father's parents had come to Switzerland from Savoy (in the south-eastern part of France) and her mother's family originated from Alsace, in north-eastern France. Simone Dunoyer states that 'the bond my parents had was not only with Geneva, but also with France, due to their origins, and also because most of the Dunoyer family resided in France' (ibid.; see epigraph five). She later confirms that those French 'contacts have never been lost' (Simone Tata 2011c). This indicates that the young Simone Dunoyer had a personal link with nations beyond Switzerland, but that her international consciousness remained within the boundaries of Europe.

As she acknowledges in this chapter's fifth epigraph, the key factor influencing her upbringing was the war across Europe from 1939 to 1945: 'The impact of World War Two started with the defeat of France and its occupation. For a family with so much French blood, it had a terrible impact' (Simone Tata, 2011). Switzerland was a neutral country, but its geographical situation at the heart of Europe meant that it was surrounded by nations at war with each other. Despite its clear privilege in her life as far as material comforts were concerned, she says that she still carries

> strong and sad memories of World War Two. These definitely had a large impact on the rest of my life, more so as the war started when I was nine years old, an age when a child is already quite aware of events and the surrounding atmosphere, which, needless to say, was extremely sad and gloomy. (Simone Tata 2011a)

She recalls that '[T]he French exodus [after the defeat of France in 1940] included many family and friends' who fled to Switzerland. She elaborates that '[t]he progress of the war was closely followed on maps and discussed at length... We used to listen to General de Gaulle on the radio and never lost hope' (Simone Tata 2011c). There was, however, a continuing terror: 'We had daily air [raid] alarms and all our windows had to be blackened. Switzerland also expected to be invaded at any time and this sent us children into panic' (ibid.). Though she did not travel abroad until after the war, the conflict showed her the fragility of Switzerland's national borders. As we will see when we examine her life as a young adult, this experience of war in childhood was to make her particularly receptive to Mahatma Gandhi's message of 'peace' (Simone Tata 2011c).

The war, however, also meant that she came into contact with children from all socio-economic groups during her schooling:

> I went first to a private school, but later moved to our village school, since because of the war and the absence of petrol, there were no more cars. The village school was a day one and also mixed, but mixed in more sense than one, as the children were of all classes of society. It could have not been more democratic! (Simone Tata 2011a)

As is so often the case, although they belong to elites in India, the women in this book do have an appreciation of other groups in society; they value that broader experience and put it to good use in their careers in India.

As regards her language repertoire, a crucial issue for the women in this book, Simone Dunoyer confirms that 'my mother tongue was French, I did not speak any other language as a child' (ibid.). That said, she 'started learning German at the age of eleven and English at fourteen' (ibid.). So, if we review the qualities of Simone Dunoyer's childhood, we see that the three elements which dominate might also be shared by many prosperous children growing up in Switzerland during the war years: an awareness of nations beyond one's own national borders, the multilingual and the socially inclusive.

As far as her knowledge of India is concerned, Simone Dunoyer is very clear: 'I had my education in French, as opposed to a British one which certainly covered far more of the Empire past and present' (Simone Tata 2011b). It is actually highly significant that she analyzes her childhood impressions in this way. This is of course the result of an adult life lived mostly in India and her awareness of that country's previous colonial link with Britain; but it is also a consequence of the fact that her knowledge of India before she travelled to that nation was mostly acquired outside Britain. At school she says that her 'knowledge of India was purely geographical' (ibid.); but this changed after the end of the war when the struggle for Indian independence entered a critical phase. Marie-France Latronche has demonstrated the importance of the representations of M.K. Gandhi in the French-speaking world from the end of the First World War onwards (Latronche 1999). For Simone Dunoyer too, a knowledge of India on the cusp of independence appears to have been conveyed through the person and the political philosophy of Gandhi. She notes that lectures on 'Gandhi happened in school' (Simone Tata 2011c). Although there were many Britons who understood the moral imperative of Gandhi's position on the independence of India, the general political consensus in the United Kingdom was far less favourably inclined towards him than in countries such as Switzerland and France.

In the wake of Independence and after the assassination of Gandhi on 30 January 1948, India became more present for her in terms of general culture. This is because Simone Dunoyer lived in London that year, learning more English and sampling the cosmopolitan mix that London offered. London 'never felt drab, but quite exciting' (Simone Tata 2011b). She recalls eating Indian food for the first time: 'with a Swiss girlfriend we ventured into an Indian restaurant and almost died from the very spicy food' (Simone Tata 2011a). Upon returning to Switzerland and taking up her literary studies at the University of Geneva, she attended 'various classes and lectures on [Gandhi's] life and mission'; as a consequence her 'interest in India grew considerably' (ibid.). She is honest and analytical in stating that the freedom struggle was an intellectual matter for her. We are not talking about India representing a spiritual quest for her. As she says: 'There was no wish yet to visit India. There was no new way of "seeing things", except the message of peace and the freedom which India attained with Gandhi as the torch bearer' (Simone Tata 2011c). This is important, since it underlines the fact that she did not subscribe to an image of India, so prevalent among young Westerners in the 1960s, as the location of a form of experience which could not be acquired in the West. Simone Dunoyer was attuned to the way in which the sovereign nation of India had acquired independence, but she had a stable sense of self. Her interest in India was intellectual and not existential. Thus, at this point in her life, her interest in India and the world outside Europe was closer to Jamsetji Tata's interest in the world beyond the British Empire. It was, however, not yet informed by actual experience.

The next stage in the rapprochement between Simone Dunoyer and India was a spell working for Air India in their Geneva office and later on at the airport itself. The fact that Tata Indian Airlines, founded by J.R.D Tata and the South African aviator Nevill Vintcent, was the pre-war precursor to Air India meant that her work brought her into the ambit of Tata Group. Simone Dunoyer is very positive about her cosmopolitan working environment at Air India, which 'had a mixture of various nationalities. All became good friends' (Simone Tata 2011b). The year 1953 was of key significance; India came to Geneva in the form of Indira Gandhi and Naval H. Tata and other Tata executives, and Simone was chosen to be at this gathering, where she met her future husband for the first time.[62] The same year she resigned from Air India and concretized her interest in India by visiting the country.

Although it may have been the meeting with Naval H. Tata that spurred her on to take her interest in India to another level, she insists that she experienced India for the first time alone. She engaged with the culture of India by means of the intellectual notions that she had discovered during her young adulthood in Europe: 'I flew from Geneva to Bombay. I had a few contacts and letters of introduction. My itinerary was planned in advance, based mostly on monuments and places having a religious or philosophical importance, such as Benares' (ibid.). This independence was a measure of her intellectual independence. She had set up a visit of personal discovery, rather than being guided or introduced to India by a Tata insider.

Thus after her India trip in 1953, there seems to be a greater emotional engagement with India; she mentions the world 'fascination' here in connection with India for the first time. She concedes that when she returned in 1954 'my interest and fascination with India brought me back the following year and this time we [Naval and Simone] had lunch together the day I was returning to Europe' (Simone Tata 2011a).

The seventh epigraphic quotation above repeats the idea of fascination during her tour of India in 1953. The modes of transport are significant. Not only is there air travel and rail, but also bus. This means that, just as with her experience of socio-economic mixing at the village school in wartime Switzerland, this journey around India gave her an experience of a cross-section of its people; 'all types' (as she calls them), not only elites. Her judgement of Indians is a touch trite, but overwhelmingly positive: she found them 'awfully polite, helpful and interesting' (ibid.). If these quiet compliments sit rather uneasily in the context of her fascination, the same seventh epigraphic quotation provides other hints as to why she was well received, and these reasons are crucial when interpreting Simone Dunoyer's account.

Her tour around India as a European came after the end of colonialism, and yet it seems that it was viewed by Indians as a voluntary engagement with a land that so many other Europeans had left or were leaving. Her journey using public transport ensured a degree of mixing with Indians from which colonists, former colonists, European travellers and many Indians generally shielded themselves. Her journey was different; it was an individual one. She was discovering India on her own, learning about the country from the people she met, and this was what appears to have been welcomed by those Indians. As she says 'they were also very curious to find a young European woman travelling alone, more so since most foreigners had long since left India and the age of the backpackers and hippies was still a long way off' (Simone Tata, 2011).[63] This positive response by Indians to a young Swiss woman travelling alone around their country was conditioned by her choice of a range of modes of transport as well as by the particular historical time frame: after Independence, but before the mass so-called spiritual tourism of the 1960s. Although her 2011 reflection on this period of travel does not stress the post-colonial dimension, the fact that Simone Dunoyer headed in the opposite direction to many Europeans does mark her apart. The future Mrs Simone Tata and managing director of Lakmé is concerned to present her undoubtedly broad-based experience of India as one of free engagement, based on intellectual curiosity. She brackets out the personal and emotional dimension and the link to the Tata family. In doing so, she is defining the evidence-based qualities of her intellectual make up as a businesswoman. Let us now examine the Tata company in the period before she became Lakmé's managing director.

1955 to 1959 Lakmé before Simone Tata and Simone Tata before Lakmé

The Tata brand name 'Lakmé' has been present in India since 1952. As recounted by Simone Tata in the sixth epigraph, the name occurred, not to her, but to her future husband Naval H. Tata after a visit to the opera in Paris. The name served an internal company purpose, as there evidently needed to be a separation between Tata's new cosmetics venture and TOMCO's existing products – soaps, detergents, shampoos, and even eau de cologne. As the portrayal of a cross section of Indian society in the 1946 advertisement for Hamam soap illustrates, these were mass market products. They were the Indian-owned competitors to Lever Brothers' products. Though these TOMCO products came in contact with human skin, they were not intended to be visible on it in the same way as make-up. These products were toiletries and not cosmetics like Lakmé's.[64] In order to be successful, the future business needed the financial backing of the Tata brand, but it was not necessary to indicate its origins within the group.

If Lakmé was different and independent, where did the word come from? Although it dates from 1952 in India, in Western Europe and in France in particular this word has existed in the public domain since 1883, as the title and principal female role in a French opera with words by Edmond Gondinet and Philippe Gille and music by the noted composer Léo Délibes. *Lakmé* the opera is a melodramatic tragic tale of a failed and entirely platonic love between a young Indian girl and a British officer in colonial India. It ends with Lakmé's suicide.[65] Clearly, therefore, there is no connection between the story and cosmetics. So when it was chosen by Naval H. Tata, it was a signifier ready to be populated with commercial meaning in India. As Simone Tata says, 'The name rolled easily off the Indian tongue and it was without any foreign connotations' (Simone Tata, 2012a). While Lakmé did not refer to any well-known pre-existing foreign enterprises, as Simone Tata's comments imply, it was, nonetheless, in its original form and from an India perspective, a foreign French word. The reason for this is that it has an acute accent on the final 'e'. This marker of its French history has had a variable existence during the time within the Tata Group. In the Tata Group advertising in the early years, from 1952 to 1959, it appeared in a French form with an accent.[66] A look at the early economic environment and the presence of French know-how in the Lakmé products and their marketing will further illustrate this co-existence of French, European and Indian elements. It will also set the scene for the intervention of Simone Tata with her first-hand knowledge of Parisian cosmetics, explored in the next section.

Of course, beauty care did exist in India before Lakmé, in the form of homemade preparations from various natural herbs, but this company was the first national brand of cosmetics, with multiple ranges of individual products made to international standards in a specialized production process. It is also important to note that the birth of Lakmé was not only a commercial initiative by the Tata Group; it was a response to a particular problem spotted by the Indian state in the nation's economy. In the early 1950s, when the economy was centrally planned, Jawaharlal Nehru's minister of finance, C.D. Deshmukh, was concerned that India was losing valuable foreign exchange on cosmetics manufactured abroad. He contacted Naval H. Tata, then head of the Tata Oil Mills Company (TOMCO), and requested that the firm should begin to manufacture cosmetics in India.[67]

The venture was launched with the collaboration of two French firms, Robert Piguet and Renoir, who provided the technical know-how to the Tata Group on a contractual basis until 1966 (though Simone Tata developed an increasingly independent marketing strategy and product development for Lakmé from the early sixties onwards).[68] As is evident from the advertisement of the late 1950s reproduced at the start of this chapter, the advertising of the Lakmé product range makes this French connection a selling point that emphasizes the products' exclusivity. The advertisements from this period before Simone Tata's involvement in the company refer to how the cosmetics are 'prepared from French formulæ' and mention that the products were 'French-inspired', 'created in Paris', 'from Paris' and, in an example which combines apparently British and French words, 'perfect in Milady's Boudoir'. 'Milady' is a contraction of 'my lady', a Continental European form of address for an English noblewoman, harking back to an indistinct aristocratic past in the West.

The significant French involvement in this early pre-Simone Tata period of Lakmé is confirmed by a *Tata Monthly Bulletin* article, which recounts how 'Lakmé made its debut by holding a gala reception at the Taj Mahal Hotel on November 18, 1953'. The report, which is entitled simply 'Lakmé', continues, 'Tastefully decorated under the personal guidance of Mrs Rodabeh Sawhny, who is on the Lakmé Board of Directors, the Banqueting Room had assumed a French atmosphere and provided an excellent setting for the introduction of Les Parfums Robert Piguet et Renoir to the elite of Bombay.'[69] The article further details a visit of Mr W. Golenko, General Manager of the French company 'of Paris [...] to have personal discussions with the Chairman and Directors of Lakmé for processing and marketing of [these] perfumes in India and for manufacturing some cosmetic products which Lakmé propose to bring out'. The rest of the article demonstrates the cultural dimension of the implantation of manufactured cosmetics in India, recalling that this was the battle to convince Indian consumers about these products that Lakmé later intensified in its advertising under Simone Tata's leadership. Before the general public were to be convinced, the Tata staff would need to understand the issue:

> From time immemorial, perfume has been an ordinary article of use for the people of the Orient, whether rich or poor, male or female. [...] attar of jasmine and roses from India [...] were the usual commodities of trade [...] which Westerners of those days valued very highly. [...] The perfumes of the Orient, however, were not the distilled scents which come from Western countries and with which the present generation are so familiar. Paris being the centre of art and civilisation for centuries in Europe, it was in France that the art of distilling perfumes from flowers was first perfected and developed into a major industry.

The article thus sets out to introduce a notion of 'different' and added value to French perfume. The décor for this product launch was overseen by Rodabeh Sawhny (née Tata), who was the third of the children of Sooni and R.D. Tata, so we can see here that the 'cultural internationalism' elaborated in the previous section was also deployed to the advantage of the company before Simone Tata joined.[70] It would be an exaggeration to see Rodabeh Sawhny, the wife of a 'Tata man', as a model for Simone Tata: their contributions to Lakmé, are poles apart. The parallel does however show that there is a pragmatic sense of the individual within the family contributing to the advancement of the company as far as her or his skills allow.

This strategy for TOMCO to sell mass-market products and for Lakmé to continue as something exotically French was still in evidence in 1958, when an advertisement for the Calypso and Gulchheri perfumes shows these Robert Piguet products as being 'offered exclusively' by Lakmé. However, as outlined in the 1953 *Tata Monthly Bulletin,* Lakmé intended to embark on the manufacture of products in India. The manufacturing process and scale of production of these products could be inspired by Piguet and Renoir of the French cosmetics industry, but there was a potential for these Indian-manufactured products not only to be aspired to by an elite audience who were using imported perfumes, but also to gain a new market share from potential consumers who might be persuaded to use products manufactured in this way if they were adapted to their Indian consumers with respect to the fragrances used and the range of colour tones offered.

From 1952 to the early sixties, before Simone Tata's involvement, this potential was far from being realized. The company was growing slowly and there was not yet a consensus that any personnel changes at the top of Lakmé were needed to realize the potential. At the start of Lakmé, in 1952, Simone Tata was not even part of the Tata family, let alone part of Tata Group, but this was about to change.

Though it was a private event, the marriage of Simone Dunoyer and Naval H. Tata on 26 June 1955 marks a crucial juncture in the story of Lakmé. As we have already seen in the case of Suzanne Brière, and as we shall see with Antonia Maino, who became Sooni Tata and Sonia Gandhi respectively, the passage of a European woman into an Indian elite family by marriage entails a change to her legal identity and lifestyle. That said, however, in comparison with these two very public marriages, the ceremony in which our subject became Simone Tata was a very low-key affair. It was celebrated with discreet modernity, very different from traditional Indian weddings in all their various religious and ethnic manifestations in the public domain. This modernity meant that the wedding had only a civil component; despite Naval H. Tata being a religious man, there was no Parsi ceremony. The bride wore a European dress and there were just five or six people present, including Naval H. Tata's adoptive mother, Lady Navajbai Tata, and his sons Ratan and Jimmy Tata from his first marriage to Soono Commissariat.[71] It is also significant that no one from the Dunoyer family attended the wedding. The consent of Simone's father François Ernest Dunoyer had been obtained only after 'pressure from my mother and friends' (Simone Tata 2011b). Simone Tata also confirms that there was another precondition to her father's consent; it concerned a legal link back to Switzerland: 'My nationality was Swiss and has remained Swiss till now, a promise I gave my father when he finally agreed to my marriage' (Simone Tata 2011a).

In the same interview Simone Tata makes a distinction between nationality and country of permanent residence. After mentioning her father's wishes on marriage in 1954, she specifies that she 'lived in India' from that moment on (Simone Tata 2011a). This mention of Indian residence (and Indian residence alone) as a positive decision on her part is crucial because it ties her to India for life. She was not able to change her nationality on account of her father, but she could easily have spent more time outside India or retired to Switzerland. This she has not done. She has continued to live in Mumbai, first with her husband's family in the so-called Tata Palace (also known as Tata House) and from 1989 in a smaller apartment. As it has been framed in this way, and because she has never stood for elected office in India, her nationality has been an issue neither within the Tata Group nor in the limited public representations of her.[72]

In one sense the last phase of Simone Tata's pre-Lakmé existence is the most transitional one. Like Suzanne Brière, she had married into one of the most prestigious Indian business families. Her own father was an industrialist, but she had had no direct experience of either the technical or the business side of his chemicals enterprise. In 1955, therefore, all was set up for a domestic existence in India as mother and wife and a contribution to the Tata Group resembling Sooni Tata's. Simone Tata and her husband Naval H. Tata might have been able to shape Tata Group over the next generation by a new branch of the family with connections to Switzerland and France. The potential for influence was great as J.R.D. and his siblings had either not had children or these children had not joined the Tata Group. There was no inkling that Simone Tata would contribute directly to the Tata Group by leading a company within it.

Simone Tata's situation was different from Sooni Tata's in two important respects. Naval H. Tata already had two male heirs (one of whom, Ratan, went on to become chairman from 1991 to 2011); and, after the Second World War and Indian Independence, the cultural argument about the value of internationalism in the company had been won. Simone Tata could capitalize on that victory. As we have seen above, in the references to Tata Indian Airways, the Tata Group under J.R.D. Tata moved into ever more international domains, and so the presence of a European woman in the inner circle of the Tata family was not remarkable in itself; but what would the future hold for Simone Tata?

Initially domestic life occupied centre stage for her: Naval H. and Simone Tata's son Noel Tata was born in 1956.[73] By her own account, Simone Tata was mainly a full-time mother in the first eight years of her son's life. Though he was ferried less often between India and Europe than J.R.D. Tata had been, Noel, like J.R.D. Tata and his siblings before him, had an international, multilingual upbringing: 'We spoke to him in French from time to time. However, during our holidays in Europe, more so in Geneva with my family, French was "de rigueur"' (Simone Tata 2011a).

As far as her own integration into the Tata family is concerned, Noel's mother confirms, referring to this period, that 'I had a very happy relationship with my mother-in-law, Lady Navajbai Tata. She told me a lot of stories about the family and her childhood and married life' (Simone Tata 2011b). In this comment, Simone Tata indicates two things: first, she was warmly accepted by the previous generation of Tatas (just as R.D. and Sooni Tata had gained Jamsetji's approval). Secondly, she is also indicating that these years were a period of a family apprenticeship close to the manner of a traditional Indian *bahu* or daughter-in-law. It is during this period of living with the Tatas that she can say that she had been integrated into the family and had acquired their values. All this meant that, had she wanted to, Simone Tata could have restricted herself to the domestic domain. This was to be the case with her friends, the other two Tata spouses who had international upbringings: Thelly Tata, the wife of J.R.D. Tata, and Fanny, the Italian-born wife of Darab R.D. Tata, the second son of Sooni and R.D. Tata.

Tata Central Archives and *Horizons: The Tata–India Century 1904–2004*, Aman Nath, Jay Vithalani and Tulsi Vatsal's landmark commemorative volume, both have photographic records that show that Simone Tata had a traditional public role as the wife of a key Tata director. These documents show the couple on either side of Jawaharlal Nehru during his visit to the Bombay Hockey Club in 1956 and also welcoming King Baudouin and Queen Fabiola of Belgium in 1960. In these photographs Simone Tata is pictured dressed in a sari, a form of dress that she did not wear in her everyday life, even in public. A photograph from the same period shows her watching tennis in Bombay wearing slacks (Nath, Vithalani and Vatsal 2004, 343). In her subsequent professional career with Lakmé she wore exclusively Western clothes.

During this time, though, Simone Tata was listening and learning. Her husband's business life and her own domestic life overlapped. She is characteristically modest about this informal business education: 'Any insight I got into the way Tata was run was by listening to my husband and his colleagues' (Simone Tata 2011b); and, 'Knowledge about specific Indian customs was acquired by listening and mixing with people' (ibid.). The following quotation indicates that she preserved her contacts with Switzerland as a private individual, while also building up a new form of international experience shadowing her husband during his work for Tata Group and the International Labour Organization: 'Apart from my annual trip to Geneva, I did accompany my husband in a few trips to the USA, England and France' (ibid.).

As Simone Tata recounts in *Creative Businesswoman,* her induction into the Tata Group was a gradual process from 1960 onwards:

> I came to join Lakmé by accident. A director from Tata Sons once asked me, 'Why don't you join the Lakmé board? ... Slowly it became a half-a-day job ... At some stage Tata Oil Mills (of which Lakmé was a subsidiary) decided that they needed a Managing Director for Lakmé. One Board member sounded me out, but my husband's reaction was a 'no, no, no'. I asked Naval how he could make such a decision on my behalf? Besides, Lakmé was so broke, it could not pay the salary of an MD. (Pandit 2008, 27–8)

This account stresses that there was no trace of financial gain in the induction of Simone Tata, but it stresses with humour that her position within the family and within her marriage meant that, once the suggestion had come from Tata Group, she was absolutely mistress of her destiny. If this was nepotism, it was also supposed to be based on merit. Furthermore, the company culture of Tata Group allowed its senior managers at least to entertain the possibility that someone who was not part of the business might have something to contribute.

In the early 1960s, Simone Tata had that rare mix; she had ten years' experience in India and possessed a specialized knowledge of Western cosmetics from the 1940s and 1950s which corresponded to the potential target market that could be developed in India in the 1960s. As part of her upper-middle-class upbringing in Switzerland, as elsewhere in the world, a special place was accorded to personal grooming for the Dunoyer sisters. As she confirms, 'My initial knowledge of cosmetics certainly came from my mother and her friends. In my generation, past high school, girls were using cosmetics. Also my mother was very particular about maintaining our skin in perfect condition' (Simone Tata 2011c).

1960 to 1998 Simone Tata joins and then leads Lakmé

Simone Tata admits in a provocative formulation in epigraph number eight, 'I started at the top in a non-existent industry'. It is probably true to say that Simone Tata was able to come into Lakmé at this level due to her Continental European experience of cosmetics and her Tata family connection, but what she did once she was in and progressively gained more influence within the business might be a surprise. She did not stay with France, or with Switzerland, but developed a composite internationalist strategy in product design and marketing. By her account, her husband was a formative influence in terms of her understanding of the global business context: 'Through his wide international exposure, Naval raised my understanding of the world's problems... His understanding of the economic, political and social systems of India and the world, their historical evolution, and business in its broad outlook, influenced my thinking' (Pandit 2008, 24). Thinking globally, according to Simone Tata, Lakmé adopted a strategy which had been successful in the sector:

> In the 1960s Revlon was the leading cosmetic company in the world. And Revlon had a number of brands (Revlon, Moon Drops, Intimate, etc.) positioned at various price levels, each price level consistent with the brands. For example, Revlon was a mass brand, Moon Drops was for the woman between 25 and 40 years, Intimate, a very expensive range, for very sophisticated older women... What worked for Revlon, with each brand, became a model for Lakmé. (Pandit 2008, 32)

The global element here is that this strategy is neither Indian nor European, but American. However, despite what Simone Tata says, it seems that Lakmé adapted the Revlon model for India. It adopted the product diversification aspect, but rather than going for two additional, more exclusive and expensive, premium sub-brands as Revlon had, Lakmé kept a single brand, except in the case of TOMCO products outside Lakmé, but brought out a range of products which were newer to India in terms of their packaging and use. The base offering in the late 1950s, before Simone Tata's induction, is presented in the advertisement at the start of this chapter. It shows five Lakmé product ranges: eau de cologne, dusting powder, talcum powder, face powder, and lipstick. Three years later, after Simone began to be active in the company, a draft of a 1962 advertisement by the Bomas Agency for Lakmé satin glow liquid foundation illustrates that the range is expanding. This advertisement features the hand selecting the product, which is a common feature of publicity from the end of the 1950s. The product, packaged in a smaller version of the usual Lakmé container, was new to the Indian market in this form, and the advertisement includes a more detailed specific description indicating how to use it and what it does: 'spreads to a satin smoothness' and 'veils every blemish'. A later advertisement in colour for the same product from the 1970s shows how it is repackaged and paired with another new product, the Lakmé compact, which is also shown; the suggestion to the consumer is that these products are to be used together.

A second comparison between product marketing at the end of the 1950s and the start of the 1960s illustrates that the French dimension of the earlier style is diversified with a new but more traditionally Indian fragrance. Lakmé talcum powder was the bestselling cosmetic product in the late 1950s, initially launched 'with a choice of three subtle perfumes created in Paris', but at the start of the 1960s, it was marketed in a more traditional Indian version. The advertising campaign that promoted this newer product portrayed the faces of Indian women in traditional Indian dresses and ornaments. It was a direct appeal to the traditionally minded Indian consumer:

> You handle with loving care your precious pieces of Gupta stone. You prefer on your table the lively sparkle of silver 'thals' to the coldness of imported pottery. You choose for yourself the dark, oiled sleekness of the Indian coiffure. In perfumes too, you prefer the traditional.

This composite strategy illustrates very well the comment at the start of this chapter that Tata Group understood Indian nationalism, but acted internationally for business and family. The talcum powder campaign from the 1964/65 season, when Simone Tata was company managing director, shows that this diversification continued apace.[74] In that year, lavender was the single fragrance of Western origin; it had been joined by Vetiver, Sandalwood, Apsara, and Nirvan.[75] The 1960s diversification is culturally aware, adding traditional Indian fragrances to a product that is manufactured and packaged as a part of a brand built up with the aid of exclusive French elements. These elements are not in the foreground any longer, but remain in the brand name and in the shape of the packaging and, which built its recognisability and market share on exclusivity based on fragrance components of non-Indian, French origin.

The French elements are a crucial and hitherto ignored portion of the heritage and composite marketing strategy which increasingly included Indian elements. This also plays itself out in the visual language of the advertisements. In the late 1950s the publicity material either advertised with the aid of drawings of the products or with a disembodied hand which was not linked to a particular physical manifestation of the human body with its cultural and ethnic markers. In the mixed strategy from the 1960s onwards, we see that form of depiction being complemented by Indian women being pictured, joined by other women who have whiter skin. For instance, a 1963/64 campaign from Bomas outlines a beauty regime with 'three steps to a fairer lovelier complexion'. Unsurprisingly perhaps, the model here is very fair skinned and there are no cultural markers regarding clothes, jewellery or bindis. Lakmé advertising does mention fairness of complexion, that most important of postcolonial issues, which is not the subject of this chapter. The principal commercial rationale of the company, however, is to produce cosmetics for and to depict women with a wide range of skin tones. The net effect of this strategy shows that Lakmé was resolutely diverse in the cultural allusions made in its product offering. This is further evident in the way that the model for the bestselling talcum powder with its five perfumes in the 1964/65 series wears a sari, but has no bindi.

In 1964, Lakmé was probably the only large enterprise in the whole of India led by a European, but Indianized, female managing director. It is an interesting paradox that Simone Tata's mix of intellectual internationalism and cultural internationalism, which was deepening with every year that she spent in India, was able to adapt the Europeanness in Lakmé's original concept and early strategy, taking the company beyond benefitting from French know-how to developing new products that were attuned to the needs of the Indian women who purchased them.

With reference to the company after 1964, Simone Tata insists that Lakmé 'was a Western concept in its choice of products', which differed from the indigenous 'beauty aids'. However, as she mentions, the products 'were tailored in their consistency and colours to Indian skins. [Lakmé] was in fact the first Indian brand to occupy this position and answered the needs of Indian women' (Simone Tata 2011a).[76] From Simone Tata's comments on 'Indian skins' above, it was clear that the products were carefully developed with a particular Indian range of tones in mind: a range of skin colours, most of which were different from Simone Tata's own. But as she makes perfectly clear, the product was not the only thing that had to be produced and packaged; there was also technique in usage that had to be communicated to consumers. Simone Tata recounts that part of the successful formula had its roots in her own acquisition of cutting-edge techniques in Paris: 'Later on, whilst in Lakmé, on my yearly visit to Paris, I went to reputed make-up artists such as Carita and Alexandre to learn the finer points of make-up (it used to make me broke)' (Simone Tata, 2011c). The Carita sisters and Louis Alexandre Raimon (Alexandre), with whom they shared a salon in the rue du Faubourg Saint Honoré in Paris, were among the most highly reputed cosmetic artists and hair stylists of their day. In 2005, Simone Tata commented that her 'forte was knowledge of cosmetic products as also developments in the cosmetics industry worldwide' (Simone Tata 2005).

As Simone Tata expounds to Shrinivas Pandit, 'knowledge of products, and a feel for the product and the category, gives you that authority. My strength was my knowledge' (Pandit 2008, 31). Pandit is correct to say that her knowledge was set within an aesthetic context – a sense of the beautiful which would function in the diverse Indian market. This aesthetic sense was set within a commercial context in which Tata and Lakmé developed means of production which would allow them to deliver new cosmetics to the Indian market at a profit for the first time. In 2008, Simone Tata gave the details on how this was achieved: 'we introduced a number of products, well ahead of their time. Some became a big success, others hardly covered their costs, but it enabled Lakmé to answer any woman's needs' (Pandit 2008, 32).

A key element of this was the consistency of the Lakmé product as far as its ingredients were concerned. It did not have the regional variation of what Simone Tata calls 'traditional Indian beauty aids', the composition of which would vary according to the ingredients available in different parts of India (Simone Tata 2011a). From their inception, Lakmé products would be the same throughout India. This is the consistency on which a brand can be built.

That said, Lakmé, with Simone Tata at its helm, did not have an easy ride. As Simone Tata (interviewed in 2011) admits, despite a progression in its sales between 1965 and 1966 to 'Rs 46 lakhs, an increase of about 43 per cent', Lakmé was initially a 'limping company' during her tenure.[77] One limiting macroeconomic factor was the fact that the business was not operating in a free market as far as its sales outside India were concerned. A *Tata Review* article from 1966 that reviews the history of TOMCO and Lakmé bemoans the lack of 'import licences for raw materials' in 1960s.[78]

In the 1970s, there was a pressing need to tap into foreign markets, since 'the Indian market became non-profitable due to the yearly hike in excise duty, which reduced margins to almost zero' (Pandit 2008, 30). Simone Tata outlines how for the reorientation of the business towards the export market she had to recruit a team of professionals as 'surveys became necessary, [as did the] appointment of agents, market developments, signing of contracts' (Simone Tata 2011b). For Madame Tata herself, this expansion meant increased international travel, 'four to five trips a year' (ibid.). The expansion was primarily in the direction of Eastern Europe, including Russia, Hungary, and the former Czechoslovakia: 'When Lakmé exported to the West [i.e., to Eastern Europe], both consistency and colours were adapted to Western fashion and the needs for these markets' (Simone Tata 2011a). Unlike Hindustan Unilever's Pear's Soap (and notwithstanding the controversy around the soap's 2009 formula change), Lakmé couldn't achieve the crowning glory of exports to Western Europe and countries such as France: 'Lakmé tried unsuccessfully to penetrate [Western] Europe in spite of many efforts' (ibid.). It was possible, however, for Lakmé to 'manufacture for other brands such as Dior and export their products under their brand name' (Simone Tata 2011b).

Lakmé under Simone Tata's stewardship overcame these macroeconomic challenges, diversifying their product range and continuing an evolution which Indianized the brand without sacrificing its exclusivity, which had been carefully built up with reference to its non-Indian heritage. Lakmé had to convince consumers of the desirability of every new product it introduced. The Lakmé advertisement from the 1970s (reproduced at the beginning of this chapter) with the strapline 'Does make-up label you "fast", "loose" or "that type"?', demonstrates clearly that Lakmé not only had to sell its products and anchor its brand, but that it also had to make a successful cultural argument for cosmetics. Indeed, this series mentioned the brand as a champion of cosmetics, but did not mention any products. The need for this public-service-style intervention was because many sections of Indian society saw make-up as morally questionable, or even 'un-Indian'. As Simone Tata puts it, 'cosmetics were taboo; there was a social implication. We ran a Lakmé campaign to try and remove the stigma' (Nath, Vithalani and Vatsal 2004, 184). Another advertisement in that series included a text-based piece which asked, 'Is it bad to look good?' and replied, 'No. And you know. You take so much care to make everything look good; your children, your home, even your kitchen.' It continued by affirming that 'looking good is your birth right. It's your heritage and tradition. Ancient scriptures, paintings, poetry [...] are full of examples which honour an Indian woman's birth right to beauty and encourage her with traditional ways to make-up. Modern science has refined this traditional art with better techniques and more convenient aids for make-up' (Nath, Vithalani and Vatsal 2004, 184).

These cultural pamphlets in favour of cosmetics (calling them 'advertisements' alone would be a misnomer) attempt to build a bridge between cosmetics and Indian traditions, before showing how manufactured cosmetics modernize those traditions. The aim is to appropriate cosmetics for as wide a section of Indian women as possible. Another advertisement affirmed: 'And this label ['beautiful'] is your birth right, your heritage and tradition, your prerogative, be you a housewife, a student or anybody' (Nath, Vithalani and Vatsal 2004, 184). While one can object to them from a feminist perspective, asking why there is a societal imperative for women to 'look good' in the first place, the pamphlets do set this up in terms of a woman's personal choice 'when you want to look your best for yourself'. The crucial point for the purpose of this chapter is to reflect that Lakmé's longevity and market size allowed it to be the self-appointed spokesperson for cosmetics in India. In responding to this cultural need and pleading the case of the sector in general, Lakmé demonstrated a sense of corporate responsibility for the sector itself. At one level, this campaign was Lakmé's novel adaptation for commercial purposes of the disinterestedness which is at Tata Group's philanthropic core. At another level, it showed how powerful the brand had become in India by the 1980s and 1990s. Lakmé had done so many forms of business, such as import, franchise, manufacture and export, but specialist companies such as Hindustan Unilever could bring huge advertising budgets into play to embed new products. The value in the company was shifting from the company's products to the brand itself. This, and the fact that it was one of the smaller companies within the Tata Group which wanted to consolidate, sealed its fate, which was to be sold. How did its managing director react to this existential challenge?

1998 to 2003 and beyond Trent and Westside: Simone Tata and Tata Group after Lakmé

Let us now move on to focus on Simone Tata during and after the sale of Lakmé to Hindustan Unilever in 1998. As she confirms in *Creative Businesswoman*, it was her role as managing director of Lakmé to develop the business strategy with the company's board. Now well-established as a market leader, Lakmé became a takeover target: 'Post 1992, several multinationals, Americans, French, Japanese, approached Lakmé with projects for joint ventures or complete buy-out. Almost all the large international brands came knocking at my door' (Pandit 2008, 38).[79] Lakmé had established itself as a very attractive company on account of its domestic and overseas markets. According to Pandit, there were both macroeconomic and Tata-specific reasons to review its future direction; these included 'competition from multinationals, liberalization, Tata Group's decision to exit from non-core areas [these were its smaller sectors in terms of profit], [and the] need for huge investment in building marketing muscle' (ibid.). Simone Tata did everything she could to protect the brand within Tata Group, but from 1992 she was managing change in a world in which cosmetics knowledge and cosmetics manufacture had become globalized. Following a joint venture in 1996 with Hindustan Unilever, an offer was made in 1998 for the whole business. In all her interviews with Pandit and with the present author, the same adjective is used to describe the Hindustan Unilever offer: 'irresistible' (Simone Tata 2011a and Pandit 2008, 39). There was no room for discussion. The only other such ineluctability in the life of this business leader was in relation to her promise to her father to retain her Swiss nationality.

In 1998, Lakmé left the Tata Group, closing the door on the workshop in which the brand was forged. In her interviews, when she looks back on the sale of the company from a personal point of view and remembers what she felt at the time, Simone Tata uses the vocabulary of mourning: 'I grieved silently' (Pandit 2008, 39). It is, however, a mark of her resilience and creativity that when she speaks in the present tense she regards the sale from a different perspective: 'I do not feel either grief or pride or sadness about Lakmé. I turned the page very quickly, especially with having to set up Westside' (Simone Tata, 2011).[80] This pattern of regret for what happened in the past combined with an optimistic vision of continuity also permeates her external perspective with regard to the sale. This is demonstrated in her comments about the people who worked for Lakmé: 'I did of course very much regret parting with the company for which I worked for over thirty-five years and parting with the wonderful people with whom I worked (to me this was the saddest part)' (Simone Tata, 2011a). Once again, however, this sentiment is mitigated in a later part of the interview: 'Quite a few Lakmé people joined Westside; especially in Finance, Engineering, HR and Management' (ibid.).

Conclusion

Simone Tata's career shares two common features with that of Mirra Alfassa – she was able to play a key role in the establishment of not one, but two organizations. For the Mother, those organizations were the Sri Aurobindo Ashram and Auroville (both of which are active today). Simone Tata transformed Lakmé and founded Westside, a Trent (Tata Retail Enterprise) business specializing in clothes. Westside is currently run by Simone Tata and Naval H. Tata's son Noel.

Another shared characteristic between Mirra Alfassa and Simone Tata is that both women had the freedom accorded to them by their reputation to name their second organizations, 'Auroville' and 'Westside' respectively. Whereas Auroville bears a French-related proper name, one of the few in use in India today, Simone Tata's follow-on venture bears an entirely Anglophone name: 'Yes, I chose the name Westside. If in the 1950s Lakmé had a French connotation associated with beauty and perfumes, Westside forty years later was intended to represent Western fashion, lifestyle and the modernity of the Western World' (Simone Tata 2001b). Paris traditionally divides itself into Left and Right Banks (*rive gauche* and *rive droite*), but the term Westside is, as Simone Tata indicates, a global division which reproduces the division of cities such as London.[81] The majority of the products on sale in Westside stores are manufactured in India; the shopping experience, however, is an idealized model of Western shopping, including valet parking at its Mumbai store.[82] Since its establishment in 1998, when it took over the Littlewoods stores in Bangalore (Bengaluru), the Westside retail business has been completely devoid of identifiable French or Swiss influence.

Thus, when we think about providing an explanation for the influence of Simone Tata, we need to return to the immediate postcolonial period (1947–62) and to a world in which information flowed much more slowly across national borders. It is probably safe to say that no woman will again have a career path within the Tata Group like that of Simone Tata. She joined the family before she joined the company and had a period of seven years to refine her skills. Nowadays businesses change at a much faster rate. A whole educational industry has grown up around the MBA, which is geared to producing multilingual graduates who, already as young people, have business experience working in other cultures. All in all, it is possible to say that the world has now come around to Simone Tata's way of doing things in 1962. At that time she was a unique resource for the Tata Group, with her cultural adaptability linked to a strong sense of self, her multilingualism and, most of all, her specialist knowledge with its exclusive Parisian components. Nowadays the world's business schools and universities produce hundreds of thousands of individuals each year who are supposed to have skills the same as, if not superior to, those of Simone Tata; however, few of them, whether male or female, will be able to achieve both economic success and transform the acceptance of the product that they sell. In commercial terms, Simone Tata has left her mark on the corporate world in India. She built Lakmé from a 'limping company' (Simone Tata 2005) to one worth $45.5 million.[83] As the twenty-first-century world is far more globalized, companies generally do not attempt to mount cultural battles for the products that they sell (they tend to wait for the market conditions to become propitious). Simone Tata's cultural achievement is to have made a major contribution to Lakmé's change in social attitudes in favour of manufactured cosmetics.

Now we have a better sense of Simone Tata's personal contribution, what can be said about Tata Group, the Indian elite that sustained her and through which her achievements became possible? What are the unique characteristics of this group that nurtured Simone Tata and Lakmé and Westside?

Given the enduring importance of the dynastic principle in Indian society, and, as historical commentators such as Patrick French (2010) have shown, that it has an atrophying influence in fields such as politics, it is interesting that the Tatas have all but abandoned dynasty in favour of developing a standard around which positive qualities can be gathered. When the chairman's baton was passed between J.R.D. Tata and Ratan Tata, both men were concerned to avoid even the slightest sense of nepotism in the handover. The outgoing chairman stated that 'Tatas is much too big to have a hereditary succession. Tatas is, thank God, a national institution and must continue to be so' (Lala 1992, 336). The incoming chairman was sufficiently exercised by the issue to write a letter to the editor of the *Economic Times*: 'Tata Sons has been, and continues to be, professionally managed by a Board of Directors and not by family members' (Piramal 1996, 395). While such statements of principle are necessary during periods of transition, the Tatas remain influential within the Tata Group and will no doubt have a role to play in it in the future; but how far they rise will be based on merit. Decisions appear to be made collectively by a board of directors in which family members are an absolute minority and will remain so. This form of meritocratic check and balance appears to have functioned since Ratanji and Dorabji's days, when Tata Group was already too large (and suitably experienced family members too few) for Tatas to take charge of each of its constituent companies. The system whereby family members have a fast track into the company, but only in order to prove themselves, and are not guaranteed influence, is a way of assuring change *and* continuity in the Tata Group.

In 2008, the acquisition by Tata Group of Jaguar Land Rover prompted a great deal of speculation about the nature and future of the Tata Group and of the role of the Tata family within it. In epigraph eleven, Gita Piramal is quoted by Randeep Ramesh as saying 'the Tatas are a reconstructed family who adopt and cobble together people to make a family. That way they do promote talent rather than blood relations.'[84] The validity of these alternatives to family was confirmed first, when Cyrus P. Mistry was named as chairman designate of Tata Group to succeed Ratan Tata, and, second, in the replacement of Mistry by Natarajan Chandrasekaran in October 2016. It is interesting that Mistry and Chandrasekaran were chosen over Noel Tata, the half-Francophone Indian–Swiss son of Naval H. Tata and Simone Tata. There are both similarities and differences between the nomination of J.R.D. Tata to the chairmanship of the group and that of C.P. Mistry. Mistry, a UK-educated Irish Indian chosen to succeed Ratan Tata in 2012 for reasons far beyond family and nationality, including, crucially, his personal qualities, is the second son in the family that is the largest individual shareholder in the group (with 18.4 per cent). So here, as in the case of J.R.D. Tata, a long-standing link brought a talented individual into the field for consideration.[85] C.P. Mistry's grandfather first bought shares in the Tata Group in the 1930s and the family increased its shareholding considerably when it purchased the shares of J.R.D. Tata's siblings. In 2011, as compared with 1938, the substantial financial nature of the interest of the Mistry family in the firm is crucial. The most significant difference between Mistry and J.R.D. Tata is that, although Mistry is a Parsi, he is not a Tata by blood or by marriage.

Clearly, controlled diversity in the large and diverse inner circle of the Tatas, which has provided the chairman of the group, not only has many faces, but also many forms. The process of transition is both feudal and federal, with the leader being chosen this time from among the leading Tata families, who are not all Tatas. Typically, the Tatas have developed for themselves a highly efficient form of Indian dynastic progression. It would be going too far to say that there is something Swiss in their mix of tradition and modernity; more relevant perhaps is the Japanese practice of adopting adult males in business families. Here, a member of the older generation who is no longer able to run the business on account of age adopts an adult son who marries into the family, changes his name to that of his new wife and takes over the family business interests.[86] We can see that this model also preserves patriarchy and male succession.

The Tata Group has evolved a system that circumvents dynastic inheritance, one of India's greatest weaknesses and also one of her most positively cohesive and powerful social forces over the centuries. In the tenth epigraph, Simone Tata makes a distinction between the wider world of business and the Tata Group. In the wider business community, where she is not as well known as in the Tata Group, misunderstandings about her supposed superficial role in Lakmé abounded. People thought that she was a figurehead, 'Brand Ambassador', rather than a managing director. While avoiding all 'self-publicity' (2011b), Simone Tata has stressed that her role in the Lakmé cosmetics business was far from cosmetic. The tenth epigraph praises the company for allowing her to establish herself. In the early 1960s, when she gradually began to be admitted into the Tata Group, it was a case of potential enlarging of the recruitment pool. The fact that she was in the frame at all was a result of the internationalism and openness of both the family and the company (Sooni Tata was the pioneer in this domain). Seen in terms of today's increasing awareness of the case for workplace gender equality in India, it might appear somewhat of a paradox that in allowing Simone Tata in at all, the Tata Group made a significant step for gender relations by affirming the special privilege accorded to family. Simone Tata made her own influence, and the family entry ticket did not guarantee a job, only a chance to shine. In January 2016, Tata executives announced that the Group was launching the Studiowest brand of cosmetics in Westside stores. This market re-entry means that Tata is back in competition with HUL's Lakmé and other international brands such as Maybelline and Revlon, both in store and via Westside.[87] At home in Mumbai, Simone Tata welcomed Studiowest dispassionately as a logical step in revenue maximization.[88]

Notes

1. 'Moi qui ne suis ici ni chien ni chat, Française pour les Parsis, Parsi pour les Françaises je dois être d'une extrême prudence, lorsqu'on est le point de mire d'un peu tout le monde, le moindre fait… court, grandit, devient grand.' Sooni Tata in a letter to her mother Mathilde Brière dated 28 January 1904. Tata Central Archives: FP NO 97 SL 44 PG 02.
2. The comments marked 'Simone Tata, 2011' in the Bibliography were made in correspondence between the author and Simone Tata.
3. The modern term 'Tata Group' will be used to refer to the whole group, including Tata Sons, the group's holding company.
4. http://www.hul.co.in/brands/personalcarebrands/Lakme.aspx (accessed 11 November 2011).
5. In 2014, the annual turnover of Trent was Rs 1284 crores. Despite the stark difference in their fields of activity, in growing two successful organizations in India, Simone Tata resembles Mirra Alfassa.

6. In the 2014 Brand Trust Report for all sectors in India, Lakmé was ranked thirty-sixth overall and third in the fast-moving consumer goods category.
7. The Tata Group occupies such a prominent place in Indian life that this is not the first time the company's history has been used as a perspective on nineteenth, twentieth and twenty-first century Indian history, e.g., Aman Nath, Jay Vithalani and Tulsi Vatsal, *Horizons: The Tata–India Century 1904–2004*, Mumbai: India Book House, 2004.
8. J.N. Tata lived from 1839 to 1904.
9. R.D. Tata's first marriage was within caste, creed and nationality. R.M. Lala states that: 'R.D. was married at an early age to a Parsee girl from the Banaji family. She died childless not too long after the marriage' (R.M. Lala, *Beyond the Last Blue Mountain: A Life of J. R. D. Tata*, New Delhi: Viking, 1992, 8).
10. The documents, among the private papers of R.D., Sooni, and J.R.D. Tata, documenting this presence are held at Tata Central Archives in Pune and were studied during an Arts and Humanities Research Council-funded research visit. They are held in the 'fireproof boxes': FP NO 096 to FP NO 099. I would like to express my gratitude to the archivists, Nawzer Lala, Rajendra Prasad Narla, Deepthi Sasidharan and Freny Shroff, for making my visit such a profitable one. The views contained in this chapter are my own, but I benefitted enormously from having been able to debate them in a spirit of academic exchange with specialists like Prasad Narla. See also Ian H. Magedera, 'Embedding an Internationalist Vision: Sooni Tata and the Transnational Identity of the Tata Family 1902–1923', *Sands of Time*, VII.3 (2008) 3–4, VII.4 (2008) 6–8 and VIII.1 (2009) 3–6. Available here: http://www.tatacentralarchives.com/publications/newsletters/main.htm and 'Desorienter l'orient et les orients désorientés: Said, Derrida et le paradoxe du GPS' in Jean-Pierre Dubost and Axel Gasquet (eds) *Les Orients désorientés*, Paris: Kimé, 2013, pp. 33–55.
11. The languages known to them were English, French, Gujarati and Hindi.
12. Sooni Tata's precursor role in this chapter thus mirrors how Jeanne Dupleix's life frames the debate for all Indian *videshinis* in the *Prélude Pondichérien* at the start of this book.

13. It was during the second leg of that journey on a ship travelling from Japan to the United States that J.N. Tata made the acquaintance of Swami Vivekananda, who was on his way via the eastern route to the World Parliament of Religions in Chicago. This meeting was recalled during a ceremony in which the prime minister of India, Narendra Modi, in 2015 unveiled an official coin commemorating the 175th anniversary of J.N. Tata's birth.
14. Sir Dorabji Tata's dates are 1859 to 1932 and Sir Ratanji Tata's from 1871 to 1918.
15. This was part of Tata and Co.
16. R.M. Lala, *Beyond the Last Blue Mountain: A Life of J.R.D. Tata (1904–1993)*, New Delhi, Penguin Books India, 1992, p. 17.
17. Tata Central Archives, FP JRDT-RDT-FAMILY COR-ENGLISH-1913-25-1-81-120.75.
18 *J.R.D. Tata Keynote: Excerpts from his Speeches and Chairman's Statements to Shareholders*, S.A. Sabavala and R.M. Lala (eds), New Delhi: Rupa & Co. 2004, p. 18.
19 One of the addresses at which they stayed in Paris was more prestigious than that of Madame Brière: 6 rue Halévy in the ninth district, a wide street close to the Opéra, which is to feature in the story of Lakmé, the cosmetics company that Simone Tata went on to lead in 1964. The copy of J.R.D. Tata's birth certificate confirms these addresses and is available at http://www.spitama.org/actedenaissance.htm (accessed 11 May 2015).
20. Tata Central Archives: FP NO 96 SL 37 PG 01 'J'ai eu ce matin ce qu'on appelle une trousse. Il était onze heures et quart and Ratan arrive en courant pour me dire que notre bateau partait à midi. La petite était déshabillée et moi dans un état de coiffure déplorable.'
21. As far as possible, the places are referred to here with their contemporary names. At the time of travel, geopolitics dictated that Carlsbad was in Bohemia, part of the Austro-Hungarian empire.
22. 'Je suis de plus en plus dans les malles, je dirai même que j'y reste, j'y vis!', Sooni Tata (1902a).
23. The quote in the postcard is from 'Pâle et blonde', the popular song by Jean Richepin and César Antonovich Cui. It is interesting that Sooni Tata does not inflect the adjective 'black' in French – it should read

'noire'; perhaps this underlines that she is just playing a verbal game. Indeed, this playfulness of a European woman taking on an Indian role is also demonstrated by Mother Teresa when she says that after she leaves the Loreto Order she would delight at being a maid with a 'fair face' at a nunnery (Kolodiejchuk 2007, 127).

24. J.R.D. Tata's recollections of his later childhood suggest that this frenetic pace eventually calmed down: 'So every two years my family – not my father – led by my mother, used to change homes'. These words are quoted from a 1986 interview with M.V. Kamath in *Sands of Time*, the newsletter of the Tata Central Archive (Kamath 2004, 4). The interview spans issues 3.3 to 4.2, but is currently incomplete. A complete run of *Sands of Time* is available at http://www.tatacentralarchives.com/publications/newsletters/main.htm (accessed 11 November 2011).
25. 'C'est cette maudite galopade qui m'a forcé à retourner vers la France et vers la science, qui j'espère me remettront sur pieds et me rendront mes forces perdues' (Sooni Tata 1905a).
26. In a letter to her mother she stresses what she has to do for herself, after nursing her daughter through a bout of serious illness: 'I have to sleep like a log, I have to recover all the fat reserves that have disappeared, melted'. Tata Central Archives FP NO 97 SL 42 PG 01 ('il faut que [...] je dorme comme un loir, il faut que je rattrape tout ma graisse envolée, fondue!').
27. 'Nous causerions en mon français si cher et si beau, que je suis forcée d'abandonner un peu pour parler anglais, puisque malheureusement le français n'est pas compris de tous. Avec Ratan je ne puis parler le même langage qu'avec toi ma petite maman, je dois employer des mots justes et correctes [the wayward 'e' here is struck through], ne donnant pas une double entente'. Sooni Tata (1902c).
28. While this letter to his former teacher might have been looked over by his native-speaker wife, the contents and the errors written in his hand do suggest that R.D. Tata might have written this independently.
29. See Tata Central Archives, FB 100.
30. 'le goujerati de ma belle mère que je ne comprends pas, le français petit nègre d'une aya qui me tutoie et que je n'écoute pas et des chamailleries avec le reste des domestiques qui ne me comprennent pas' (Sooni Tata 1904d).

31. 'Moi qui ne suis ici ni chien ni chat, Française pour les Parsis, Parsi pour les Françaises je dois être d'une extrême prudence, lorsqu'on est le point de mire d'un peu tout le monde, le moindre fait… court, grandit, devient grand' (Sooni Tata 1904c).
32. 'C'est extraordinaire la facilité et la persévérance avec laquelle les Parsis apprennent les langues' (Sooni Tata 1904d).
33. 'Ma petite mère. Hier matin donc j'ai pendant une demie heure étudié le goujerati (c'est dur)' (Sooni Tata 1903b).
34. Sylla Tata, born 27 August 1903; Jehangir ('Jeh'), later known as J.R.D., born 29 July 1904; Rodabeh, born 24 August 1909; Darab, born 26 February 1912, and Jimmy/Jamshed, born 29 February 1916.
35. In a letter to her mother, Sooni notes with relief that her daughter who had been ill with malaria for a week, is better now. Tata Central Archives, FP NO 97 SL 42 PG 01.
36. 'un mélange de goujerati, d'hindi et d'anglais' (Sooni Tata 1906c).
37. 'Quand je pense que Sylla va avoir 4 ans! C'est une petite femme déjà et comme elle sera drôle et amusante quand nous la reverrons, et Jehangir cheri? 3 ans bientôt quel changement nous trouverons en lui, il saura parler comme un grand. Quand je songe à tout ce que je perds en ne les voyant pas, je suis prise d'une indicible mélancholie et je voudrais partir sur l'heure pour accourir vers vous, avec Ratan bien entendu' (Sooni Tata 1907a).
38. The children returned to India on a regular basis for Parsi ceremonies, such as the navjot (or induction) of Sylla and J.R.D. in Bombay in 1911, and the following reference from 1910 written for a governess by Sooni Tata in English certifies that the person in question 'was in charge of our children for four months to teach them Gujaratee. She performed her duties completely [underlined] to our satisfaction and we part from her as we have to leave Poona' (Tata Central Archives: FP NO 100 02 SOONI MAID 02 11 1910 PG 01).
39. A 1947 office skit at Tata headquarters paired each of the Tata directors with the title of a song. The song chosen for Darab Tata, R.D. and Sooni's Tata's second son, was 'The Last Time I Saw Paris'. See Nath, Vithalani and Vatsal (2004, 106).
40. Le Touquet was known before and after Sir John Whitley's time as Paris-Plage (Paris-by-the-sea).

41. See Laurent D'Aubreby, Rajendra Prasad Narla, Ian H. Magedera, Freny Schroff and Isis Vernier, *De Bombay à Hardelot: 50 ans de presence de la famille Tata*, exhibition catalogue, Hardelot: Office de Tourisme, 2011, p. 5.
42. Ibid., p. 5, 'la reine des plages et la plage des reines'.
43. In fact, though an integral part of France, it only became an official part of the communal structure of local government in 1954. The town's coat of arms is probably unique in France in including the British Union flag alongside the French tricolour. http://www.ville-neufchatel-hardelot.fr/Quelques-mots-d-histoire/Le-Blason-de-Neufchatel-Hardelot (accessed 18 May 2015).
44. Laurent D'Aubreby, Rajendra Prasad Narla, Ian H. Magedera, Freny Schroff, and Isis Vernier (2011, 11).
45. In Paris they lived at number 140 on the prestigious Avenue Victor Hugo, from where J.R.D's sister Rodabeh Tata wrote to her brother in 1921.
46. B.-J. Thobois, *Le Château d'Hardelot*, Paris: Le livre d'histoire-Lorisse, p. 240.
47. See Laurent D'Aubreby, Ian H. Magedera, Rajendra Prasad Narla, Freny Schroff and Isis Vernier, *De Bombay à Hardelot: 50 ans de presence de la famille Tata*, exhibition catalogue, Hardelot: Office de Tourisme, 2011, p.10.
48. Rajiv Gandhi's first choice of profession was as a commercial pilot for Air India; but aviation also exacted a tribute from two of the most flyer-friendly families of the women in this book: two of their sons, Jimmy (Jamshed) Tata and Sanjay Gandhi, died in flying accidents in private aeroplanes.
49. As quoted in the second epigraph, when the time came for J.R.D. to find his own spouse, it appears that he wanted to carry on the family tradition of multiple belonging which characterized his parents' lives: 'I was very Europeanized, I'd lived half in Europe, in Japan, India and France. I wanted to have a wife who would be as comfortable in India as elsewhere. I was waiting to find a girl who was like me, half and half, where there were foreign parents. My wife had an English mother and a Parsi father. Which was born in America and educated partly in Italy and spoke Italian' (Kamath 2005, 6).

50. Darab Tata worked in various capacities within the Tata Group. As reported in the *Tata Review* from 1965 (vol. 1, no. 2, p. 16), Rodabeh Tata 'took a personal interest' in a sympathetic new redesign of Taj Mahal Hotel. She is pictured in the sitting room of the Dutch Suite.
51. The issue of her family connections will be explored later.
52. B.J. Padshah (1864–1941) was director-in-charge of Tata Steel, 1907–24, leaving Tata in 1931. Padshah is an extremely interesting figure because as a young man he had an association with Theosophy and Madame Blavatsky.
53. Aparna Basu, 'Indian Higher Education: Colonialism and Beyond' in Philip G. Altbach and Viswanathan Selvaratnam (eds), *From Dependence to Autonomy: The Development of Asian Universities*, Dordrecht: Kluwer 1989, pp. 167–86. See also http://www.tatacentralarchives.com/history/biographies/05%20bjpadshah.htm (accessed 11 November 2011).
54. I am grateful to Rajendra Prasad Narla for bringing to my attention the B.J. Padshah/R.D. Tata correspondence.
55. J.R.D. Tata stresses the level of education of both his mother and his maternal grandmother, who was '[h]ighly educated [and] who really was responsible for the high standards of education of my mother' (Kamath 2004, 4).
56. A section of it can be consulted at www.tatacentralarchives.com/history/family_tree/family_tree.pdf (accessed 11 November 2011). A family genealogy prepared by A.T. Butler in 1928 has also been published (Nath, Vithalani and Vatsal 2004, 12–13).
57. Since the late 1970s, with the advent of cheaper international scheduled air travel (something that J.R.D. and Tata Group were instrumental in establishing in India) and a mobile global Indian diaspora, these forms of internationalisms are coalescing.
58. Sooni Tata's understanding of the situation of the Parsis had its limits, as it was based on the Tata family and their acquaintances and friends. Indeed, her sense of religious belonging was not shared by all sections of the Parsi community and, as the 1908 *Petit vs Jeejeebhoy* case (commonly known as the 'Parsi Panchayat case') indicates, recourse to the law was necessary to confirm that Sooni Tata, as a convert to the faith, should enjoy all the rights and privileges of those born into it (see [no author] 2005, i–vii, 1–195 and 265–71).

59. In a letter dated 4 March 1903, Sooni Tata asks her mother to send Gaston Stiegler's *Le Tour du monde en 63 jours*... (1901): 'Comme il doit aller en Chine... il voudrait avant lire les notes de Gaston Stiegler' (As he [R. D. Tata] has to go to China... he would like to read Gaston Stiegler's notes beforehand) (Sooni Tata 1903c). In contrast, Lady Navajbai Tata, the widow of Sir Ratan Tata, was a director on the board of Tata Sons from 1918 to her death in 1965 ([no author] 2008, 6).
60. Tata's human capital is the sum total of the actual and potential skills possessed by the Tata workforce and management. Sooni Tata's contribution is necessarily 'secondary' because she was not a direct employee of the firm.
61. A note on sources: Simone Tata provided written responses to the author's questions on 6 September 2011, indicated in the text as '2011a'. These were then followed up by three sets of answers to supplementary questions on 29 November 2011, 30 November 2011 and on 1 March 2012, which appear as '2011b', '2011c' and '2012a'.
62. In August 1953, under the provisions of the Air Corporations Act, the Union of Indian States also nationalized Air India by becoming a majority stakeholder in the company.
63. A similar case of positive reception is found, at the end of *Les Fous de l'Inde*, where Régis Airault describes the journey to India that he and his wife made when one of their children was very young. Their presence in India was taken up in an overwhelmingly positive manner by the Indians whom they met: 'Les douaniers nous avaient souhaité la bienvenue en embrassant notre fils, le bénissant pour ce premier séjour dans leur pays: "You trust India. You bring your baby."' (The customs officials welcomed us and kissed our child, blessing him for this first stay in their country: 'You trust India. You bring your baby') (Airault 2000, 206).
64. This remained the case over several decades as the 1971 advertisement for Kastela Hair Oil illustrates.
65. Here is a summary of the plot: India is British and Nilakantha, a priest, dreams of revenge. His daughter Lakmé meets Gerald, a British officer, by chance; he soon swears undying love, although he is engaged to the governor's daughter Ellen. Lakmé protects him from the wrath of her father and her servant Hadji helps him to escape. A fellow officer finds

them and tries to bring Gerald to his senses. Lakmé does not allow him to keep his promise to stay with her because she has swallowed the fatal datura flower. The librettists were inspired by the novel *Le Mariage de Loti* or *Rarahu,* whose author, Pierre Loti, was a French naval officer. Plot summaries of other French operas set in India can be found in Granger et al. (2003, 110–12).

66. In the 1970s, however, it has appeared both in an internationalized form without any accent and also in an idiosyncratic artistic form with the incorrect accent. One of those adverts is reproduced at the head of this chapter; in it the name is written with a circumflex accent pointing not upwards, but to the right. Images which illustrate this can be found at Tata Central Archives. I am grateful to Rajendra Prasad Narla for introducing me to these images. This variability suggests that, though it is clearly present in terms of marketing strategy, Tata Group did not want to stress the French dimension of its cosmetics brand name in an overpowering way, for fear of alienating any of its traditional customers.
67. See Nath, Vithalani and Vatsal (2004, 184).
68. Robert Piguet, a Swiss-born couturier and perfumer closed his fashion house in 1951; he died in 1953. His 1952 tie-up with TOMCO was probably intended to reap cash value from his brand, which is still active today. See http://www.robertpiguetparfums.com/profile.php (accessed 11 November 2011). Renoir perfumes produced products between 1939 and 1959 ([no author] 1968a, 24).
69. *Tata Monthly Bulletin*, vol. 8, nos 11 and 12, p. 109.
70. Her husband was TOMCO's director-in-charge in 1966, having been director-in-charge of the Indian Hotels Company in 1965.
71. This first marriage had ended in divorce in 1945 (Piramal 1996, 370).
72. The only photos to have had significant public exposure appear in Nath, Vithalani and Vatsal (2004, 197, 205, 241, 338 and 343).
73. 'His full name is Noel Nusserwanji Tata, though he is known as Noel only. Noel was the name of Simone Tata's favourite uncle and Nusserwanji was the name of J.N. "Jamsetji" Tata's father' (Simone Tata 2011a).
74. Simone Tata: 'While developing Lakmé, I knew that without an array of products to answer the needs of all women, we would remain marginal' (Pandit 2008, 32).
75. 'Apsaras' are female spirits of the clouds or waters and 'Nirvan' means

salvation; it was the name of a TOMCO-produced perfume and eau de cologne from the period between 1943 and 1948, so before Lakmé was founded.

76. This is confirmed by the S.H. Benson advertising, which refers to '8 complexion-toned shades to suit your skin'.
77. See Simone Tata (2005). The sales figures are recorded in an article entitled 'The Tata Oil Mills Company, a Saga of Perseverance' in *Tata Review*, vol. 2, no 1 (June to September 1966), 15–16 and 21, p. 21.
78. *Tata Review* ([no author] 1966, 21).
79. It is interesting to note that, just as Lakmé was courted by 'several multinationals', Carita, one of the French companies from which Simone Tata drew her early expertise, passed into the Japanese ownership of Shiseido in 1986.
80. Westside is one of the leading clothing, household and lifestyle retailers in India, with forty-nine stores across the country each with between 15,000 and 30,000 square feet of sales space.
81. The western parts of many but not all cities in Western Europe have been considered the more exclusive, particularly since the advent of heavy industry in the nineteenth century. This is because the prevailing winds blew pollution from west to east. This polarization is intensified in London because the docks are located on the eastern (seaward) side of the city and also because the river flows from west to east.
82. Valet parking features prominently in an article by Roshni Jayakar (2002) on Noel Tata and Westside.
83. This is attested to by public recognition, including the New Delhi Institute of Economic Studies Udyog Rattan Award 1988, the IFA (Images Fashion Awards) Visionary of the Year Award 2003, Bombay Management Association's Special Recognition Award 2003, Indore Management Association's Lifetime Achievement Award 2005, and the Amity Woman Achiever Award 2010.
84. http://www.guardian.co.uk/business/2008/mar/28/automotive.mergersandacquisitions (accessed 11 November 2011).
85. In a modern manifestation of the desirability for Indians of non-British Europeanness, it should be noted that Cyrus's father, Pallonji Mistry, became an Irish citizen in 2003. One of the reasons this was possible was because his wife, Pat Perrin Dubash, was born in Ireland. Naturally, as her son, the current Tata Group chairman also has Irish nationality.

86. See Mariko Oi, 'Adult Adoptions: Keeping Japan's Family Firms Alive.' http://www.bbc.co.uk/news/magazine-19505088 (accessed 20 September 2012).
87. Reeba Zachariah and Partha Sinha, 'Tatas back in Beauty Biz 18 yrs after Lakme Exit', *Times of India* (Kolkata Edition), *Times Business*, p. 23.
88 Simone Tata, Interview with Ian Magedera, 25 January 2016.

STATE AND NATIONAL POLITICS: PRINCESS DURRU SHEHVAR; PRINCESS NILOUFER

She [Durru Shehvar] was always essentially and indefinably royal, and it seems to me that if fate had so willed she might have been one of the great queens of the world. She would have been as imperious as Elizabeth of England.

– Sir Walter Monckton, as reported by his biographer Lord Birkenhead in 1969

But by wanting the best education and training [for her son], Durru Shehvar had also estranged Jah from his Indian roots ... She had done the state a great service through her relief work during the war and her patronage of hospitals, educational institutions and welfare bodies, but even now many Hyderabadis feel that she looked down on them.

– John Zubrzycki, 2006

She [Durru Shehvar] had the honour of being the first royal lady from the Nizam's family to attend a public function when she presented a silver cup to the winning team of a public garden tennis tournament in 1933.

The Hindu, 2006

In April 1932, an unnamed staff writer on the *Asiatic Review* gave the following lavish account of a Hyderabadi homecoming of two newly-wed couples:

> From early dawn on the long-expected day every street in the great city of Hyderabad in the Deccan, every road that leads to it from the many suburbs and adjoining villages, was thronged with people going all in one direction – towards the railway station at Nampalli. There were other railway stations in the city, which is vast and populous and which of later years had become quite up to date in its convenience, but this was the terminus at which travellers arrive from Bombay, and Bombay is the port at which travellers arrive from Europe. Everybody in the city, from the Ruler downward, had long been expecting the return of certain travellers from Europe with a longing which those who know the tie which bind the Ruler to his people in an Indian State will understand. The heir apparent and his brother, who had been for more than half a year in Europe, were to return that day. To increase the popular excitement they had lately married and were bringing back their brides with them. The bride of the Crown Prince was the only daughter of the Khalifa of the Muslims, a princess of the House of Osman, her name was 'Royal Pearl' [Durru Shehvar], while the bride of the other prince was a descendant of the same great family, and her name was 'Water Lily' [Niloufer]. ([no author] 1932, 330)

This account mentioning 'Royal Pearl' and 'Water Lily' sounds like a fairy story, but there were two real women behind the airy English translations of their names. Durru Shehvar was born in 1914 in the Çamlica (Chamlidcha) Palace in the Üsküdar district of Istanbul and died in London in 2006.[1] She spent her formative years in Geneva, Paris and Nice from 1924 to 1932 and lived in India from 1932 to 1948, before settling in London for the rest of her life.[2] Princess Niloufer was born in 1916 at the Göztepe Palace in Istanbul and died in Paris in 1989. She had a principal residence and matrimonial ties to India from 1932 to 1952. Both women display the non-British status of Indian *videshinis*, but their defining origins in an Ottoman royal house in European exile mean that tagging them with a single nationality is difficult. As a whole, their lives spent in West Asia, India and Europe demonstrate a to and fro mobility at the crossroads of Europe and Asia (with the majority of their lives lived in Europe, first as exiles and then by choice). From the point of view of the Hyderabadi crowds who came out to see them, there was certainly a non-British 'different difference' evident in the curiosity about these new princesses. And what of their influence in India? Durru Shehvar in particular had significance in emboldening elite women in Hyderabad to organize themselves for the good of their state and to understand how that state could contribute in the 1930s and 1940s to the wider project of Indian freedom. Both Durru Shehvar and Niloufer endowed major hospitals which are still treating Hyderabadis today.

The second noteworthy feature of the *Asiatic Review* article is the complimentary references to the modernity of Hyderabad, 'which of later years had become quite up to date'. There is no colonial disdain evident in this account, rather an apparently genuine enthusiasm for the spectacle: 'everybody in the city [...] had long been expecting the return [...] with a longing which those who know the ties which bind the Ruler to his people in an Indian state will understand'. We will find this favourable disposition towards Hyderabad and its ruler the Nizam again and again in British accounts – an enormous princely state, approximately the same size as the British Isles, which had sat in the middle of the Deccan since Aurangzeb's death in 1707. What was the reason for this? The familiarity, or even benevolent affection, in the tone of this and many other accounts originates in a pact between the Nizam and the British Crown, in which Hyderabad had officially been Britain's 'most faithful ally' since the rebellion of 1857, when the Nizamate took the British side. Deep-seated political ties bound the parties to this alliance, demonstrating the cold, hard politics behind the fairy-tale return of the princesses 'Royal Pearl' and 'Water Lily' into the kingdom of Hyderabad.

The 1930s dream of a Caliphate: The geopolitical context of the double marriage and its objectification of Durru Shehvar and Niloufer

As the *Asiatic Review* article states, the double wedding – between the elder son Azam Jah and Durru Shehvar, and between his younger brother Moazam Jah and Niloufer – had taken place in Europe; to be precise, it was celebrated in Nice on the French Riviera, on 20 December 1931.[3] Durru Shehvar and Niloufer were cousins. Before turning to Durru Shehvar's individual actions, we must first consider the political implications of the proposed unions. These implications operate at a regional level in India as the princesses married into the royal family of Hyderabad, one of the largest and richest Indian states before Independence ([no author] 1948, 11), occupying a strategic position in the centre of the Deccan peninsula. The princesses' Ottoman origins, however, also invoke a global geopolitical level from the end of the First World War, the end of the Ottoman Empire, the exile of its spiritual power, the Caliph (Abdul Mejid Effendi II was Durru Shehvar's father and related to Niloufer), in 1924.[4] Furthermore, as *The Times* reported, the marriage was a unique event in the culture and history of statecraft in Hyderabad and other Indian princely states:

> Since the British connexion with India [that is since the start of British colonialism], no Indian ruling family has intermarried with the royal house of a foreign country and the present exception is the more striking in that it has always been the rigid rule in the Dynasty of Hyderabad, unlike the House of Othman, to confine its marriage alliances to a narrow circle of immediate kinship. ([no author] 1931c)

The double marriage, therefore, was an eminently political alliance, in conception as well as execution, because it entailed the 'union of two great dynasties' (Venkateshwarlu 2006, 11). As a double marriage, it was also intended to demonstrate the strength of the intended ties. The bridegrooms were the sons of Osman Ali Khan, the seventh Nizam (1886–1967) and the brides were Durru Shehvar and Niloufer, the daughter and the niece of Abdul Mejid Effendi (1868–1944), the former Caliph, who, though in exile and deposed, was last in the line of Ottoman Caliphs who went back to 1517.

The gently nostalgic title of K. Venkateshwarlu's 2006 article in *The Hindu* celebrating Durru Shehvar's life is 'When Marriage Brought Continents Closer'; these words, referring to Europe and Asia, belie the significant strategic considerations which lay behind the alliance between Hyderabad and the house of the last Caliph. The key contextualizing element in this prehistory predates the 1931 marriage by nearly two decades. The Ottoman Empire had fought on the side of the Central Powers alliance (including the German and Austro-Hungarian Empires and the Kingdom of Bulgaria) that was defeated in the First World War. This meant that the Ottoman Empire, which first emerged in the thirteenth century, was under threat after the end of the First World War.[5] The Treaty of Versailles of 1919 initially only reduced the territorial extent of the Ottoman Empire, while preserving the status of the Caliph as spiritual ruler of the world's Sunni Muslims.

The Treaty of Sèvres of 1920 was the de facto peace agreement between the Ottoman Empire and the Allies. The terms of this treaty saw constituent regions of the Ottoman Empire, such as Syria and Lebanon, as well as Mesopotamia and Palestine, become the protectorates of Allied countries such as France and Britain. Resistance to this state of affairs and to the terms of the Treaty of Sèvres came from two different quarters and for two different reasons. A Turkish nationalist movement under the leadership of Mustafa Kemal rejected the terms of the treaty, wanting to decouple spiritual and political authority. Mustafa Kemal's forces were victorious and thus, before it was ratified, the Treaty of Sèvres was rejected and superseded by the Treaty of Lausanne of 1923. The second oppositional grouping was the Khilafat movement (which aimed to preserve the dignity of the exiled Caliph); its real politik objectives in the ruins of the Ottoman Empire were less clear. Of far greater geopolitical significance was the transnational manner in which they asserted themselves as the 'faithful of the Caliph' – this was a reciprocal claim echoing the spiritual leader's formal title 'Caliph of the Faithful'.

It is in 1923 that the European and Asian strands of this story begin to intertwine. Mustafa Kemal wanted to go further than simply decoupling political and religious authority. He campaigned for the abolition of the Caliphate and the exile of Durru Shehvar's father, Abdul Mejid Effendi. Indeed, Omar Khalidi suggests that the involvement of an international dimension via Indian Muslims came to precipitate the end of the Caliphate. Mustafa Kemal used a letter sent on 24 November 1923 by

> the Aga Khan and Sayyid Amir Ali, a renowned scholar, [who] wrote to the Grand National Assembly voicing their concerns. They were expressing the deep commitment of Indian Muslims – the largest body of Muslims in the world – to the caliphate as an institution. But their letter gave Mustafa Kemal a pretext to denounce the move as foreign intervention. The Caliph had been in office barely four months when the caliphate was abolished by the assembly on 3 March 1924. (Khalidi 2004, 35)

The former Caliph and his immediate family, including Durru Shehvar, were forced into exile. Theirs was an exile to Western Europe. The family lived first in Geneva, in somewhat straitened circumstances; they then moved to Paris and finally to Nice. Their relocation to southern France was made possible by the Nizam, who supported the Abdul Mejid Effendi family to the tune of £4,000 per year. By his own admission, the former 'Caliph of the Faithful' lived in Nice, 'apart from the worldly vanities' ([no author] 2004, 24).

The first substantive contacts between the Sultans and South Asia with a view to supporting the Caliphate had occurred in the late nineteenth century with the embassy of Jamaluddin Afghani sent to India by Abdul Hamid II. The year 1919 saw the establishment of the Khilafat movement in India. Its ambitious aims were to turn the clock back and 'preserve the boundaries of the Ottoman Empire as they had been in 1914, and to preserve intact the spiritual and temporal authority of the Ottoman sultan as caliph of Islam' (Minault 1982, 1). As might be expected, the focus of the movement was not only outside India's borders. As Gail Minault has argued, it had an important self-affirmatory quality and

> it can be viewed as a quest for 'pan-Indian Islam'. A united, pan-Indian Muslim constituency, if it could in fact be mobilized, would in turn permit genuine Muslim participation in the Indian nationalist movement. This seeming paradox can be explained in the reasoning of the Khilafat leaders: Muslims in India, if united, could offset their minority status by their ability

> to bargain from a position of strength, whether with the British government or with the Hindus in the Indian National Congress. (ibid., 2–3)

The annulment of the Treaty of Sèvres (1920) and its superseding by the Treaty of Lausanne (1923) was a significant event; it confirmed the passing of de facto authority in the region from the Ottoman Empire to the Turkish Republic under Mustafa Kemal. Furthermore, the exile of the former caliph in 1924 brought to an end the European raison d'être of the Khilafat movement. Despite this, however, the marriages in 1931 of Azam Jah and Durru Shehvar, and Moazam Jah and Niloufer, can be seen as a rearguard action by the leaders of the movement to promote its aim of maintaining the Caliphate. It was probably thought that the flame of the Caliphate might be kept alive better in Hyderabad State in India rather than in the former Ottoman lands in the Middle East.

A crucial agent in this old-fashioned attempt at alliance building was the Indian activist Maulana Shaukat Ali (1873–1938), elder brother of the founder of the movement, Maulana Mohammed Ali Jouhar (1878–1931). He knew that the male offspring of Abdul Mejid Effendi's daughter would have the legitimate claim to be the Caliph, in the event that his son Şehzade Ömer Faruk Effendior, his male offspring, did not accede. But King Faud I of Egypt, King Faisal of Iraq and Reza Shah Pahlavi, the Shah of Persia, had also realized this and were actively interested in the hand of Princess Durru Shehvar, who was seventeen in 1931. This alliance was then emphasized by offering not one, but two women from the family to marry into the Hyderabadi Nizamate.

Depictions of the women from this period onwards objectify them, portraying them only in terms of their physical attributes and, at best, via their skills. In effect, Walter Monckton's enthusiastic comments about the elder princess having something 'essentially and indefinably royal' belong to this same type of pen portrait (Birkenhead 1969, 111). According to Lucien Bénichou, Shaukat Ali is said to have adjudged Durru Shehvar to be 'attractive and well-educated' (Bénichou 2000, 48).

The British Resident in Hyderabad, T.H. Keyes, was actively involved in all aspects of the government of the state. This included giving advice on the upbringing of the princes and who they were to marry. Keyes' comments about Durru Shehvar, made in a confidential correspondence sent to London, are in the same vein as those of Monckton and Ali, though they are more expansive. He reports that Durru Shehvar is

> extraordinarily well-educated and has excellent style in English and French. Her contributions to French magazines show real poetic feeling, and I believe that the verses she has written in Turkish show remarkable talent. She intended, before her marriage was arranged, to adopt the profession of letters, and had begun to write in three languages … She is beautiful, has great dignity and *savoir faire* and a very strong character. (Keyes 1932, 1)

At one level, the depiction of the young woman in these summary terms is quite understandable, as it is a case of making a quick assessment rather than concentrating on detail. Keyes also produced the following hopeful portrait of Crown Prince Azam Jah, suggesting that he would be more temperate and less true to the British view of the oriental despot:

> Azam Jah is of a very kindly disposition, and, while weak, has excellent intentions. He is devoted to his wife, and though he is of course quite incapable of appreciating her literary and musical tastes, I have little fear that they will fail to make a success of it. (Keyes 1932, 2)

The marriage would last sixteen years. However, as time went by, and as the princess's public roles in Hyderabad increased, one would expect the portrayals of Durru Shehvar to become more detailed and to move from surface representation to a sense of how she expressed herself. The most important element of such a representation would be direct quotation, conveying a sense of the woman in her own words. But this never happened: verbatim quotation is extremely rare in representations of Princess Durru Shehvar and Princess Niloufer. What we do have is reported speech and, later, photographic portraits by first-rank practitioners, such as Cecil Beaton, Boris Lipnitzki and Jack Birns.[6] The unattributed form, such as in the expression 'sources close to Buckingham Palace indicate that…', is associated with monarchs even today; the near total absence of actual words reliably attributable to Durru Shehvar tells us a great deal about the stark limitations on the public actions of elite women in Hyderabad in the 1930s and 1940s. The starting point was that they should remain at home, but if they ventured out the assumption was that, like stereotypical Victorian children, they should be seen but not heard.

The marriage in 1931 had a very important political dimension. Hyderabad resembled a throwback to Mughal times, with a Muslim monarch and nobility ruling over a Hindu-majority population in the ratio of approximately one to eight. When the time of the wedding came, tradition meant that the ruling seventh Nizam could not leave Hyderabad to attend the ceremony; the main Hyderabadi witnesses to the wedding on 14 November 1931 also served as part of the negotiating team led by the Aga Khan at the second Round Table Conference in London, which took place from September to December 1931 and which discussed constitutional reform in India. These witnesses included Shaukat Ali, instrumental in the early stages of the arrangement, and Sir Akbar Hydari (1869–1941), who as finance minister was the personal representative of the Nizam and had led the Hyderabad delegation at the first Round Table Conference a year earlier.[7] He would become more prominent in Hyderabadi political circles, serving as prime minister of Hyderabad from 1937 until his death in 1941. Furthermore, as is shown by his negotiations with Mirra Alfassa about transplanting the Sri Aurobindo Ashram to Hyderabad, Hydari was attuned to the prestige of international alliances which were not channelled through the British. His wife, Lady Hydari, was also at the centre of liberal influence in the state during the period when her husband was prime minister. She founded an elite women-only social club in her own name, of which Durru Shehvar was a patron.[8] In her address to the 1937 Hyderabad State Women's Conference, Durru Shehvar pays public tribute to the politician's wife: 'Lady Hydari, one of the earliest pioneers of enlightenment amongst the women of Hyderabad' (Durru Shehvar 1937, 1).

The day of the marriage was pronounced a public holiday in Hyderabad and when the couples returned home in 1932, the

Nizam is said to have broken the protocol and gone to the station to meet and greet his new daughters-in-law with pecks on the cheek. British documents on the run-up to the resettlement of the Ottoman princesses traced by John Zubrzycki indicate that the fairy-tale homecoming reported in the *Asiatic Review* was not the whole story. First, according to an unnamed British official, a factor militating against the marriage from the start was the princes' mother, Dulhan Pasha, who feared that an exogamous marriage would mean her losing whatever small influence she had over her sons ([no author] 1931a, 11). Although the Nizam referred to his elder daughter-in-law Durru Shehvar as *nagina* (the gem) in public in the early years of her marriage, the absolute ruler also feared increased Ottoman influence in Hyderabad. Moreover, giving the princess too many privileges would, according to the Nizam, allow her to 'maintain a large alien establishment, [would] jeopardise her relations with her husband and upset seriously the tenor of Hyderabad society'.[9] It was as a result of this royal plan to severely curtail the freedoms and comfort of the princesses, that Keyes had to intervene to ensure that their accommodation was closer to that which they had enjoyed in Nice with Durru Shehvar's father (at the Nizam's expense, let it be remembered), rather than 'the two miserable little *zenana* cottages' that the Nizam initially planned for them (Keyes 1932, 1). Accordingly, both couples eventually settled in the Bella Vista Palace, an imposing European-style residence in the Saifabad district of the city which, when it was built, had a view of the Hussain Sagar Lake.

The union was politically useful for both Britain and Hyderabad State. As the colonial power, Britain attempted to use the alliance to promote Hyderabad as a powerful counterweight to the pan-Indian consensus. Ever since 1857, when Hyderabad fought on the side of the British, the two parties had cultivated a mutually beneficial alliance cemented by the Nizam's cash and British titles. For instance, the Nizam made a contribution of $100,000,000 to the war effort during the First World War, as well as providing supplies for the Hyderabadi regiments posted in Europe ([no author] 1937, 4).[10] In return, Britain styled Salar Jung, the sixth Nizam, and his descendants, 'most faithful allies' of the Crown, and gave the seventh

Nizam an honorary knighthood.[11] The order of precedence placed the Nizam in first position among Indian nobles, with the right to a twenty-one-gun salute – the only one of the Indian princes to have this. Britain's approval is clear from the reporting of the marriage in English-language media, including publications based in the United States. In 1937, *Time* magazine thus reported on the seventh Nizam, Durru Shehvar's father-in-law: 'Some Indian sovereigns are lecherous, champagne-quaffing wastrels with a taste for French women [sic] and English horses which they spectacularly gratify from Monte-Carlo to Epsom Downs and Hollywood, but decidedly the Nizam is different' (ibid.).[12] Although, in private, officials despaired at the Nizam's character, which paired extreme miserliness with greed, public reporting stressed only his modest lack of ostentation and his desire to better his kingdom through public works. It should be noted that, quite apart from the actual civil liberties (or the lack of them) under the seventh Nizam in Hyderabad, the notion of the enlightened Muslim monarch is in representational terms as much a stereotype as its opposite, the oriental despot. Both representations are propagated by imputation, depending on the viewpoint of the Western commentator.

1932 to 1937 The Ottoman princesses begin to assert their independence in Hyderabad

One of the Nizam's many stipulations about the marriage was that the princesses and their husbands should not be allowed to leave Hyderabad for Nice 'every hot weather'.[13] In the event, though Durru Shehvar was held to this, she imposed her will regarding travel to France as she neared the end of her first pregnancy. This too was an affair of the state, as she was carrying the heir to both the Asaf Jahi dynasty and the Caliphate. It was clear for her which had precedence. In the case of her offspring, the key issue, in addition to safeguarding her own health and that of the unborn child, was to capitalize on the religious inheritance of the future baby's Ottoman grandfather. Therefore, Durru Shehvar returned to Nice to give birth.

Her first son, Mukarram Jah, was born in 1933 and her second son Mufakham Jah in 1936. Although Durru Shehvar chose Europe over India for medical and political reasons, both she and her cousin Princess Niloufer were actively involved in improving the obstetrics facilities in the state and then (finally realized after 1948 in bricks and mortar) in the city of Hyderabad. This activity was significant for the internal politics of the country. This is because it attempts to quell resentment among the Hyderabadi population, who might have considered it unfair that a 'foreign-born' princess went abroad to give birth when Hyderabadis had to make do with far more limited resources at home. The first concrete gesture came from Princess Niloufer, who lobbied her father-in-law to establish a hospital for women and children. The process started in April 1949, with the hospital opening after benefitting from a personal donation of funds from her 1952 divorce settlement. The hospital, located in Red Hills, Hyderabad, is named Niloufer Hospital for Women and Children.[14] The second foundation, the Princess Durru Shehvar Children's and General Hospital in Purani Haveli, dates from 1989. The hospital grew from the Medical Aid Society of the same name, of which the princess was a patron when she resided in Hyderabad in the 1930s and 1940s. Her second son, Mufakham Jah, appears to have played an active role in the founding of the hospital.

Ever since their marriages and very public arrival in Hyderabad in 1932, Durru Shehvar especially appears to have maintained a prominent public ceremonial role. This is clear from the final epigraphic quotation about her presenting the trophy at a public garden tennis tournament in 1933, which stresses the way in which she established the visibility of female members of the royal family in public life. However, the event, a garden tennis tournament in the pre-television era, was definitely patronized by the local elite and not by the local masses. It is not clear if the tournament was a mixed affair in gender terms, but the tradition in domestic and public life was a segregation of the sexes.

These small victories in public visibility continued, and appearing outside the palace not only anchored Durru Shehvar in the public imagination, it was also a form of permissible royal work. For example, in 1937, she opened the new terminal building at Begumpet Airport, one of the first, if not the first woman to open an airport in India.

Being able to perform these public ceremonial duties was a testament to her own influence there and to the public persona that she was carving out for herself.

1937 to 1942 Princess Durru Shehvar's commitment to Hyderabadi women's organizations

Looking at the range of fields of female activity that are catalogued in a bibliography such as Tahera Aftab's *Inscribing South Asian Muslim Women*, it is noteworthy how limited the material is on Hyderabadi women (Aftab 2008, 209). There are only a few pages of publications, compared with tens of pages for other locations such as Lahore. The material that exists is determined by the social conservatism operative in Hyderabadi society at that time. Durru Shehvar, however, was able to secure personal victories against the status quo when she not only performed silent or quasi-silent ceremonial duties, but on occasions spoke at length on her own account.

In 1937, Durru Shehvar addressed the 11th session of the Hyderabad State Women's Association Conference (Anjuman-e-Khawateen) as president.[15] This organization was restricted to women and was probably deliberately parochial in scope. It was a Hyderabadi organization for Hyderabadi women (people from that state only began to integrate themselves into national structures after 1948). This limitation raises the issue about whether we are also dealing with an organization for only Muslim women, but it is clear from her 1937 address (analysed below) that this was not the case. This indicates that female activism in Hyderabad was in its very early stages and that the social and religious conservatism of that particular time and place were the determining factors. It is a measure of Durru Shehvar's courage that she was willing to take a stand under these circumstances and, as we shall see, she was prepared to broaden the horizons of the women she addressed by implementing initiatives similar to Swadeshi and Khadi (the self-sufficiency and home-spinning movements) that were already active at a national level.

That said, it is important not to overplay Princess Durru Shehvar's role and suggest that she was the originator of the women's rights movement in Hyderabad. This would be to ignore the importance of figures such as Mohib Hussain. Forty years before Durru Shehvar and Niloufer arrived in India, and in a similar manner to Sister Nivedita's historically grounded educational activism, Hussain 'edited three journals and carried on a campaign for social and educational reforms amongst women. He was also an opponent of the purdah system. This created a furore amongst the orthodox Muslims and the government stepped in to close one of the journals dealing with the problems of women' (Luther 2006, 182). Durru Shehvar's importance and her effectiveness stemmed from the fact that she was a modernizer who came from the innermost circle of the establishment, and because she was attempting to modernize at a crucial time when the national liberation movement in India at large had begun a process of political transition. She is one of the few examples of social liberalism in the rather atrophied upper echelons of Hyderabadi society.

Let us now examine the only surviving verbatim record of a political intervention by Durru Shehvar.[16] It is Resolution XII of the 1937 Hyderabad State Women's Conference. This was an address, delivered in the Hyderabad Town Hall, in support of a particular motion: 'This Conference appeals to every Hyderabadi to fulfil loyally the behest of our Gracious Sovereign and encourage the development of Cottage Industries by an extensive use of local products' (Durru Shehvar 1937, 1). It is remarkable how many bases Durru Shehvar touched with her exhortation. She demonstrates the sure-footedness of a good politician by subsuming anything that she has to say under a pre-existing proclamation by the absolute ruler of Hyderabad. Once again, as in the case of the 'Caliph of the Faithful' and Britain's 'most faithful ally', we see a word such as 'loyally', which appeals to tradition (ibid., 1).

The focus here on local products cannot but benefit Hyderabad as a princely state, but these ideas of self-sufficiency have a pedigree. In an Indian context they make their first appearance (with specific reference to textiles) in connection with the Khadi Movement propounded by M.K. Gandhi in the 1920s and before that, in relation to anti-colonial Indian self-reliance, in the Swadeshi Movement sponsored by Aurobindo Ghose (later Sri Aurobindo), among others. Although, as we shall see, textiles are specifically mentioned by name, Durru Shehvar does not evoke either Sri Aurobindo or M.K. Gandhi. Wherever these ideas came from, she wants to apply them to a very specific Hyderabadi context; therefore the Nizam himself should be the first reference.

Once this nod in the direction of pan-Indian movements has been made, demonstrating common ground between Hyderabad and the rest of the country, Durru Shehvar, however, clearly wants to spur her female audience to action rather than confine herself to worthy principles. This is reiterated in the rhetorical structures of her address: 'The trend of modern life has shifted its focus from tradition to reasoned action, from vague and pious impulse to organized endeavour' (Durru Shehvar 1937, 1–2). The proponents of Swadeshi and Khadi used their movements for the purposes of national self-affirmation. Durru Shehvar gives her particular form of pragmatism not a nationalist, but a clear gender-based twist:

> [O]ur awakening marks the point of transition from a position of subordination to a desire for independence. It has always been my earnest prayer, that no woman should bend her head for the sake of a little support for herself and her children and that she should be able to maintain the pride and dignity of her womanhood, by the skill and labour of her hands. (ibid., 2)

The point of view from which these words are spoken will presently be discussed in detail, but the important thing to note at this point is that the women who were actually making the products are referred to in the third person here. Durru Shehvar's common position with the women of Hyderabad, therefore, is not as inclusive as the first person plural of Sister Nivedita, which her Calcuttan acquaintances, such as Mrs J.C. Bose, found so remarkable. This further indicates that Hyderabadi society was more stratified than that of Calcutta and that Durru Shehvar's mobilization of different social groups would be a challenge.

As she continues her address, the princess does acknowledge a context for these ideas that is wider than Hyderabad alone:

> Indian women all over are anxious to offer convincing tokens of their readiness and capacity to make their contribution towards national life; we in Hyderabad are no less eager to play our part right and prove by our actions not merely by our intentions that we are able to fulfil the duties and functions of complete citizenship and therefore entitled to demand it. (Durru Shehvar 1937, 2)

Calling her audience 'Indian women' is as nationalistic as Durru Shehvar allows herself to become. The stress on Hyderabad prevents her from spelling things out. However, as she continues, the social position of her audience and the particular task she wants them to perform become ever clearer:

> One of the most beneficent and far-reaching ways of serving the state, which is within the means of every woman whether she be poor or rich, whether she follow the old tradition or belong to the new school, is by the encouragement of local industries. This can unite all of us into the sisterhood of a common aim and ideal without any discrimination of rank, community, class, creed or wealth. (Durru Shehvar 1937, 2)

There is a shift in this section from nation back to state, from India to Hyderabad. She appears to be tacitly recognizing the diversity of her audience in both confessional and caste terms; but the key point she is proposing is that all the women in front of her can perform a positive political act through consumer choice. As she puts it towards the end of her address: 'Every yard of home-made cloth that we buy, and every coin that we spend on the products of our own villages are the concrete symbols of food and shelter for the poor' (ibid., 5).

Here, Durru Shehvar finally lays her cards on the table and reveals herself and her audience as consuming patrons who are the sort of elite women who can provide relief for the poor through targeted purchases. It should also be noted that her address has a physical form, which puts both its inclusivity and pragmatism into practice. The document is bilingual, with the Urdu text starting on the back cover; read from right to left, it finishes on the right-hand centre page of the pamphlet. In addition to this, a colophon declares: 'Printed on hand-made paper'. No one could say, therefore, that the princess did not practise what she preached. There is integrity here and it seems she wanted to unite the diversity of her elite audience. It is clear that Durru Shehvar understood that female liberation could start with those women who were in a materially secure position to reflect on what they could do for others. In Durru Shehvar's text one has the sense of her building a common project, but she was not able to have a lasting concrete influence on achieving gender equality in Hyderabadi society, because the collapse of the state deprived her of her position and the context in which to effect change.

At the same time as Durru Shehvar was attempting to change Hyderabadi society, she was also taking active steps to integrate herself into it. As with the other Indian *videshinis* in this book, language was a key theatre of their integration into India. It has been possible to collect unpublished eyewitness testimony about Durru Shehvar's learning of the languages spoken at the Nizam's court.[17] With the possible exceptions of Annie Besant's knowledge of Sanskrit and Sister Nivedita's good command of Bengali, Durru Shehvar is the subject in this book who achieved the greatest degree of fluency in a South Asian language.[18] The offspring of the Urdu instructor who accompanied her on official visits around India confirms that she acquired a competence in '"Taksaani zabaan", or the Urdu spoken by merchants and jewellers in the Gold Bullion market of Delhi. This language was the more colloquial Urdu' (Shanaz 2012) in which the interlocutor is addressed via the first person singular. The wife of the Crown Prince, however, could do better: Professor Agha Hyder Hassan Mirza also taught her the more 'exclusive "Begumati zabaan", the Urdu spoken in the royal quarters of the Red Fort of Delhi and by the Mughal royal family. With this language, Durru Shehvar was taught to use the "royal plural", or "royal we" manner of speech' (ibid.). In an early audience with the Nizam, Durru Shehvar was not only able to demonstrate that she could command the highest linguistic register, but also that she could show an appropriate degree of subservience:

> During this meeting Princess Durru Shehvar did not, however, use the 'royal we' while addressing the Nizam. She used the humble Taksaani form of

> the commoner, addressing the Nizam as Allah Hazrath, and saying that his humble *bandi*, or 'slave', stood before him. (Ibid.)

It is almost certain that after a few years Durru Shehvar would also have been familiar with the colloquial 'Deccani Urdu', which was the lingua franca of the ruling elite in Hyderabad (ibid.).

Despite her efforts to acquire the tools for her integration into Hyderabadi society in public, her relationship with her husband Prince Azam Jah became ever more estranged. There might have been many reasons for this of course, with some of them attributable to Durru Shehvar.[19] He was vice-president of the Hyderabad Executive Council from 1932 to 1949; this post was the full extent of his political existence, otherwise he seems to have been a military man. From 1933 to 1948, he was commander-in-chief of Hyderabad State Forces (and was promoted to the rank of general in 1936). He was colonel-in-chief of the Nizam's own Hyderabad Lancers and an honorary major attached to the 7th Light Cavalry. His service medals include the Tunis Victory (1942), British Defence (1945), British War (1945), and Hyderabad War (1945). The only honour that might give an indication about his personal preferences is his patronage of the Hyderabad Kennel Club.

So while Durru Shehvar was patron of the Lady Hyder Ali Club, her husband went to the dogs, as it were. Apart from the documents quoted above, there appear to be no further surviving records of either Azam Jah or his younger brother Prince Moazam having dealings with the British. There must, however, have been some interaction at an official level because as we have seen the elder son was vice-president of the Executive Council and the younger son was the chairman of the City of Hyderabad Improvement Board (1932–1949); however, the nature of these contacts does not seem to have been personal. This is very different in the case of his wife. Before these contacts are explored, it should not be forgotten that the British were all things to all men in Hyderabad. To the Nizam they were constitutional advisors and the de facto guarantors of the sovereignty of the Nizamate. He had no reason to distrust them, but they were unable to keep the state independent. To Durru Shehvar they must have been discreet supporters of her drive for modernity in the princely state, particularly insofar as this related to the status of women. Them probably reasoned that this project would give the intelligent Durru Shehvar an aim in life and that she would be grateful to them for their support. Just as the Nizam had been advised about using his resources for enlightened projects in the domains of transport and energy infrastructure, the wife of the heir to the throne could try to help Indian women from all communities to attempt to realize their potential, thus making Hyderabad a model of Indian modernity and possibly, just possibly, helping the state to act as a bulwark against the gathering perfect storm of pan-Indian sovereignty. The tacit support of the British as advisors to Durru Shehvar is not fully documented; but the handwritten dedication to 'Lady Tasker, in appreciation of her work' on a copy of her 1937 address to the Hyderabad State Women's Conference does appear to demonstrate at least a degree of closeness between the princess and the wife of the British Resident (Durru Shehvar 1937, n.p.).

All through this period of Durru Shehvar's activism, her integration into the life of Nizamian Hyderabad and her marital difficulties, the constitutional situation of Hyderabad and British India continued to be negotiated. The consensus between the British and the Hyderabadis in the 1930s was that a stronger form of independence could be retained. Commenting on the situation in 1937, an article from *Time* magazine refers to the struggle for influence between the princely states and the proponents of an 'All-India Federation' as a 'constitutional crisis' ([no author] 1937, 20). The article continues:

> [The] [s]trongest figure on the princely stage was the Nizam of Hyderabad's trusty Sir Akbar Hydari, firmly demanding of the British Raj the virtual amendment of the new Constitution by the insertion in the Acts of Accession… of such ultra safe clauses as 'Nothing in this instrument affects the continuance of [the Nizam's] Sovereignty in and over this State.' (Ibid.)

As the 1940s drew on, however, it was becoming evident that there was a clear unifying and unitary logic to the project of the Union of

Indian States. Hyderabad State, with its majority Hindu population, a Muslim ruler and a small Muslim aristocracy, was appearing more like a historical anachronism, propped up by the British as a surrogate structure through which power could be exercised. As outlined in a personal minute to the prime minister of the United Kingdom from the minister of state for Commonwealth relations in 1947, the crucial issue for the Nizam and his statesmen was to attempt to 'negotiate an alliance with India, rather than an amalgamation into India.'[20] This position of wanting to 'resume the status of independent sovereign after the lapse of the [British] paramountcy' (Tirtha 1967, 174) was restated by the Nizam in a *firman* or royal proclamation dated 26 and 29 July 1944. This was countered by the fledgling State Congress:

> This vital declaration has been made without any reference to the people of the State and does not represent their will expressed by the State Congress on behalf of the people of the State. No decision can be accepted unless it is endorsed by the people ... The place of Hyderabad, therefore naturally lies in the Indian Union only. The Government by their declaration have, however, sought to align themselves with the disruptionist forces of the vested interests and feudal hierarchy, which can only mean perpetuation of autocratic rule. (Ibid., 174–75)

Thus, as time went on, the continued existence of the State of Hyderabad was being directly threatened by the accelerated moves towards Indian independence after the end of the Second World War.

After the end of the Second World War, three problems came to a head for the Nizam: Hyderabad's status in the emerging constitution; the preservation of his own privileges in the new order; and the power struggle with the formidable Durru Shehvar regarding the education of her sons and his heirs. The mother sought and obtained the counsel in this matter of British officials (before August 1947) and of Prime Minister Nehru (Prasad 2010 [1984], 347). The dissolution of the Hyderabadi State and the irretrievable breakdown of Durru Shehvar and Azam Jah's marriage happened at the same time. The de facto end of the seventh Nizam's kingdom came at the end of Operation Polo on 17 September 1948. The de facto end of the princess's marriage happened just a few days earlier when she boarded a private aeroplane and flew to London with her two sons, Mukarram Jah and Mufakham Jah. Durru Shehvar moved to London just before the euphemistically named 'police action' between 13 and 17 September 1948, in which the Indian Army took Hyderabad by force of arms.[21]

1947 and the hidden scandal of 1932 The objectification through photographs of Princess Niloufer

Princess Durru Shehvar's married life in India has left a few select written traces on account of her activity in public bodies, elite associations and with British representatives. It is much more difficult to reconstruct her cousin Niloufer's twenty years in Hyderabad between her arrival there in 1932 and her divorce in 1952. In her case, visual depictions dominate and, as anyone who has had a photograph taken of themselves by a professional knows, it is difficult to control how one is represented due to the technical demands of both the photographic process and the medium in which the resulting photographs will appear. News magazines such as *Time* are content to depict women like Niloufer and Durru Shehvar as children in the way that they represent them, as in this extract from an article in 1937 which stresses their Indian rather than Ottoman credentials: 'unlike their husbands, who follow their father's example in dress, the Caliph's girls dress as Indian ladies do' ([no author] 1937, 4). This phrasing bears witness to a false reduction to 'girls' and 'Indian ladies'. This view is contradicted by Durru Shehvar's discreet activism and her new public visibility as outlined above. The reference in *Time* magazine is also refuted by both women's mobility back and forth from Nice, Paris and London to Hyderabad. So, while it is true that one of the best known official photographs of Durru Shehvar is the sumptuous image from 1934 at the head of this chapter – where she is dressed in a magnificent heavy silk sari, holding a one-and-a-half-year-old Mukarram Jah[22] – it should not be forgotten that the official wedding photo taken in Nice in 1931 showed her in a European-style wedding dress. When performing their public duties in Hyderabad the women dressed in saris, but they wore Western clothes when in Europe.

In Niloufer's case, photographic representation cross-referenced against key events in the build-up to and breakdown of her marriage to Moazam Jah bear testament to a battle of representation and to the limited options to influence society open to a woman like Niloufer who did not take part in women's activism in Hyderabad. Currently the most widely available images of Niloufer are part of a series of her photographs taken in Paris by Boris Lipnitzki in March 1947. Those dozen or so images, now the property of the Roger-Viollet agency, show a composed and self-assured princess posing in both Western dress and in a white sari with fabric flourishes. It was these images, taken during a Spring break in Paris away from Hyderabad in March 1947 that cemented Niloufer's reputation as one of the leading beauties of her age.[23]

Why were these photographs taken at this time? There are at least two possible scenarios. These photographs resemble a modern portfolio shoot for an aspiring top model: no image is the same and there are multiple wardrobe changes. The aim is to showcase Niloufer's beauty. The photographs were taken in March 1947 at the photographer's studio in Paris. The Court Circular of 2 April 1947, published in the *Times*, suggests that the royal couple travelled on to London after this: 'Prince Muazzam [Moazam] Jah and Princess Niloufer have arrived in London and are staying at the Savoy Hotel' ([no author] 1947a, 7). It is probable, therefore, that the couple were in Paris together when the photographs were taken. This was the last trip that they were to make to Europe together, as the Prince took a second wife in October 1948 and Niloufer left Hyderabad before the start of Operation Polo in September 1948.[24] Could it be that these lavish photographs were an attempt at a rapprochement between Niloufer and her husband, Prince Moazam Jah? The accounting records of the photographer's studio have not survived, so we do not know whether it was the Prince or the Princess who commissioned the series. If it was the princess, then it would concur with the relaxed and happy way that she is being portrayed here. Her cultural hybridity is also evident, for even the saris that she wears are embellished in a way that adapts the classic form. As the curator's comment on one of her saris in the Fashion Institute of Technology records: 'As the consort of an Indian prince, she was required to wear saris, but having grown up in France, she often commissioned designs that reflected a

Western fashion sensibility in their colour, motif, and placement of embellishment.'[25] Niloufer is at ease in these photographs, but alone.

There is another possible scenario, however, which revolves around the way that her husband had apparently sought to both objectify both her and another woman with whom Prince Moazam was infatuated at the time of his marriage with Niloufer. We should not forget that the ceremony in Nice took place one month before her fifteenth birthday. A private and confidential report from 1932 sent to London by the British Resident mentions two sets of photographs resulting from an episode that had taken place fifteen years earlier, also in Paris. Commenting on those events, the Resident writes: 'The Nizam doesn't know the full story or the full amount paid (£1,000) for photographs – but he knows enough to be furious and to have taken a special dislike to the making of pictures' (Keyes 1932, 2). Here, then, in the words of the British Resident, is the story of the events from 1932 that had given rise to the first set of photographs (currently untraceable) from Paris:

> One incident of [Prince Moazam Jah's] tour is illustrative of his character and tastes. When he was taken to Paris to make the acquaintance of the Khalifa's niece, Nilofer (she was not really entitled to the style of Princess), he also renewed his acquaintance with a famous demi-mondaine, the head mannequin at a fashionable establishment and, after consenting to marry Nilofer, arranged with an expensive photographer to take several photographs of his future wife and of his demi-mondaine friend. As the photographer could not get payment he flew to London and besieged the controllers [the Nizam's treasurers at large] with two bills of £500. He accounted for the size of the bills by explaining that the two ladies had arrived on a Saturday afternoon at nearly the same time and that he had to recall his staff by taxi from their suburban homes and keep them at work all Sunday so as to have the photographs ready for Muazzam [Moazam], as demanded, by the Monday morning. The controllers paid the bill of the photography of Nilofer, and in the course of their enquiries discovered that Muazzam Jah had subsequently had the mannequin over to stay in the same hotel for a week without any of the suite discovering it, and had never even paid her hotel bill. Eventually, just as the party was leaving Nice, the photographer

> flew down from Paris with a lawyer and an order for the attachment of Muazzam Jah's baggage; and Hydari [Hyderabad's finance minister] had to pay the bill and costs. (Keyes 1932, 2)

This account cannot be corroborated; however, if it is true, it indicates that the Prince had a scant regard for his wife. If Niloufer was not aware of any aspect of this previous episode, it illustrates the great extent of her powerlessness and lack of knowledge, particularly as the Prince would go on to marry another woman just over a year later. If she was aware of all the details, it demonstrates that she was resisting this definition of her as a merely decorative being. She turned this objectification around, possibly deliberately, by looking so radiant and by showcasing the personal haute couture designs that she had made for herself. It is quite possible that she was thinking that this series of pictures was not just the personal possession of herself and her then husband, but that the copies that remained in Paris might be seen more widely by those who might help her at a time when she was no longer married and no longer in Hyderabad.

Indeed, in terms of the subject's self-confidence the Lipnitzki photographs contrast very starkly with those taken by the American *Time–Life* photographer Jack Birns in the very month of Operation Polo, September 1948. Niloufer looks into the camera in a rather startled manner.[26] The Birns shots appear to depict the last throes of Hyderabadi court culture; the set includes an image of Durru Shehvar's twelve-year-old younger son Mufakham Jah in his royal robes. They are quite flat documentary portraits with one image devoted to each subject.

September 1948 The end of the Nizamate and Durru Shehvar's departure from Hyderabad

We return now to state and national politics. Jawaharlal Nehru was clear that an independent Hyderabad was not admissible. The continued existence of Hyderabad State after August 1947 was an anomaly that would need to be remedied as soon as possible. In Nicholas Seton Mansergh's *Transfer of Power*, Nehru states that he and Congress would 'encourage rebellion in all states that go against us' (Mansergh 1982, document 124). On the ground, the majority Hindu population had little loyalty to the State of Hyderabad.

In Hyderabad, politics had long moved along linguistic lines, and the major players, including the Andhra Mahasabha and the faction of the Congress Party led by Swami Ramananda Tirtha, favoured the break-up of the state. The People's Democratic Front, the socialists and the Peasants' and Workers' Party participated in the campaign for the disintegration of the state as well (Sherman 2007, 513).

The de facto end of the possibility of an independent Hyderabad State, after five days of armed conflict (between 13 and 17 September 1948), left the Nizam in a situation in which he was, by his own admission, 'completely helpless' (Bénichou 2000, 237). Whereas under British rule the Nizam, and by extension his daughters-in-law, had had power and influence in religious, cultural and economic matters (on account of the royal family's heritage and immense personal wealth), the situation now was very different. They were thrown back on themselves as a dynasty. However, the Asaf Jahs were clearly a highly dysfunctional dynasty. The personal battle between Durru Shehvar and the seventh Nizam over the education of the future heir of the dynasty had begun at his birth and continued into the late 1940s. As mentioned earlier, a few days before Operation Polo, Durru Shehvar boarded a private aeroplane and flew with her sons to London. The Nizam let her go, probably to assure the safety of Mukarram Jah, the boy whom he had secretly designated as his heir. As soon as the 'police action' was over, however, his Most Exalted Highness wanted them to return to Hyderabad. This led to the Nizam having a telegram sent to Durru Shehvar at the Savoy Hotel with an offer to pay the hotel bill. The expenses in London, however, would only be settled if the boys and their mother returned home. Durru Shehvar's reaction on reading the message was recorded by Philip Mason: 'Imagine the vulgarity of my in-laws. He says he will pay my bill at the Savoy if I bring the children back!' (Mason 1978, 224–25). She did return, but the de facto end of the dynasty's power also exposed the irreconcilable nature of the breakdown of her marriage; by 1952 both she and her cousin Niloufer had shifted their principal residences to Europe, Durru Shehvar to London and Niloufer to Paris.

It is at this point, namely after the so-called 'police action' by which the newly formed Union of Indian States asserted its right of sovereignty over Hyderabad State by force of arms, that it is appropriate to assess the overall impact of the presence of Durru Shehvar and Niloufer on the Nizamate, from their arrival in 1932 to their definitive departure in around 1952. As we have seen, the princesses were brought to Hyderabad not for themselves, but in spite of themselves; the alliance was made because Durru Shehvar in particular held symbolic value as a place-holder of the Caliphate. We shall see this notion of 'place-holder' again in the case of Sonia Gandhi, the subject of the next chapter, though the circumstances are entirely different, involving a woman who herself made a personal decision to maintain a dynasty which she appears initially to have wanted to keep at arm's length. In Durru Shehvar's case, the discussion above has shown that it was external geopolitical considerations of preserving, transplanting and possibly resurrecting the influence of the Ottoman Caliphate in the person of her male heirs. It is important also to acknowledge that, at the time, the Caliphate's power was symbolic rather than real.[27] Abdul Mejid Effendi, as we have seen, had already been in exile for seven years. Although it was a marriage whose real politik element was more a potential than a reality, it is possible to see quite clearly that the elder princess in particular began to modernize the distaff side of the dynasty and fought and won the battle for a Western education for her sons. As Rajendra Prasad puts it, the princesses

> brought with them the graces and elegance of the East and something of the emancipated femininity of the West. It was about time too – the world of the Asif Jahs could well do with a whiff of fresh air from outside. It has been in a state of airless isolation for too long. (Prasad 2010 [1984], 201)

Until Durru Shehvar came to Hyderabad, it appears that wives and concubines asserted what little power they had in the name of the Nizam; they were invisible in their own right. It is important not to make sweeping statements about the nature of purdah; however, it is clear from a list of the organizations that Durru Shehvar patronized that she was the first royal wife in the history of the dynasty to have taken up a significant public role. Omar Khalidi goes further, suggesting that

> a lasting legacy of the marriage of the two princesses was the fading of purdah among the Muslim elite in Hyderabad. Masumah Begum, a social worker and politician, recalled how the change took place gradually. Before the princesses arrived, a wife might stay at home if men would be present at a gathering who were not friends of her husband. But when the princesses issued an invitation [directly to both members of the couple], it was a 'command performance' that could not be refused, nor could one inquire who would be there. (Khalidi 2004, 38)

In this way, purdah began breaking down in a state that was about to collapse as well. We have seen that the first part of this role concerned simple appearances in public, representing the monarchy at opening ceremonies and prize-givings. This was extended to activism for female causes.

It can be seen that, although Durru Shehvar had been brought to India for her symbolic role, she nevertheless had an important influence; not only was she visible, but she also took the further step of speaking to women to raise their awareness about female empowerment. These addresses took place within a clearly defined elite context; but as we can see in her patronage of the Hyderabad Girl Guides and the Durr-i-Shahvar College for Girls, they did at least reach out to the younger generation.

Operation Polo spelled the end of a dynasty whose destiny had long been out of its own hands. Hyderabad was the second largest Indian princely state, but it was also the second largest empty symbol. As we have seen from the confidential correspondence, the British Resident wielded a defining influence in both external and domestic affairs. The 'police action', despite the way in which it was dressed up as a civilian matter, was the last stage in the slow-burning end of Mughal power in India. The founder of the dynasty, Nizam ul-Mulk, who ruled over Hyderabad from 1724 to 1748, had carved out his empire against a backdrop of not only the fading central power of the emperor in Delhi, but also the regional threat from the Marathas in the west and competition from local Telugu-speaking zamindars. Given this inherent instability, there is little surprise that his successor, Nizam Ali Khan (1762–1803), became dependent on military alliances with the British to maintain his power. In the course of the nineteenth century, this working *with* the British gradually mutated into a working *under* the British. In 1931, the British approved the alliance with the Ottoman princesses, confident that it would only operate at a symbolic level. Hyderabadi hopes for prominence as the seat of a possible international pan-Islamic alliance disregarded the demography of the state, with Hindus outnumbering Muslims eight to one. This rearguard action was also doomed because the Caliphate was, just like the Nizamate, a spent force, exiled to a villa on the French Riviera. After Operation Polo the Nizam remained in place, but now his political power was reduced to nought. The annexation following the 'police action' was the de facto end in all domains apart from the symbolic. What then followed from 1948 to 1956 was the break-up of Hyderabad, and the question raised by that was how Durru Shehvar would negotiate her identity as a symbol of royalty, rather than as an active princess.

In personal psychological terms the end of the Nizamate must have brought back for Durru Shehvar memories of herself as a ten-year-old child during her family's forced departure from the Dolmabahce Palace where she had grown up. In the final chapter of his *Constantinople: City of the World's Desire 1453–1924*, Philip Mansel recounts the hurried way in which they had to leave their homeland. On 3 March 1924, Abdul Mejid Effendi was told by Adnan Bey and the prefect of police that he had to leave Constantinople at dawn:

> His family and servants began to weep. The freedom of life in the West was offered as consolation ... Durru Shehvar is said to have remarked in tears: 'I do not want that kind of freedom'... For fear of demonstrations, the government obliged the Caliph to leave from outside the city. At 5.30 a.m. ... they were taken in three cars followed by a lorry of luggage ... to Catalca [railway station, where they arrived at 11 a.m.] ... All day they remained in the railway station ... At midnight the Orient Express arrived. As the party began to board, watched by the other passengers, the Governor of Istanbul

> gave the Caliph an envelope containing passports, visas for Switzerland, and £2,000 sterling. While the train sped through the Balkans, past the site in Hungary where the heart of Suleyman the Magnificent is buried, the Caliph lamented: 'My ancestor came with a horse and flags. Now I come as an exile.' (Mansel 1995, 413–14)[28]

Having experienced this wrenching westward journey from home into exile, it is a measure of the strength of Durru Shehvar's character that she did not succumb to dynastic malaise after the end of Hyderabad, but remained engaged with the very particular battles that she was waging – such as that with the Nizam about the education of her sons. It is a measure of the level of conservatism in Hyderabad that she had to struggle so hard to achieve the internationalist dimension that R.D. and Sooni Tata had embraced for their young family thirty years earlier. That branch of the Tata family were pioneers, well ahead of their times. Durru Shehvar, however, did prevail in the end, and her son attended Harrow School, Peterhouse at Cambridge University, and the Royal Military Academy Sandhurst.

The break-up of the State of Hyderabad was recommended by the States Reorganization Commission, which began work in 1953. That year,

> the state of Andhra Pradesh was carved out of Madras. In 1956, the Telugu-speaking regions of Hyderabad, including Telangana, were joined with the new province [this continued to be opposed by a minority who wanted an independent Telangana state, granted in June 2014]. And Hyderabad [State's] Marathi speakers were eventually amalgamated into the new state of Maharashtra, and its Kannada speakers into Karnataka. (Sherman 2007, 513)

Key voices such as B.R. Ambedkar raised issues about the lack of safeguards against casteism under the new linguistic regime. Ambedkar wanted quantitative data to show that dividing in that way was not going to reincarnate caste oppression in the guise of democracy. He also raised what had become a crucial question regarding the justice of having what were always multi-caste cities such as Mumbai also serving as the capitals of states carved along linguistic lines. He argued that all social groups in India needed to have a legally-anchored stake in the economic potential of these cities. The division went ahead notwithstanding these concerns. Hyderabad was dismembered in this way because of the fundamental injustice of its religious composition, which harked back to Mughal rule and gave no voice to individual citizens. The States Reorganization Commission appears not to have considered the status quo with universal suffrage as an option; their plan was to rationalize as well as to democratize. Clearly, the debate that took place regarding the formation of the State of Telangana in 2014 is an indication that a perfect solution is rarely achievable in such complex matters. Despite the problems, the democratic gain achieved by the current situation is clear to see.

The traditional lack of visibility of female members of a family, which was discussed in the *prélude pondichérien* in relation to Jeanne Dupleix, defines the basic context for Durru Shehvar's public activism in Hyderabad; but the death of the state in whose name she undertook it also influenced the way that her work on behalf of women fell into obscurity. A further factor which contributed to Durru Shehvar's lack of prominence was that her sense of decorum prevented her from engaging in self-publicity. There are no self-authored documents about her life. There is not even a full-length biography; the only documents entirely devoted to her are on the scale of articles in periodicals, such as Omar Khalidi's 'The Caliph's Daughter' from 2004. This is clearly an injustice in view of her influence on the ground in Hyderabad in the sixteen years between 1932 and 1948. The main reason she is a neglected figure today, despite her importance, is because the dissolution of Hyderabad and the dominance of pan-Indian nationalist accounts of the period have removed the context in which her story can be told.

1948 to 2004 Durru Shehvar's commitment to Hyderabadi heritage

Durru Shehvar's father-in-law, the seventh Nizam Asaf Jah, died in 1967; his son, her former husband, survived him by only three years. Her cousin Niloufer died in Paris in 1989; the limited prominence of these other members of the dynasty during their lifetimes and Durru

Shehvar's longevity enhanced her importance as she carved out a new role for herself in heritage preservation after 1948. Her last public appearance in Hyderabad was at the inauguration of the Nizam's Silver Jubilee Museum in 2000; her last private visit was in 2004.

Paradoxically perhaps, Durru Shehvar became one of the most widely recognized symbols for an institution – the Nizamate – against whose core traditions regarding the position of women she fought. This is indicative of how influence in India can be maintained despite an Indian *videshini*'s mobility between Europe and India. The present situation in Hyderabad since her death is not very different from when she was alive; legal cases about the ownership of dynastic property and possessions inch their way through the courts of India at a snail's pace. This web of litigation is a fitting indictment of the elephantine error committed by the Asaf Jahi dynasty in continuing the *zenana* tradition without adequate modern property law.

If we enquire about the position of the former Hyderabadi royal family today, we will discover that there is an eighth Nizam, though in title alone. He is Mukarram Jah, the son of Durru Shehvar and Azam Jah; after being initially attracted to Hyderabad and being enthroned in 1967, he clearly distanced himself from the dynasty. Durru Shehvar's influence can be felt in the love–hate relationship that her son appears to have had with Hyderabad. Commenting on Mukarram Jah's upbringing, John Zubrzycki states that the fact that he 'felt more at home in England and then in Australia than he did in India owed much to his mother's prejudices and her insistence on sheltering him as far as possible from the tradition-bound confines of palace life' (Zubrzycki 2006, 231). In the footage that was taken of his visit to Hyderabad, he appears rather ill at ease at being made a spectacle of.[29] He moved to Western Australia in 1973, where he lived in splendid near isolation at the sheep station he owned. According to Zubrzycki, he chose this part of Australia because it reminded him of the countryside around Hyderabad. Above all, it is in his practice of monogamy – albeit serial monogamy – that his mother's influence can be felt. Mukarram Jah's matrimonial practice is not that of the Nizamian Hyderabad of old; he married and divorced his first four wives in succession. In a curious twist of fate, given the enforced exile from Istanbul of her father the Caliph, Durru Shehvar's son now lives in Turkey, taking no part in the ongoing bitter litigation regarding the ownership of the Hyderabadi dynasty's palaces and jewels. His first wife, the Turkish architect Esra Birgin, whom he married in 1959, holds his power of attorney in all legal matters. Princess Orchedi, who is wife number five, also happens to be Turkish. While they certainly fall far short of the Caliphate and the Ottoman Empire, one has the sense that Durru Shehvar might have approved of these two fragments of female Turkish influence in India.

Conclusions

Both Durru Shehvar and Niloufer belonged to Hyderabadi royalty and, therefore, were part of the super-elite. It is also true, however, that they had an extremely limited sphere of movement and action on account of the social conservatism of the Hyderabadi court, which did not accord a public role to any woman, whether she was of the royal house or not. Previous commentators have used the term 'purdah' to describe the princesses' position, but different benchmarks were in place for the Ottoman Empire-born princesses. These benchmarks are crucial; they helped to determine the women's actions, and also how those actions have been portrayed. The fall of Durru Shehvar's activism into obscurity is a result of both the power of the social conservatism that she was struggling against, and the abolition of Hyderabad State and its absorption into the Union of Indian States. The attempts at modernization of civil society in the Hyderabad of the 1930s and 1940s by this female member of a princely elite were not part of the grand narrative of Indian Independence; this is why Durru Shehvar's deeds have not yet received the attention they deserve.

The main subject of this chapter has been the elder of the two brides, Princess Durru Shehvar. She distinguishes herself on account of her sustained activism for women's causes in Hyderabad, her ongoing struggle to internationalize the education of her sons, and her commitment over decades, until her death in 2006, to the cultural heritage of Nizamian Hyderabad. This ongoing engagement contrasts with Princess Niloufer's single, though magnificently munificent, donation of the capital from her divorce settlement to finance a hospital. Durru Shehvar's and Niloufer's marriages were a result of a geopolitical project for the Caliphate and thus extend back to the 1920s, and Durru Shehvar's engagement with Hyderabad lasted for the whole of her adult life with her travelling from London to Hyderabad at the age of eighty-six to open a museum. Durru Shehvar is also significant because she maintained contact with Hyderabad from Europe; she did not campaign for the heritage of the Ottoman Empire, the realm of her birth, although it was physically closer to her location in London. Instead, she made a reasoned choice for the world-class heritage of a defunct state within the new national picture. There were few internationally recognized champions of Hyderabad who had the distance to be disinterested participants in the preservation struggle. So what she achieved was an embracing of art and architecture and the securing of her own modest legacy beyond the lifetime of the state. She became a figurehead for Hyderabadi heritage preservation in India, who divorced that heritage from the autocratic minority rule by the Nizam's elite to which she had once belonged, but which she had fought against as far as it impacted on women. This thoroughly modern engagement deserves credit and is certainly a partial justification for her inclusion as the main Indian *videshini* in this chapter (it also accords with the long-view perspective of this study). Niloufer was different from Durru Shehvar: she was not an activist, she had no children, and after her divorce in 1952 she maintained no ties with Hyderabad that entailed public appearances. She remained president of the Association for Women and Children's Medical Aid (AWCA), however, and continued her patronage of the Niloufer Hospital for Women and Children. Indeed, she never returned to Hyderabad after 1950. Her legacy, therefore, is more personal; on rare occasions it has surfaced, generally in connection with her beauty and sense of fashion, which were perpetuated by the images of her that were taken in Paris. Niloufer's agency is thus submerged; whereas, in embracing Hyderabadi cultural heritage, Durru Shehvar demonstrates that she shared the creativity and dynamism of Indian *videshinis* such as Mirra Alfassa and Simone Tata. All three of them had a second life-project.

Notes

1. This chapter adopts the spelling of this name, which means 'great pearl' (and not 'royal pearl' as in the 1932 *Asiatic Review* article), adopted by the princess herself. Some variant spellings are Durrushehvar, Durru Shevhar, Dur-i-Shahvar, Durru Shehwar, Durru Shahvar, Durrai-Shehvar, Dur-e-Shawar, and Dürrüşehvar.
2. While the *Asiatic Review* is correct to state that she was the only daughter of her mother Atiye Mehisti Kadınefendi (1892–1964) and the Caliph (called Khalifa here), he actually had had a son in 1898 and three daughters (in 1921, 1923 and 1926) with Şehsuvar Kadınefendi. Although Durru Shehvar's mother only married the Caliph in 1912, Durru Shehvar was born after the son, Şehzade Ömer Faruk Effendi, but before the three daughters, Princesses Fatma, Zehra and Necla.
3. This was the date of the *zifaf*, the public civil ceremony; the religious ceremony, the *nikah*, took place at the Hilafat Palace (also known as the Villa Carabacel) in Nice on 14 November 1931. Azam Jah was born in 1907 and died in 1970. Moazam Jah was born in 1907 and died in 1987.
4. The Caliph was the spiritual and temporal leader of the world's Sunni Moslems. Niloufer was the only daughter of H.E. Damad Moralizada Salar ud-din Bey Effendi, by his wife H.I.H. Princess Adila Sultana. According to Begum Bilkees I. Latif, both women are great-granddaughters of Murad V, who was Caliph from the end of May to the end of August 1876. See 'Princess Niloufer Sultana of Hyderabad', *You & I* (10 August 2009), 37, http://emag.youandi.com/Editions/YouandI/issue80/Downloads/10_08_2009_039.pdf (accessed 11 November 2014).
5. The Ottoman Empire joined that alliance secretly on 2 August 1914. Its membership was only made public on 29 October 1914.
6. Beaton's portraits were taken during a visit to Hyderabad in 1944, Lipnitzki's in Paris in 1947 and Birns's in Hyderabad in 1948.
7. The arrival of the delegation of the 'premier Indian state' at London's Victoria Station was reported in *The Times* ([no author] 1930, 13).
8. An article in *The Hindu*, 'Lady Hydari Club yearns for past glory', traces the fate of the historic club building; once so important for the 'twilight generation', the building now lies unused and inaccessible (Rangan 2011).

9. Telegram from the Resident, Hyderabad to Polindia (quoted in Zubrzycki 2006, 147).
10. During the Second World War 'the seventh Nizam gave the Royal Navy a corvette called "Hyderabad" and three squadrons of the R.A.F' ([no author] 1943, 8).
11. Hyderabad's faithfulness to Britain between 1857 and 1859 also spawned celebratory tomes, such as the 507-page work by Hastings Fraser (1865).
12. It is interesting to see how demeaning references to women are applied to Frenchwomen. The introduction shows that, in fact, both British and non-British European women first met their future royal husbands when they were dancers. The cases of the English cabaret dancer Florry Bryan and the Maharaja of Patiala and Anita Delgrada, a Spanish flamenco dancer, who was briefly married to Jagatjit Singh, the Maharajah of Kapurthala, in 1910 attest to this fact. In an even wider context, bayadère and nautch dancers are a mainstay of European male representations of Indian women, as illustrated by Johann Zoffany's painting of the Frenchman Antoine-Louis Henri Polier watching a nautch, produced circa 1786–88 in Faizabad or Lucknow (opaque water colour on paper, 25 x 32 cm). An image of this portrayal is available in the Wikimedia Commons.
13. Telegram from the Resident, Hyderabad to Polindia (quoted in Zubrzycki 2006, 148).
14. See www.nilouferhospital.com (accessed 11 November 2011).
15. The princess was patron of the Anjuman-e-Khawateen Baraye Taraqqi Taleem wa Mashrat (Organization for the Improvement of Women's Education and Social Life), the Lady Hydari Club, and the Hyderabad Ladies' Recreational Club. See http://www.royalark.net/India/hyder11.htm (accessed 11 November 2011, authored by Christopher Buyers). Royal Ark is a most useful online resource.
16. We owe the survival of this record to a British civil servant, Sir Theodore Tasker (1884–1981), who was seconded to the Government of Hyderabad from 1927 to 1942. See the papers of Sir Theodore Tasker, British Library shelf mark MSS. EUR. D798/39.
17. These invaluable accounts were most graciously collected by Dr Fatima Shanaz from her uncle Nawab Agha Sirtaj Hassan Mirza, her mother Meherunissa Hassan Mirza and her father Nawab Mir Moazam Husain.

Her mother and her uncle are the children of Professor Agha Hyder Hassan Mirza, who was Durru Shehvar's instructor in Urdu and court etiquette.

18. There is no record as to whether Princess Niloufer learnt Urdu.
19. Christopher Buyers' Royal Ark website gives a sense of Azam Jah's activities during the 1930s and 1940s.
20. The minute is dated 22 September 1947 and is found in the National Archives of the UK ([no author] 1947b). In the 1930s, this position had gone by another name: 'We believe – as I made clear at the last [Round Table] Conference – that Federation is the only possible basis for the future constitution of India' (Sir Akbar Hydari quoted in *The Times* ([no author] 1931b, 9).
21. The use of this term and the more common 'Operation Polo' encompass the official Union of Indian States' view of the clash of arms, which they considered to be an internal matter. However, the abiding visual images of the end of the conflict, depicting an official surrender with two stern generals clasping hands (a scene familiar to newspaper readers from the reporting of the Second World War), send a contradictory message: namely, that the five-day battle was a conflict between states. The war was fought between 13 and 18 September 1948; there were thirty-two fatalities among combatants on the Indian side and 490 regular soldiers and 1,373 Razakar irregulars were killed on the Hyderabadi side. At the surrender, Major General Joyanto Nath Chaudhuri represented the Indian side and Major General El Edroos represented the Hyderabadi side.
22. http://commons.wikimedia.org/wiki/File:AsafJahVIII-D%C3%BCrr%C3%BChshehvar_1stOfficialPic_1931.jpeg (accessed 11 November 2011).
23. These images can be found at http://www.parisenimages.fr/en/ (accessed 11 November 2011).
24. See http://www.royalark.net/India/hyder11.htm (accessed 11 November 2011, authored by Christopher Buyers).
25. http://fashionmuseum.fitnyc.edu/view/objects/asitem/search$0040/0/dynasty-desc?t:state:flow=b7fcea7a-4d68-4c0a-bd87-7b126da6dad7(accessed 11 November 2014).
26. The copyright for this image is held by Getty Images.
27. However, as the philosopher Jean-Paul Sartre states, concepts such as nothingness 'can produce effects in the real' (Sartre 1952, 411). In

2016, we have a Caliphate without a Caliph, a manifestation based on an ideology of a society at war without a nominated headman calling himself the Caliph, and without many of the externally recognized characteristics of most other states in the world.

28. It is interesting to note that only three years later, in 1927, the 'Occident Express' carrying the prospective novice Anjezë Gonxha Bojaxhiu on her way to the Loreto convent in Ireland must have travelled along the same railway tracks.
29. A video of the ceremony is available at http://www.youtube.com/watch?v=aBrnCbBZKqI (accessed 11 November 2011).

STATE AND NATIONAL POLITICS: SONIA GANDHI

As time advances such unions are bound to multiply with benefit to society… No religion which is narrow and which cannot satisfy the test of reason will survive the coming reconstruction of society in which values will have changed and character, not possession of wealth, title or birth, will be the sole test of merit.

– M.K. Gandhi in 1942 on the marriage of Indira Nehru and Feroze Gandhi, a Parsi

I am marrying Rajiv the person.

– Sonia Gandhi speaking at her first press conference in 1968

I became part of India thirty years ago when I entered Indira Gandhi's home as her eldest son's bride. It was through her heart that I grew to understand and love India.

– Sonia Gandhi in January 1998 at a political rally in Sriperumbudur, Tamil Nadu

Throughout these past six years that I have been in politics, one thing has been clear to me. And that is, as I have often stated, that the post of prime minister is not my aim. I was always certain that if ever I found myself in the position that I am in today, I would follow my own inner voice. Today, that voice tells me I must humbly decline this post.

– Sonia Gandhi's statement to a meeting of the Congress Parliamentary Party, 18 May 2004

Thirty-six momentous years of Indian history separate the 1968 and the 2004 quotations above by Sonia Gandhi, our next Indian *videshini*. The earlier statement marks her entry into public life and the second her renunciation of the post of prime minister of India. Among many other difficult periods for India, the years between 1968 and 2004 encompass the Indo-Pak War of 1971, the Kargil War, the Emergency and the Kashmir Insurgency. We have entered the political arena of a sovereign nation state and the Nehru–Gandhi dynasty was at the helm of the country for nineteen of those thirty-six years.[1]

Those unstable years for India did witness some happy events for the Nehru–Gandhi family itself, events that pointed towards its continued central role in Indian life. These included the marriage of Rajiv and Sonia Gandhi in 1968; the births of Rahul and Priyanka Gandhi (in 1970 and 1972 respectively); the marriage of Sanjay and Maneka Gandhi in 1974; and the birth of their son Varun in 1980.[2] The 'business' of the dynasty is politics, however, and two political defeats in national elections impinged on the family's dominance in the post-Independence period: Indira Gandhi lost in 1977, and her son Rajiv in 1989, and to this we can add the defeat of Sonia and her son Rahul in 2014. However, even more than these political setbacks, which might always be reversed, the dynasty was shaken to its very core by no less than three deaths from unnatural causes during this period. Sanjay Gandhi, the dynasty's heir apparent, met with an accidental death in an aeroplane crash in 1980; Indira Gandhi died at the hands of her bodyguards Beant and Satwant Singh in 1984; and Rajiv was killed by a Tamil Tiger suicide bomber Thenmozhi Rajaratnam in 1991. These three interrupted Nehru–Gandhi lives may have potentially negated the family's ability to be active in national politics at the highest level, but one after the other they propelled Sonia Gandhi from the periphery of the dynasty to its very centre.[3] The final killing in 1991 meant that her small family unit had been decapitated, her children deprived of a father and she of a husband; the question then arose of what role she could play in the party now that she was no longer the wife of its head.

Between the early 1980s (when she, Rajiv and their children returned to India after the end of the Emergency and after the death of Sanjay Gandhi) and the day in 2004 when she uttered the words of the 'inner voice' epigraph, Sonia Gandhi's position changed: the foreign wife of the non-political son became the main standard bearer of the family in national politics. On the morning of 18 May 2004, before her renunciation that evening, she was an entirely credible candidate for the office of prime minister of India (though an enormously controversial one).

If we compare the statement from 1968 with that from 2004, the first is charming in its simple and clear attempt to state the obvious. However, it is also a courageous and ultimately doomed attempt by the bride-to-be to exclude herself and her husband from the symbolic dimensions of the position that the family occupied in peri-colonial India. The unspoken proper noun in her reference to 'Rajiv the person' is 'Gandhi'. Of course, we understand that she is speaking from the heart here – in her first public appearance with her groom-to-be, one would expect no less. That said, with the benefit of hindsight it is rather paradoxical that she speaks here from the standpoint of Sonia Maino, the Italian-born woman who met Rajiv in Cambridge in 1965; that non-Indian standpoint is the very thing that her detractors would reproach her for as soon as she entered public life. In the 2004 quotation she not only speaks as the head of the Gandhi dynasty, but utters words (whether chosen by her or by her speech writers) which make a knowing reference to a turn of phrase also used by M.K. Gandhi. Mahatma Gandhi used this expression 'inner voice' in a 1931 article in *Young India*: 'Penances with me are no mechanical acts. They are done in obedience to the inner voice' (M.D. 1931, 60). In this quotation the voice gives authenticity, but it also acts as an arbiter of the truth in moral questions. This second function of the voice as a moral guide is similar to the notion of conscience in the Christian tradition.[4]

Returning to consider what she said in 2004, she states that she has been 'in politics' for six years; that would take us back to 1998, when she accepted the Congress Party presidency. One of the most important elements in politics is the interpretation of the past to suit the present. Politics is the permanent and repeated manipulation of past events; one of the greatest challenges is to present interpretations of the past by Sonia Gandhi and others (both her supporters and her opponents) in a *fair manner*, while at the same time being critical of any gross manipulations by either party.

For example, some people would argue that Sonia Gandhi began her political life when she started campaigning for her husband in 1984. Others would say that she had been in politics since her marriage in 1968. That is obviously a more extreme view. The point here is that she does not count her apprenticeship, but starts the clock on her political life in the year she was elected to the post of Congress Party president, a position on a pan-Indian level and one she still holds. Crucially, it is a party position in which she is subject to relatively little hostile critique. Her submitting herself to the voters of the Amethi parliamentary constituency in Uttar Pradesh came later, in 1999.

Sonia Gandhi's decision to renounce the post of prime minister in 2004 was seen in a number of ways by Congress Party members and by people in India more widely. Many Indians were relieved that her stepping aside might herald a period of greater political stability (Dasgupta 2004, 11). A significant number of party members, however, made very public displays of dismay that a Gandhi would not lead the country now. The most extreme of these displays was probably that of Gangacharan Rajput, a former Congress MP, who threatened to commit suicide if Sonia Gandhi did not reconsider her decision.[5] (He was dissuaded, it seems.) But the great majority of Indians, irrespective of whether or not they were members of the party, would have recognized the strong positive spiritual implications of stepping aside for conscientious reasons. In classical Indian thought, a self-effacing act of public renunciation can be referred to by using the term tyaga or sacrifice. In her statement, Sonia Gandhi stresses her passivity: she says in the first person that 'I found myself in the position' of having the prime ministership offered to her. So it is not a refusal to serve, but the act of respectfully declining an offer that was made to her by others. In this reference to M.K. Gandhi, the spiritual father of the modern nation, Sonia Gandhi could keep the moral high ground and be flexible because there was nothing definitive about this act of listening to the inner voice. She could potentially consider another offer at a later date (for herself or for a member of her family). In his 2005 addendum to his critical study of the dynasty, Tariq Ali writes:

> Ironically, the refusal to accept the Prime Ministership of India enhanced the dynasty and made the ultimate accession to power of her son [...] or her daughter [...] a virtual certainty. [...] Will Rahul or Priyanka be leading the Congress in 2015 under the slogan of 'Remove Poverty'. [...] The rules that apply to the Kennedy and Bush clans in the United States, also apply to the Nehrus–Gandhis of India. The electorate is sometimes prepared to give them the benefit of the numerous doubts that exist, but once they betray the hopes (or illusions) of those who have supported them, they crumble just like any other politician. (Ali 2004 [1985], 342)

Ali displays perspicaciousness in the scenarios that he sketches out at the time of writing, Sonia remained in a position of political power within the party, but until December 2017 the Party had been unwilling to give the benefit of any doubt to her male offspring. We will look further at the situation of her daughter in the conclusions of this book. Meanwhile, Rahul Gandhi continues his work attempting to be an effective political opposition. His once much vaunted struggle for democracy, and renewal within the party's organization, is less present in the media than when the Congress was in power. He has an anti-dynastic platform that was outlined in 2008: 'it is undemocratic that the Congress is still led by a Gandhi. But it's the reality... My position gives me certain privileges. It is a fact of life in India that success in politics depends on who you know or are related to. I want to change the system' (Singh 2011, 220). These comments on nepotism imply a link between his own positions as general secretary, chairperson of the Indian Youth Congress and chairperson of the National Students' Union and his mother's presidency of the party, but these words spoken in 2011 are also supposed to justify his own reformist creed. But some Indians, both inside and outside the Indian National Congress, felt and continue to feel that the authenticity of Rahul's reforms would have been enhanced if his mother had resigned and there had been a new election for the post of party president rather than the mandate being renewed automatically. Rahul's predecessor for the post of general secretary was his mother and he was the first holder of the other two posts. Passing these posts to others could be a first step in his 'want[ing] to change the system' (Singh 2011, 220). Many would also go on to question the credibility of Rahul Gandhi's desire to reform as he put himself forward and was duly elected to the new post of Congress Party vice-president in 2013.

This chapter on Sonia Gandhi aims to analyze, in a selective way, how representations of her are dominated by controversies surrounding her nationality and sense of her own national affiliations. As she became more and more active in politics, this identity became public property; but was she Indian or was she Italian? Her supporters had one opinion, her opponents another. Rupa Chatterjee, expressing the perspective of those who approve of her, describes her as 'Indira Gandhi's Italian or foreign *bahu* [daughter-in-law] who was more Indian in thought and deed than the Indian daughter-in-law Maneka' (Chatterjee 2000, 27).[6] The opposite view is stated by G.P. Mohanty: '*Videshibahus* [foreign daughters-in-law] are welcome, but we cannot have them as prime ministers. That will be a security risk' (Mishra 1999, 11). For the first group, she was more Indian than the Indians; for the second, her mere presence in Indian politics was seen as an intolerable injustice and even a threat to national security. They justify such a position by maintaining that her loyalties would automatically lie with Italy, rather than with India; though, as we shall see, some commentators do not get as far as mentioning the land of her birth – for them, the fact that she is not Indian is enough.

The most important point to understand when considering her identity is the historical context. The representation of national allegiance in her identity, which was constructed at key points during the period from 1979 to the present, must be contextualized historically. In precise terms what occurred was the building-up of a public persona, beginning gradually in the 1980s and, as she became ever more involved in politics, reaching a climax in 2004.[7] The key stages of this move into the political fray coincide with the deaths of members of the family: Sanjay Gandhi in 1980, Indira Gandhi in 1984 and Rajiv Gandhi in 1991. It is important to analyze how she charts her own induction into the dynasty in the ten years between 1965 and 1975. Surprisingly perhaps, we shall see that she describes this as having been a more gradual process than that described by Congress-supporting biographers such as P. Sood in his *Sonia Gandhi: Trails of Triumph* (Sood 2009, 1). Sood argues that a fast-track integration occurred; and even a more circumspect commentator such as Rupa Chatterjee writes that 'Sonia metamorphoses from daughter-in-law to daughter' (Chatterjee 2000, 58). Chatterjee is referring here to the period between 1980 and 1984 which saw Maneka's estrangement from her mother-in-law Indira Gandhi after Sanjay's death; but Sonia Gandhi begins the story of her integration in the 1960s.

It is also important to include the perspective of her political opponents, who refer to the same gender-laden markers of her supposed Italian identity – dress, dietary preferences and tastes in interior design – that are used by her supporters to justify her Indianness. (These markers have been chosen here because they occur frequently, both in accounts of the politician by others and also in Sonia Gandhi's writing about herself.) Gender features as a positive element. Her attempts to recount the lives of dynasty members underline her own growing importance as a woman within the dynasty (one who is now a senior member in her own right, as well as having perpetuated the dynasty through her childbearing). Her contributions attempt to create a matrilineal line that runs directly from Indira Gandhi to herself. She presents this as a relationship based on love, obedience and respect; the subtext, however, is that this is not only a relationship between daughter-in-law and mother-in-law, it is also a link between the prime minister of India and a political aspirant.

In the period from 1984 to 2004, Sonia Gandhi moved from the periphery to the centre in this most political of Indian families. Any examination of her place in public life, therefore, must also concern itself with the status of the dynasty. The most important aspect of this status is how it compares with other groups in Indian society, more generally in its attitude towards women and foreigners. The place of these groups in society is guaranteed by the constitution (specifically by Article 15, about the prohibition of discrimination on grounds of religion, race, caste, sex or place of birth). Though the question of legitimacy of the Nehru–Gandhi dynasty, from a wider societal point of view, lies outside the scope of this chapter and this book, one topic that needs to be considered is the dynasty's ability to transform itself in order to retain its place in society.[8] We shall look at the strategies that the dynasty has adopted in order to retain its place, faced with direct and brutal challenges from a variety of different sources, including legitimate political challenges by the Janata Dal in the late 1980s and the Bharatiya Janata Party (BJP) in the 1990s and in the first two decades of the present century, as well as the altogether different matter of political assassination. In looking at these strategies, including those of allowing female 'succession', in the form of Indira Gandhi's 1966 accession to the post of prime minister, and permitting the integration of a foreigner like Sonia Gandhi, it is legitimate to ask whether the controversial 'first family' of India is estranged from the cultural practices followed by the majority of Indians or whether, counter-intuitively, the Nehru–Gandhi dynasty actually provides a model of progressive family organization for India. After all, an organization that allowed Indira Gandhi as a woman to establish the crucial second generation of the dynasty in 1966 and then offered Sonia Gandhi as a foreign-born Indian the possibility of continuing it in 2004 is, on both counts, far ahead of its time.

Let us now consider the early history of our subject, from her birth as Edvige Antonia Albina Maino to the start of her married existence as Sonia Gandhi. She was born on 9 December 1946 in Lusiana in the province of Vincenza, northern Italy. It is indicative of the ambition of those who seek to Indianize her that the distance of her birth from South Asia is sometimes abolished retrospectively. Mani Shankar Aiyar is quoted as suggesting that 'her life began with the Indian Republic' (Sood 2009, xxi). This rather far-fetched claim comes about because December 1946 marked the 'start of deliberations on the Indian constitution' (ibid). This is a narrative of mythic birth in the best Indian tradition, where the events of the mid-1960s and Sonia Gandhi's life choices are read back to the earliest moment of her past and seen as indicating her destiny. The scenario would not be out of place in a Bollywood movie. Indeed, the spoof trailer for the fake film on Saint Teresa uses exactly the same device in the scene in which the sultry novice spins the globe roulette-like; when it stops spinning her finger is pointing to Calcutta.

The fifteen-page introduction by Sonia Gandhi to the lavishly illustrated and produced commemorative book *Rajiv*, which appeared in 1992, one year after her husband's assassination, traces the entire span of their life together from 1965 to 1991. The text achieves a credible degree of authenticity by making no uncharacteristic detours into high-end political theory and preserving the personal and populist touch that was the hallmark of Sonia Gandhi's campaigning in the 1999, 2004 and 2009 national elections. It is also a canny text which, just like the 2004 renouncement, adopts a perspective many of her Indian readers might share. For instance, in her 1992 account of the period after Indira Gandhi's assassination, she first presents herself in a good light protecting her family when she states that she 'fought like a tigress' (Sonia Gandhi 1992, 6) to dissuade her husband from entering politics. (The reference to the national animal of India is another illustration of an attempt to create a common perspective with her fellow Indians.[9]) But after this she states that she will follow the example of her husband in his duty towards his family and will help him in his political career: 'If he felt that he ought to offer his help to his mother, then I would bow to those forces which were now beyond me to fight' (ibid., 7). This is a strategic and, in the eyes of many of her readers, wholly laudable admission of weakness; it is both an act of self-abnegation and a display of obedience to the family and service to the nation.

After increasing suspense by describing how the first meeting planned between Sonia Maino and her future mother-in-law had to be aborted because of the younger woman's blind panic, the account foregrounds Indira Gandhi's active hospitality towards her elder son's chosen partner. We saw the same phenomenon in the case of Lady Navajbai Tata and Simone Tata. The mother-in-law's welcome of Sonia Maino even went as far as the language used: 'She spoke to me in French, knowing I was more fluent in it than in English' (Sonia Gandhi 1992, 1). We shall return to the role of French within the dynasty; but here we are dealing with an expression of Mrs Gandhi's generosity: Sonia Gandhi is implicitly basking in the approval of a woman who had positioned herself to become the first female prime minister of India (taking office on 24 January 1966). The question being asked of the sceptical reader is, perhaps, 'If the prime minister of India can welcome me with open arms, why shouldn't you?'

It is remarkable that, in her introduction to this volume about Rajiv Gandhi, Sonia Gandhi should give such prominence to her mother-in-law, quoting her far more than her own husband. The reason behind this is to establish a female kinship link, which was essential for the survival of the dynasty at the time. The first thing that Sonia Gandhi does is to adopt a cross-generational perspective that links Indira Nehru and Feroze Gandhi's experiences with those of herself and Rajiv Gandhi. This is done by her quoting of M.K. Gandhi's positive opinion of the kind of 'mixed marriage' typified by the union between Indira Nehru and Feroze Gandhi (it is found in the first epigraph at the start of this chapter). For her detractors, Sonia Gandhi's drawing of a parallel between her own case and M.K. Gandhi's vision of a meritocratic India is the height of bad taste; indeed, for them, her political career is entirely the result of the connections of the family into which she married. The BJP parliamentarian Sushma Swaraj was quoted as stating that 'as a daughter-in-law of this country I will give her love, respect and security. But if she wants to be become PM by virtue of that, I won't take it' (Hasan 1999, 8). In a later interview the future minister of external affairs added: 'the only issue on which she was asking for votes was that "I'm the daughter-in-law of Indira Gandhi" and "I'm married in India"' (Skoda 2004, 279).

On these cross-generational foundations Sonia Gandhi builds the woman-to-woman relation. The daughter-in-law states that Indira Gandhi told her that she too was once 'young, extremely shy, and in love, and that she understood me perfectly' (Sonia Gandhi 1992, 2). Indira is then quoted as saying: 'I see some glimpses of myself in you and many of my husband in my son who is your husband' (ibid., 3). The repetition of the kinship link here underlines the solidarity between Indira and Sonia Gandhi.[10] For her readers, this impression of an implicit understanding between the two women was probably intended to stand in stark contrast to the animosity between Indira Gandhi and her other daughter-in-law, Maneka Gandhi, the widow of Sanjay Gandhi, from whom the prime minister was estranged in the wake of her elder son's death in 1980.[11] The falling-out between Maneka and Indira Gandhi was sealed when the daughter-in-law founded a political party in 1983, the Rashtriya Sanjay Manch, intended to keep alive the supposed political ideology of her husband. In doing this she went against the wishes of Indira Gandhi for her son Rajiv to take over the mantle of the heir of the dynasty. Maneka Gandhi joined a head-to-head battle with her brother-in-law for her husband's former seat in the Amethi constituency in 1984. (It was during this election campaign that Indira Gandhi was assassinated.) Maneka lost; Rajiv won for Congress. His detractors pointed to the sympathy vote, saying that he had only won because the nation's voters wished for continuity. Four years later, in 1988, Maneka merged her party with the main Janata Dal opposition, becoming its general secretary. Her son Varun has also embraced the path of opposition to Congress; in 2009 he was elected in Pilibhit constituency for the BJP.

Returning to the 'good' daughter-in-law, the specific female-to-female relationship across the generations between Indira and Sonia Gandhi also had a cultural dimension that valorized European cultural heritage. Sonia Gandhi herself draws discreet parallels between India and Italy, such as in the comment about her obedience to the Nehru–Gandhi matriarch: 'The power of a man's mother is not exclusively an Indian phenomenon' (Sonia Gandhi 1992, 1). The implication here is that Sonia Gandhi is familiar with these conventions of respect for female elders from her own upbringing in Europe. This argument is also used by Rupa Chatterjee in her *Sonia Gandhi: The Lady in Shadow* – 'Of all the Western communities, Italy is perhaps closest to India. A lot of importance is given to tradition and family bonds' (Chatterjee 1998, 2).[12] Inevitably, perhaps, the Italian aspect is an ambivalent one. It is also evoked by Gautham Siddharth, who mentions the Mafia, saying that Octavio Quattrocchi, one of those involved in the 1980s Bofors howitzer procurement scandal, is 'a don-like figure in the corridors of power' (Siddharth 2004, 123).

Sonia Gandhi's induction into the family is referred to in an ambiguous manner. In some accounts by Sonia Gandhi herself, it is described as a gentle process where her choices matter: 'I was allowed… to find my own way of fitting into Rajiv's world. I began gradually to take an interest in the running of the household [the joint household, including Mrs Gandhi senior]' (Sonia Gandhi 1992, 2). The link between Sonia Gandhi's free choice in her actions on one hand and the gender-stereotyped daughterly duty on the other is notable here.[13] At other times, particularly if the impersonal forces of the perspective of the Indian populace at large are involved, the induction is considered as already having occurred. In this account, written in 1992, of how she felt not long after setting foot in India for the first time, some twenty-seven years after the event she asks herself

> why those eyes [of the Indian populace were] so insistent. I was to discover in time that this unnerving stare was not simply because I was a stranger and a foreigner. I was also a new member of a family that had lived for years in the public eye. (ibid., 2)

Here she is conscious of already belonging to the dynasty and, years later, foregrounds that belonging as an important element in her identity as 'a stranger' and a *videshini* ('a foreigner'). She demonstrates that her sense of belonging is anchored in rituals, and these include death as well as betrothal and marriage: 'on [Rajiv's] becoming Prime Minister in the wake of his mother's death, there were precise instructions for ancestral cremation of both or one [of us] by Rahul… [the] ashes [were to be delivered] into the Ganga at Triveni near Allahabad' (ibid., 9). This account of events in 1984, written after her husband's assassination in 1991, mentions Indira Gandhi's assassination as part of the process of shaping Sonia's identity within the dynasty. Triveni is held in high esteem by many Hindus, but it is also of course remembered as the place where M.K. Gandhi's ashes were released into the water. This is yet another example of the wide-ranging chronological perspective that links her, via the dynasty, to the spiritual father of the modern Indian nation. Sonia is stating that the family had already decided to use the same location that was used for the immersion of M.K. Gandhi's ashes.

There are other confluences (Triveni Sangams) and the seven Sapta Puri as well as many other sites, but the Yamuna and Ganges was the location for M.K. Gandhi's immersion.

Although Sonia Gandhi seeks to underline the thoroughness of her transformation from European to Indian, her account includes candid admissions, so as not to trivialize the substance of change and to underline that it needed determination on her part; for example: 'I felt awkward and uncomfortable wearing Indian clothes. My palate would not accept the unfamiliar pungent flavours' (Sonia Gandhi 1992, 2–3). These references pick up on two of the key markers of identity: dress and dietary preferences. However, the way in which these difficulties and differences are presented confirms that Sonia Gandhi understands they are desirable prerequisites for her acceptance by Indians, just as Sister Teresa understood the importance of 'living like the Indians', though the thought of it 'filled [her] with fear'. They are clearly also difficulties and differences which will be overcome; indeed the viewpoint from which the text is written suggests that by 1992, when the book was published, they had already been overcome.

The mention of the difficulties in Sonia Gandhi's induction into Indian life via the dynasty, and of their resolution, raises an important point about the sequence in which events are presented, which fits into the wider point about being wary of how past events are presented in accounts of Sonia Gandhi's life, both by herself and by others, whether her supporters or detractors. In her account there is no one particular transformation scene in which she sees herself becoming an Indian. As we have seen, her identity is constructed in a paradoxical fashion: she is a free agent at some points, such as in the period from 1965 to 1991, for example, and, at others, an individual who is 'bow[ing] to those forces which [are] now beyond [her] to fight' (Sonia Gandhi 1992, 7). This construction of identity and time is multilayered and non-linear. There are several objectives: some are high-order ones, such as the commemoration of her slain husband; but there are others that are just as important, such as acquainting readers with her own induction into the dynasty, her mother-in-law's role in that induction, and the place that she occupied within the family at the time of her publication in 1992. In a recognition which is diametrically opposed to her attempt to bracket out the family's public identity in 1965, she now acknowledges that its members belong to India (and the implication is that they live and die for India too): 'Rajiv did not belong to any group or caste or community. He was Indian and everyone saw him as their own' (Sonia Gandhi 1992, 11).

Sonia Gandhi's introduction is a tribute to her husband, but it is also written with a clear consciousness that the role of being the dynasty's standard-bearer had now fallen to her; all the more so in that her children were still to come of age in political terms in 1992 (Priyanka was aged twenty and Rahul twenty-two).[14] Her technique in this book is to illustrate her sensitivity to Indian sensibilities positively, rather than to deal directly with her opponents' reproaches about her foreign origin. Sonia Gandhi was not above portraying herself as having been humble and obedient when her mother-in-law and her husband were alive. After 1991, though, she saw herself as being under an obligation to act for the family and also for India. Her introduction to *Rajiv* is the narrative that expertly prepares the ground for stepping into the political arena. In 1997 she cut her political teeth in the relatively safe environment of the Calcutta Plenary Session of the Congress Party before submitting herself to the Indian electorate in 1999, winning the seats of both Bellary and Amethi. She was a Lok Sabha member for Bellary for just one year, but occupied the seat of Amethi until 2004, when it was contested and won by her son Rahul. In 2004, Sonia Gandhi became the member for Rae Bareli.[15]

How can we best describe the relation of Sonia Gandhi to foreignness, to the non-Indian elements in her make-up? As with the other Indian *videshinis* in this book, we need to consider how this is viewed by the woman herself as well as in the opinion of others. Maybe such identities and perspectives on identity simply flow effortlessly around each other as if dissolved in water, but with the non-standard ability to reconstitute as separate elements if circumstances change? If the temperature drops sufficiently, water freezes. Although low temperatures are not a natural feature of most of India, cold fronts do indeed form in politics whenever the question arises of Sonia Gandhi's foreign origins. And that question has been asked at the top of some people's voices at every election since 1999. Immediately before and during the election campaign in 2004, there was a feeling amongst those who opposed Sonia Gandhi that the issue of her origins and hence her implied loyalties was the most pressing matter facing India. It was the subject of her biographies from both sides of the political divide. For her detractors, it was the single issue which barred or should have barred her from holding executive positions in India. The subtitle of *Sonia Under Scrutiny* (New Delhi: India First Foundation, 2004), edited by A. Surya Prakash, is 'Issue of Foreign Origin'.[16] As Jaya Jaitly, one of the contributors to the volume, puts it, she 'is unable to realize the extent to which India can be humiliated if it cannot find a real Indian to lead it' (Jaitly 2004, 53). This stance is directly countered by a supporter like Janak Raj Jai in his study *Sonia's Foreign Origin: A Non-Issue* (Raj Jai 2004). This book is a point-by-point rebuttal of Prakash's. However, as long as Sonia Gandhi occupies a position in Indian public life, she will continue to be reproached for her foreign origins. K.N. Bhat, one of the contributors to Prakash's book, advances a republican-based legalistic argument, that India should follow the lead of the United States and bar foreign-born people from the two highest offices of state, those of president and vice-president (Bhat 2004, 24).

For other opponents, the principal issue is that, although she came to India and married Rajiv Gandhi in 1968, Sonia Gandhi did not take up Indian nationality until 1983. This means that, although they do not necessarily dispute that she was a citizen of India in 2004, her citizenship is under suspicion. As someone not born in India, it is argued that she is a 'citizen of the second class' (Prakash 2004, 12), implying that her citizenship can be revoked if she violates the letter of the law of the land (as her critics maintain she has already done in the Bofors Scandal). The rallying cry of the opponents of Rajiv Gandhi at the time was: 'Videshi biwi, videshi paise!' ('Foreign wife, foreign money!') (Sood 2009, 53).

A few lone voices, such as that of Barun Mitra, can be heard arguing that the 'foreign origin' issue is an example of unreflective political nationalism:

> behind this veneer of concern for the future of the country in the hands of one 'foreign born', the true sovereign in any democracy – the *demos*, the voting citizens – is being subjected to an ultimate insult. What these self-proclaimed champions of national self-respect are saying is that the voters are politically too dumb, emotionally too naive and therefore prone to being swayed by just one inexperienced foreigner. (Mitra 1999, 11)

But despite such voices, this issue has the potential to be reincarnated whenever her political opponents desire it: 'Once a foreigner, always a foreigner', they say (Jaitly 2004, 43). Another of the volume's contributors calls her a 'naturalised alien' (Siddharth 2004, 120).

Compared with Brahm Datt Bharti, whose rabid views in *Vatican–Teresa–Sonia* extend to casting sectarian slurs on Moslems and Christians in an indiscriminate manner (Datt Bharti 1995, 27), the contributors to the Prakash anthology are discerning individuals. Their education and intelligence, however, do not protect them from faulty logic in this question. They ground their blanket objection to any foreign-born individual in Indian politics by looking back in time both to the Second World War and to the final stages in the struggle for Indian independence. In this world view, it is possible to object to the presence of Sonia Gandhi in politics on the grounds that she is both 'white' and an Italian.[17] Her Italianness associates her with the Axis powers, who were defeated by the Allies supported by Commonwealth troops which included Indians. The introduction to the Prakash volume alludes to her father's supposed sympathies for Mussolini and her 'fascist upbringing' (though other commentators emphasize Stefano Maino's communist sympathies) (Prakash 2004, 11). The anachronism of these points, applied to a woman born in 1946, does not trouble the contributor, who writes that Indians 'defeated' Italians in the Second World War (Siddharth 2004, 124) and then immediately goes on to allude to the struggle for independence, in which, he states, 'we… got killed in hundreds for asking the white men to leave India. Liberalization seems to have removed the *Swadeshi* resistance not just to foreign goods, but to foreigners in general' (Gurumurthy 2004, 129). This is of course the amalgamating of two partly contemporaneous, but nonetheless very different struggles, one in which Indians were fighting for the Empire and another in which they were fighting against it.

If one is going to object to Sonia Gandhi's political career, it seems more coherent to do so from an anti-dynastic point of view. Even this anti-elitist discourse cannot flourish alone, it seems; it is also swamped by the anti-foreigner rhetoric, as in the following quotation: 'Can any foreigner, regardless of the family he or she is married into, be considered fit for the Prime Ministership merely on grounds of marriage?' (Siddharth 2004, 119). It is, however, the arguments employed to further this and similar objections that have an anti-white bias, which affects their legitimacy. The following objection to continued domination of the Indian political scene by the Nehru–Gandhi dynasty (made before Sonia Gandhi listened to her inner voice) is invalidated by its racism. According to this contributor, Sonia Gandhi displays the 'arrogance and superiority that comes from belonging not only to a white-skinned race, but to a family that believes in dynastic principles and its divine right to rule' (Jaitly 2004, 50). Surely, if Sonia Gandhi is arrogant, this has something to do with her as an individual rather than the colour of her skin?

The racist argumentation that is employed in these objections to foreigners originates in the colonial wound. The pain of this humiliation inflicted over several generations survives in many of those with first- or second-hand experience of the Independence struggle. Despite their roots in a desire for justice, arguments of this sort only perpetuate injustice and do not contribute to sophisticated political debate in the country. However, we have seen the nationalist card being played from the Balkans to Zimbabwe and how prevalent anti-foreigner rhetoric can be in such places, where it can frequently be linked to the former colonial power. As one of the contributors to the Prakash volume mentions, Indira Gandhi herself used the technique in the 1970s, 'with frequent references to the "foreign hand"' in Indian affairs' (Siddharth 2004, 116). One example of this was Indian disquiet at the supposed Central Intelligence Agency involvement in the marriage between the Chogyal of Sikkim and the American citizen Hope Cook in 1963. In the final analysis, this facile use of nationalism will be prevalent indefinitely and as long as there is political capital in it. The 'foreign issue' is an easy rallying point for politicians who oppose Congress. In a sovereign democracy they cannot question the free and fair decisions of voters; they can, however, dispute the right of Sonia Gandhi to stand for election and occupy high political office.

In 2002, in a lecture at the Oxford Centre for Islamic Studies entitled 'Conflict and Coexistence in Our Age', Sonia Gandhi sought to project the value of India's constitutionally anchored secularism: 'India is not a Hindu country, or a Moslem country or a Christian country... India is thus a multi-religious, multi-linguistic, multi-ethnic and multi-regional civilization without parallel' (Sonia Gandhi 2002, 12 and 15). This statement is eminently political, of course. As the then leader of the opposition, she was seeking both to distance herself from the pro-Hindu policies of her rivals and to position herself as a public spokesperson for non-sectarian values. This manoeuvre appears to be part of a conscious strategy, in the same vein as her 2004 renunciation and shift from being a prime ministerial candidate to being the holder of what appears to be a job for life as Congress Party president. She also seems to want to give the impression that she is above the cut and thrust of daily political life in India. The discourse of the 'inner voice' that she alluded to in 2004, when she moved into one of the most important backseats in Indian politics, associates her with a transcendental element in political life. As we have seen in the cases of both Saint Teresa and Mirra Alfassa, the Mother, the *shakti* or transcendent female principle is one of the ways in which Indian traditions allow women to hold and exercise power.

While outer voices drive the Indian politics that goes on around her, she can now maintain an aloof position, at least as long as the Congress Party remains a significant political force in India. For her critics she is not 'above' Indian politics, but 'behind' it, enjoying a powerful unelected position in Congress that gives her a key role in determining the party's prime ministerial candidate. In party terms she is a gatekeeper.

As far as the Nehru–Gandhi dynasty is concerned, the position of party president is ideal. It shields her from the political front line (except when she fights for her parliamentary seat at election time), but is a position of national importance nonetheless. This combination of attributes helps her in maintaining her position. She is currently the only member of the dynasty who has a significant level of international recognition outside India. It must be said that this recognition, however, derives from her appearance on television screens around the world in 1991 as Rajiv Gandhi's widow, rather than from any stateswoman-like activity on the international political stage. Therefore, despite her 2002 address at Oxford University, quoted above, her recognition belongs to the domain of institutions such as the *Forbes Magazine* list of the hundred most influential women in the world and *Time* magazine's one hundred most influential people. She has not forged a reputation for independent political thought on India's internal situation, though she did take a leading role in pushing through the Women's Reservation Bill in March 2010. In visual terms, the images of Sonia Gandhi that are prominent in the public domain (particularly those online) feature her with her two political forebears who held the position of prime minister (Jawaharlal Nehru and Indira Gandhi) and with visiting foreign heads of state and prime ministers who frequently pay her courtesy visits when they are in India. This status has earned her two Hindi epithets: Rajamata (the king's mother) and Mata Sonia (Mother Sonia).[18] Both terms indicate that her position is understood in both historical and symbolic terms.

Sonia Gandhi has been propelled into her current position by her brother-in-law's flying accident and by two acts of gross political violence (against her mother-in-law and her husband) that were beyond her control. Both criminal and both taking place during election campaigns, these last two acts were results of the religious and political fault lines present in Indian society and in South Asia more generally – the first concerning Operation Blue Star (the 1984 military operation to remove supporters of Damdami Taksal from the Golden Temple at Amritsar) and the second relating to the problems of India's neighbour Sri Lanka (and the bitter opposition of Tamil Eelam's Liberation Tigers to the presence of an Indian peacekeeping force in Sri Lanka between 1987 and 1990 under the Indo-Sri Lankan

Accord). These conflicts incited people to bring violence to the heart of the Indian state. They were tragic external events, but they were essential parts of the conveyor belt that took her to the brink of prime ministership and then to her role as a 'place-holder' Congress Party president. Sonia Gandhi's choice not to withdraw from public life has also maintained a form of political continuity for the dynasty. Her 'service to the nation' since 1998 has meant that the younger Nehru–Gandhis, such as Priyanka Gandhi and especially Rahul Gandhi, remained in the spotlight during their period of political infancy. Priyanka tried her hand at political campaigning and Rahul has continued his political apprenticeship via his parliamentary seat at Rae Bareli and through his work as chairperson of the Indian Youth Congress (2007 onwards), the National Students' Union (2007 onwards), general secretary of the Indian Nation Congress (2007–2013) and Party vice-president (from 2013 onwards).

Sonia Gandhi's holding role is particularly important given the continuing effects of the Maneka Gandhi schism. In the years since 1983, her sub-branch of the dynasty, including Sanjay and Maneka Gandhi's son Varun, has been developing a pro-Hindu ideology which elaborates a different type of Indianness from that for which Sonia Gandhi and Congress might be said to stand. Sonia Gandhi's statements about her own Indianness, for all their reliance on dynastic power structures, put forward the case for an inclusive, non-ethnic form of Indianness. In this, one might even say that she is a figurehead for the constitution in the manner of a non-executive ceremonial president in countries such as Ireland and Austria. Given that she has declined the prime ministership and that the Indian presidency has been held by individuals from a number of different regions and communities in India, is it possible that Sonia Gandhi might put herself forward for the post of president of India? For her detractors, the privilege that defines her political career invalidates any positive effect she may have had, such as her defence of secular values.

Indian political life remains driven by identity politics; birth and family allegiances often have a significant influence on political identity. For politicians, this frequently determines the constituencies they represent and the groups for which they seek to speak. In rural areas this manifests itself in feudal thinking (by both lords and labourers); at a national level, identity politics surfaces as paternalist thinking in which the Nehru–Gandhis are the nation's 'first family'. This accords with the statements by Sonia Gandhi in *Rajiv* (quoted above) that 'everyone [in India] saw him [Rajiv] as their own' (Sonia Gandhi 1992, 11). But the dynasties that exist at state level have not been able to occupy the highest offices of state on a sustained and frequent basis.[19] This has left the field free for Sonia Gandhi to occupy a holding position.

Lurking in the background is hereditary politics, a recessive effect of identity politics, the negative effects of which it concentrates and amplifies. Patrick French's *India: A Portrait* outlines these effects in a rather graphic way. The author demonstrates that, since 1947, there has been a consolidation of political power in India through family networks. With a team of Indian researchers, French investigated the family backgrounds of all 545 MPs in the Lok Sabha, the Indian lower house of Parliament. He defines a hereditary MP as one who has a close relative in politics. He found that, whereas only 10.5 per cent of MPs aged between seventy-one and eighty were hereditary, this rose to 65 per cent for those aged between thirty-one and forty and to 100 per cent for MPs under thirty. Also, over 66 per cent of all women MPs were hereditary. French states:

> If the trend continued, it would be possible that most members of the Indian Parliament would be there by heredity alone, and the nation would be back to where it had started before the freedom struggle, with rule by a hereditary monarch and assorted Indian princelings. (French 2011, 120)

Though French evidently does not feel the need to spell this out, 'hereditary monarch' is a reference to Rahul Gandhi.

This book has mentioned fictional representations in the case of Jeanne Dupleix, Saint Teresa (in passing) and in more detail with reference to Mirra Alfassa. We have seen that, if the posthumous representation of a particular Indian *videshini* is important for the organization that supported her, measures will be taken to monitor the representation and to defend a version which enhances the institution. This is the raison d'être of the Mother Teresa Center (which will probably be renamed the Saint Teresa Center).

In recent years, Sonia Gandhi has been robustly defended by the lawyer A. Manu Singhvi. In 2006, a biopic directed by Jagmohan Mundra with Monica Bellucci in the role of the party president was halted by the threat of legal action by Congress Party lawyers. The publication of the English-language translation of Javier Moro's *El Sari rojo* (*The Red Sari*) was also resisted until January 2015, after the Congress Party's defeat. Both the director of the film and the novelist claim to offer sympathetic portraits of this most prominent Indian *videshini*, with Mundra saying rather wistfully that the film was intended to be 'positive without being reverential'.[20] (Defenders of Sonia Gandhi would probably respond, 'They would say that, wouldn't they!') It appears that the strategy that was followed when Congress was in power was one of total media management. The reputation of this politician appears to have been so precious that all fictional portrayals were too risky. The novel's publisher, Pramod Kapoor, is quoted as saying: 'The pressure [not to publish] was more political than legal. When [Congress] was defeated that pressure was very much less.' In his opinion, 'the law should remain the same whether or not a party is in power, but what makes India different from other places is that there are laws beyond laws.'[21]

The content of the book suggests that Moro is aiming for an epic register to depict the blood sacrifice of the whole Nehru–Gandhi dynasty; hence the reference to red saris – though the cover images of the original Spanish text and of the Brazilian Portuguese and Catalan translations depict a Sonia Gandhi look alike in the more usual widow's white sari. For all the controversy surrounding its publication in India, the book is quite conventional in some respects; for instance, it does not stray from the position officially sanctioned by Sonia Gandhi and her lawyers as far as the controversial 'foreign origin' issue is concerned: 'She feels very Indian, she has learned to love the people of this country and she feels loved by them' (Moro 1998, n.p.).

This being fiction, Moro dramatizes competing instincts of fight or flight in Sonia Gandhi's mind after her husband's assassination. It contains passages which might be considered extremely sensitive, such as the following exchange:

> 'Madam, these are the times of the flights to Milan.' Sonia Gandhi does not remember having asked her husband's secretary for that information. Perhaps she did, in the confusion at the beginning, when she sought protection from the enormity of the tragedy... all her body language evokes that of a genuinely Indian person. (Moro 1998, n. p.)

In the opinion of those who advise Sonia Gandhi it is not admissible to mention the possibility of emigration in a fictional depiction. Moro is no doubt aware of the sensitivities here; that is why he has his protagonist fail to remember enquiring about flights to Europe.

In an article which praises Vinod Mehta's autobiography for breaking the mould as 'a rare and salacious Indian tell-all', Soutik Biswas makes a fascinating sidelong comment about life-writing in India:

> For a country obsessed with people's life stories, Indians don't write absorbing autobiographies or biographies. Most of them turn out to be long-winded hagiographies or self-absorbed and pedagogic narratives. India remains a deeply hierarchical society where criticism is often taken as a personal affront.[22]

One does sympathize with the readers for the meagre fair that is offered to them; this is certainly the case with many of the biographies of Sonia Gandhi analyzed in this chapter. The tragedy is that some people only consume works written from the point of view of which they are already convinced. There will be the anti-Sonia camp who will read only Brahm Datt Bharti's book (Datt Bharti 1995) and Surya Prakash's edited anthology (Prakash 2004), and the pro-Sonia people who will only deign to open Raj Jai (2004) and Sood (2009). The truth about Madam President would contain selected elements from both camps, with Chatterjee's two books as an overall moderating influence (Chatterjee 1998 and 2000). The answer to the question as to why the minders of Sonia's public image are so sensitive to competition from fictional forms must include the element of transcendentality mentioned above. For certain commentators, her *tyaga*-like renouncement of the worldly prize of the prime ministership 'transformed her from a political leader to a deity' (Dasgupta 2004, 11). This is the reverence for the individual senior women which is expressed in a singular and a wholehearted manner for a limited duration. The minders seem to believe that the transcendental element is something fragile which needs an unsullied space devoted to it in public life in order to continue to grow. It is this purity that they will go to any length to defend. The aspect that they cannot seem to embrace yet is that the reverence for Sonia Gandhi is a natural phenomenon in a nation with many religions and whose largest religion is polytheistic. This reverence will ebb and flow at its own pace, without the need for minders.

It may be that India is now on the cusp of an end of one form of the age of dynasties. That is the age of unbroken dynasties where every member of the clan who took part in public life gained a high public office by virtue of a mandate of the general population. In listening to her 'inner voice', Sonia Gandhi broke that unbroken line and her son is struggling to re-establish it. This struggle will go on no doubt, and could well be taken up by Priyanka Vadra's children. This non-linear succession is a trickle over rocky ground which flows down (through the generations) but can also be interrupted and flow sideways (across those generations) or even run dry for one season before returning the next. The situation of this elite family in India is now closer to the mixed picture in the United States with the past political achievements of the Kennedys and Bush families and the dynastic media profile of family of the 45th president.

In examining how others have represented her, going right back to her birth one discerns an ever-present polarization of opinion about Sonia Gandhi as a positive or negative influence in Indian politics. Sonia's own writings about herself are equally important for a full picture and their publication history teaches us to be extremely attuned to the historical context of each intervention. These autobiographical pieces were published at key moments – in the wake of the killing of her mother-in-law and, particularly, after her husband was assassinated – when she and her advisors felt it was necessary for her to address the nation in her own words.[23] Sonia Gandhi's contributions to these books, therefore, function as acts of commemoration in which she deepens her link with the family by representing it during a period of public mourning. She takes it upon herself to do this rather than withdrawing into a private space after a tragedy.[24] This public act of commemoration for a shocking attack on Indian democracy enhances her own position within that system. She has systematically provided a commentary on each generation of the dynasty, first editing a volume of letters between Indira Gandhi and Jawaharlal Nehru (1988, republished in 1992) and then contributing introductions to two commemorative volumes: *Rajiv* (1992) and a volume of photographs, *Rajiv's World* (1994).

What emerges is a triangular relationship between Sonia Gandhi's identity as an Indian of Italian origin, her identity as a woman, and her position within the Nehru–Gandhi dynasty. The main focus of the first part of the chapter was on personal and gender identity in the induction period, as constructed in accounts written by Sonia Gandhi after Rajiv's death and published in 1992 and 1994. The implication is clear: Sonia's own personal and gender identities had to be anchored in the hearts and minds of Indians so that the family would continue to occupy a position at the core of Indian public life. This was done in an act of public commemoration for her assassinated husband. The second part of the chapter focuses on Sonia Gandhi's changing place in Indian public life after 1984, 1991, 2004, and 2014. These representations are taken from biographies and contributions by both her supporters and her many detractors and include biographies, journalism and fiction. In the final analysis, at a national level, Sonia Gandhi is now marooned as a placeholder for the next generation of a family that cannot yet capitalize on its historical legacy. She is dependent on what her own son and political heir acknowledges as 'undemocratic' structures. The situation is confused and Congress appears not yet to have made up its collective mind whether Mrs Gandhi is part of the solution or part of the problem. That said, though, the story of Sonia Gandhi's political career demonstrates how the power of the dynastic myth in India propelled this Indian *videshini* to the cusp of the most powerful executive position in the Union of Indian States.

Notes

1. That figure includes fourteen years under Indira Gandhi: the ten years of her first three terms as prime minister from 1966 to 1977, followed by the four additional years of her fourth term between 1980 and 1984. Those fourteen years were followed by the five years of Rajiv Gandhi's tenure from 1984 to 1989.
2. For readers unfamiliar with India, let it be stated that there is no family relationship between M.K. 'Mahatma' Gandhi and the Nehru–Gandhis.
3. Rani Singh has called this 'the greatest transformational journey made by any world leader of the last four decades'. While we will have to wait for the verdict of history on whether Sonia Gandhi is a 'world leader' (Singh 2011, 240), there is no doubt that Singh is right about the distance that this Indian *videshini* travelled in public life.
4. This concept of an internal voice was so important for M.K. Gandhi that he also used other expressions for it in the same period, as illustrated by a quotation from *Young India* from the 1920s: 'There are moments in your life when you must act, even though you cannot carry your best friends with you. The "still small voice" within you must always be the final arbiter when there is a conflict of duty' (M.K. Gandhi 1920, 3).
5. Sanjoy Majumder, 'Why did Sonia change her mind?', http://news.bbc.co.uk/1/hi/world/south_asia/3726081.stm (accessed 11 November 2011).
6. Sood echoes this in the statement that Sonia Gandhi was 'more Indian than any Indian girl' (2009, 16).
7. Though not exhaustive, the following list, showing (in parentheses) the number of biographies of Sonia Gandhi published each year between 1997 and 2009, demonstrates the pattern of interest around a clear peak in 2004: 1997 (1), 1998 (2), 2000 (1), 2002 (1), 2003 (1), 2004 (6), 2005 (4), 2006 (1), 2009 (1) and 2011 (1). If the numbers of book-length biographies in English are anything to go by, the star of the dynasty's male scion has some way yet to rise: Lakshmi Priya's 2011 study, rather hopefully entitled *Rahul Gandhi: The Great Warrior*

of Indian Politics, bills itself as the first biography of the man (Priya 2011, xiii).

8. For a critique of the legitimacy of the dynasty, see Tariq Ali, *The Nehrus and the Gandhis: An Indian Dynasty* (2005).
9. Another example of this technique is her gentle mocking of British food ('boiled cabbage and gooey spaghetti on toast') and weather ('cold and gloomy') in her account of her first meeting with Rajiv in Cambridge (Sonia Gandhi 1992, 1). Her supporters would say this demonstrates her Indian perspective on life, whereas her detractors would probably call this an example of ingratiation.
10. A biographical note on an unofficial pro-Sonia website states that Rajiv and Sonia were married in a 'simple ceremony [that] was held on Vasant Panchami day in February, the same day when Indira Gandhi married Feroze decades earlier'; www.soniagandhi.org (accessed 11 November 2011).
11. Maneka Gandhi went so far as to make a counterclaim questioning the legitimacy of Indira Gandhi's marriage in terms of Hindu rights. The aim of this was to dispute Mrs Gandhi senior's share of $47,500 worth of shares owned by her deceased son ([no author] 1984, 11).
12. Rupa Chatterjee also quotes Gautam Kaul, Sonia's uncle-in-law, who refers to the Italians 'strong clannish spirit' and states that 'Sonia transferred that feeling to her family and relations once she came into our family' (1998, 92).
13. In 2004, her political opponents present her interest in running the joint household: 'Sonia, in the meanwhile, had been busy serving and taking care of her mother-in-law's guests. Her service to the nation until then consisted of serving on a government committee to purchase gifts for foreign dignitaries on behalf of her mother-in-law' (Jaitly 2004, 44–45). The emphasis here is on triviality and foreignness.
14. Seven years later, in 1999, Priyanka Gandhi helped her mother to campaign in the Amethi constituency.
15. Both Amethi and Rae Bareli are Nehru–Gandhi family seats. Rae Bareli had been won by Indira Gandhi in 1967 and by Sonia Gandhi's father-in-law Feroze Gandhi in 1952. Amethi had been held by both her brother-in-law Sanjay in 1980 and by her husband Rajiv from 1981 to 1991.

16. In *Vatican–Teresa–Sonia,* Brahm Datt Bharti propounds a conspiracy against India linking the United States and Rome (Datt Bharti 1995, 2), which, together, are aiming for 'political subjugation through ecclesiastical annexation' (ibid., 16). He evokes 'a plot being hatched and fostered by some people from within' (ibid., Preface, n.p.) and warns that 'the mediums to be used will be Indian citizens more than aliens' (ibid., 26).
17. Her political opponents would have a field day if they knew that 'Albina', her third given name at birth, means 'white'.
18. The first is advanced by Jaitly, who lambastes her expectation to be called upon 'as if she were the dowager Empress of India or the *Rajamata* of a feudal court' (2004, 48–9); the second is found in a rather jocular account by a more neutral commentator, Swapan Dasgupta (2004, 11).
19. Four of the many examples of such families and their main regions of influence (in parentheses) are the Bansilals (Haryana), the Anugrah Narayan Sinha/Singh family (Bihar and Nagaland), the Karunanidhi family (Tamil Nadu) and the Nandamuris (Andhra Pradesh).
20. http://sawfnews.com/Entertainment/16344.asp and Agence France Presse (accessed 11 November 2011).
21. http://www.theguardian.com/world/2015/jan/23/india-congress-party-decline-sonia-gandhi-book (accessed 11 August 2015).
22. http://www.bbc.co.uk/news/world-asia-15719679 (accessed 11 November 2012).
23. 'Sonia Gandhi was helped [in the editing of her contribution to *Rajiv*] by Manjulika Dubey, a former editor with Roli Books and the wife of Suman Dubey, Rajiv's old friend and associate from the Doon School till [his assassination at] Sriperumbudur' (Chatterjee 2000, 145).
24. 'Anyone who says Sonia Gandhi is ordinary ignores her will not to withdraw after the assassination [of her husband]' (Chatterjee 2000, 121).

CONCLUSION

The span of this study starts in 1893, a year of arrival, travel and return. It was the year in which Annie Besant arrived in South India, the year Swami Vivekananda travelled to North America and the year Sri Aurobindo returned to West Bengal. A hundred and twenty-four years later, the end point in the span has not yet been reached: although Sonia Gandhi celebrated her eighteenth and final anniversary as Congress Party President for life in March 2017 and Simone Tata is very much involved in work for the Tata charitable foundations.

If we step back for a moment and consider the organizational legacy of these Indian *videshinis* – which includes the Home Rule League, the Central Hindu College, the All India Women's Conference, Auroville, the Missionaries of Charity, Lakmé cosmetics and Westside retail – it is clear that these women have had a profound and diverse influence on civil society across India. But how do things look if we change tack and attempt to discern their particular legacy for Indian women? We recall that such an attempt is unrepresentative in terms of the book as a whole, since only four out of eleven aimed specifically to improve conditions for women: Sister Nivedita, Margaret Cousins, Princess Durru Shehvar and Princess Niloufer. The institutions that they sponsored and helped to found continue in adapted form in 2016. Of these institutions, the Princess Niloufer Children's Hospital and the Princess Durru Shehvar Children's Medical Aid Society, the All India Women's Conference (AIWC) and the Ramakrishna

Sarada Mission Sister Nivedita Girls' School, only the last two have a specifically female focus. Sister Nivedita has a hallowed placed in the school *daalaan* or entrance hall and Margaret Cousins has a library named after her at the AIWC headquarters in New Delhi.[1]

Although these two cases of commemoration and veneration are culturally important, identifying a living legacy for the Indian *videshini* needs a wider frame. Simone Tata helped the women who purchased Lakmé cosmetics to achieve a paradigm shift in their social acceptability in India, but the economic effects of their consumer choice was felt across the economy and not only by women. The same applies to Mirra Alfassa's Auroville, which is a mixed community, not only in terms of nationalities, but also in terms of gender. Sonia Gandhi is also in a similar situation, and will probably continue to exert her influence over all members of the Congress Party, regardless of gender. These conclusions underline the point made in the Introduction that the gender-based components in the analysis need to be considered in tandem with social and economic ones.[2]

Perhaps we might consider the legacy of Indian *videshinis* not *for* women, but *through* women. This is to personalize their legacy and to examine whether women play a predominant role as their successors. Just as it has been essential constantly to factor into their activity the role of their respective elites, so it is as far as their legacy is concerned. Viewed through their elites, however, the picture is a rather depressing one, suggesting that their specifically female legacy is very much under pressure. Moreover, since the official working lives of all of these women have come to an end, the patriarchal structure inherent in the elites re-exerts itself. This phenomenon accords with continuation of a restrictive notion of class among elites in the United States:

> [T]he increased diversity in the power elite has not generated any changes in the underlying class system... The elite is no longer exclusively wasp [white Anglo-Saxon protestant], but members still share perspectives and values that favor narrow class interests regardless of where they come from. (Zweigenhaft and Domhoff 2006, 11)

In attempting to examine the Indian *videshinis'* legacy through women, it is useful to divide the group into those who had children during the period of their engagement with India and those who did not. In the first group, therefore, we are dealing with a genetically individualized legacy by offspring and in the other with a legacy by representatives. Applying this distinction yields Jeanne Dupleix, Sooni Tata, Simone Tata, Princess Durru Shehvar and Sonia Gandhi as mothers on one side, and Sister Nivedita, Saint Teresa, Margaret Cousins and Princess Niloufer as women without children on the other. There is a third group of women, including Annie Besant and Mirra Alfassa, who had children before they arrived in India. These children can be bracketed out of the equation because they had no lasting influence in India in their own right, nor did they transform the organizations founded by their mothers.[3]

What, then, has become of the daughters of the Indian *videshinis*? Over the centuries, and all over the world, there have been societies that have sanctioned interference in human reproduction in order to manipulate the probability of having children of a particular (usually male) gender. This interference, the desperately sad techniques it uses and their destabilizing demographic effects are ongoing problems in many countries, India included. It is probably safe to assume that selective female abortion did not come into play in the case of these women and that the low frequency of surviving female children within the group of Indian *videshini* mothers is the result of chance (in any case the sample of five women is not statistically significant). Even taking this into account, the influence of their girl children still makes dismal reading; none of the seven female offsprings born to Jeanne Dupleix, Sooni Tata and Sonia Gandhi have had anything approaching the influence enjoyed by their mothers.

This analysis of the influence of the girl children of the Indian *videshinis* begins with the tragic legacy of Jeanne Dupleix's six female children. Of these six, four survived into adulthood, but all four died young or in childbirth.[4] The only one to be taken to France was Marie-Gertrude, known by her nickname 'Chonchon'. She survived her mother by only three years, dying in childbirth in 1759. The only thing known about the Marquise's only female grandchild, the daughter of Anne-Christine and the Chevalier d'Epremesnil, is the little girl's nickname 'Mimi'. Thus the end of the Dupleix's distaff line is similar to the pitiful end of all the dreams and pretensions of Madame Bovary in the landmark nineteenth-century French novel by Gustave Flaubert. Young Berthe Bovary's life is summarized in half a sentence. The bourgeois life is no more and Emma Bovary's daughter is sent to work in 'une filature de coton' (cotton mill) to earn her living (Flaubert 1971 [1856]).

As far as the distaff line of the family is concerned, there is an additional factor in the way that the family was remembered in France, which obscured the role of women within it. We have seen in the references to historical and fictional texts in the *prélude pondichérien* that posthumous writing about the Dupleixes is one of the main ways that French presence in India has been memorialized since the eighteenth century. We have also noted, however, that Jeanne Dupleix features in these works very much as an adjunct to her governor-general husband.

Sooni Tata, who had five children with her husband R.D. Tata, was the most reproductively fertile Indian *videshini* after the Marquise Dupleix. Her daughters were the first- and fourth-born of her children. Although Sylla Tata (1903–93) and Rodabeh (Dabeh) Tata (1911–94) continued to live in India, they appear not to have taken any active role in the Tata business empire. Sylla married Sir Framjee Dinshaw Petit, third Baronet (1901–83). Rodabeh married Leslie Sawhney who became director-in-charge of the Indian Hotels Company. Although she had no formal training in the field, Rodabeh is acknowledged and remembered within the Tata Group for the significant contribution she made to the interior design for the refit of the Taj Mahal Palace Hotel in 1965 (Simone Tata 2012). Princess Durru Shehvar had two sons, but no daughters. (As we saw in her chapter, the power of attorney of her elder son, Mukarram Jah, is held by his first ex-wife, Esra Birgin, who is generally acknowledged to have played a disinterested and positive role in partially re-establishing the cultural legacy of the dynasty in Hyderabad.) Simone Tata had one son, Noel Tata, who holds an important position within the Tata Group, but she had no female children.

When we come to Sonia Gandhi, however, these highways and byways populated by men lead us to an interesting woman: Priyanka Vadra, Rajiv and Sonia Gandhi's only daughter and the younger of their two children. The difference in the involvement in politics between Priyanka and her sibling Rahul is similar to that between the siblings Sanjay and Rajiv Gandhi in the previous generation. Sanjay pursued a political career from the start whereas Rajiv kept his distance from politics. Priyanka, like her father before her, has been able to enjoy the luxury of not standing for election. With her husband, Robert Vadra, she has, however, helped regularly with local party organization and campaigning on behalf of first her mother and then her brother in the constituencies of Amethi and Rae Bareli (the second of these is the curiously Italian-sounding headquarters of 'Gandhi Inc.'). This activity that serves to keep her in the public eye has occurred regularly: in 1999, 2004, 2007 and 2012. According to an NDTV interview with Barkha Dutt in 2009, Priyanka wants to remain in this background role. It is interesting that the discourse she uses to ground this decision not to run for public office is the same as her mother's, that of an 'inner voice'. Her interiority is based on a period of Vipassana meditation in 1999.[5]

If she does decide to stand for election at some future date, the full force of public scrutiny will fall upon her. The arguments that will be levelled at her will be objections in terms of her dynastic allegiances, rather than concerns about foreign origin. Unlike her Italian-born mother, Priyanka is beyond reproach as far as her birth is concerned; moreover, she is married to an Indian.[6] Her brother pursues a political career and he is the heir apparent, Priyanka Vadra's political potential, however, remains unfulfilled. Her mother now occupies an office to which she is elected by Congress members and not by the public at large; this makes her position relatively secure for now, enabling her to continue to function better as a placeholder for her son, although there is no democratic justification for her continued tenure, particularly after the defeat of 2014. As far as her daughter is concerned, direct female political filiation remains a potential; such is the unpredictable nature of politics that the time might come when Priyanka or her daughter Miraya might decide to stand for election in her own right.

Given this balance sheet and the fact that their single female torchbearer has not yet started her race, there is no option but to conclude that these Indian *videshini* mothers reproduce power for their dynasties with no apparent pro-female gender bias. This conclusion seems to be borne out if we consider that the intended symbolic offspring of Annie Besant, Jiddu Krishnamurti, was a man (and he was accompanied by his brother as a companion and potential replacement). Fortunately for all those concerned, this project for succession in Theosophy, in which the unlikely couple of Charles Leadbetter and Annie Besant begot an Indian 'world teacher', ended in 1929 when the 'son' rejected both the project and its particular form of filiation. Krishnamurti pursued an independent path as a teacher of spirituality.

Looking now at non-genetic, symbolic filiation among those Indian *videshinis* without children, it would seem that the only gender-specific legacy of the Indian *videshinis* is the small army of nuns belonging to Saint Teresa's order. These are the massed ranks of the Missionaries of Charity, now predominantly of Indian origin. This is indeed an incongruous legacy. Although they have a long tradition of attending to personal suffering in Kolkata, in other Indian cities and around the world, the elite to which they belong, the Roman Catholic Church, is an organization that is entirely unreconstructed in terms of its supranational hierarchy.[7] Its power structure includes the Catholic Church in India of course, but the spiritual authority at its centre is European in origin. Ultimate authority sits with the pope in the Vatican.

As we have seen in the case of Margaret Cousins, it was possible for Indian *videshinis* to see themselves as symbolic midwives for Indian daughters who would continue their work once capacity was built in their organizations. The feminists in the Abala Abhivardini Samaj (Weaker Sex Improvement Society) and the Tamil Women's Association were enriched by the international dimension of Cousin's contribution to their organization. In institutional terms, it is clear that the Missionaries of Charity is a success and serves to harness the aspirations for services of Indian Catholics, particularly those from South India. In personal terms, however, compared with the richness of the active intercultural negotiation of a Simone Tata, a Princess Durru Shehvar and especially of a Sister Nivedita, the hybridity of Missionaries of Charity nuns does appear to be rather impoverished. This is because they live as individuals in a single-faith community, and the majority of a sister's contact with individuals outside that community is with destitute people. Perhaps we are all better off waiting for the next female avatar of the Nehru–Gandhi dynasty. There is clearly no other woman who has Priyanka Vadra's prominence. Social activists' circles and students in Madurai might well mention Gabriele Dietrich (born in Berlin in 1943) as a possible candidate. She is a professor of social analysis and a social activist and tells the following tale of her long path to acquiring an Indian passport:

> I had applied for Indian citizenship because of my conviction that a full engagement with people's organizations required me to be a citizen. I had begun the process in 1984 but the difficulties I encountered require an article of their own! [...] [A]mong all the hurdles I encountered was a local clerk [who said] "Waste, madam. This will never work. Let your hubby apply first and you'll get it automatically". My husband, though supportive of my decision, had never dreamt of applying for citizenship himself. I am, in all likelihood, the only example of a woman married to a foreign citizen to be naturalised ... (Dietrich 2011, 13)[8]

One of the only women under forty who might merit being called an Indian *videshini* in the future is Kalki Koechlin, the Indo-French film actress gradually gaining prominence in India (Bobin 2012). That said, however, prominence is one thing; achieving influence on Indian society in the manner of the Indian *videshinis* is quite another matter.

Attempting to discern a legacy for Indian *videshinis* through women, therefore, leads to a series of dead ends. Their most significant legacy is an organizational one and the material trace that they leave in the street signs of a few Indian cities.

If we grant that Indian *videshinis* were so numerous and influential in the period in question, this leads us to ask why there are hardly any of them making their mark in Indian society today? The recessive patriarchy of elites and the reproductive accident of the preponderance of boy children among their offspring provide only partial explanations. The more complete explanation can be found by examining the cross-border availability of opportunity though globalization. In 1947 the elites were content that independent India anchored their social position in a narrative of nation, but they were also anxious to give their sons and daughters an international edge in education and work experience. Now globalization has internationalized Indians and perhaps made the position of the Indian *videshinis* redundant. If by some chance an elite family in post-liberalization India does not have any international experience of this sort and wants to internationalize in a rapid manner, another option open to it is integration via arranged marriage with a person of Indian origin (PIO) or a non-resident Indian (NRI). There are approximately twenty-seven countries around the world that have an Indian-origin population of more than 100,000. In total, the Indian diaspora numbers over thirty million, with the United States of America and the United Kingdom being the home to populations of 2.8 and 1.4 million respectively. The fact that we are unlikely to see the return of the Indian *videshini* as typified by the subjects of this book only goes to enhance the value of these examples. Taken together, the women studied here are a unique group, whose collective influence in India represents an important historical phenomenon, but it is one which gives us an insight into how elites function in today's India.

As we move into the final phase of this book, let us recall our wariness, signalled in the Preface, about applying grand theories to India and its peoples. This is particularly important to bear in mind in a summative conclusion. Reviewing the book's source material and its content, there is no simple single characteristic common to all the Indian *videshinis*; what they do share, however, is identities negotiated in different ways between Indianness and foreignness. As we have seen, their writing about themselves makes an active contribution to the ways in which they are perceived. Their identity for others, however, is also defined by the background political situation in the period between 1893 and 2017.

The female subjects of this book are notable for their diversity. This has been referred to in the Introduction using the notion of a 'plural Europe'. This diversity includes western European nations such as France (Sooni Tata, Mirra Alfassa), Italy (Sonia Gandhi) and Switzerland (Simone Tata). The most striking part of this diversity, however, is the decentred Europe that results when we take into account the Ottoman Turkish origins of princesses Durru Shehvar and Niloufer, the Irishness of Annie Besant, Sister Nivedita and Margaret Cousins and the Albanian-speaking otherness of Anjezë Gonxha Bojaxhiu before she became Sister, Mother and then finally Saint Teresa. The Europeanness of these women is not limited to the colonizer nations of western Europe; it includes peoples, nations or empires that were or had been under the sphere of others: the Irish in thrall to the British; the Albanian-speaking Macedonians controlled by the Ottoman Empire until 1912 and by the Serbs after that; and, finally, the Ottoman Turks, defeated by the Great Powers, by the emerging Balkan states and by the internal nationalist movement from within Turkey itself.[9] The resulting plurality of the female subjects of this book taken as a group is interesting; but it is important to note a caveat as far as the identity of individual women is concerned: it would be incorrect to essentialize the Indian *videshinis* according to their countries of birth or the citizenship that they hold, in spite of the origins of some of them in a decentred Europe. It would be an error to think that there is something essentially and immutably French, Italian, Swiss, Turkish, Albanian or Irish about them. To understand this we need to remind ourselves that they engaged not only with an abstract notion of India, but, in some way or the other, every one of these women passed through England en route to India.

That the passage to India was a journey through England can be illustrated first by the role of the English language. All the women in this book (except Jeanne Dupleix) either already had (in the case of the 'Irishwomen') or had to acquire a level of competence in English, which was such that they could do their business in that language. (In the elite circles in which they moved, knowledge of Indian languages was desirable, but not essential.)

This transiting through Britain can be understood in a quite literal sense. As shown by passenger lists, Southampton, London and Tilbury were the main ports of departure for India.[10] There is also the interesting factor that, while it was the colonial power, Britain controlled access to India. Thus, Mirra Alfassa, then called Mirra Richard, and her husband Paul were kept waiting in Japan for several months before they were granted permission 'to travel to India through British ports' (Heehs 2008, 321).

The passage through Britain can also be understood in a more fundamental manner that affected the individual women's cultural make-up. For instance, Annie Besant and Margaret Noble were educated in Britain; and we have seen that in 1948, for Simone Tata London was like a waiting room for India. We have also seen that when, again in 1948, Princess Durru Shehvar and her sons boarded a private aeroplane, as the armed forces of the newly independent Union of Indian States gathered around the Nizamate of Hyderabad, their destination was neither Istanbul nor Nice (the cities of Durru Shehvar's birth and marriage), but London and its Savoy Hotel. Sonia Maino and Rajiv Gandhi have an even closer connection with the United Kingdom, having met in Cambridge in 1965. She was at a language school and he was at Trinity College studying engineering. It is because of these instances of cultural contact that Britain and the British Empire in India do not function as constant and absolutely opposite poles in the formation of the women's identities. This means that the structures of difference mentioned in the Introduction also contain an unavoidable engagement with the British in the whole of the peri-colonial period, from 1893 to 2011, the year of Sonia Gandhi's last visit to London, where she delivered the 14th Commonwealth Lecture entitled 'Women as Agents of Change'.[11]

These women's lives also include multiple itineraries, all of which have influenced their plural cultural identities. It is not just a case of a simple single journey from a European country to India. The epigraphic quotations that open each chapter are intended to give a sense of this plurality, as viewed by the women themselves and also by others. For example, the self-proclaimed composite identity of Saint Teresa quoted in the epigraphs includes the following elements: 'Albanian', 'Indian', 'Catholic Church', 'whole world', and 'Jesus'. This dimension is elaborated in the cosmopolitan, internationalist or even transnational elements of their activities, dress and multilingualism. This is about a plural identity practice which goes beyond parochial nationalism – that type of nationalism would be the sort of arrogance that says that European is always best. This limiting form of nationalism is eloquently criticized by Sooni Tata when she lambastes the 'stay-at-home' Frenchman.[12] The implication of the plurality of their identities is that the Indian *videshinis* will be unlikely to consider the Indianness of Indians in monolithic terms. This is because the only form of Indianness that could include them would be one which is plural and not predetermined in terms of religion and caste. Thus for our first Indian *videshini*, Annie Besant, to suggest that she was 'cradled in England but Indian by choice' (Besant 1917, 2) would only be logical and morally defensible if she supported the same plurality for Indians. In the event, as we saw in her references to the Brahmins taking their 'rightful place again as leaders' (Besant 1918, 5), she favoured a return to Brahmin privilege.

The analysis of this book has examined two distinct aspects of these women's identity. We have observed, first, a certain nimbleness in the women's negotiation of their own multiple identities; and, second, a tendency for Indians to consider the European-born women either as Indians (Sister Nivedita, Saint Teresa), or as foreigners. This tendency co-exists with the women's plural identities. Of course in the case of some women, most notably Sonia Gandhi, we have one group of Indians arguing for her adoption and another group condemning her as an alien.

Following this schematic overview of the ways in which the identities of the European-born subjects in this book are constructed, it is now time to consider their influence. Where the women's identities displayed a plural representation of nation, their influence is dependent on a singular expression of the Indian nation.

Indeed, the crucial factor that positively influences the careers of these non-British, European-born Indian *videshinis* is that they were better able than British women to be co-opted onto the nationalist journeys of their respective elites or support groups (even if some of those journeys began in the final decade of the nineteenth century, over forty years before Indian independence was achieved). The Indian *videshinis*' elite support groups were strong enough (precisely because they were pro-Indian and not British) to sustain them by making a space for their differences – an advantage that, clearly, was unavailable to British women.

The more contact that these women had with the British, the more vehemently their difference could be harnessed by their elites in the service of Indian nationalism or in the context of increasing national consciousness. Their difference and plurality then becomes reified as political resistance, although in reality the attitudes of Annie Besant and Sister Nivedita towards Indian nationhood were much more nuanced. This might be expected given the enormous variations in the political situation between the arrival of Besant in 1893 and her death in 1933. It also applies to Sister Nivedita, who arrived in 1898 and died in 1911. Annie Besant styled herself as an Irishwoman in relation to the Irish Home Rule project that she transplanted to India. Although she is monumentalized today as a freedom fighter, her political position favoured an alliance between India and Britain rather than a clean break. Sister Nivedita was seen as an Irishwoman by her Indian spiritual guide, Swami Vivekananda, and by those responsible for her reputation after her early death: her Indian publishers, her biographer, her translator and the writers of the prefaces to her works. The discourse of nationalism is so strong that the English elements within her self-description were elided in favour of an Irish national identity defined in opposition to it. Her early death, her lack of overt political activity and the fact that her Indian support organization, the Sri Ramakrishna Mission, was engaged on a path that was less elitist than that of Annie Besant, all conspired to make Sister Nivedita's legacy less connected with Indian nationhood and thus more limited in influence than Besant's. However, the chapter shows that the depth of the intellectual engagement with India in Sister Nivedita's writing is only now getting the attention it deserves.

Additionally, since the influence of an Indian *videshini* depends on the intensity of the engagement of her elite or support group with the ideal of the Indian nation, the potential for influence moved to a higher level when the Indian nation was actually established in 1947.

The connection between influence and the difference in this intensity can be illustrated by comparing Simone Tata with Sonia Gandhi. The Tata Group is one of India's most prominent multinationals, but the logic of a business whose leaders work to benefit the company's bottom line meant that Simone Tata and Lakmé were at the service of the nation only when company and national interests coincided. The Nehru–Gandhi dynasty on the other hand gains its significance from an unwritten covenant linking it with the foundation of India as a nation.

In the second decade of the present century, both the Nehru–Gandhi dynasty and India are at a generational crossroads. For how many more generations can dynastic influence constructed via the narrative of nation have such a prominent role in Indian politics? It may be that Sonia Gandhi is still to fulfil her life's work, by durably transmitting the family's influence to the next generation despite the plurality of her identity. With all its missing elements, linguistic and cultural, and without a claim by birthright, hers is a fragile Indianness, a performance of Indianness, a willed Indianness. Though she has used it in an increasingly questionable way to occupy a senior position in a major Indian political party, it is a testimony to India's hospitality in the peri-colonial period that such a form of Indianness can continue to exist. There is a political slogan she has spoken in front of crowds at hundreds of election rallies over the years, words which are full of controversy because they are spoken by her as an Italian-born woman. These words are preposterous to many Indians, but to those in Congress they are the crutch that the party and the country still need because they reconnect the most elite family with the narrative of nation in what Natwar Singh has called an 'elected dynasty'.[13] They do this in spite of the complex past of the person who is speaking them. If she campaigns in the Lok Sabha elections in 2019, perhaps with Rahul or Priyanka at her side, Sonia Gandhi's slogan will still stress her Indianness and the continuation of her family's power: 'Jai Hind', Sonia will say, 'Victory to India!'

Notes

1. http://sisterniveditagirlsschool.org/photogallery/pages/School-Dalan.html and http://www.aiwc.org.in/photo-gallery.html (both accessed 11 November 2011).
2. The ability of the activity of Indian *videshinis* such as Saint Teresa, Simone Tata and Sonia Gandhi to influence the generality of civil society after 1947 defines the difference in emphasis between this book and Kumari Jayawardena's path-breaking study *The White Woman's Other Burden: Western Women and South Asia During British Rule* (1995).
3. Mirra Alfassa's son, André Morisset, was sympathetic to both the Sri Aurobindo Ashram and to Auroville, but he did not play a leading role in either institution. Similarly, Besant's daughter Mabel Emily Besant-Scott (1870–1952) had no involvement with the organization of the Theosophical Society headquarters at Adyar, Chennai.
4. These four daughters were Marie-Rose (1722–48), Anne-Christine (1727–48), Jeanne-Suzanne-Ursule, called Suzon (1729–45) and Marie-Gertrude, called Chonchon (1736–59).
5. See http://www.youtube.com/watch?v=hzW9nCOxUq0 (accessed 11 November 2012).
6. However, if she enters the political fray, 'evidence' will probably be found to cast doubt on her Indian nationality, as it was in the case of her brother on company documents which were widely reported on in the media in March 2016: http://www.ndtv.com/india-news/rahul-gandhi-asked-to-explain-british-citizenship-charge-by-ethics-panel-1286870 (accessed March 2016).
7. Aroup Chatterjee's objections concerning the modus operandi of Mother Teresa and the Missionaries of Charity have already been noted.
8. 'Upholding Each Other' in Ritu Menon, ed. *Making a Difference: Memoirs from the Women's Movement*, New Delhi: Women Unlimited

in collaboration with *Women's World India*, 2011, pp. 1–19.

9. Although it will be contested by some, the inclusion of Turkish-born women as Europeans is deliberately inclusive; it recognizes the ragged edge of Europe's eastern border.
10. For example, Annie Besant left from the Port of London in 1893 and Sooni Tata appears to have left from Tilbury in 1919.
11. The full lecture with its prominent dynastic references and uncontroversial content is available here: https://www.youtube.com/watch?v=IlvnWDU-YzI
12. In a letter to her mother, Mathilde Brière, dated 7 January 1904 (Sooni Tata 1904a).
13. Natwar Singh in an NDTV interview with Nidhi Razan (1 August 2014) https://www.youtube.com/watch?v=OXuTEWSWAW8.

Appendix 1
BIOGRAPHICAL INFORMATION

Name in India	Birth name	Place and date of birth	Date of arrival in India	Region of activity in India	Indian elite or support group	Organization she founded and/or developed
Education and Activism						
Annie Besant	Annie Wood	London, 1844	1893	India-wide, Chennai	The Theosophical Society	Home Rule League Central Hindu College Indian National Convention
Sister Nivedita	Margaret Noble	Dungannon, Northern Ireland, 1867	1898	Kolkata (Bagbazar)	Ramakrishna Mission	Girls School Bagbazar, Kolkata
Margaret Cousins	Margaret Cousins	Boyle, Southern Ireland, 1878	1915	India-wide, Chennai	The Theosophical Society	All India Women's Conference
Religion and Spirituality						
The Mother	Blanche Rachel Mirra Alfassa	Paris, 1878	1914 (visit) 1920 (settled)	Puducherry, Tamil Nadu	Sri Aurobindo Ashram	Auroville
Mother Teresa	Anjezë Gonxha Bojaxhiu	Skopje, Macedonia, 1910	1928	India-wide, Kolkata	Roman Catholic Church in India	Missionaries of Charity

Name in India	Birth name	Place and date of birth	Date of arrival in India	Region of activity in India	Indian elite or support group	Organization she founded and/or developed
International Business and Commerce						
Sooni Tata	Suzanne Brière	Paris, 1880	1902	Mumbai	R.D. Tata	Next generation of Tata family
Simone Tata	Simone Dunoyer	Geneva, 1930	1953 (visit) 1955 (settled)	India-wide, Mumbai	Tata family and Naval H. Tata	Lakmé Cosmetics Westside Retail
State and National Politics						
H.H. Nawab Durru Shehvar Durdana Begum Sahiba, Princess of Berar	H.I.H. Princess Khadija Hayriya Aisha Durru Shehvar, Sultana	Istanbul, 1914	1932	Hyderabad	Nizamate of Hyderabad	Hyderabad State Women's Conference and Durru Shehvar Children's Medical Aid Society
Nawab Niloufer Farhat Begum Sahiba	H.H. Niloufer, Khanum Sultana	Istanbul, 1916	1932	Hyderabad	Nizamate of Hyderabad	Princess Niloufer Hospital
Sonia Gandhi	Edvige Antonia Albina Maino	Lusiana, Italy, 1946	1968	India-wide and New Delhi	Nehru–Gandhi dynasty	Next generation of the Nehru–Gandhi dynasty

Appendix 2
SAINT TERESA'S KEY LETTERS

Date	To	Content	Page(s)
January 1947	Archbishop Périer	First request to found her Order. Its name, its dress, an invocation of Cabrini and the voice of God; living with Indians (though she fears this).	Kolodiejchuk 2007, 47–52
February 1948	Cardinal Prefect of the Sacred Congregation of Religious in Rome	Plea for secularization, because must 'live like an Indian with the Indians'.	Kolodiejchuk 2007, 115
September 1948	Fr. Van Exem	Playfully enjoys a subaltern position, though she has a 'fair face'.	Kolodiejchuk 2007, 127
October 1954	Jacqueline de Decker	Sketches out the notion of 'second self', allowing non-resident incapacitated individuals to help the cause.	Kolodiejchuk 2007, 147

BIBLIOGRAPHY

[no author]. 1894. 'Indian Affairs.' *The Times,* 5 February: 8.

[no author]. 1930. 'Round-Table Conference.' *The Times,* 6 October: 13.

[no author]. 1931a. 'Report on the Internal Situation of the Hyderabad State for the Fortnight Ending 30 November.' British Library, IOR R/1/1/2063 1931–32.

[no author]. 1931b. 'Round-Table Conference.' *The Times,* 5 September: 9.

[no author]. 1931c. 'Wedding of the Nizam's Sons.' *The Times,* 12 November: 13.

[no author]. 1931d. Court Circular, *The Times,* 27 January: 17.

[no author]. 1932. 'The Home-Coming of the Hyderabad Princes.' *Asiatic Review* 28, no. 94 (April): 330–4.

[no author]. 1937. 'Hyderabad: Silver Jubilee Durbar.' *Time* 29, issue 8 (22 February): 4–5.

[no author]. 1943. 'Nizam of Hyderabad's War Gifts.' *The Times,* 18 March: 8.

[no author]. 1947a. 'Court Circular.' *The Times,* 2 April: 7.

[no author]. 1947b. 'negotiate an alliance with India, rather than an amalgamation into India', a minute dated 22 September 1947. National Archives of the UK, PREM 8/568.

[no author]. 1948. 'A Map of Hyderabad State.' *Chicago Sun,* 16 September: 11.

[no author]. 1966. 'TOMCO, a Saga of Perseverance.' *Tata Review* 2, no. 1 (June–September): 15–16 and 21–22.

[no author]. 1968a. 'Lakmé: from Strength to Strength.' *Tata Review* 3, no. 4: 24.

[no author]. 1968b. *Auroville.* Pondicherry: Sri Aurobindo Society.

[no author]. 1969. 'Scéance commémorative de Sri Aurobindo à la Sorbonne, le 5 décembre 1955.' Pondicherry: Sri Aurobindo Ashram Trust.

[no author]. 1974. *Auroville, the First Six Years 1968–1974*. Auroville: Auropublications.

[no author]. 1977. *Matrimandir, August 1970–February 1977*. Auroville: Auropublications.

[no author]. 1984. 'Mrs Gandhi Not Hindu – Daughter-in-Law Says.' *New York Times* (2 May) http://www.nytimes.com/1984/05/02/world/around-the-world-mrs-gandhi-not-hindu-daughter-in-law-says.html (accessed 11 November, 2011).

[no author]. 1988. Auroville International Information. [n.p.]: Auroville International United Kingdom.

[no author]. 1990. Auroville International Information. [n.p.]: Auroville International United Kingdom.

[no author]. 1998. Sri Aurobindo Ashram: The Story of the Main Building. Pondicherry: Sri Aurobindo Ashram, 1998.

[no author]. 2005a. 'Burjorji Jamaspji Padshah.' *Sands of Time* 4, issue 2 (April): 1–5.

[no author]. 2005b. *Judgments*. Bombay: Parsiana Publications Private Ltd.

[no author]. 2006. 'Obituary for "Princess Dürrüsehvar of Berar".' *Daily Telegraph*, 11 February: 24.

[no author]. 2008. 'Navajbai Tata.' *Sands of Time* 7, issue 1: 6.

[no author]. 2010. 'Nevill Vintcent, a Casualty of World War Two.' *Sands of Time* 9, issue 2: 6.

Aftab, Tahera. 2008. *Inscribing South Asian Muslim Women: An Annotated Bibliography and Research Guide*. Leiden: Brill.

Airault, Régis. 2000. *Fous de l'Inde: délires d'Occidentaux et sentiment océanique*. Paris: Payot.

Aldrich, Robert. 1996. *Greater France: A History of French Colonial Expansion*. Hampshire: Macmillan.

Aldrich, Robert. 2005. *Vestiges of the Colonial Empire in France*. London: Palgrave Macmillan.

Alfassa, Mirra. 1977. *The Mother on Auroville*. Pondicherry: Sri Aurobindo Ashram Trust.

Alfassa, Mirra. 1978. *Collected Works of The Mother*. 12 vols. Pondicherry: Sri Aurobindo Society.

Alfassa, Mirra. 1987a. *Prayers and Meditations. Collected Works of The Mother*, vol. 1. Pondicherry: Sri Aurobindo Society.

Alfassa, Mirra. 1987b. *Questions and Answers 1956. Collected Works of The Mother*, vol. 8. Pondicherry: Sri Aurobindo Society.

Alfassa, Mirra. 1987c. *Questions and Answers 1957–1958. Collected Works of The Mother*, vol. 9. Pondicherry: Sri Aurobindo Society.

Alfassa, Mirra. 1987d. *Some Answers from the Mother. Collected Works of The Mother*, vol. 16. Pondicherry: Sri Aurobindo Society.

Alfassa, Mirra. 2000. *The Spiritual Significance of Flowers.* Pondicherry: Sri Aurobindo Ashram Publications Department.

Ali, Tariq. 2005 [1985]. *The Nehrus and the Gandhis: An Indian Dynasty.* London: Picador.

Atmaprana, Pravrajika (ed), *The Complete Works of Sister Nivedita,* 5 vols Calcutta: Ramakrishna Sarada Mission and Sister Nivedita Girls' School, 1955.

Atmaprana, Pravrajika. 1969. *The Story of Sister Nivedita.* Calcutta: Ramakrishna Sarada Mission, Sister Nivedita Girls' School.

Aurobindo, Sri [Aurobindo Ghose]. 1970a. *Letters on Yoga. SABCL (Sri Aurobindo Birth Centenary Library)*, vol. 22. Pondicherry: Sri Aurobindo Ashram.

Aurobindo, Sri [Aurobindo Ghose]. 1970b. *The Mother. SABCL,* vol. 25. Pondicherry: Sri Aurobindo Ashram.

Aurobindo, Sri [Aurobindo Ghose]. 1970c. *Supplement.* SABCL, vol. 27, Pondicherry: Sri Aurobindo Ashram.

Aurobindo, Sri [Aurobindo Ghose]. 1997a. *Letters on Himself and the Ashram. Complete Works of Sri Aurobindo,* vol. 35. Pondicherry: Sri Aurobindo Ashram.

Aurobindo, Sri [Aurobindo Ghose]. 1997b. *Autobiographical Notes. Complete Works of Sri Aurobindo*, vol. 36. Pondicherry: Sri Aurobindo Ashram.

Aurobindo, Sri [Aurobindo Ghose], Mirra Alfassa and Paul Richard. 1914–1920. *Arya.*

Aurobindo, Sri [Aurobindo Ghose], Mirra Alfassa and Paul Richard. 1914. 'The Society has its headquarters at Pondicherry…' *Arya*, 1, no.15: 58.

Bakshi, Haradhan. [no date]. 'Mirra is my Shakti. She has taken charge of the new creation. You will get everything you need from her. Give consent to whatever she wants to do.' Papers, notebook 3. Sri Aurobindo Ashram Archives.

Barbier Saint Hilaire, Philippe. 2001. *Intinéraire d'un enfant du siècle: de l'École polytechnique à l'Ashram de Sri Aurobindo*. Paris: Buchet-Chastel.

Bartlett, Thomas. 1997. 'The Irish Soldier in India, 1750–1947'. In *Ireland and India: Connections, Comparisons, Contrasts*, ed. Michael Holmes and Denis Holmes, pp. 12–28. Dublin: Folens.

Basak, Sudeshna. 2004. *Glimpses of the Past: Essays on Sister Nivedita, and Her Contemporaries*. Kolkata: K.P. Bagchi & Co.

Beaulieu, Augustin de. 1905. *Relations anciennes de voyageurs celebres: Augustin de Beaulieu, sa navigation aux Indes orientales (1616–1622)*, ed. Eugène Guénin. Paris: Hachette.

Benichou, Lucien. 2000. *From Autocracy to Integration: Political Developments in Hyderabad 1938–1948*. Hyderabad: Orient Longman.

Benson, S.H. c1970. 'Lakmé Beauty Preparations Prepared from French formulæ'. Lakmé advertisement (undated but probably from the 1970s). Tata Central Archives, L1 ADVT 04.

Besant, Annie. 1885. *Autobiographical Sketches*. London: Freethought Publishing Co.

Besant, Annie. 1893. *An Autobiography*. London: T. Fisher Unwin.

Besant, Annie. 1894. 'Indian Affairs'. Letter to the editor of *The Times*. *The Times*, 30 March: 14.

Besant, Annie. 1913a. *Wake up India: A Plea for Social Reform*. Adyar: A. Besant.

Besant, Annie. 1913b. 'The Education of Girls in India.' London: The Theosophical Publishing Society and Madras: The Theosophist Office.

Besant, Annie. 1914. 'England and Ireland.' *New India*, 13 October: 11–13.

Besant, Annie. 1915. *War Articles and Notes*. London: The Theosophical Publishing Society.

Besant, Annie. 1917. 'The Case for India: The Presidential Address Delivered by Annie Besant to the Thirty-Second Indian National Congress Held at Calcutta 26 December 1917.' London: The Home Rule for India League (British Section). http://archive.org/details/caseforindiapres00besauoft (accessed 11 November, 2011).

Besant, Annie. 1918. 'A Letter.' *New India*, 27 November: 5.

Besant, Annie and C.W. Leadbetter. 1908. *Occult Chemistry: Clairvoyant Observations on the Chemical Elements*. Adyar: Theosophist Office and London: Theosophical Publishing Society.

Besant, Annie, et al. 1891. 'Constitution of the Theosophical Society.' *The Theosophist* (January), 65–72.

Bhat, K.N. 2004. The Bofors Case: Any Reason to Feel Good? In *Sonia Under Scrutiny*, ed. A. Surya Prakash, pp. 85–90. New Delhi: India First Foundation.

Bhattacharya, Alak. 2010. *Nivedita: Synthesis of East and West*. New Delhi: Northern Book Centre.

Birkenhead, the Earl of (Frederick Winston Furneaux Smith). 1969. *Walter Monckton: The Life of Viscount Monckton of Brenchley*. London: Weidenfeld & Nicolson.

Bishop, Anthony. 1967–68. 'John Nicholson in the Indian Mutiny', *Irish Sword* 8: 277–87.

Bobin, Frédéric. 2012. 'L'Égérie frenchie du cinéma hindi.' *Le magazine du Monde*, 9 June: 58–61.

Boisserolle. 1759. 'Réponse à un article du Mémoire du sieur Dupleix.' Paris, Bibliothèque Nationale de France, fonds des nouvelles acquisitions françaises, vol. 9154, p. 72.

Bose, J.C. 1911. 'Sister Nivedita.' *Modern Review* 10, no. 5 (November): 483–8.

Boucher d'Argis, Antoine-Gaspard. 1756. 'Régnicole.' In *Encyclopédie ou dictionnaire raisonné des sciences des arts et des métiers*, ed. J. le rond d'Alembert and D. Diderot, facsimile edn, 36 vols. Stuttgart-Bad Cannstatt: Friedrich Frommann, 1967. http://alembert.fr/ (accessed 11 November 2011).

Bowen, H.V. 1998. *War and British Society 1688–1815*. Cambridge: Cambridge University Press.

Brosse, Thérèse. 1984. *Sri Aurobindo-Mère: Shiva–Shakti*. Paris: Dervy-Livres.

Brown, Mick. 2000. 'Gurus and Gauloises.' *Daily Telegraph*, 1 April: 1, 12 and 13.

Burton, Antoinette. 2003. *Dwelling in the Archive*. Oxford: Oxford University Press.

Cadell, Patrick. 1953. 'Irish Soldiers in India.' *Irish Sword* 1: 79.

Champaklal. 1975. *Champaklal Speaks*. Pondicherry: Sri Aurobindo Ashram Press.

Champaklal. 1976. *Treasures*, part 2: *Notes, Prayers and Reflections of the Mother*. Berkeley: Sri Aurobindo Association.

Chatterjee, Aroup. 2003. *Mother Teresa: The Final Verdict*. Kolkata: Meteor Books.

Chatterjee, Rupa. 1998. *Sonia Gandhi: The Lady in Shadow*. Delhi: Butala.

Chatterjee, Rupa. 2000. *The Sonia Mystique*. New Delhi: Virgo Publications.

Chawla, Navin. 1992. *Mother Teresa: The Authorized Biography*. New Delhi: Gulmohur Press.

Chinmoy, Sri [Chinmoy Kumar Ghose]. 1985. *Flower-Frames*. Jamaica, NY: Agni Press.

Clément, Catherine. 2007. *Les Derniers Jours de la déesse*. 2nd edn. Paris: Librairie Générale Française/Le Livre de Poche.

Cook, Scott B. 1987. 'The Irish Raj: Social Origins and Careers of Irishmen in the Indian Civil Service, 1855–1914.' *Journal of Social History* 20, issue 3: 521.

Cousins, Margaret E. 1922. *The Awakening of Asian Womanhood*. Madras: Ganesh.

Cousins, Margaret E. 1923. *What Women have Gained by the Reforms*. Madras: General Secretary's [of the Women's Indian Association] Office.

Cousins, Margaret E. 1941. *Indian Womanhood Today*. Allahabad: Kitabistan.

Cousins, James H., and Margaret Cousins. 1950. *We Two Together*. Madras: Ganesh and Co.

Daguerches, Henri. 1906. *Consolata*. Paris: Calman-Lévy.

Das, Nilima. 1980. *Glimpses of the Mother*. Pondicherry: Sri Aurobindo Ashram.

Dasgupta, Swapan. 2004. 'The Inner Voice of Sonia.' *Outlook*, 31 May: 11.

Datt Bharti, Brahm. 1995. *Vatican–Teresa–Sonia*. New Delhi: Era Books.

David, Georgette. 1999. *Pondichéry: Porte de l'Inde*. Paris: L'Harmattan.

Denson, Alan. 1967. *James H. Cousins, 1873-1956, and Margaret E. Cousins, 1878–1954: A Bio-Bibliographical Survey*. Kendal: Alan Denson.

Devi, Savitri [Maximiani Portas). 1939. *A Warning to the Hindus*, Calcutta, Hindu Mission.

Devi, Savitri [Maximiani Portas). 1965. *Long Whiskers and the Two-Legged Goddess, or the True Story of a "Most Objectionable Nazi" and .... half-a-dozen Cats*, Calcutta, n.pub.

Dupleix, Joseph-François. 1737. 'On appelle mestices les enfants nées d'un Européen et d'une femme noire' (We call the children born of European men and black women mestizos). Correspondance de Dupleix (1731–40). Bibliothèque Nationale de France, manuscript 8979–8982.

Dupleix, Joseph-François. 1748. 'Relation du siège de Pondichéry attaquée en août 1748' (An account of the siege of Pondicherry, attacked in August 1748). Bibliothèque Nationale de France, manuscript 12086 and fonds des nouvelles acquisitions françaises, manuscript 9364.

Durru Shehvar [H.H. Nawab Durru Shehvar Durdana Begum Sahiba, Princess of Berar]. 1937. 'Address to the Hyderabad State Women's Conference.' Papers of Sir Theodore Tasker. British Library, MSS. EUR. D798/39.

Dutta, Krishnan. 2008. *Calcutta: A Cultural History*. Northampton, MA: Interlink Books.

Edwards, Penny. 2010. 'A Strategic Sanctuary: Reading *l'Inde française* through the Colonial Archive.' *Interventions: International Journal of Postcolonial Studies* 12, issue 3: 356–67.

Egan, Eileen. 1985. *Such a Vision of the Street: Mother Teresa – the Spirit and the Word*. London: Sidgwick & Jackson.

Falkiner, Suzanne. 2008. *Joan in India*. Kew (Victoria): Australian Scholarly Publishing.

Flaubert, Gustave. 1971 [1856]. *Madame Bovary*. Paris: Garnier Frères.

Foley, Tadhg and Maureen O'Connor eds. Ireland and India; Colonies , Culture and Empire (Sallins: Irish Academic Press, 2006).

Foucault, Michel. 1984. *Histoire de la sexualité*. Paris: Gallimard.

France, Peter, ed. 1995. *The New Oxford Companion to Literature in French*. Oxford: Clarendon Press.

François-Denève, Corinne, Mircea Itu, Ian H. Magedera and Kate Marsh. 2011. *French Books on India: from Dupleix to Decolonization*. Glasgow: University of Glasgow French and German Publications.

Fraser, Hastings. 1865. *Our Faithful Ally, the Nizam, Being an Historical Sketch of Events, Showing the Value of the Nizam's Alliance to the British Government in India, and his Services During the Mutinies*. London: Smith, Elder & Co.

Fraser, T.G. 1996. 'Ireland and India.' In *'An Irish Empire'? Aspects of Ireland and the British Empire*, ed. Keith Jeffery, pp. 77–93. Manchester: Manchester University Press.

Frauenfeld, Alfred Eduard. 1938. 'Dr Karl Lueger.' *Zeitschrift für Politik* 28: 85.

French, Patrick. 2011. *India: A Portrait*. London: Allen Lane.

Friedan, Betty. 1963. *The Feminine Mystique*. New York: W.W. Norton and Co.

Frykenberg, Robert Eric. 2008. *Christianity in India: From Beginnings to the Present*. Oxford: Oxford University Press.

Gaebelé, Yvonne Robert. 1934. *Créole et grande dame: Johanna Bégum, marquise Dupleix, 1706–1756, sa famille, la vie aux Indes dans la première moitié du XVIIIe siècle, Pondichéry en ce temps-là*. Pondicherry: Bibliothèque coloniale and Paris: Leroux.

Gaebelé, Yvonne Robert. 1937. *Une Parisienne aux Indes au XVIIIe siècle.* Pondicherry: Bibliothèque coloniale and Paris: Éditions Leroux.

Gambhirananda, Swami, ed. 1955. *Sister Nivedita: The Web of Indian Life.* Calcutta: Advaita Ashrama.

Gandhi, M.K. 1920. 'The Congress and Non-Co-operation.' *Young India* 2, no. 31 (New Series) (4 August): 3.

Gandhi, Sonia. 1992. *Rajiv.* New Delhi and New York: Viking.

Gandhi, Sonia. 1994. *Rajiv's World.* New Delhi and New York: Viking.

Gandhi, Sonia. 2002. 'Conflict and Co-existence in Our Age.' Lecture given to the Oxford Centre for Islamic Studies.

Gautier, Judith. 1887. *Le Lion de la victoire: La Conquête du paradis et La Reine de Bangalore.* 2 vols. Paris: Frinzine.

Gautier, Judith. 1913. *L'Inde éblouie (Dupleix, De Bussy, La Touche).* Paris: Armand Colin.

Geetha, V. and S.V. Rajadurai. 1995. 'One Hundred Years of Brahminitude: Arrival of Annie Besant.' *Economic and Political Weekly* 30, no. 28 (15 July): 1768–73.

Gherlardini, Paolo. 1997. *Mother Teresa: Missionary of the Impossible.* Milan: Gruppo Editoriale Sirio.

Gondinet, Edmond and Philippe Gille (libretto), and Léo Délibes (music). 1883. *Lakmé.* Paris: Heugel.

Granger, Serge, Ian H. Magedera, Kate Marsh and Dhana Underwood. 2003. '"Aux délices de Mahé": a Selected, Critical and Annotated Bibliography of French-Language Representations of India 1763–2002.' *International Journal of Francophone Studies* 5, no. 2: 104–27.

Greene, Meg. 2004. *Mother Teresa: A Biography.* Westport, CT: Greenwood Press.

Guët, Isidore. 1892. *Origines de l'Inde française, Jân Begum (Mme Dupleix), 1706–1756.* Paris: Baudoin.

Gupta, Nolini Kanta. 1969. *Reminiscences.* Pondicherry: Sri Aurobindo Ashram Trust.

Gurumurthy, S. 2004. 'Is Sonia Lying to Save her Friend?' In *Sonia Under Scrutiny,* ed. A. Surya Prakash, pp. 80–4. New Delhi: India First Foundation.

Hanbery MacKay, Carol. 2001. *Creative Negativity: Four Victorian Exemplars of the Female Quest.* Palo Alto, CA: Stanford University Press.

Hasan, Mushirul. 1999. 'She is here to stay: The rights of Citizen Sonia.' *Indian Express,* 22 May: 8.

Heehs, Peter. 2008. *Lives of Sri Aurobindo*. New York: Columbia University Press.

Heelas, Paul. 1996. *The New Age Movement: The Celebration of the Self and the Sacralization of Modernity*. Oxford: Blackwell.

Hindocha, Huta D. 1999. *The Story of a Soul*. Pondicherry: Havyavahana Trust.

Hitchens, Christopher. 1995. *The Missionary Position: Mother Teresa in Theory and Practice*. London and New York: Verso.

Hojman, David E. 2011. 'A Critical Juncture and Counterfactuals Approach to the Dutch Invasion of Colonial Chiloe.' In *Primer Congreso Chileno de Historia Economica: Actas*, ed. C. Donoso Rojas and M.G. Huidobro, pp. 31–6. Vina del Mar (Chile): Universidad Andres Bello.

Holmes Michael. 2000. 'The Irish and India: Imperialism, Nationalism and Internationalism.' In *The Irish Diaspora*, ed. Andy Bielenberg, pp. 235–50. Harlow: Longman.

Holmes, Michael and Denis Holmes, eds. 1997. *Ireland and India: Connections, Comparisons, Contrasts*. Dublin: Folens.

Hulin, Michel and Christine Maillard. 1996. *L'Inde inspiratrice*. Strasbourg: Presses Universitaires de Strasbourg.

Jaitly, Jaya. 2004. 'Sonia's Craze for Power.' In *Sonia Under Scrutiny*, ed. A. Surya Prakash, pp. 36–53. New Delhi: India First Foundation.

Jayakar, Roshni. 2002. 'The Other Tata.' *Business Today* (15 September), http://archives.digitaltoday.in/businesstoday/20020915/features3.html (accessed 11 November 2011).

Jayawardena, Kumari. 1995. *The White Woman's Other Burden: Western Women and South Asia During British Rule*. New York and London: Routledge.

Kamath, M.V. 2004a. 'The Unknown Tata.' *Sands of Time* 3, issue 3 (July): 3–5.

Kamath, M.V. 2004b. 'The Unknown Tata.' *Sands of Time* 3, issue 4 (October): 3–5.

Kamath, M.V. 2005. 'The Unknown Tata.' *Sands of Time* 4, issue 1 (January): 5–6.

Kaur, Manmohan. 1968. *Role of Women in the Freedom Movement 1857–1947*. New Delhi: Sterling Publishers.

Keramet Nigar, Salih. 1964. *Halife Ikinci Abdulmecid (Abdul Mejid Effendi)*. Istanbul: [n. pub.].

Keyes, T.H. 1932. 'Report on the Sons of His Exalted Highness, The Nizam of Hyderabad and Their Turkish Wives. Behaviour of Sahibzada Muazzam Jah during his stay in Europe' (21 January). British Library, R/1/1/2260: 1–2.

Khalidi, Omar. 2004. 'The Caliph's Daughter.' *Cornucopia* 31, issue 4: 34–8.

Kinealy, Christine. 2006. 'At Home with the Empire: the Example of Ireland.' In *At Home With the Empire: Metropolitan Culture And the Imperial World*, ed. Catherine Hall and Sonya O. Rose, pp. 77–100. Cambridge: Cambridge University Press.

Kolodiejchuk, Brian, ed. 2007. *Come Be My Light: The Private Writings of the 'Saint of Calcutta' / Mother Teresa.* New York: Doubleday.

Kuch, Peter. 1986. *Yeats and A.E.* [G.W. Russell]. New York: Barnes & Noble and Gerrards Cross, UK: Smythe.

Kumar, Raj, Rameshwari Devi and Romila Pruthi, eds. 2003. *Sister Nivedita: Social Revolutionary.* Jaipur: Pointer.

Lala, R.M. 1992. *Beyond the Last Blue Mountain: A Life of J.R.D. Tata.* New Delhi, Viking.

Latronche, Marie-France. 1999. *L'Influence de Gandhi en France, de 1919 à nos jours.* Paris: L'Harmattan.

Le Fèvre, Claude-Noël. 1818. *Éloge historique de Dupleix.* Paris: Le Fèvre.

Levy Bensusan, Samuel. 1910. *Lawrence: Masterpieces in Colour.* London: T.C. & E.C. Jack and New York: F.A. Stokes Co.

Loti, Pierre [Julien Viaud]. 1880. *Le Mariage de Loti: Rarahu.*. Paris: Calmann-Lévy.

Loveman, Brian. 2001 [1979]. *Chile: The Legacy of Hispanic Capitalism*, Oxford: Oxford.

Luther, Narendra. 2006. *Hyderabad: A Biography.* New Delhi: Oxford University Press.

M.D. [full name unknown]. 1931. 'Under the Canopy of Heaven.' *Young India* 13, no. 14 (2 April): 54–5 and 60–1.

Magedera, Ian H. 2010. 'Arrested Development: The Shape of "French India" after the Treaties of Paris of 1763 and 1814.' *Interventions: International Journal of Postcolonial Studies* 12, issue 3: 331–43.

Mansel, Philip. 1995. *Constantinople: City of the World's Desire 1453–1924.* London: John Murray.

Mansergh, Nicholas Seton, ed. 1982. *The Mountbatten Viceroyalty: Announcement and Reception of the 3 June Plan, May 31–July 7, 1947. Relations Between Britain and India: The Transfer of Power, 1942–47*, vol. 11. London: HMSO.

Marny, Dominique. 1999. *Du Côté de Pondichéry.* Paris: Presses de la Cité.

Marsh, Kate. 2009. *India in the French Imagination: Peripheral Voices 1754–1815*. London: Pickering & Chatto.

Martin, Claude. 1789. Letter to Ozias Humphrey, dated 11 March. Royal Academy, London, HU/4/24-5.

Mason, Philip. 1978. *A Shaft of Sunlight: Memories of a Varied Life*. London: André Deutsch.

McKendrick, Neil. 2009. 'Joseph Needham: The Bridge Builder.' *Once a Caian…* 9: 6–9, http://www.gonvilleandcaius.org/Document.Doc?id=133

Miles, Malcolm. 2008. *Urban Utopias*. London: Routledge.

Minault, Gail. 1982. *The Khilafat Movement*. New York and Guilford: Columbia University Press.

Mishra, Saroj. 1999. 'Middle Classes Didn't Want Her.' *Hindustan Times*, 30 May: 11.

Mitra, Barun. 1999. 'Who is a Foreigner?' *Economic Times*, 22 May: 11.

Mokyr, Joel and Cormac Ó Gráda. 1989. 'The Height of Irishmen and Englishmen in the 1770s: Some Evidence from the East India Company Archives.' *Eighteenth-Century Ireland* 4: 90.

Montecrossa, Michel. 2002. *Mirapuri*. Gauting: Mirapuri-Verlag.

Montecrossa, Michel. 2010. *Filmaur Multimedia Germany, DVD and BLU-RAY Catalogue*. Gauting: Mirapuri-Verlag.

Morgan, Jenny (director), Christopher Hitchens (writer) and Tariq Ali (producer). 1994. *Hell's Angel*. Bandung Productions for Channel 4 Television.

Moro, Javier. 1998. *El Sari rojo* (*The Red Sari*). Barcelona: Planeta Publishing Corporation.

Morris, Morris D. 1983. 'The Growth of Large-Scale Industry to 1947.' In *The Cambridge Economic History of India*, vol. 2, ed. Dharma Kumar and Megnad Desai, pp. 553–676. Cambridge, Cambridge University Press.

Muktiprana, Pravrajika. 1992. *Bhaginī Nivedita*, 6th ed. Kolkata: Sister Nivedita Girls' School.

Muggeridge, Malcolm. 1971. *Something Beautiful for God*. New York: Harper & Row.

Namakkal, Jessica. 2012. 'European Dreams, Tamil Land: Auroville and the Paradox of a Postcolonial Utopia', *Journal for the Study of Radicalism*, 6, 59–88.

Nandy, Ashis. 1983. *The Intimate Enemy: Loss and Recovery of Self under Colonialism*. Oxford and New York: Oxford University Press.

Naravane, Vaiju. 1998. 'In Maino Country.' *Frontline* 15, issue 9 (25 April – 8 May): 11, http://www.frontlineonnet.com/fl1509/15090140.htm

Nath, Aman, Jay Vithalani and Tulsi Vatsal. 2004. *Horizons: The Tata–India Century 1904–2004*. Mumbai: India Book House.

Nirod [Nirodbaran]. 1966–86. *Talks with Sri Aurobindo*. 4 vols. Calcutta: Sri Aurobindo Pathamandir.

Nirod [Nirodbaran]. 1977. 'Introduction.' In *Causerie au lendemain du départ de la Mère*, by Pranab [Pranab Kumar Bhattacharya]. Auroville: Éditions Auropress.

Nivedita, Sister [Margaret Noble]. 1908. *Love and Death*. London: Longmans & Co.

Nivedita, Sister [Margaret Noble]. 1910. *The Master as I Saw Him: Pages from the Life of Swami Vivekananda*. London and New York: Longmans & Co.

Nivedita, Sister [Margaret Noble]. 1913a. *Notes of Some Wanderings with the Swami Vivekananda*. Calcutta: [n.pub.].

Nivedita, Sister [Margaret Noble]. 1913b. *Studies from an Eastern Home*. London: Longmans & Co.

Nivedita, Sister [Margaret Noble]. 1915a. *Footfalls of Indian History*. London: Longmans & Co.

Nivedita, Sister [Margaret Noble]. 1915b. *Religion and Dharma*. London: Longmans & Co.

Nivedita, Sister [Margaret Noble]. 1916. *Myths of the Hindus and Buddhists*. London: G.G. Harrap & Co.

Nivedita, Sister [Margaret Noble]. 1950. *Hints on National Education in India*. Calcutta: Swami Atmabodhananda and the Udbodhan Office.

Nivedita, Sister [Margaret Noble]. 1955 [1904]. *The Web of Indian Life*. Calcutta: Advaita Ashrama.

Nivedita, Sister [Margaret Noble]. 1967. 'The government must be mad, or at least prove so if Swamiji ....' Letter to Mrs Eric Hammond, dated 22 May 1898. In *The Complete Works of Sister Nivedita*, vol. 1. [Calcutta]: Ramakrishna Sarada Mission, Sister Nivedita Girls' School.

Padshah, B.J. 1906. 'We all absolutely agree with you [R.D. Tata] that we need to travel outside India for promising recruits.' Letter to R.D. Tata, dated 21 June. Tata Central Archives, BJ PADSHAH/RDT/COR/1904–18/1-66.

Padshah, B.J. 1918. 'Don't worry about the Tata name. It won't suffer if strangers are introduced into the shrine or home.' Letter to R.D. Tata, dated 23 July.

Tata Central Archives, BJ PADSHAH/RDT/COR/1904–18/1–66.

Pandit, Shrinivas. 2009. *Creative Businesswoman Simone Tata.* New Delhi: Tata McGraw Hill.

Patenaude, Monique. 2004. *Made in Auroville.* Montreal: Tryptique.

Paxton, Nancy L. 1992. 'Complicity and Resistance in the Writings of Flora Annie Steel and Annie Besant.' In *Western Women and Imperialism,* ed. Nupur Chaudhuri and Margaret Strobel, pp. 158–76. Bloomington and Indianapolis: Indiana University Press.

Pocha, Jehangir S. 2012. 'Passing the Baton at Tata.' *Forbes India* (1 April), http://www.forbes.com/2012/01/04/forbes-india-passing-the-baton-cyrus-mistry-appointment-ratan-tata-successor_3.html

Praeger, Jack. 1982. 'Calcutta's destitute.' *The Tablet,* 23 January: 78–9.

Pranab [Pranab Kumar Bhattacharya]. 1977. *Causerie au lendemain du départ de la Mère.* Auroville: Éditions Auropress.

Prasad, Rajendra. 2010 [1984]. *Asif Jahs of Hyderabad: Their Rise and Decline.* Hyderabad: Prachee Publications.

Procida, Mary A. 2005. 'Kumari Jayawardena: *The White Woman's Other Burden: Western Women and South Asia during British Rule.*' *Journal of Social History* 30, issue 2: 11.

Purani, A.B. 1958. *Life of Sri Aurobindo.* Pondicherry: Sri Aurobindo Ashram.

Purani, A.B. 1982. *Evening Talks with Sri Aurobindo.* Pondicherry: Sri Aurobindo Ashram.

Raj Jai, Janak. 2004. *Sonia's Foreign Origin: A Non-Issue.* New Delhi: Regency.

Ramji, Kamala, ed. 1977. *AIWC [All India Women's Conference] Golden Jubilee and Margaret Cousins Birth Centenary Commemoration Volume.* New Delhi: AWIC.

Ramusack, Barbara N. 2004. 'Margaret Cousins.' In *Dictionary of National Biography,* ed. Laurence Goldman, online edn. Oxford: Oxford University Press. http://www.oxforddnb.com/ (accessed 11 November 2011).

Rangan, Pavithra S. 2011. 'Lady Hydari Club yearns for past glory.' *The Hindu* (4 July), http://www.thehindu.com/todays-paper/tp-national/tp-andhrapradesh/article2157375.ece (accessed 11 November 2011).

Rangappillai, Ananda. 1917. *The Private Diary of Ananda Ranga Pillai.* Trans. Henry Dodwell. 12 vols. Madras: Government Press.

Rao, Amruta. 1996. *Occidental Daughters of Mother India.* 3 vols. New Delhi: APC Publications.

Ratcliffe, Samuel Kerkham. 1913. *Sister Nivedita: Studies from an Eastern Home.* London: Longmans & Co.

Reymond, Lizelle. 1953. *The Dedicated: A Biography of Nivedita,* trans. Jean Herbert. New York: John Day. (First published as *Fille de l'Inde* (*Daughter of India*). Neuchâtel: Attinger, 1946.)

Richard, Michel Paul. 1987. *Without Passport.* New York: Peter Lang.

Richepin, Jean (words) and César Antonovich Cui (music). 1891. 'Pâle et blonde.' Paris: Heugel http://conquest.imslp.info/files/imglnks/usimg/8/89/IMSLP105301-PMLP53532-Cui_-_44_-_20_Poemes_de_Richepin.pdf (accessed 11 November 2011).

Satprem [Bernard Enginger]. 1977. *Agenda de la Mère.* Paris: Institut de Recherches Evolutives and Mysore: Mira Aditi.

Satprem [Bernard Enginger]. 1988. *Mother's Agenda,* vol. 5. Trans. Michel Danino. Paris: Institut de Recherches Evolutives and Mysore: Mira Aditi.

Saurel, Louis. 1937. *Un prodigieux roman d'aventures: la vie de Dupleix.* Paris: Nathan.

Sebba, Anne. 1997. *Mother Teresa.* New York: Doubleday.

Sengupta, Anjali. 1984. *Cameos of Twelve European Women in India 1757–1857.* Calcutta: Rddhi-India.

Sengupta, Ramprasad. 2007. 'Steel Industry.' In *Oxford Companion to Economics in India,* ed. Kaushik Basu, pp. 498–503. New Delhi: Oxford University Press.

Sethna, K.D. 1999. *The Development of Sri Aurobindo's Spiritual System and the Mother's Contribution to It.* East Lyme, CT: Integral Life Foundation.

Shanaz, Fatima. 2012. Correspondence with the author.

Sherman, Taylor C. 2007. 'The Integration of the Princely State of Hyderabad and the Making of the Postcolonial State in India, 1948–56.' *Indian Economic Social History Review* 44, no. 4: 489–516.

Siddharth, Gautham. 2004. 'Sonia Gandhi for PM? Not on Indian Soil.' In *Sonia Under Scrutiny,* ed. A. Surya Prakash, pp. 113–25. New Delhi: India First Foundation.

Singh Bhatia, Harbans. 1979. *European Women in India: Their Life and Adventures.* New Delhi: Deep & Deep.

Skoda, Uwe. 2004. 'The Politics–Kinship Nexus in India: Sonia Gandhi versus Sushma Swaraj in the 1999 General Elections.' *Contemporary South Asia* 13, no. 3: 273–85.

Smith, Vincent Arthur. 1904. *The Early History of India*. Oxford: Clarendon Press.

Sood. P. 2009. *Sonia Gandhi: Trails of Triumph*. New Delhi: Vitasta Publications.

Spear, Richard E. 2008. 'Colonial collectors: the Tata bequests of nineteenth-century European paintings in the Mumbai Museum.' *Burlington Magazine* 150 (January): 15–27.

Spink, Kathryn. 1997. *Mother Teresa, An Authorized Biography*. London: HarperCollins.

Srinivasa Iyengar, K.R. 1978. *On the Mother: The Chronicle of a Manifestation and Ministry*. Pondicherry: Sri Aurobindo International Centre of Education.

Stiegler, Gaston. 1901. *Le Tour du monde en 63 jours*. Paris: Société française d'imprimerie et de librairie.

Surya Prakash, A. 2004. *Sonia Under Scrutiny*. New Delhi: India First Foundation.

Tadman, Michael. 2002. 'Class and the Construction of "Race": White Racism in the Antebellum South.' In *The State of American History*, ed. Melvyn Stokes, pp. 327–47. Charlottesville: University of Virginia Press.

Tagore, Rabindranath. 1955. *Sister Nivedita, The Web of Indian Life*. Calcutta, Advaita Ashrama.

Tata, J.R.D. 1924a. Letter dated 1 January. Tata Central Archives, FP NO 123 JRDT SOONI 57 PG 04.

Tata, J.R.D. 1924b. 'Tu dois être maintenant de retour à ~~Paris~~ Bombay' (You must be back in ~~Paris~~, Bombay by now). Letter dated 3 September. Tata Central Archives, FP NO 123 JRDT SOONI 58 PG 01.

Tata, Simone [Simone Dunoyer]. 2005. 'Mental make-up.' An interview with Simone Tata by Christabelle Noronha of (Tata) Group Corporate Affairs, http://www.tata.com/media/interviews/inside.aspx?artid=ivCKuWMihdk= (accessed 11 November 2011).

Tata, Simone [Simone Dunoyer]. 2011a. Correspondence with the author (6 September).

Tata, Simone [Simone Dunoyer]. 2011b. Correspondence with the author (29 November).

Tata, Simone [Simone Dunoyer]. 2011c. Correspondence with the author (30 November).

Tata, Simone [Simone Dunoyer]. 2012a. Correspondence with the author (1 March).

Tata, Sooni [Suzanne Brière]. 1902a. 'Je suis de plus en plus dans les malles'

(The trunks are becoming more and more of a second home to me). Letter dated 3 November. Tata Central Archives, FP NO 095 SL 13 PG 06.

Tata, Sooni [Suzanne Brière]. 1902b. 'Sommes-nous assez réussis?' (How good are we on this photograph?). Postcard from New York dated 10 November. (Reproduced in Nath, Aman, Jay Vithalani and Tulsi Vatsal, *Horizons: The Tata-India Century 1904–2004*. Mumbai: India Book House, 2004, p. 345).

Tata, Sooni [Suzanne Brière]. 1902c. 'Nous causerions en mon français si cher et si beau' (We would chat in my beloved and beautiful French). Letter dated 12 December. Tata Central Archives, FP NO 95.

Tata, Sooni [Suzanne Brière]. 1903a. Letter dated 1 January. Tata Central Archives, FP NO 96 SL 23 PG 02.

Tata, Sooni [Suzanne Brière]. 1903b. 'Ma petite mère. Hier matin donc j'ai pendant une demie heure étudié le Goujerati (c'est dur)' (Mother dearest, yesterday I studied Gujarati for an hour and a half (it's difficult)). Letter dated 23 January. Tata Central Archives, FP NO 96 SL 25 PG 15.

Tata, Sooni [Suzanne Brière]. 1903c. 'Voilà toute cette génération qui se marie qui s'éparpille aux mille coins du monde' (So here's all of this generation getting married and being scattered to a thousand corners of the globe). Letter dated 4 March. Tata Central Archives, FP NO 96 SL 27 PG 20 and 21.

Tata, Sooni [Suzanne Brière]. 1904a. 'En général le Français d'aujourd'hui est pot au feu [sic] et craint de quitter de vue son toit' (In general the Frenchman of today is the stay-at-home type and is afraid of venturing to a place where he can no longer see the roof of his own house). Letter dated 7 January. Tata Central Archives, FP NO 97 SL 41 PG 01.

Tata, Sooni [Suzanne Brière]. 1904b. 'Si tu es à Bombay et prie Lady Jenkins de te présenter ses hommages, kind regards en English. Voilà!' (If you [Sooni's mother] are in Bombay and ask Lady Jenkins to offer you his [a third party's] compliments, 'kind regards' in English. There we are, done!). Letter dated 22 January Tata Central Archives, FP NO 97 SL 43 PG 04.

Tata, Sooni [Suzanne Brière]. 1904c. 'Moi qui ne suis ici ni chien ni chat' (I, who am neither fish nor foul here). Letter from Bombay dated 28 January. Tata Central Archives, FP NO 97 SL 44 PG 02.

Tata, Sooni [Suzanne Brière]. 1904d. 'Le goujerati de ma belle mère que je ne comprends pas, le français petit nègre d'une aya' (the Gujarati of my mother-in-law that I do not understand, the pidgin French of a children's nurse). Letter from Bombay dated 8 February. Tata Central Archives, FP NO 97 SL 46 PG 03.

Tata, Sooni [Suzanne Brière]. 1905a. 'C'est cette maudite galopade qui m'a forcé à retourner vers la France' (It is this accursed mad rush which forced me to return to France). Letter dated 22 September. Tata Central Archives, FP NO 98 SL 110.

Tata, Sooni [Suzanne Brière]. 1905b. 'Le roi futur' (the future king). Letter dated 10 December. Tata Central Archives, FP NO 98.

Tata, Sooni [Suzanne Brière]. 1906a. Letter dated 16 February. Tata Central Archives, FP NO 96 SL 81 PG 01 and 02.

Tata, Sooni [Suzanne Brière]. 1906b. Letter dated 8 June. Tata Central Archives, FP NO 98.

Tata, Sooni [Suzanne Brière]. 1906c. 'un mélange de goujerati, d'hindi et d'anglais' (a mix of Gujarati, Hindi and English). Letter dated 10 September. Tata Central Archives, FP NO 98.

Tata, Sooni [Suzanne Brière]. 1907a. 'Quand je pense que Sylla va avoir 4 ans! C'est une petite femme déjà' (When I think that Sylla is going to be four soon! She is a little lady already). Letter dated 1 March. Tata Central Archives, FP NO 99.

Tata, Sooni [Suzanne Brière]. 1907b. Letter dated 15 March. Tata Central Archives, FP NO 99 SL 126 PG 01.

Tata, Sooni [Suzanne Brière]. 1907c. Letter dated 20 April. Tata Central Archives, FP NO 99 SL 131 PG 01.

Taylor, Anne. 1992. *Annie Besant: A Biography*. Oxford: Oxford University Press.

Teo, Hsu-Ming. 2004. 'Romancing the Raj: Interracial Relations in Anglo-Indian Romance Novels.' *History of Intellectual Culture* 4, no. 1: 2–18 http://www.ucalgary.ca/hic/files/hic/teo.pdf (accessed 11 November 2011).

Teresa, Mother [Anjezë Gonxha Bojaxhiu]. 1929. Untitled poem. *Blagovijest* [*Annunciation*] [Skopje] (25 March), 3–4.

Tirtha, Swami Ramananda. 1967. *Memoirs of Hyderabad Freedom Struggle*. Bombay: Popular Prakashan.

Todorov, Tzvetan. 1982. *Conquête de l'Amérique*. Paris: Le Seuil.

Tuohy, Frank. 1976. *William Butler Yeats*. London: Macmillan.

Twain, Mark. 1896. *Personal Recollection of Joan of Arc*. New York: Harper and Brothers.

Underwood, Dhana. 2004. 'Victime ou déesse sexualisée? la représentation de la femme indienne à l'époque coloniale de 1744 à 1930, étude des œuvres littéraires de langue française.' Ph.D. dissertation, University of Liverpool.

Van Vrekhem, Georges. 2004. *The Mother: The Story of Her Life*. New Delhi: Rupa & Company.

Venkateshwarlu, K. 2006. 'When Marriage Brought Continents Closer.' *The Hindu* (10 February), http://www.hindu.com/2006/02/10/stories/2006021011660400.htm (accessed 11 November 2011).

Vigié, Marc. 1993. *Dupleix*. Paris: Fayard.

Vij-Aurora, Bhavna. 2012. 'Politics is in the Heir.' *India Today*, 10 February: 11.

Vincent, Rose. 1982. *Le Temps d'un royaume: Jeanne Dupleix, 1706–1756*. Paris: Le Seuil.

Vir Gupta, Pankaj and Christine Mueller. 2005. 'Golconde: The Introduction of Modernism in India.' Washington, D.C.: American Institute of Architects, http://www.aia.org/aiaucmp/groups/ek_public/documents/pdf/aiap080052.pdf (accessed 11 November 2011).

Vivekananda, Swami [Narendra Nath Datta]. 1972. Letter to Margaret Noble, dated 29 July 1897. In *The Complete Works of Swami Vivekananda*, vol. 7. Calcutta: Advaita Ashrama.

Voltaire [François-Marie Arouet]. 1764. 'Des Brames' (On Brahmins). *Dictionnaire philosophique*. Geneva: Gabriel Grasset.

Weber, Thomas. 2011. *Going Native: Gandhi's Relationship with Western Women*. New Delhi: Roli Books.

Wright Mills, Charles. 1956. *The Power Elite*. Oxford, OH: Oxford Press.

Younger, Coralie. 2003. *The Wicked Women of the Raj*. New York: HarperCollins.

Zubrzycki, John. 2006. *The Last Nizam*. Sydney: Pan Macmillan Australia.

Zweigenhaft, Richard L. and G. William Domhoff. 2006. *Diversity in the Power Elite*. Lanham, MD: Rowman & Littlefield.